CW00485121

A Twisted
Prophecy

Happy Reading

PAUL CUDE

Paul M Cude

CONTENTS

1 TRICK OR TREAT

The king had a face like a bulldog licking vinegar off a nettle, while the doctor looked on, suitably chastised. As the bright lights assaulted Peter's eyes and the waft of industrial cleaning agents raced up his nose, the sheer scale of the ward he'd walked into mesmerised him. It was huge... at least the size of a hockey pitch, if not bigger. Steering the group along the wall to their left, the decidedly grumpy doctor weaved in and out of blood pressure monitors, laughing gas bottles and one or two commodes. All the time the three friends were aware they were skirting around what could conceivably be the biggest bed in the world, off to their right. A gargantuan dark blue curtain twenty feet high circled at least twenty five yards around whatever lay inside; it was captivating, but clearly off limits, judging by the scowl on the doctor's face as she looked back over her shoulder at them. Directly in front of them another dark blue curtain, about the size you'd expect in a human hospital, concealed whatever was inside it.

'It has to be her,' thought Peter, barely able to contain himself. As one, the group stopped and watched as the doctor marched around the far side, grasped the curtain and, in one swift stroke, pulled it all the way back, revealing the hospital bed. Peter exhaled loudly as happiness ebbed through him, for the most part anyway. Though hugely grateful she was alive, his stomach churned when he noticed the state she was in. When Richie's body had been recovered at the sports club, he hadn't really paid much attention, due mainly to his surprise at the fact she hadn't perished in the bomb blast that had destroyed the clubhouse. But here and now, she looked as though she'd been beaten by a crowd. Her eyes were barely visible, they were so badly bruised and swollen, and the entire left side of her face was a brilliant purple from some trauma or other. Leaving her face, he glanced downwards, noticing that her right wrist was in plaster, along with her left ankle, and what was left was generally covered in bandages.

'Why the hell haven't they healed her?' was the singular thought that ran through his mind. And he wasn't the only one.

Tank was well and truly appalled. Not knowing what to expect, the joy at hearing his friend had managed to cheat death had been ripped away as soon as that curtain had been drawn back and he'd seen the state of her. Boiling rage threatened to consume him, that is until the cool, calculating part of his brain beat it into submission. Knowing exactly what to do, he'd never before been this well equipped. The knowledge he now possessed was immense, even his sometimes ill-tempered employer couldn't deny that. So instinctively, without hesitation, he acted. Deep inside the repository of his mind, he found what he was looking for. It wasn't fancy or clever, but exactly the right mantra to heal the vast majority of her wounds, here and now. Reciting the words in his head, he closed his eyes and focused his thoughts and belief on his injured friend.

Taken aback, a very unusual occurrence for Flash, in all his time, he'd never seen a dragon in such a state. Clearly something out of the ordinary was going on. The question was: what?

Like never before, the king felt... hassled. A million things scuttled through his head, threatening to overwhelm his very being, in this, the very worst thirty-six hours of his life. Hundreds of thousands of beings across the planet had died, beings that he was responsible for, and he'd been powerless to intervene, only able to sit and watch events unfold. The terrorist attacks, as that's what they'd been, had seemingly stopped, and it was hoped that there were no more to come, the thinking being that the stolen laminium from Cropptech had been all but spent. It wasn't known for sure, but that was the dragon council's reasoning. And now he was here, at the request of the doctors, on a matter of the utmost importance. What could be more important than what was going on across the planet, he simply didn't know. But he was here anyway, and shocked to find the dragon he regarded almost as his own son waiting outside the sealed off ward with his friends. Still having no idea what was going on, his patience was very quickly running out. He needed answers, and he needed them now.

Clearing her throat in a kind of school teacher sort of way, the doctor tried to get everyone's attention, but as time slowed right down, all eyes fixed on Tank standing, eyes closed, right in front of his mangled friend, concentrating for all he was worth. Instantly, the look of authority on the doctor's face turned to one of horror as she suddenly realised what Tank was attempting. Before she could shout, "Stop," the young rugby playing dragon let rip a mantra, the full force of his belief and magic behind it.

In that instant, Flash knew. He didn't know how, but he knew, and as Tank cast his mantra, the ex-Crimson Guard reacted as only he could.

Opening his eyes, expecting to see positive results from his handiwork, Tank instead watched open mouthed as Flash launched himself at the king, rugby tackling him to the hard, mezzanine floor. A moment later, a ferocious burst of magical energy whizzed through the exact spot on which the king had been standing only a split second before, zipping off across the ward, smashing resoundingly into a fancy looking heart rate monitor attached to the far wall, that burst instantly into flames, sending fragments of glass and plastic scattering across the area. Crashing to the floor, Flash had the presence of mind to cast a shield mantra, even though he was currently atop the king. Bullet-like pieces of glass and plastic impacted on the invisible shield, halting in mid-air, while the tinkling sound of them then hitting the floor echoed around the massive room.

Standing stock still, apart from his hands which were shaking violently, Peter couldn't believe the scene before him. Tank was too shocked to move, as Flash scrambled to his feet, pulling the winded king up from the floor. During all this the look on the doctor's face changed from horror to pure rage. Crimson cheeks and a vein pumping like a child inflating a balloon made her look like she might yet be in need of the facilities here.

"ENOUGH!" bellowed the doctor. "You stupid children!" She turned to face the king, her head only inches away from the monarch's tired and weary face. "Now do you see why I didn't want them admitted, why it was they were made to wait outside? Perhaps in the future *Your Majesty,* instead of demanding and insisting, you'll listen to reason before you countermand my instructions."

It was all Peter could do not to close his eyes, as the last thing he wanted to do was watch the king quite rightly tear the poor doctor apart, thinking too highly of him for that. Tank felt exactly the same way, while Flash hovered behind the king, ready to intervene should things get out of hand. Although quite what he was going to do, he had no idea.

Easing his face forward a fraction, the king was surprised that the doctor didn't move at all, matching his stare all the way. Tense didn't begin to cover it. After what felt like hours, but in reality was actually only a few moments, he sighed, before whispering,

"I'm sorry doctor. You're right of course. I hope you can forgive me. I've had a lot on my mind the last day or so."

Swallowing nervously, the doctor replied,

"I fully understand Your Majesty, and I apologise for speaking to you in such a way. We seem to have gotten off on the wrong foot. Perhaps we could start again from the very beginning?"

"I think that might be best all round," answered the king. "And don't worry about these three. Braver and more committed dragons it would be hard to find. I trust each of them with my life, as should you."

"Understood."

"So what's going on?" enquired the monarch. "I still have no idea why I've been dragged down here."

"Two halves of a problem Sire. The first is this young female, who has been through quite an ordeal. Brought into us from the blast site at Salisbridge sports club, I have absolutely no idea how she's even still alive. What I can tell you though, is that she's paid a considerable price to still be residing in the world of the living."

On hearing this, Peter's head turned to meet Tank's steely gaze. This was not something that either of them had bargained for, or wanted to hear, on this they could agree with just a look. The good doctor continued.

"The reason," she started to explain, turning and glaring at Tank, "that the healing mantras don't work on her, is that her DNA has been changed, rewritten if you like, and is unlike anything we've ever seen before. I've spoken to dragons across the world about this, and nobody has any answers."

Opening his mouth to speak, the doctor held up her index finger to halt the king. Flash looked on with great respect for her, given what had just happened.

'She's either incredibly brave, or unbelievably stupid,' he thought.

"Essentially her DNA has been completely transformed into something we of course recognise... a human! As far as we can tell, apart from the fact our mantras don't have any effect on her, she's totally and utterly human. No trace at all her dragon heritage."

On hearing this, Peter was stunned and glancing around at the others, he could plainly see he wasn't the only one.

"What can be done?" piped up Tank, meekly.

Turning to face him, the doctor had a scowl of epic proportions plastered across her face.

"NOTHING! Not a damn thing. Even if we knew how this happened... and we don't, finding a way to reverse it is all but impossible. It would be like taking a normal human and turning them into one of us. It simply can't be done."

Fighting back the urge to vomit, Peter's legs suddenly turned to jelly.

"You mentioned that there were two halves to this problem. What's the other?" queried the king.

"You remember out little conversation... just a minute ago?" whispered the doctor.

The monarch nodded.

"You and I need to have a little chat in private."

"Okay."

Grabbing a fistful of curtain, the good doctor yanked it two thirds of the way around Richie's bed, enclosing Peter, Tank and Flash. Turning to the friends, her scowl having all but disappeared, she said,

"You can stay for fifteen minutes. After that, you'll have to go. She drifts in and out of consciousness, and might well wake up. She's coherent but pumped full of some rather powerful painkillers, so you can expect her to be a little confused. Make sure you don't tax her too much. At some point tonight we're looking to move her upstairs to one of the human wards. There's nothing more we can do for her down here."

Peter started to protest. Again the doctor's index finger came out.

"She'll be just fine. We'll make sure, wherever she is, that the ward is staffed by dragons familiar with her condition. But it's better this way... trust me. Also, you'll be able to visit whenever you like, something I'm sure will boost her recovery. And you, mantra boy," she exclaimed, using her well exercised index finger to point at Tank, "no more of the clever stuff. We've tried everything, and none of it works. You'll only get someone else hurt. Understand?"

Sheepishly, Tank squeaked the tiniest, "Yes."

"This way Your Majesty," declared the doctor, holding back two parts of the surrounding curtain to form a doorway. Taking one step towards the gaping hole, the king turned back to look at Peter.

"I'll catch up with you... I promise. It might take me a few days with everything that's going on, but I will. If there's a problem, or she," he nodded his head sideways, indicating Richie, "needs anything at all, you know how to get a message to me."

Peter croaked a, "Thank you," in reply, his throat really dry from not having had a drink all day.

The king turned to face Flash.

"I'm going to need your particular skill set, so don't get too comfortable."

"Ready as ever Sire," replied the ex-Crimson Guard, bowing his head slightly.

With that, the monarch waltzed through the gap in the curtains, followed swiftly by the doctor, leaving the three friends in total silence, none of them quite knowing what to say. It was Peter who spoke up first.

"What does it all mean?"

Tank shrugged his shoulders despondently. Flash considered the question carefully before replying.

"It has implications on so many levels. First and foremost, her health. If she's a fit and healthy human, and we've no reason to doubt that's the case, then she should make a full recovery. We all know what a superb athlete she is, so on that front things should be fine. As for the mantras not working on her, I for one have never come across anything like it. But as a group, I would suggest we're ideally placed to try and find out more. I can search the king's library, and Tank can pump Gee Tee for information. It might be a little complicated and confusing now, but together we're in a unique position to get to the bottom of it."

Silence resumed briefly, that is until Peter plucked up the courage to ask,

"And what is it you're not telling us?"

Burying his face in his hands, Flash exhaled deeply. In the normal course of his duties, it would be about now that he'd be deciding if a little white lie was in order. But ever since the cruel twist of fate that had left him trapped in human form, the three dragons with him had become his friends. Never having had friends before, he really didn't want to lie to them. But he also didn't want to hurt them either. In the end, the decision wasn't a difficult one.

'Friends always tell each other the truth, no matter how hard the subject matter, don't they?' he thought, as he straightened up to face Peter.

"If she's human when she leaves hospital, she'll have to live as one of them."

Peter's face brightened.

"That's not a problem; that's what she does now."

Flash caught sight of Tank's troubled face out of the corner of his eye, realising he was much further along with where this was going.

'Here we go then,' he thought. 'Might as well get it out in the open.'

"She won't be allowed to carry on as she is, Peter. Under no circumstances will the council allow it."

"I don't understand," replied the young hockey playing dragon.

"I think I do," cut in Tank. "You mean the council won't allow her to live as a human and retain her dragon memories, don't you?"

"I'm afraid so," Flash nodded.

"That's preposterous!" exclaimed Peter.

"I'm really sorry Peter, but I'm pretty sure that's what'll happen."

"Why, why, why would they do that?" Peter stuttered, starting to get in a tangle.

"If she's fully human, then they simply can't take the risk that she might reveal our existence to the rest of the world. As well, to them, it will be easier casting her out than actually trying to help her recover and fit back in, without any of her dragon abilities. To them, it will seem like the perfect answer to a very uncomfortable question."

"You can't know this for sure," Peter spluttered, getting more upset by the second. "Anyway, the king would never allow such a thing."

Tank wandered around the bed to his friend. Putting one of his giant arms around his shoulder, he said,

"Just calm down a little... okay? Getting upset won't do anyone any good, and there's certainly no reason to take things out on Flash. You asked him the question, and he answered truthfully. For what it's worth, I think he's probably right." Peter started to open his mouth at this point, but taking a leaf from the good doctor's book, Tank held up his index finger and then carried on. "But the point at which that happens is a long way off. For now, we need to help her recover. We need to be there for her. And while we're doing that, we can look into how the change occurred and what, if anything, we could do, should the council try and cast her out. But for now, let's just support her. That's what she needs the most."

Tank had a way of cutting to the heart of the matter. Feeling so stupid, Peter knew his friend was right. But deep down, he was afraid, afraid for his friend, unable to bear the thought of her being cast away, tossed aside like a little loved or played with rag doll.

'If the council want to do that, then they're most certainly going to have to go through me,' he mused, embracing his friend and apologising to them both. Quickly, he shook Flash's hand, thanking him for his honesty. Then the three of them just sat and waited, all the time watching over their stricken friend. Her breathing was a little ragged, Peter noticed, as her chest rose and fell, but he was glad that she was sleeping, and hoped that the pain from her injuries didn't trouble her so much in that state.

In the blink of an eye, their visiting time was over. A large dragon nurse pulled back the curtain and escorted them back out of the ward, the way they'd come in. As they shuffled back towards the entrance, the sound of muffled voices rang through the air from behind the giant, all encompassing curtain, now off to their left. It certainly sounded like the king, in a rather animated state. Intrigued, the three of them tried to get a little closer, but the nurse was having none of it. Having been suitably reprimanded, they continued on their journey, with Flash and Tank both having the same idea at almost exactly the same time. Casting barely noticeable mantas that enhanced their hearing many times over, they waited patiently to hear what was being said, but to no avail, as the voices remained muffled and incoherent. Flash figured it out before Tank. The curtain! Clearly the curtain was imbued with some kind of magic, a noise scrambling mantra if he wasn't mistaken. Whatever was going on in there, the medical staff certainly wanted it to remain a secret.

Reaching the end of the ward, the dragon disguised as a nurse held the door open for them to leave. Tank and Flash walked straight through, while Peter glanced back over his shoulder, hoping to glimpse the king one more time before they left. Disappointment spread out from his chest like a spilled drink when he couldn't spot the monarch. Just as he was about to turn round, he noticed the giant curtain had got snagged on something, leaving a gap from foot to knee height. And through that gap he caught sight of something extraordinary, something that just shouldn't have been. Before he had a chance to take stock, he was grabbed by the arm and thrust through the door.

"Come on sonny, you've done enough gawping for one day. Be on your way," cackled the nurse. And with that, she slammed the door shut behind them, leaving all three alone in the eerily darkened corridor.

Lagging behind his friends, mulling over everything that had happened not only in the ward just now, but the events of the previous week, Peter, despite having lived through it, and there had been moments (particularly in the clubhouse when Tank was laying down the mantras to contain the laminium bomb's blast) when he'd thought he wouldn't survive, it still seemed like a whirlwind of a dream to him. Things had happened so fast, and had gone from nothing to everything in the blink of an eye. As if saving everybody at the sports club wasn't enough, even though it came at the cost of the building itself, the loss he felt at losing Janice's friendship, well... love actually, cut deep. And then to find that Richie had been in the cellar when the building had been obliterated was nothing short of heartbreaking, only to be negated by the fact that she had, amazingly, survived. That had all been combined with a short spell in jail until everything had been sorted out, and with the much bigger picture: the devastating terrorist attacks across the globe which had wreaked havoc both above and below ground.

'The earth,' he thought, as he continued to follow his friends, 'is a much more dangerous place now than at any other time I can remember. I just want things to go back to how they were... safe, secure, playing hockey, with the clubhouse intact, and my beautiful Janice tucked up in my arms. Oh why did it all have to go so wrong?'

2 A WING AND A PRAYER

A dragon call to arms went out across the kingdom to every living and breathing dragon. The world had been savagely attacked, the like of which had never been seen in its history. Even the darkest days of the previous World Wars paled in comparison with this outrageous, audacious act of violence.

Of course they all knew about it, each and every one of them. It had been plastered across the telepathic papers, with signs and banners flashing and pulsing away at the local storage nodes, making sure every dragon consciousness that arrived there got the message. As if that weren't enough, the king himself made a personal plea, compelling dragons to drop what they were doing and join the rescue efforts in any way they could. And they did, in their hundreds of thousands across the planet, those who were able taking human guise, infiltrating the world above and offering as much aid and assistance as was dragonly possible. Other, mainly subterranean, dragons made their way to the underground areas that had been hit in the attack. In his plea, the king had issued orders that everything was to be used in their fight against whoever had perpetrated this heinous act of barbarity, and in repairing the damage that had been wrought across the globe. So everything was. Both above and below ground, dragons wove their magic in two totally different ways. Below ground, dragons openly used their magical energies to cast mantra after mantra, some to the point of near exhaustion. Most were moving wreckage, some were reinforcing damaged structures, others carefully recovered the bodies of the slain. It was a grim task for sure, but by working together and drawing strength, both physically and emotionally, from each other, progress was made. Dragon towns and cities were made safe and the dragon corpses were recovered with as much dignity as possible.

On the surface, dragons used their power in much the same way, following the king's appeal. Small groups operated across the stricken sites, openly using their power, careful not to reveal themselves to the humans, well... mostly, but more concerned with time ticking by, and rescuing those that remained trapped or badly injured. The use of their power wasn't casual or reckless, but more measured, controlled, and just... MORE! It was almost as if they'd stepped out of the shadows and into the light. Things got done. For the most part the humans were in disarray, and had little chance of noticing the speed with which things were progressing, or indeed how much of the heavy work had been completed without the need for cumbersome machinery. Survivors were found... mothers, sons, fathers, daughters, animals in all different shapes and sizes, all saved because the rulebook had been thrown away, at least for the time being.

Efforts, however, didn't stop there. Magical mantras were used to repair electrical sub-stations and the infrastructure they needed to provide power. Water was also an issue, but this was child's play to the dragons on the ground. With their eidetic memories, creative minds and wealth of magical power, they almost resembled gods in what they could do. Hospitals in the midst of a blast radius sprang up from virtually nowhere, as good as new, having been obliterated only days before. Sewage systems were not only repaired, but made more efficient and effective. All this was achieved without the humans' knowledge. How? Groups of police, fire and other government bodies, all dragons in disguise, manned (or dragoned) each and every perimeter cordon, at each and every site. Some were harder to maintain than others, some required extra resources which duly arrived, thanks in no small part to the plea from the king. In most cases, humans couldn't get within a mile of the edge of each blast. It was teamwork on a massive scale, with parties of dragons numbering in the hundreds, purely devoted to organising the hundreds of thousands of volunteers who were answering the dragon king's call.

Human media were the thorn in the side of all this, but dragons had worked their way up the ladder over time in nearly every organisation, with newspapers and television being no exception. Top level executives began issuing unusual orders about who should be covering the story, or stories, depending on how you looked at it. Helicopter pilots and the news reporters who travelled with them were selected not because of their reporting experience, but because they too were dragons, and they too were being co-ordinated by the groups underground, making sure not to film or record the dragon squads working at the scene of each blast, instead only filming or snapping pictures of the devastated areas that were unattended. It was a little clumsy, a little chaotic, but most importantly... IT WORKED! Everything the news channels and newspapers featured had been vetted by a dragon at some point. No human on the entire planet had any idea of the actual scale of the unseen dragon aid, and would be surprised at the pockets of infrastructure and vital services that remained untouched over the coming days, having actually been swiftly rebuilt or repaired.

But of course there were still bodies. Tens, hundreds, thousands... more! It was hard going, even for the dragon recovery teams, who it had to be said for the most part were pretty much detached, mainly because most of them regarded humans as far below their equal, equating them more with a beloved pet, than something worthy of sharing the planet with. These were much older and rapidly diminishing views, in an ever changing world, but still they existed, not quite widespread, but common enough. It hardly mattered though. Each and every dragon went about their business, whatever it was, with utter professionalism, dedication and ruthless efficiency. Minutes turned into hours, hours into days, days dragged on until finally, the whole dragon operation was called to a halt.

Once the order had been given, schedules and rotas were changed back, allowing tired and weary dragons to be substituted for their grief stricken charges. Over the course of twenty four hours, deployment was pretty much as it should have been, with the odd dragon here and there, but for the most part, it was mainly humans who inhabited and covered the devastated areas.

3 ALL HAIL OUR SAVIOUR IN SCALE

A patchwork of images faded in and out of his mind almost constantly now. For the most part, he couldn't tell whether he was awake or not. Reaching back into his mind, he tried to recall how it had all started. Remembering being somewhere... somewhere he shouldn't have, then... it all became dark and he'd awoken here, wherever here was. It was one of the many questions 'THEY' wouldn't answer.

Thinking of them mainly as 'THEY' because of their continued evasiveness, he'd asked what had happened, where he was and how he'd got here, all eliciting the same response..."All in good time." What the hell was that supposed to mean? Why were they being so restrictive with the truth? What was going on? And why couldn't he remember exactly what had happened? All these things constantly nagged at him, but nothing like the big question, the one that stood out like Batman in a Marvel production, the elephant in the room: why could he not feel, or move, any part of his body? And why were his neck and head surrounded by some kind of tiny metal scaffolding frame? Had he broken his back and become permanently disabled, or suffered massive trauma to his head? It might explain a few things if he had. Politely he'd asked these questions, only for the nursing staff (if indeed that's what they really were... sometimes he wondered about that, however ridiculous it seemed) to change the subject very quickly and awkwardly, all of them saying that he'd have to be a patient patient and wait to speak to the doctor, who was on his way. That was days, if not weeks ago. It was hard to remember and keep track of time with all the drugs they were feeding him. On waking up, they'd give him a drink, but before he knew it, he felt sleepy again. Trying to fight it, he gave everything he had in an effort to stay awake, but the pleasant, almost joyful feeling of the medication starting somewhere lower down in his body, was just too hard to resist. In the end, sleep won every time.

But he was awake now, and more alert than he could remember being for some time. Hearing the door to his room open with a tiny little squeak, followed by the expansive whooshing rush of air which normally preceded footsteps, he knew instantly this time was different, because there was more than one set, three or four if he wasn't mistaken. This was something... NEW!

"Good evening... Tim, is it?" whispered a soft, soothing, reassuring voice.

Trying to turn his head in the direction of the sound, he failed miserably, just like all his previous attempts.

"Ahhh... of course, you can't move. Let me come over to you."

Right at the bottom of his vision a smiling face swam into view, nothing like he'd expected. Tim was glad that someone was here finally, someone to answer all his questions, though this guy looked nothing like any sort of doctor he could ever remember seeing, apart from the smile of course. They nearly all had that. For a start, there was the hair. Long, straggly, grey hair, down past his shoulders. Unkempt was the most fitting way he could think to describe it, and his clothes weren't much better, looking very much like they'd been slept in for days on end. The matching grey stubble etched across nearly every part of his lower face did nothing to ease Tim's very real concerns.

"It's nice to finally meet you son," uttered the figure hovering over Tim.

"You too," Tim felt compelled to say, feeling completely and utterly helpless and out of control, having hoped the anger at being trapped here for so long without any answers would have fired him up enough to demand to know exactly what was going on. But it wasn't the case. His life was most certainly in their hands, and he felt this now more than ever.

"You've been through a lot son. Can you tell me what you remember?"

"Very little in fact," replied Tim honestly. "I recall being somewhere... somewhere I shouldn't have been. But I can't for the life of me remember where. And then it went dark, and then... NOTHING! Sorry I can't be more help than that."

"That's alright," answered the... KING! For that's who was standing over Tim right at this very moment, here at the earliest available opportunity, given everything that had happened across not only the dragon domain, but planet wide. Knowing he should have got here sooner and not just demand the staff continue to sedate Tim until he got there, of all the options, it just seemed like the easiest thing to do. As well, a part of him was secretly terrified of dealing with anything to do with the prophecy. Having always known it was a possibility, what ruling monarch didn't, he'd never truly believed the fabled white dragon would turn up on his watch, and certainly not under these circumstances, here and now, during all this.

"I'm sure, son, you have plenty of questions about what's been going on and how it is we're going to treat you?"

"Uh huh," he mumbled, trying to nod his head, but of course being unable to.

"What I'm going to do, is get them to remove the restraint stopping your neck from moving. Is that okay?"

"Yes," Tim remarked enthusiastically. "Is it possible to take all of this scaffolding away?"

"That, my young friend, is known as M.U.C.U.S. and is rather important at the moment."

Tim tried to smile, but it turned into more of a grimace than anything else. Hoping desperately that Tim wouldn't ask him what M.U.C.U.S. stood for, the king knew that it would only raise more questions that he didn't want to answer. M.U.C.U.S. actually stands for Mantra Universal

Containment Unit Subjugator, and was currently keeping Tim's head in human form, because the rest of him, which he couldn't feel or see, was residing in a perfectly pure white dragon shape.

"Before I go on though, there are some things I need to tell you," announced the king. "I know that you've been bracing yourself for bad news regarding your condition. I know, because that's exactly what I would be doing in your place. On that front, you should know that there's good news and... interesting news. Note I didn't say bad news."

Tim just smiled at the monarch nervously. The king continued.

"What I need for you to do, is take me at my word, and try your hardest to remain as calm as is humanly (a poor choice of words in the situation) possible. Do you think you can do that for me?"

Gulping and swallowing almost at the same time, Tim just about managed to get out a squeaky, "Yes."

"Good man," quipped the king. "Remove the M.U.C.U.S.," he ordered.

Two nurses appeared on either side of Tim's head and began fiddling about with the brace-like structure encompassing his neck and skull. All the time the grey haired figure hovered in view, a comforting smile imprinted on his face.

Moments later, the nurses retreated, nodding in the king's direction as they did so. Holding his breath, knowing that the next few moments could prove to be some of the most momentous ever in the dragon kingdom, and had been foretold thousands of years ago, the king watched closely, waiting to see what would happen.

As the nurses retreated, Tim carefully tried to move his neck. Stiff didn't begin to cover it, but after a few seconds he was at least able to roll his head and shrug his shoulders. Just as he was about to sit up and inspect the rest of his body, the most peculiar feeling started to attack him right behind his eyes. Instantly his vision blurred.

Thinking that something had got into his eyes, he blinked furiously. If only it were that simple.

You see, when Richie broke her *'alea'*, using it in conjunction with the simple shield mantra to save them from the explosion and the collapsing building, the magical properties of the mantra and the laminium in the bomb combined to produce an even more unpredictable side effect. It forced Richie's DNA to lock itself into a perfect human form, in a very different way to say that of Flash, and in doing so, her dragon abilities, magic, DNA, call it what you will, all overwhelmed Tim, turning him into a dragon. At first, the change wasn't apparent. On recovering his body from the blast crater, it fully resembled a human, in every single aspect. It was only once it was taken to the secluded part of Salisbridge District hospital, the area deep below ground reserved only for the worst dragon cases, that the changes to his physiology became apparent. It was a shock to each and every one of the dragon staff there, because they'd known him to be a human... he'd been checked out before arriving. And the surprises didn't stop there. His transformation wasn't like a normal dragon's transition between forms. For Tim, it was one body part at a time, over a much longer period. Whereas most dragons only take a matter of moments to change forms, Tim's body parts required minutes or even hours in some cases, for the full effect to become permanent. With his left arm changing first, and then the right wing springing out almost as if from nowhere, the staff had little idea of what they were dealing with, or what exactly they should do. Only once his stomach and back had converted, did they realise that they were likely dealing with an all white dragon, and given the prophecy about such a beast, the one prophecy all dragons adhere to above all others, the king had been immediately informed.

Iron being beaten into submission on an anvil, that's what the pain behind his eyes felt like. All thoughts of sitting up or moving at all were washed away when the excruciating pain rippled through his jaw. Wanting to scream, yell or shout for all he was worth, just the very thought of moving any part of his mouth even a millimetre was enough to dissuade him. With his vision barely there at all thanks to the pain behind his eyes, he wished he could move his arms, really to check what he knew couldn't be true. It just couldn't. Because it felt as if not only were his teeth actually growing, but that his entire face and jaw had got... BIGGER! Making to swallow, he found that his tongue, something he'd never had any problems with before, had never even noticed in fact, was lopping about inside his mouth, flailing around like a blind anaconda searching for a mate. It felt as though it were that size as well. Just when he thought it couldn't get any worse, with the pain at its most horrific, a sensation tickled deep down within his face.

'Oh no,' he thought to no one but himself. Trying to push it away, having done so on previous occasions, it was no good with the pain and the unfamiliar sensations breaching all of his defences. Lacking both the concentration and willpower required, the sensation snowballed out of control, growing with each moment that passed, until inevitably it happened.

'Aitchooooooo!' he sneezed, oddly accompanied by a whooshing and wheezing sound, as well as a burning feeling all around his mouth and nose.

He wasn't king for nothing, and had seen it coming... well, only just. Flinging himself off to one side, the streak of blue and orange flame shot past where he'd been standing, bouncing off a metallic bedpan, smashing into one of the glass panels that made up three quarters of the room. An ugly, smouldering, brown mark was now splattered against the specially toughened glass, just where the flame had struck.

With the pain starting to recede, Tim's vision started to clear, showing the elderly man still smiling at him, albeit off to one side of where he'd previously stood. Feeling odd, his face seemed... longer! No, not longer... bigger, heavier, more difficult to balance. It was weird. With his lolloping tongue dangling out of his mouth, the need to look down at his body became more pressing than ever. Sitting up, he arched his very heavy head forward, concerned that he might not have the strength to bring it back up again, and gazed down at the rest of his body. It didn't register at first, figuring he must still be asleep... dreaming! But of course he wasn't, he was wide awake, gawping down at a huge, bright, white scaled belly that rose up and down in time with his own breathing, two perfectly folded wings, and razor sharp talons on the end of scraggy looking feet which spread out from beneath the most powerful set of legs he'd ever set eyes on. Flimsy looking arms lay neatly pointed towards the bottom of the bed. It was the most bizarre out of body experience any being on the planet had ever had... only it wasn't! It was him... his mind, in the body of a dragon. Yet it was real. As real as it gets.

"To be honest, I expected a little more... panic!" remarked the king.

"It's not real," answered Tim, wiggling his strange and protruding jaws from side to side. Sucking his lips together, the king rubbed his stubbly chin.

"I'm afraid it is."

Tim just sat there, gazing across at the dragon ruler, all the while taking in the prehistoric body laid out before him.

"Would you allow me to explain?" asked the king.

"If you can explain all of THIS," said Tim, "then you're a better man than I am, which at the moment... wouldn't be difficult at all."

Smiling at the thought of sharing a joke with the 'white dragon', he thought it a good omen, and a glimpse into a calm, thoughtful and strong personality.

'And by God is he going to need that,' mused the

monarch.

"While I appreciate you trying to describe me as a better 'man' than yourself, the truth of the matter is much more complicated than that. You see, I too am a dragon. In fact, I'm the king of the dragons, in charge of just about everything there is."

Automatically, Tim's giant scaly jaws started to open, but he managed to stifle the laugh that threatened to come out. Something about the individual before him commanded respect and authority. Instinctively he'd already recognised it, and despite the fear, terror, panic, and questions numbering in their hundreds, currently running through his newly shaped head, he was now paying absolute attention to this very unusual individual.

"So will you let me explain? I warn you now, it's going to take some time, and quite a lot of what you will hear will be beyond your wildest imagination. But given where you are, and what's happened to you, this is as important for you as it is for me. What do you say?"

Fighting for control of his immense head, Tim came to the only logical conclusion... to listen. He was in no condition to do anything else, particularly given he had no idea where he was, or who, or what else inhabited the building that he was currently receiving care in. If nothing else, he supposed that it might just fill in some of the missing gaps in his memory. Nodding his agreement, the king perched on the bottom of the very large bed and started from the beginning.

They sat and talked for hours... many hours. I say talked, Tim had of course mainly listened. To his credit, the king had let the newly discovered 'white dragon' interrupt whenever he felt the need to know something so obvious to the monarch that he wouldn't have thought to explain it to a dragon who'd only been one for a matter of days. To say it had blown Tim's mind was an understatement. But as he'd hoped, it had at least cleared up some of his missing memory. Sitting on the bed, feeling more than a little sorry for himself, his thoughts drifted off to the woman he loved... Richie! A smile crept across his face, in a much different way than he was used to. Before it could have been used to charm the wits off any woman, but now... it would probably terrify most of the human population. In anticipation of the food he'd been promised, his stomach gurgled ever so slightly. Normally a chicken and fish kind of guy, when they'd asked what he'd like to eat, just after the king left, he instantly told them he wanted rare steak and well cooked bacon. Oh how things had changed.

As the delightful aroma of the bacon, done to a turn, filtered through his super sensitive nose, wafting across from somewhere else in the building, he once again thought about the superstar lacrosse player, wondering just how she was adapting to her change in bodily circumstances. Although hers was a change as dramatic as his, the shock and realisation would be vastly different. On reflection, he should have realised she was something different, something special. Of course, he had thought of her as something unique, but would never have had her down as another species. All the bravado, showing off, taking on men twice her size and beating them at goodness knows what... It was all so obvious now, with hindsight and his new knowledge about dragons. A small part of him wondered why she hadn't visited. The king had said she'd been forbidden to do so, but that wouldn't stop the Richie he knew. Quite the opposite in fact. It would have spurred her on, wanting to put one over on authority, as she had so many times before. But had the reversion to a fully fledged human being changed her, or was it something else? Perhaps, like him, she had gaps in her memory too, and was even now unable to remember their time together. Feeling as though his heart was being squeezed, he hoped not. Just as he turned this over in his mind, a tall, rather attractive, red haired woman who he now knew to be a dragon, slipped through the door, carrying a gigantic tray with a cover on the top. It was so big and wide that her slender arms struggled to contain it as she headed his way. Once again he smiled, at least he hoped that's what he was doing, supposing there was every chance he was doing something else, what with all this being so new to him. Perhaps at some point he'd have to ask for a mirror, not only to see the new him, but also to practise getting his brand new face to work properly.

With a friendly, "There you go," the nurse plonked the tray down on his lap... well, more like his belly actually, before lifting off the lid. Watching her leave the room, he felt a brief pang of disappointment. Part of him wanted a conversation, in the hope that perhaps she could answer some of the many questions he had, or show him just the smallest hint of kindness. But she was gone, so he glanced down at the tray and his eyes nearly popped out. It looked as though the entire dragon kingdom's supply of bacon and steak had found its way onto a plate the size of a sofa. Starting to count the rashers, he stopped when he reached fifty, realising that he'd not even got halfway. There must have been over thirty of the finest steaks, not just any old things either, T-bones if he wasn't mistaken. And someone had taken the liberty of adding some fried eggs, at least three dozen by the look of things.

'It does look appealing,' he thought, pleased that someone had added the eggs, the human in him really appreciating the gesture.

'But hang on,' a sudden thought occurred to him, 'they've only gone and forgotten all the cutlery. How on earth am I supposed to eat all of this?' And then he remembered. He was a dragon, and cutlery was no longer an option. Chuckling came from nowhere, tears winding their way across the new landscape of his prehistoric face, with much further to travel now than before. Indiscriminate guffaws of laughter pierced the wolfing down of bacon rashers for the next thirty minutes or so.

4 A TOUCHING MOMENT

Waiting for everything to come to fruition drove him mad. Constantly having to move about, avoiding built up areas, swapping cars, dodging CCTV cameras even at service stations... the monotony was just staggering, though part of him knew it would be worth it in the end.

Opening the fridge, he grabbed a beef salad sandwich sealed in a plastic carton, something they'd picked up the day before at a remote service station, his stomach turning at the thought of eating the ropey looking snack. It had most certainly seen better days, but there was little else. So, unwrapping it, he discarded the plastic on the floor and, walking through to the living area, sandwich in one hand, cane in the other, took a bite. Moments later, he wished he'd thrown away the sandwich and taken a bite of the plastic, sure it would have tasted better. Striding down the steps that led into the lounge, he glanced across at the television that his father was watching with the sound turned down. Some news channel was still harping on about the destruction caused by the laminium bombs. His laminium bombs. That made him smile. Slowly, he eased down into the plump arm chair opposite his father, the legendary dragon incarcerated for so many years for his crimes against the entire underground population, all those years ago... TROYDENN!

The wizened old man glared across at him. At the moment, there was little love lost between the two of them. Both loving and despising his father in equal measures, he loved him because he'd shown him his true potential, nurtured his new found abilities and, in the end, granted him the power to become the new super dragon that he was, eclipsing his father in ways the old dragon could only dream of. But he also hated him because of how he'd treated his mother. Of course he couldn't actually remember, but he'd been told what had happened, deep down in that frozen hellhole of an icy dungeon where the rogue dragons had been left to die, and where he'd been both conceived and born. How she was used and abused by everyone, including him. No respect, no rights, no say in anything because she was female, one of just a handful. She'd meant nothing to his father, that much he did know, just an experimented on shell, used for one purpose and one purpose alone: to give birth the human way, to continue the bloodlines of the dragons trapped there. Such a simple idea, and one to which their dragon captors had given little thought, because if they had, then they most certainly wouldn't have been imprisoned. To think, all it took was the tiniest sliver of power to turn their DNA fully human, and that was it. Reproduce the human way, and then just wait for the opportunity for freedom to come along, which of course it had, in the form of the very trusting and very gullible nagas. An added bonus to the whole thing presented itself in the guise of the very different powers those born there had been granted, as well as the fact that normal dragons (if there's even such a thing) are unable to detect even the tiniest hint of anything even remotely not human. All in all, like a phoenix rising from the ashes, some good had come from the forced captivity. And with these new found powers, the opportunity to change the fate of the world still very much existed.

"Uhhhh," he shook his head in disgust. Just the thought of that cold, dark place made him shudder. No one should be brought up in a place like that. He had been, and it had shaped him into the being he now was. And he was determined to make those that had put him and his father there, pay dearly for doing so.

"What's the hold up?" his father demanded, grumpily.

"No hold up. We're just moving assets into place. None of this is easy. It's not as if we have a superfast underground monorail system to move them all around. Everything takes time." Not to be harsh in the slightest, he'd meant it in a no nonsense kind of way, but that's not how his father took it at all.

For an old dragon, in a desperately old, frail and fragile human form, he was quick. Off the scale quick. Instantly he straddled his son. Troydenn's index finger pressed firmly into his son's forehead. For Manson it was surreal and not the first time it had happened, not by a long way, and he had no doubt it wouldn't be the last either. Unable to move, paralysed, with even the tiniest of his muscles incapable of operating as they should, getting shallower with every second that passed, his breathing slowed. There was no pain, just the frightening prospect of his father not letting him go. Soon, he wouldn't be able to pull any air into his lungs, his vision would start to blur and things would go very badly. Briefly he wondered just how far his father would go this time, just to get his point over.

"YOU... don't speak to me like that! Understood?" Troydenn spat, knowing full well his son couldn't reply, even if he'd wanted to. "I don't want to hear about hold ups and delays. We need to get this done now. I've waited as long as I can for all of this. I don't care about your plans for the dragon domain and the rest of the planet. I just want him to PAY! I want to hear him scream, shout and beg for forgiveness. I want to take him to the very edge of death and then bring him back, over and over again. HE MUST PAY! AND IT MUST BE DONE SOON!"

Having heard the words, how could he not? But it was becoming hard to focus now, and he felt as though he were drowning. It was odd. A pervasive black had started to invade the edge of his vision, moving ever closer to the centre with every moment that passed. Wanting to close his eyes, shake the vision of that fearful face which sat right in front of him, he didn't. Having done so once before, he'd paid a frightful price that time, upon waking up. So, willing his eyes to stay open, he looked straight ahead, for as long as he could before the blackness finally took him.

5 DEBT COLLECTOR

Preceding the opening of its see-your-own-reflection shiny doors, the shrill 'ding' of the lift started him out of his reverie. Quickly adjusting his tie and posture, he stood up straight, shoulders as far back as they would go. Before the doors had withdrawn fully, he stepped through the gap, feeling the luxurious, thick carpet beneath the soles of his brown suede shoes. Nodding to the secretary on the way past, knowing that she was more than just that, he did all he could to hide the nervousness he felt from her as she flashed him a sparkling smile.

'Oh how things have changed,' he mused, walking up to Garrett's office door, that nervous feeling weighing heavy on his mind, given that once again he was about to have to lie to his boss. Sometimes it seemed as though each lie tore off a tiny piece of him, never to be seen again. Knocking twice in quick succession, a voice from within uttered,

"Come."

Entering, he sat down in the chair that Garrett proffered.

"Peter my boy, how are you?" his boss asked cheerfully.

"Fine thank you si... Al," he replied, remembering both Garrett's and Paul Simon's advice.

Leaning forward, the owner's expression changed from cheerful to concerned.

"Your request to meet sounded urgent. There's nothing wrong, I hope?"

"Uhhh... no, no, well... kind of," he stumbled. "It's just that I wanted to let you know about... uh... Richie Rump. She... uh... works in the training department."

"Mr Bentwhistle," announced Garrett formally, "am I to believe that you think I don't know the names of all the people in every single country throughout the world that this company employs?"

'Of course he knows their names. That's just him... isn't it?' Peter chastised himself.

"From the directors to the janitors, the scientists to the grounds staff, the engineers to the lorry drivers, both full time and temporary staff, I make it my place to know their names, more so now than I ever used to. And I used to," announced Garrett, a little miffed. "I know who Miss Rump is, and indeed how close the two of YOU are," he added.

'Of course he does,' he thought, shaking his head. A tiny voice deep inside him was currently screaming, "Stupid, stupid, stupid," over and over again. He tried to ignore it.

"Please... you were telling me about Miss Rump," Garrett continued.

Swallowing nervously... he was having trouble with this as it was... not with the Richie part of things, but the next bit. Hoping he could go through with it when the time came, he turned back to the matter at hand.

"I just wanted you to know that she won't be able to return to work for a few weeks. She's been really badly hurt and is currently in hospital."

This took Garrett aback.

"How?" he asked.

"The explosion at the sports club, the one that's been all over the papers. She was caught up in it."

"But I thought everyone got out safely, and that there were no casualties," exclaimed the 'bald eagle'.

"That's how it appeared at first, but apparently she was caught in the periphery of the blast, something that with all the confusion surrounding it, wasn't realised until much later.

"Is she badly hurt?"

"She has some burns," answered Peter, "as well as some broken ribs, other broken bones and major bruising. While her injuries aren't life threatening, she does seem to have been very badly roughed up."

"I see," said Garrett, a faraway look in his eyes. "What can I do?" he asked. "I can have the finest doctors in the land at her bedside in hours. They'd know what to do. We can have her moved to a private hospital, with the finest treatment. Money's no object."

More than a little taken aback by the very generous offer, he shouldn't really have been surprised given Garrett's caring disposition both before, and more so after, the whole incident with the dragon Manson. The offer he'd just made would almost certainly apply to every single one of his staff.

"That's really not necessary Al," remarked Peter, remembering. "She just needs some time to recover, and in her own words, she's getting wonderful treatment and care."

Garrett nodded.

"Then I'll pay her a visit and see if there's anything else she needs."

Afraid this would happen, although she'd been moved to a different ward, he was pretty sure the dragons keeping an eye on Richie at the hospital would be deeply disappointed to have Garrett sniffing around.

"I'm pretty sure she would rather not have any visitors," he stated. "She's rather embarrassed about the whole thing, and ashamed that she's having to miss work. On that score, she's also worried about her workload. There are a couple of important training courses that she's supposed to be running next week, and she's concerned about someone else taking over."

Garrett nodded thoughtfully.

"So... it's probably better if I don't go and you just pass on our get well wishes," he said diplomatically.

"That's pretty much how I see it."

"Okay. Tell her I'll make sure her courses are covered and that she's not to rush back. In fact, tell her that she's barred from the building for at least three weeks. That should do it, shouldn't it?"

Peter smiled.

"That would be great."

"Thanks for letting me know."

"You're welcome," he replied, staying in his chair, despite Garrett expecting him to stand up.

"Is there something else I can do for you?" Garrett asked.

Swallowing nervously, Peter had never envisaged being here, asking about this. For all intents and purposes, he'd forgotten about the whole thing. But as things stood with the situation at the sports club, he figured it was worth a shot. I mean, what exactly was the worst thing that could happen?

Garrett's short, sharp cough startled Peter back to the present.

"Ummm... I was wondering about the... about the conversation we had some time ago."

Scratching his chin, Garrett tried to recollect, eventually shaking his head.

"You're going to have to be a little more specific I'm afraid."

This was tearing him apart, not least because he hadn't really wanted to revisit all of this, finding it more than a little embarrassing, wondering if his employer had forgotten all about it, or even whether it had been a genuine offer in the first place. But from what little he knew, the sports club was in serious trouble, and he felt obliged, and simply wanted, to help them out if he could. So he just came out with it.

"You said some time ago that you owed me a debt, because of all that business with Manson, and saving the laminium, you offered me all sorts of rewards. I was wondering if the offer still stood?"

Running his thumb and forefinger through his bushy moustache, Cropptech's owner pondered his young charge's question. Surprised that the boy had come in to ask, he assumed it must be something important, resolving to hear him out.

"I'm certainly willing to listen to what you have to say. Whether I can promise you what you want, well, until I've heard you out, I just won't know."

Pleased that he'd got this far, Peter nodded.

"You see I play hockey at the weekends, at the sports club, the one that was destroyed in the explosion, the one that Richie got caught up in."

Garrett nodded, urging the young man to continue, fully aware of all this, just as he knew the young lady, Miss Rump, played lacrosse there, as well as a good number of his other employees, in one form or another.

"With the clubhouse obliterated, it has now come to light that the insurance policy covering everything at the club has long since been cancelled. How that's happened, I have absolutely no idea. What I do know is that the sports club and the individual clubs that make it up, are a very long way off having the funds to even begin to contemplate a rebuilding effort. I was hoping that you might consider helping out, in any way possible. I know it's asking a lot, and truth be told, in no way do I feel I need rewarding for what happened with Manson and all the laminium. But you did offer, and you did say at the time that if I ever thought of anything in the future then I should just ask. Well, this is me just asking."

And with that, he sat back in the chair, not having realised he'd moved further and further forward, letting out a huge sigh of relief.

Scribbling on the jotter that was on his table, Garrett dared not look Peter in the eye. Although surprised at the youngster coming in and making the request, he wasn't shocked that the request itself wasn't really for him. Part of him found it intriguing that the youngster didn't want money, or a house and was desperate to find out what sort of person would turn down that kind of offer, and indeed, learn a lot more about them. But in his mind, it did at least confirm that he was indeed exactly the right person to be in charge of security of not only this facility, but of all the Cropptech sites across the entire globe. Inside he smiled.

"While I cannot promise to help until I know a little more, I will certainly look into it and see what I can do. Is that okay?"

Peter smiled in approval.

"That's all I ask si... Al."

"Well, if there's nothing else?"

Rising to his feet, Peter said, "Thank you," and left quietly, closing the door behind him on the walk back towards the lift. Glad that was over, he was off to see if he had a spare shirt in his office, as the one he was currently wearing was now wetter than a dad bathing his baby.

6 THE MOURNING AFTER THE WEEK BEFORE

The time had come to stop. Take a breath. Get some kind of perspective on the horrendous events of the last seven days. Injuries insurmountable, the loss of life had been catastrophic. Infrastructure had been ruined and would undoubtedly take years to reach its previous levels, despite the tireless work by dragons across the globe, most in teams, most exhausting their supply of mana on a daily basis.

'It could have been worse,' was what most ordinary dragons were thinking. It could have been much worse. Regardless of their efforts, the monorail was still severely crippled in places, hampering rescue and recovery efforts, in spite of seven whole days passing. They'd done as much as was dragonly possible, and now it was time for a pause, a lull in proceedings. Time to remember those lost, both human and dragon alike.

So they'd come together, a gathering like none before it in the history of their race, every single one of them donning a cloak of some sort, many colourful, a few... not so much. Even the King's Guard, of which there were many, given that the terrorists were still at large, each wore a cloak, looking mighty odd in some cases. For the entire underground community, it was the ultimate form of remembrance. Days earlier protesters had pounded the streets, complaining about the mass of bodies filling the Bereavement Grottos, all at the same time. But that decision had already been made by the council and backtracking wasn't something it was renowned for, so nearly every dragon on the planet came together, showing unity for their kind, the council, and ultimately their king, in this, the most trying of times.

And so it was, on this early morning, that each and

every dragon spread across the earth made their way to the nearest Bereavement Grotto, or one of the specially assigned mourning areas that had been set up in town and city centres, market places, parks and historically significant sites. From London and Purbeck, to New York and Sydney. From Rio to Calcutta, from Auckland to Oslo. Each designated site had one thing in common... a huge LCD screen. All across the globe, dragons garbed in cloaks congregated, showing their solidarity not only with one another, but with the humans as well. With anything from hundreds to tens of thousands gathered at each location it was, as you might well expect, a very sombre occasion. Almost silent for the most part, even the dragons that knew one another only really offered each other a nod of recognition. That is until exactly 10.45 GMT, when the giant screens burst into life after a momentary fizzle of static, the face on the screen instantly recognisable, stirring emotions like no other could. Not one amongst them (apart from the pretenders within) would not lay down their life for him in a heartbeat. Honourable, courageous, fair-minded and an excellent leader, were just a few of the many terms used to describe him as far as those watching were concerned. Having led them for decades now, on an enlightened course, with barely a blip along the way, they knew he must be suffering, but they had no idea just how much. Across the silent spaces, his powerful yet compassionate voice rang out.

"Seven days ago, the world changed. The very nature of this planet changed. It wasn't predicted or forecast. No one either here or above had a clue what was coming. But come it did. As your king, the responsibility for defending not only our realm, but that of the humans above... falls to me. It was I, who let you down. It was I, who should have been aware of the threat. And let me assure you now, the burden of this failure will live strong in me for the rest of my life."

There was a long pause while the king just stared

silently into the camera, almost as if taking the measure of each and every dragon out there.

7 THE MARK OF TRUE EVIL

Strangely, the underground world which the dragons inhabited wasn't quite the idyllic realm that most liked to think. Much like its counterpart on the surface, it had its fair share of squalor and deeply shady depths. In one of those depths, in a run down, long since forgotten about suburb of London, beings that didn't belong, outsiders, were up to no good.

Through a heavy, metal, rusting, side door, a steady stream of nagas slithered into the dark, abandoned building. A cowled human form stood silently at the front next to an authoritative looking naga who was overseeing operations. As the shop floor of what had previously been a thriving laminium ball merchandise factory, which had moved on to bigger and better premises, filled up with many hundreds of nagas, an overpowering smell of decaying fish pervaded every last part of the run down building. Only when all the available space had been filled did the naga in charge speak.

"You know why we're all here. The debt to our captured king must be honoured if he is to be free again. It won't be long before we can leave all of this and return to the cold solitude of the waters we call our own. Until then, we have instructions to follow, a mission to help accomplish. You are here to swear a magical oath to the future leader of not only the cursed dragons, but of the entire planet itself. When this has come to pass, you will be released from your bond, any obligations forgotten. You will now repeat the chant."

At that, every naga made themselves that bit straighter, that bit taller, in anticipation of what was to come.

Drawing back his cowl, the human shape that had stood unmoving at the front revealed a scarred and disfigured face. Humans, or even dragons, would have gasped, that's how bad it was. But it made no difference to the nagas; they cared not for aesthetics of any kind. Intricately moving his fingers while at the same time weaving his hands out in front of him, he began to recite the chant.

"Droch me ha. Nee somme so ta vecht ma recht."

"DROCH ME HA. NEE SOMME SO TA VECHT MA RECHT," the beasts repeated loudly.

"Tol va diemme growd rolle simme so dul vedre nol rol sect burreme."

Like robots duplicating their master, the nagas continued.

"TOL VA DIEMME GROWD ROLLE SIMME SO DUL VEDRE NOL ROL SECT BURREME."

Swirls of multicoloured energy poured forth from the disfigured man's fingertips, creating a ribbon of rainbow coloured tentacles, stretching out in front of the gathered cast. This time he shouted the commands he wished the nagas to follow.

"AUTARUM ASISIES CONDULT SPERONUM TRACTORIN REDONC VASSIL EARONIST. SEDORST SECRETE SANTORUM FOREVST."

"AUTARUM ASISIES CONDULT SPERONUM TRACTORIN REDONC VASSIL EARONIST. SEDORST SECRETE SANTORUM FOREVST."

A multicoloured rainbow of magic exploded out across the assembled crowd, causing them all to close their eyes, taking more than ten seconds to dissipate. On opening their eyes, they weren't in the least bit surprised to find that they now all bore the same marking, imbued on their bodies. It was a starburst, only instead of being orange, it was the darkest shade of black known, beams of dark light springing out at all angles.

The ceremony seemingly over, one by one the nagas filed out, the same way they'd come in. With one difference. As they left, they were all, to a being, issued with massive, evil looking bastard swords, some with scabbards, others attached to bandoliers, the rest hanging from futuristic belts.

With this going on, it took some time before the building was empty. When it was, the whole process started over again. And that wouldn't be the last time either.

8 A BROKEN PROMISE?

A shiver ran down her spine as she shook her head, glad to be away from the father... he was an odd one, and scary too. Footsteps crunching on the gravel as she walked across the courtyard between buildings, well... wooden barns actually, this had been their home for a while now, but that was all coming to an end, hence her little walk in the freezing cold. Opening the wooden framed glass door, she edged through and then pulled it shut behind her, relieved to be back inside. Stopping to pull the zip down on her coat a little, hating that feeling of her breathing being restricted in any way, shape or form, feeling better able to breathe, she followed the maze of narrow corridors until she stood at the entrance to the biggest room. Manson was on the phone, and she knew better than to interrupt him. It would have to be something really important for that, so she waited... and listened.

"Yes... I'm looking at the chaos now, as we speak. The pathetic humans' desire to cover every news event anywhere, in graphic detail, never ceases to amaze me. They're even showing the blast crater in Thailand. Pathetic really," he said, holding the phone to his right ear while gazing steadily at the pictures from the news broadcast on the shiny, metallic television in the corner of the room. Silence followed as he listened intently to what the voice on the other end had to say.

"And you've done exactly as we agreed. I couldn't be happier. More chaos and mayhem than the planet is experiencing now, would be hard to imagine. Ahhh... now just a second," he said, turning on the spot, acknowledging his visitor with a nod of his head. "What we agreed was that I would deliver him to you as soon as I had control of the dragon kingdom, and while I'm the first to admit that this has all been a huge step in the right direction, we're not quite there yet. It should only be a matter of days now if everything goes to plan, and then you'll have him back. I PROMISE!"

She could hear the caller on the other end go very quiet, before eventually letting out a soft, "Okay," that echoed out through the phone's speaker.

"Now I need the coordinates and time of the transfer." There was a short pause before he started repeating what was being relayed to him down the phone. "37° 31'32.28N, 75° 56'42.34W at 1.15am," he confirmed, picking up a scrap piece of paper and a red biro from the desk, and while holding the phone to his ear with his shoulder, writing the information on the paper, using the side of an old wooden bookcase to lean on.

"I'll be in touch," he announced, before hitting the red hang-up button shaped like a phone on his key pad, and looking up at his visitor.

"Problems?" she enquired.

"Uhhhh... just the sweet little nagas wanting their king back." He smiled at the thought. "Of course... they will get him back, just in a few more pieces than they bargained for, when their usefulness is all but up."

Just the thought of the double cross the nagas were about to be on the end of brought memories of the disillusioned sewer worker in Chicago flooding back. Having done her bidding, he'd expected the promised 'big payoff'. Instead all he got was a bullet in the head and a swim with the fishes. Some beings could be so gullible.

Grinning like a deranged clown, he strolled over and put his arm around her shoulders.

"So, how are things progressing?" he asked, gently caressing her cheek.

"Your father's ready to go. Everything is packed up and either ready to be destroyed, or taken with us. I've wiped clean the parts of the buildings we're no longer using, and will do the rest before we go."

Smiling, he shrugged his shoulders a little and said,

"All we need now is our ride. England here we come!"

9 RESISTANCE IS FUTILE

Droplets of lava sizzled and steamed as they plummeted down the side of one of the rock walls that made up the abandoned cellar. Watching fascinated, buoyed by the warmth the lava gave off, she was intoxicated by the slow and steady movement and the change in colour. At the moment there was little else for her to do. Most beings would have been disappointed, fed up, bored even. Not her though, fully understanding the need to be here, and to be patient. And so she was. With the squad of nagas in the room next door assigned as her bodyguards, her safety was as assured as it could be, despite being back where she'd been born. Back where, in theory at least, she was a wanted criminal. Assuming that no right minded dragon was actually still on the lookout for her, given that her crimes had been committed well over six decades earlier, still she remained nervous at the very thought of being tucked away in their domain. You never actually knew with dragons. They had the longest memories of all, and because of exactly who she was, and what she'd done, she always assumed that the hunt was still on.

Probably the biggest downside of being stuck in this room, decked out with only a simple bed, a sink and a toilet off to one side, was that in waiting to be called forth, her mind had little else to do but wander off, mostly to events far in the past, pondering the decisions that she'd made, going over each and every last detail.

Blowing her long brown locks back behind her head, the warm evening breeze tickled her face. With the spitting rain having just stopped, she loosened the belt on her long grey raincoat, all the time taking in the stunning landmarks surrounding her. Directly in front of her stood the magnificent Notre Dame in all its glory, the intricate brickwork of the amazing walls that lined the river captured the real essence of the beautiful architecture as the sun started to set. Green, brown and red hues of the trees and hedges in the foreground looked like something from a fairytale, while the river itself flowed gently on its way, too important to stop, ignoring the passage of time, here in 1941. Things had been going brilliantly over the last couple of weeks, particularly with regard to this new contact that she'd cultivated. If all went well, then tonight she would once again strike at the heart of the British and French Resistance, earning herself more credit with her Nazi puppet masters. Reluctantly turning away from the timeless view, she casually looked along the bridge, in the direction of the Sorbonne. Reminiscent of their last three meetings, her contact stood on the bridge, stunning red locks whipping out behind her, waiting for their planned encounter. But here and now, it was time to force their hand and take control of the situation. After all, that's why she'd been feeding them the information for nearly the last month or so, she thought as the dying light from the sun's last rays disappeared over the horizon.

Not daring to glance round, she already knew he was there, they'd done this so many times before. It was time to start the show. So she speeded up. Doing so in the ridiculous high heels was a challenge, but less to her than most. With the red headed contact gazing in her direction, she held up three fingers in front of her body, running her other hand through her wavy hair, giving out the signal that there was trouble. From the look on the other woman's face, she'd picked up on what was happening and had a plan to deal with it.

'Good,' she thought, ambling quickly towards her, 'all is going according to plan.' Only a few feet away now, the Resistance operative, who she knew by the name of 'Kitty', glanced over her shoulder, back up the bridge, no doubt taking in her pursuer, a brawny male in a dark coat and hat who went by the name of Wolfgang, though of course she wasn't supposed to know that. Breathing heavily, she stumbled into Kitty's arms.

"I'm... I'm so sorry. I didn't realise he was following me until a few moments ago. I don't know what to do. I'm so scared," she lied, hamming it up for the good of the moment.

Instinctively Kitty grabbed her hand and pulled her in the opposite direction to her brawny pursuer, just as she was supposed to. It was too easy!

"Come with me," whispered the slim redhead in perfect English. "We'll get you somewhere safe, and then we can talk."

In return, she nodded, a false mask of fear etched across her face. High heels scraping against the cobbles, the two of them jogged along the bridge, neither daring to look back over their shoulder. Cutting across the Pont Saint-Louis, they rushed ever onwards, ignoring the odd looks from passersby. Once across the Pont Louis-Philippe, they veered left alongside the river, heading towards the world renowned Louvre. Daring to glance back, the Resistance officer, Kitty, spotted the man about the same sort of distance away as he had been on the bridge. Squeezing Earth's hand reassuringly, much to her disgust, it had the desired effect, as she made the fear disappear from her face, albeit only briefly. Another hundred yards or so on, Kitty glanced again. Their gentleman follower had gained considerable distance on them. Earth guessed that Kitty's aim would be to get her to the safe house, which probably wasn't far away, and that was the haven which Earth was trying to penetrate.

"DITCH THE SHOES," Kitty suddenly shouted to Earth, pulling one off and tossing it towards one of the trees lining the street, followed quickly by the other. Slowing to a halt, Earth followed the instructions, the man chasing them only a matter of yards away now. Both women took off, able to take full advantage of their bare feet now, Kitty's red hair trailing out behind her, as did her own. Panting heavily, not daring to look round, the two women sprinted right into Rue du Pont Neuf, glad of the darkness that now shrouded the entire city. Silently, they cut left along Rue Saint-Honoré, crossing the main thoroughfare, Kitty trying desperately to stick to the smaller, darker, quieter streets. Pausing to catch their breath, there was no sign of their tail, but she knew better than to get complacent. They had to get to the safe house, only then could they relax, or at least that's what Earth hoped the simple girl would think. Muscles in her legs burning fiercely; she wondered if her new found friend felt the same. If she did, she was hiding it well. The Resistance officer, clearly quite experienced from the extent of her spy craft, despite her age, led them sharply right and then immediately left, all the time darting in and out of the

shadows, avoiding the sporadic placement of street lamps, despite the fact that she must be exhausted by now. Another right and sharp left led them to the entrance of a darkened Rue des Bons-Enfants. Kitty pulled her up against the wall, both of them barely able to pull in a breath. There were no street lights here... it was totally dark. Heart racing, Kitty poked her head ever so slightly round the corner, hoping to prove that they'd lost their shadow. After a few minutes, it seemed evident that they had. Embracing briefly, the two women looked and felt more than a little out of place in their bare feet. It was enough to make Earth feel sick.

"I'm pretty sure we've lost him. We have a house, just up here. It'll be alright for you to stay. My associates and I will protect you, I promise."

Earth nodded in response, desperately trying to keep the smile off her face, all the time pretending to be far too shaken up to do anything else. Together, both of them crept along the street in near total darkness, both still holding hands, both pleased to get something of their breaths back. Kitty had done this hundreds, if not thousands of times before and could probably have done it just with the feel of her bare feet on the cobbled street, rather than using her eyes, which made little difference in the all encompassing black.

Edging further and further down the tiny little street, full of narrow three storey buildings, few if any showing any light at all coming from the inside, they quickly reached their destination. Like its neighbours, it was a tall, narrow building with its windows boarded up and a solid looking door, white paint flaking off the surround. Still holding her hand, Kitty sneaked around a set of rubbish bins, leant down and ever so carefully pulled back a huge piece of metal, all the time trying to be as quiet as she could. The metal was thick, and weighed an awful lot. Even using her full force, Kitty could only manage to slide it a little way. With a gap barely bigger than the women's waists showing, Kitty slipped through. Earth duly followed. A metal handle had been welded to the underside, which Kitty used to pull the metal back in place. Then she led them down the steps, stopping at a wooden door. Quietly, she tapped the door with her knuckles. Tap, tap, tap. She waited. A single tap came back. Tapping twice more, she stopped and then tapped twice more again. Silence ensued. It felt like an age, but moments later, rustling could be heard from behind the door. Eventually, it opened, well... a little anyway. A startlingly handsome man with a perfectly trimmed moustache poked his head through the gap.

"Ahhh... Kitty," he gasped in a distinctive English accent. "We weren't expecting you. Sorry, you set us all a bit on edge."

"We had a bit of a problem... a tail, but completely shaken off now."

"Excellent, excellent," whispered the man, pulling open the door and allowing the women to squeeze through, then bolting it thoroughly once he'd done so.

"Come on through, come on through," he urged.

Both followed into the basement that was... rather nice, all things considered. Apart from the boarded up windows, the rooms could have been taken from any city across Europe. It held comfortable furniture and was neat and tidy, with the smell of home cooked food mingling vicariously with cigarette smoke.

Seconds after entering the room, Earth clutched her head momentarily, feigning feeling a little faint, while actually sending out a signal to her comrades. The gentleman that had let them in rushed to her aid.

"I'm okay, I'm okay," she muttered. "Just felt a little light headed there for a moment."

"Understandable really," put in Kitty. "We have, after all, just spent the last twenty or so minutes running through the streets of Paris."

"Those damn Nazis will be the death of us all," added the gentleman.

'That's the idea,' thought Earth.

"I jolly well hope not," added another man, striding through the only other door to the room, clutching a steaming mug of something.

"I for one second that," chipped in a blonde haired woman from right behind him.

Before anyone else had a chance to say anything, a small bell attached to a line coming down from somewhere up above, dangling precariously over the fireplace, jingled uncontrollably. Each and every one of them stopped, too shocked to move. Kitty was first to speak.

"It can't be. It just can't be! We lost him... I'm sure of it."

The bell jingled again, more furiously this time.

"Questions for later!" exclaimed the man with the moustache, who had let them in. "Seems we definitely have company of some sort. Might even be time to bug out."

Nodding in agreement, they all made for the far door, all except Earth, who knew that the time had come. Kitty tried to urge her out through the door, but she was having none of it. To the young Resistance officer's surprise, Earth produced her best smile, knowing full well that once again, she'd won. Everyone in the room stood stock still, taking in a very different character from the one they'd so warmly welcomed only a few moments ago.

"YOU!" accused Kitty.

"Of course," replied Earth nonchalantly, slipping a cigarette between her crimson lips and lighting it.

"I... I... I... I don't understand," stuttered Kitty, to no one in particular.

"Ahhh..." said Earth, taking a long drag on the addictive nicotine stick separating her lips. "It was all so easy."

From nowhere, the other man in the room pulled out a .38 revolver.

"You may think you've caught us, but I can assure you it's the last thing you'll ever do," he announced.

Earth took another long puff on her cigarette, savoured the moment, and then blew out a long stream of smoke in the direction of the man holding the gun. You could have cut the tension in the room with a knife, along with all the cigarette smoke. Bizarrely, Earth burst out laughing. It wasn't just any laugh though. It was the kind of laugh that sent a chill through your very bones.

"What's so funny?" enquired the other woman in the room.

"Ohhh," said the Nazi stooge, looking up at the ceiling, "THIS!"

Instantly the air in the room became thick; the hum of static electricity pulsed through it. Earth dropped her cigarette and held out her hands towards the group of British Resistance operatives. The man with the revolver fired. One, two, three shots. Bright blue, blinding bolts of forked electricity arced from Earth's fingers, destroying the bullets mid flight, as the Resistance fighters looked on horrified. The bell in the fireplace rang constantly against the backdrop of something smashing down the basement door through which they'd previously entered. Acrid smoke and the smell of burning engulfed the room, overpowering the disgusting stench of the misguided dragon's cigarette. Both male Resistance fighters looked at one another, each with the same thought. Charging, giving it all they had, the one with the gun ending with a flying leap towards Earth. A deafening crackle whistled around the room as forked electricity streaked forth from Earth's fingers once again. Caught firmly in the neck, mid leap, the man with the gun promptly slumped to the floor, a sizzling black wound eating into his flesh as he did so. Taken off his feet by a massive static charge, the man with the moustache had come within a whisker of reaching his goal, only to be thrown backwards, smashing into the far wall where he remained, smoke steaming from his wound, totally unconscious.

Kitty and the other female Resistance fighter shared a look of resignation, but were determined, however helpless the situation, to follow the example of their friends. Before they had a chance, the basement door disintegrated in a blast so loud it knocked them off their feet. By the time they got back up, half a dozen uniformed Nazis had burst into the room, all pointing their Walther P38's at them.

Kitty looked bereft, heartbroken. Only a few minutes earlier things had apparently been going so well, and now here she was, captured by the people she feared, loathed and hated the most. Scared at the thought of what they would do to her, it didn't stop her asking.

"Who the hell are you?" she challenged, terrified by everything that surrounded her.

Earth, cigarette back in her hand from somewhere, smiled evilly, smoke pouring from both her nostrils, which was something of an irony really, given exactly what she was. Padding over to Kitty in her bare feet, she grabbed her by the chin and looked her straight in the eyes, a despicable snarl on her face.

"My name is Earth, and I'm your worst nightmare!"

Kitty, trembling by now, tried frantically to find a retort. But before she could do so, a blinding blue light, followed by an uncomfortable tingling, burned in and around her jaw. Earth smiled as Kitty struggled against the pain, before the darkness finally consumed her.

10 BREAKING NEWS

It drove him mad, the pomposity of it all. Dressing up, the coming in, the words to begin the meeting, the feast... oh, he didn't mind the feast, he was a dragon for goodness' sake, and they aren't exactly renowned for turning down food. Plus, of course, he hadn't had anything to eat for the last seven days. But the rest of it was outdated and unnecessary.

'In that respect,' he mused, 'we could learn so much from our wingless charges on the surface.'

Starting pretty much as normal, the council assembly had now nearly reached the end of the feast, the mood of which had been lively, despite the tragedy of a week ago and the ongoing hunt for survivors and bodies. Most councillors had totally forgotten about everything outside the chamber, with the tone from the sombre worldwide gatherings that morning having been totally turned on its head. All but the king it seemed. Not wanting to tell them either piece of news, he knew that he had little choice. If he didn't tell them today and they found out about it, there was a chance they could have him removed, and given the importance and significance of the white dragon (he couldn't bear to call him Tim) showing up at this time, he felt it his duty to see through whatever fate was going to throw his way. Over the last few days he'd come round to thinking that his destiny was in some way intertwined with that of the white dragon detailed in the ancient prophecy. Reaching forward, he clutched the last charcoal and jam doughnut from a pile that had originally been two feet high, flipped it into the air with his index finger and opening his jaws wide, allowed it to sail in, the tiniest of satisfied burps echoing around the back of his throat. Savouring the sweet taste and crunching the last remaining chunks of charcoal, he stood, grabbed the two empty silver plates in front of him and crashed them together, before announcing,

"The time for merriment is over. Please be seated."

And so against the backdrop of crackling fires, spitting lava and an overpowering smell of roasted meats, they started. Reports of dead being found, dragon and human alike, kicked off the business end of the meeting. Status updates were read out on the repairs going on above ground across the globe, and tales of just how much difference it made having laminium ball teams from across the planet helping out the emergency dragon search and rescue units. For the most part, it was all pretty depressing. Trying to listen, in all honesty he struggled. No doubt the other councillors had got their nightly four hours of sleep, but he hadn't had that much in the past week, and he was weary, exhausted, drop dead tired. As he watched the spitting and hissing lava wiggle its way down the nearest marble pillar, transfixed by its colour, movement, and in particular the heat and steam that it gave off, slowly his eyelids began to close.

At that very moment, Councillor D'Zone stood up and announced that he had something to say. It was a break from protocol; he should have either waited for his turn, had he booked a place in the order of things, or until the end of the session for any other business. But given his reputation as a solid, dependable and hardworking councillor, whatever he had to say was important. Instantly, the king became alert, along with all the councillors in the room.

"With everything that has transpired over the last week across the planet, I propose we withdraw any and all efforts to send a force of dragons to Antarctica. Even before this worldwide catastrophe, it made little or no sense to do so, but now, with the human and dragon bodies still being recovered, with infrastructure the world over, both dragon and human, in need of repair and overhaul, and with the threat from whoever committed this heinous crime still hanging over us, now is not the time to consign forces anywhere, least of all Antarctica. Given how important, and indeed how obvious, to any dragon, this decision is, I say we vote here and now, the old fashioned way, and get this one topic over and done with."

Echoing murmurs of, "Here, here," reverberated around the ancient room.

Councillor Rosebloom looked on, more than a little agitated, as even his cronies nodded in agreement with D'Zone's proposal. So far he hadn't had a chance to convey to them just how vital it was that the force was dispatched to Antarctica. How could he? Frustration boiled up inside him, because as far as he was aware, the bombs weren't supposed to have gone off now; it was all supposed to have happened after the force had left for the South Pole. It was all coming apart and he didn't know what to do.

With a quick glance over his shoulder at the king, in return receiving an almost imperceptible nod to carry on, Councillor D'Zone pronounced,

"All those in favour of cancelling the mission to Antarctica, raise their left wings now."

Every dragon in the room did, including the king who wasn't even obliged to vote. What was noticeable though, was that Rosebloom was incredibly slow in raising his wing, almost as if he was just following suit. The king hadn't missed this, no not at all.

"Motion carried unanimously," bellowed Councillor D'Zone. "Thank you very much for indulging me."

Some of the other dragons applauded, others nodded in appreciation.

Giddy with excitement inside, the king sat outwardly stony faced. For him, it was one less thing to worry about, and could now stop the master mantra maker moving forward with his plan to construct a fake ring and have a second vote that way. Any way you looked at it, it was good news, especially as he'd had no idea D'Zone was going to do it. He was, however, jolly glad he had.

Fires reached their dying embers as the council ploughed through some of their normal business. It wasn't anywhere near the usual volume, with their efforts mainly focused on the ongoing disaster that had transpired from the laminium bombs. Once again, the king struggled to stay awake, despite maintaining a façade of thoughtfulness.

Councillor Rosebloom wrapped things up on the ongoing topic of graffiti in urban areas throughout the dragon kingdom, with South America and India having been hit particularly hard. This moved nicely into any other business. Just as it looked to all and sundry that the session was going to come to a close early, the king breathed out a huge stream of fire to attract everybody's attention.

"I have some information to pass on to you regarding the terrorist events of last week," he announced.

Simultaneously, the councillors started chatting, mainly about a possible lead in tracking down those responsible.

"BEFORE you all get worked up," the king declared, "this has nothing to do with catching the perpetrators of this villainous act, but I regard its importance as being equally valuable."

That had their undivided attention.

"The bomb that exploded in Salisbridge, Southern England, the one that was thwarted, had some rather unexpected consequences."

Rosebloom was all ears.

One of the councillors made to ask a question, but the king held up his hand to cut him off.

"At the time, it was thought that no one had been caught up in the blast. This opinion has since been revised. Two individuals were struck by the explosion. How they survived... we're not sure, and is still being looked into. Anyhow, the result of being caught in the blast, combined with whatever magic saved them, has produced some very serious side effects. First, the young female dragon who tried desperately to save herself and the human she was with (he didn't feel it necessary to go into graphic detail about what they were doing there in the first place) has lost all her dragon abilities and has been rendered entirely human."

A collective intake of breath from all the dragons listening ran around the room.

"As far as we can tell, this is irreversible."

All the councillors sitting in front of him were wriggling around like a class full of reception children all needing a wee, eager to ask a question. Ignoring them, he continued.

"While I'm sure you all have many questions, you will need to hear the entire story before you pass judgement. The human that was with our young dragon nearly died in the incident. How he didn't, who knows? Not us, that's for sure. But that's not the most remarkable thing about it all. On regaining consciousness, the doctors discovered the human in question had inherited the young female dragon's powers and abilities, and in essence had completely transformed into one of us."

Instead of an intake of breath, this time it was the sound of collective whispers that rang around the room.

The king continued.

"Our best scientists do not know how all this has come about, but are working around the clock to try and find out. Our historians assure us that something like this is totally unprecedented in the entire history of our race."

The king paused to let his words sink in.

"Unfortunately, I still haven't reached the most remarkable part. The human hasn't just transformed into any old dragon, or taken on the form of the female dragon with him. It would appear, and I can personally confirm this, that the 'human dragon', call it what you will, is entirely WHITE in colour."

Arms and wings flailed as the room erupted. Every shade of flame possible crackled from mouths and nostrils.

No one could hear themselves think. Giving it thirty seconds or so, the king once again smashed the silver plates in front of him together, causing the room to fall silent.

"Now I have told you everything there is to know, and I promise to keep you updated if the situation changes. I'm sure you're all aware of just how important these developments are, and should all be in no doubt about the security implications around these events. Under no circumstances are you to reveal any of this to anyone outside this room. There's too much at stake with everything currently going on. I really can't think of much more to add..." At this point there was much more arm waving and fidgeting. He knew what they wanted to say, "... except to discuss how we deal with the stricken young female who has lost all her abilities."

And so it started, pretty much as the king figured it would. Determined to use what little influence he still wielded to help Peter's young friend, from the outset he feared that it would not be enough.

Four hours later... it was all over. The councillors had all filed out, with Rosebloom smugly leading the way. One or two had stopped to chat briefly with the king, but now he sat alone, not even the burning embers of the fire for company. He'd tried, God knows he'd tried, using up almost every favour owed to him in the process. But in the end, it had all proved fruitless. He'd lost and knew the cost to him would prove dear. Peter would undoubtedly be devastated, and rightly so. But it was well and truly out of his hands now. THE DECISION HAD BEEN MADE!

11 SUB-JUGATE

Cold metal hatches slammed shut behind him, simultaneously evoking a tiny sliver of dread at being entombed, and a full on surge of adrenaline at the thought of what was to come. Passing a long line of saluting crew, he casually nodded back to each one, knowing that some would never see the cold light of day ever again. Finally, he reached the command centre. As he entered, the officers all stood, backs straight, uniforms crisp, all offering their best salutes. All except the helmsman, who remained at his station, ready to enact the orders he knew to be coming. Quickly he snapped off a salute, adding a firm, "At ease." The officers relaxed, just a little anyway, except perhaps the captain, who seemed more than a little anxious. It was he who spoke first.

"This is an unexpected surprise... Admiral."

A long, uncomfortable silence ensued as the admiral surveyed the group of officers. Perturbed at this unusual course of events, the captain started to open his mouth. As he did so, the admiral gave the officers either side of the captain an inconspicuous signal. From out of nowhere, faster than the eye could see, both officers drew blades and slit their captain's throat, before even a hint of sound had escaped him. A dumbfounded look of astonishment covered his face briefly as his body crumpled to the floor. An eruption of blood splashed his pristine white uniform as his mouth tried in vain to cry out for help. With the dying captain ignored like a child vying for attention, the others got on with their assigned tasks. In only a matter of minutes the engines had fired into life, with the helmsman having already plotted their destination. Three of the officers were dispatched to 'take care' of the four members of the crew that weren't part of the plan, or even part of the same race.

Twenty five minutes later, all five bodies were strewn

across the floor of the captain's cabin, the fetid aroma of decaying flesh not quite in full swing. As the sub's crew gave their individual tasks their undivided attention, the black metal beast, in whose belly they sat, disappeared beneath the surface on its way to a most unlikely and most unofficial rendezvous.

12 A MESSENGER (LIKE NONE OTHER) OF BAD TIDINGS

His agents had sent a message to say that Peter was here, now. Not able to put it off any longer, here he was, about to break two hearts.

Not looking at the signs crisscrossing the walls of the busy hospital, instead he used the information in his eidetic memory, gleaned earlier from some of his high level guards. Nodding and smiling at the nurses as he casually strolled down the sparkling white corridors, his destination nearly in sight, he thought just how unfamiliar this part of the hospital was to him, well... not in his mind, but he'd never been here before. It had always been the extremely secret and covert part of the building, right in the very basement, that he'd visited, all but once. It felt odd to him to be in the main part of the hospital, amongst all the humans going about their daily lives. Every now and then he'd pick up on somebody talking about the global tragedy that he held himself responsible for. Part of him knew that it wasn't true and that he could have done little to prevent it. But deep down, another part felt responsible for all the lives lost and the heartache caused. Supposedly the most important and powerful being on the planet, he did, however, feel a long way short of that most of the time. Approaching his destination, he couldn't remember the last time he'd felt this nervous or afraid. This was most definitely a task he did not want to perform, but despite that, he willed himself on, knowing it was better all round to get it out in the open.

Turning sharp left, and skipping out of the way of an oncoming wheelchair with more speed and grace than anyone as old as he was had a right to, he walked solemnly towards the second door on the right, passing two innocuous patients, one male, the other female, sitting on a row of metallic chairs, both reading magazines. Nodding almost imperceptibly at both, he silently thanked them for the sterling job they were doing of keeping him safe while he was on the surface. Stepping up to the white door with a fire resistant glass pane in the middle of it, he knocked once, opened the door and flitted inside.

Perched halfway up Richie's hospital bed, the covers all dishevelled, magazines and books scattered haphazardly, Peter jumped to his feet on seeing the king. Moving all the junk off her bed, Richie sat up straight.

"Settle down... there's no need for all of that. It's not an inspection you know."

Smiling at the frail looking old man, Richie knew underneath that he was nothing of the sort.

"Sire," whispered Peter, approaching the king.

"What have I told you youngster?" the monarch replied.

"Sorry... George."

"That's better."

"Let me get you a chair," ventured Peter, rushing off into the far corner of the room, retrieving a high backed bright blue chair for the king to sit in."

"Thank you," said the king sitting down. "Hmmmm... this is comfortable. I like this chair very much. Do you think they'd allow me to take this and swap it for my throne?"

"I think that might be frowned upon Si... George," added Peter.

"Oh well," huffed the king. "So my dear," he said cheerfully addressing Richie, "how are you?"

"Getting better bit by bit," replied Richie softly.

"You still looked quite banged up, if you don't mind me saying so," stated the king, referring to the plaster on Richie's right wrist and her left ankle, as well as the fading purple mark down the left hand side of her face and the bruising around her eyes.

"It's not too bad," she mumbled, knowing how hard all

the doctors and nurses around her (all dragons) were working to try and put things right.

"Well, if there's anything you need," added the king thoughtfully, "don't hesitate to drop my name into the conversation. All the staff know I'm on the lookout for you, and have explicit instructions to contact me on your behalf should you ask."

"Thank you," replied Richie, genuinely touched.

"It's great to see you," put in Peter. "How come you're here? Did you have business this way?"

It was then that the king's expression turned sour, and Richie cottoned on to the real reason for his visit. She didn't even have to wait for him to say it. But he did.

Having had decades of experience in the top job (in the world), not knowing how to say something was rather a novel experience, not one he'd recommend though. In the end, all he could think to do was come out with it, and deal with the repercussions as they arose.

Ignoring Peter, and taking Richie's right hand, he stared deeply into her beautiful brown eyes.

"I'm sorry my dear, I truly am. I tried everything in my power, and more, to get them to overturn their decision, but in the end, I could do nothing."

Richie just nodded, her eyes starting to water. Unlike the young lacrosse player, Peter still hadn't realised what was coming next.

"It has been overwhelmingly decided by the council that because of your irreversible condition, you are to undergo a stage three memory wipe that will allow you to recall your time above ground, but nothing else, enabling you to keep the life that's been your cover ever since you left the nursery ring."

"WHAT?" Peter exploded.

"I'm sorry. I truly am."

"You can't be serious, not in a million years!" exclaimed the young hockey playing dragon.

Standing, the king's demeanour turned grim.

"But I am. I understand Peter, I really do. And when I said I tried everything in my power to change things, you couldn't possibly know what that might yet cost me. But it was all for nothing, almost as if things have been taken out of my hands. The council's decision on this matter is final, with it already having been passed over to the priesthood for them to deal with. My understanding is that young Richie here will be discharged towards the end of the week. After that she'll be given three weeks to get all her dragon affairs in order. It will then be a matter of the priests tending to her somewhere above ground, probably her home I would guess. And then it will be done. It can't be changed by anyone I'm afraid."

Tears streaked down Richie's cheeks as she lay propped up by her pillows in bed. Peter still faced the king.

"I'm really sorry to have caused you both so much pain. I did think, however, that you'd both really prefer to hear the news from me, rather than some faceless official."

"Thank you Sire," sniffed Richie through her tears.

"I'm so sorry it's come to this. You do understand that you'll never again remember all this, everything you've come from, once the memory wipe has been carried out?"

Richie nodded.

Peter just stood looking at the king, his face almost set in stone.

"I know that look, CHILD," scolded the monarch.

"Never say never," exclaimed Peter.

"I know you're angry and upset, but there's nothing you can do. If I can't change things, how on earth do you hope to do so?"

Saying nothing, mainly from fear of crying, already his mind whirled through the possibilities, but he could only come up with one. One hope, one chance. Letting his face morph into a cold, calculating smile, right in front of the king, he hadn't meant it to be mean or cutting, but that's what it turned out to be.

Apologising once more before taking his leave, the

monarch claimed he had to get back to his huge backlog of work, which was partly true.

After that, the two friends were at a loss. Peter stayed a while, but it was awkward as he had no idea of what to say or do. Richie tried to stay positive, even cracking the odd joke or two, but she couldn't fool him. He could see just how badly hurt she'd been by the news, and vowed to himself there and then that he would stop them from wiping her memory at all costs, no matter what it took. Walking out of the door twenty minutes later, he prayed that his one hope would choose to help him, and would indeed have the answer he was looking for.

13 TIME TO DRAGON UP

Needing the air, he'd decided to walk, giving him yet more time to consider where he was going and why. It had been over two weeks now, and he'd heard nothing from her. Not a word. No phone call, text, email or letter. She, of course, had no job at the moment, well... as far as he knew, what with the devastation of the clubhouse and all. And although she may have been out of the loop so to speak, she must have known that he and Tank had been cleared of having anything to do with the clubhouse's destruction. Somehow he'd assumed that she would have got in contact by now, not saying sorry, but just to see how he was. But all was quiet on the Janice front. Strolling along below the shivering boughs of tall trees lining the road inundated him with thoughts of future possibilities. With everything that had happened since that fateful day, and everything going on, seeking her out had become all but impossible... well, for a week or so. After that, it just became... awkward, scary. The more he thought about going to see her, the more excuses he made to himself to put it off. He had to go to work to see Garrett about the clubhouse, to go to the hospital to see Richie. More and more excuses he'd made for himself, until there were no more and he could put it off no longer. The mere thought of seeing her brought a lump to his throat, made his legs go weak and set his stomach rumbling in cruel anticipation. One of the reasons he'd come on foot was that it was easier not to be spotted and therefore easier to turn round and head back without anyone knowing that he'd ever been there. In his mind, he knew there was still a very good chance that he would get within sight of her house and be too afraid to go any further. Given all that he'd been through these last couple of years, this excursion should have been quite painless and relatively easy. But it wasn't. Hurting from an almost physical pain inside, that day, when the clubhouse had been destroyed, had been harder than facing Manson on the icy cold Astroturf pitch when the dark dragon had tried to steal the majority of Cropptech's laminium. And not because he and Tank had barely made it out alive or even because, at the time, they'd thought Richie's life had been extinguished. No! It was the look on Janice's face when the police officers arrested them and bundled them into the back of their cars. That look still haunted him every day, and every night in his dreams. A look that said, 'I trusted you. I loved you... and you BETRAYED ME!' Just the very thought of that moment made him choke.

Abruptly he stopped and leant up against one of the mighty trees right outside someone's lovely four bedroomed detached house. Noticing the curtains twitching, the person inside watching his every move, he couldn't have cared less. What mattered was that he was just round the corner from her house, and he knew that he needed to find the extra courage to take him there.

'Come on,' he thought. 'You can do it.' What was that phrase he'd heard so often, the one that annoyed him so much? Oh, that's right. Man up! He didn't so much need to man up, as dragon up!

Breathing threatening to overtake him in short, sharp bursts, he focused on everything he had to say, having spent days preparing it, thinking about the words and how they might sound. But here and now, the words seemed to spill from his head, letters drifting casually off into the wind, floating away, well beyond his reach. Feeling light headed and as though he were about to throw up at the same time, out of the corner of his eye once again he noticed movement behind the curtains. Knowing that if he waited any longer he risked someone coming out to see what was going on, or worse still... calling an ambulance if they thought him unwell, or both. All of which he could do without. Taking a deep breath, his head vacant of all the words he'd prepared, he straightened up, strode purposefully round the corner and headed directly for her front gate, both disappointed and excited in equal measure to see her pink car parked outside. Resolutely he paced up the path to her front door, determined to carry out what he'd spent days planning and thinking about. His body knocked on the door, while ironically, his brain RAN AWAY!

A few shuffling footsteps later, the lock on the door started to turn, giving rise to a general feeling of weakness and nausea. As the door started to move, he wished he'd followed his brain. A beautiful face with gorgeous blonde hair slinked around the gap in the door, its expression of neutrality changing instantly to a frown on noticing who was there.

"Oh... it's you!" uttered Janice.

"Uhhh... h... h... hi," was all he could get out.

"What do you want?" she asked circumspectly.

With his brain laughing at him from far off in the distance, not offering up any help at all in the way of an intelligent response, and the rest of him unable to ascertain the reason for her unhappiness, he barely managed to mumble,

"Can I come in please?"

It was all that he could think of to say.

To say there was an awkward pause was an understatement.

"I don't think that's a good idea," answered the downcast bar worker.

Feeling as though his head would explode, he hadn't gone through all of this only to be turned away... NOT NOW!

"PLEASE!" he begged, "just for a moment."

Against her better judgement, she held open the door and let him pass. Scuttling through, he started to head towards the lounge as she closed the door. It took him a second or so before he realised she hadn't followed and was in fact standing angrily, back against the front door.

"Say whatever it is you've come to say and then... go."

At that moment, he would have done ANYTHING to rid her face of that look. Anger, resentment, derision and betrayal were all there in equal measure.

'Perhaps she hasn't heard,' he thought hopefully. 'In which case, as soon as I tell her... BOOM! Back to normal.' And that was what he wanted most, as he'd come to realise long ago that he loved her, more than anyone or anything.

"Tank and I were cleared of having anything to do with the destruction of the clubhouse," he stated emphatically.

But before he got any further, his hopes were all dashed at once.

"I know."

This time it was his body that wanted to run away, as every molecule within it screamed,

"Uh oh!"

"Then I'm not sure I understand?" was all that he could babble.

Fire, anger and rage tore across her face. Before today, he'd never seen a human so angry. Storming up to him, her face having lost its delicate complexion, replaced by a not very becoming shade of scarlet, she poked her index finger firmly into his chest, looked him right in the eye and bawled,

"YOU LIED TO ME!"

Nearly falling backwards, that's how startled he was, he tried to stay upright but it was difficult with his mind spinning this way and that, thinking back on so many things, trying to see where he'd slipped up and just how he could put things right. More information, that's what he needed, at least that's what his very confused mind was telling him.

"About what?" he whispered gently.

She went ballistic. For a moment, his body felt as though he were back on the Astroturf on that cold, fateful night, once again facing the dark dragon Manson.

"Oh, I don't know... how about EVERYTHING?!"

His head spun more than before.

'What does she know? How does she know it?' he just about managed to think, using all his effort.

"What happened at the clubhouse?" she growled.

"Uhhh... you know what happened. The... the... there was a bomb, Tank and I tried to defuse it, but we couldn't and... BOOM!" he replied, waving his hands in the air for effect.

"And that's it?"

The question wasn't yelled, it was asked softly, meaningfully and with intent, the words ringing right through him, shaking him to his very foundation. It felt as though he'd reached a tipping point, balancing precariously, his very soul on the line. Another lie to the one he loved would be enough to send him over the edge into the abyss, into oblivion, losing everything that he believed in, stood for and ultimately... her! Sensibly he kept quiet.

"Cat got your tongue?" she asked sarcastically.

This wasn't how he'd planned things at all.

"You might have been cleared by the police," she commented passionately, "but there was certainly more going on in that clubhouse than you let on. You must think I'm a very stupid little girl."

Shaking his head ever so slightly, he didn't dare to interrupt her well deserved, and ultimately correct, rant.

"I struggled at the time to understand how nobody heard your friend break down the office door, but looking back on it, it seems all but impossible. As well, both of you knew all about the bomb, what it was, and more importantly... what was going on, something you didn't share with me then, and seem more than a little unwilling to share with me now, despite coming over here for what seems like some kind of forgiveness. And then of course," she continued, "the mysterious bright yellow light which flashed around the clubhouse, and this is but a guess... contained the explosion!"

Peter swallowed hard. This was very, very, very... bad!

"Am I wrong? Feel free to tell me if I am."

Unable to bring himself to say anything, tears started to build in the corners of his eyes. It broke his heart that he'd brought her to this.

"I don't understand!" she spat. "You were cleared by the police, and from everything that I know, it does seem that you were both doing your best to save everybody and the clubhouse. Tell me the truth... please!"

More than anything in the world, he wanted to tell her. In fact, he'd never wanted anything more in his entire life. But he knew if he did, it would go very badly indeed. Almost certainly the best that would happen would be a memory wipe for her and a life underground for him. And that was the best scenario he could come up with. Silence seemed the better option.

"I can't..." he uttered.

Tears raced down her beautiful face, leaping off at her chin and with a little gravity added to the mix, ended up splashing delicately onto the hallway floor. Head bowed, he watched the tiny teardrops fall in exquisite detail, anxiously searching for any way to get their relationship back onto an even keel.

"I thought you were different from other men," Janice sniffed, totally oblivious to the irony of her words.

"I am," he whispered.

"And yet you continue to lie to me. After everything. Forget what I did on that day! That I lied and colluded with you and your rugby playing friend. Lied to all the staff and everyone inside the clubhouse. Lied to the fire service and the police when they turned up. Forget all that... all of which I did for you. I trusted you!" she yelled. "I fell in love with you. You were all I ever wanted. But all it got me was LIES! LIES, LIES, AND MORE LIES!"

Shaking violently, her tears threatened to flood the building, a mixture of anger and sadness indelibly etched on her face.

"GO," she ordered, pointing at the front door. "GET

OUT!"

Feeling numb, almost as if it weren't his body he was in and that he was just watching it all unfold, happening to someone else, he had but one thought.

'It can't end like this. Can it?'

Head spinning like a tumble dryer, he did the only thing he could. He told her the truth.

"I love you," he whispered.

"Then tell me exactly what happened," she spluttered.

"I can't... I'm sorry."

"GET OUT!" she demanded. "I never want to see you again."

Knowing then that it was done, despite his overwhelming desire to, he just couldn't tell her. And all he was doing at the moment was causing her misery and pain. It was the hardest thing he'd ever done in his life, harder than fighting Manson, harder than coming here tonight. Dodging past her, he turned the lock and walked out, the door slamming firmly shut behind him. Not needing his enhanced dragon senses to hear her wailing and crying on the other side of the door, on automatic pilot his legs walked down the path and back onto the street, where they headed in the direction of his house, the rest of him failing to notice the mysterious stranger walking behind him in the shadows, in much the same direction. Later, he would have no recollection of the journey home, even though he'd most certainly done it. Sleep eluded him, his thoughts centred on what he'd put the young woman through, wondering whether he'd ever see her again.

'Perhaps,' he mused, 'this is why dragon/human relationships were banned in the first place.'

Alone in the dark, Janice spent the entire night crying herself to sleep.

14 SUITS YOU SIR!

Strolling down the poorly lit path, dipping in and out of the shadows, so many things played on his mind. Normally life was good, but he'd been plagued by dark dreams and dreadful nightmares ever since that fateful day, and they were so bad now that even his wife had commented on it. So here he was, on his way to do something about it, however small that might be in the scale of things.

By now the lighting had dropped away to virtually nothing, but that didn't bother him, as he'd walked this way hundreds, no... thousands of times, and felt securely shrouded in the dark. The thick juicy sound of mud squelching beneath his dark brown leather boots jolted him back to the present. Almost there, he was looking forward to their reaction to the unusual request he was about to present. Extending his dragon senses, he found solace in knowing he was totally alone down here. Pausing between two run down stone houses, he slipped into an impossibly small gap between them, glad for once that in his human form he was incredibly thin and gangly. Even a few more extra pounds would probably have prevented him from taking this route, one that only he, and he alone, knew. Squeezing sideways quietly between the homes, wary of scraping either wall, even a little, eventually he reached the end, facing a solid wall of rock, some forty feet or so tall. Reaching out with his mind, he found the tiny switches embedded in the wall, that had so long ago been installed there. Giving each one a nudge with his mind, he automatically moved his feet and hands, knowing that hand and footholds would now appear as if from nowhere. Scampering up and over the wall, he leapt down into a small, dark, secluded cobbled courtyard with a solitary metal door set into the moss covered rock that tailed off into the distance. It was cold here and his breath froze as he exhaled on landing. This was not a particularly pleasant place for a dragon, given the damp and chilly conditions. On the plus side, he had managed to acquire the property at an absolutely knock down price. And despite its drawbacks, it was perfect for the use that it had been put to. Blowing on his hands to warm them up, he proceeded to run them over the protruding rivets that framed the outside door, his bony fingers depressing some while ignoring others. Six seconds later the door slid sideways, revealing a darkened interior. Glad to have returned, he weaved past a couple of grubby sinks hanging off the wall, making his way towards the faint sound of voices. Thirty seconds later, having crisscrossed the maze of twisted corridors, he walked into what can only be described as an abandoned hangar, littered with desks, strewn with the latest high tech computer equipment from the human world above. By now the voices had stopped, each one replaced with a smile.

"YOYO!" came the shouts of joy from a dozen or so scruffy looking human shaped youngsters. A young girl launched herself into his arms as if shot from a cannon, while the others surrounded him in a much more calm and concise manner. The show of affection lightened his dark and thoughtful mood. Giving some of them hugs, while tousling the hair of others, eventually he managed to get them all seated. Gathered round, most in their chairs, some sitting on table edges, the youngsters eagerly waited to hear what their mentor and saviour had to say.

For days, his thoughts had been centred on exactly this. Thinking about that fateful day when he'd rescued Flash from the pool of lava as he'd been passing, and then carted him off to London for an impromptu audience with the king himself. Part of him still couldn't believe that Flash hadn't died, and for that he was hugely grateful. But everything that had come out... the details about Flash's mission and the deadly threat the nagas presented... had bothered him ever since. It hadn't helped that he'd sworn an oath of secrecy to the king himself. Figuring others in his position would have at least told their partner, or in his case, wife, what had gone on, however he was a dragon of his word and once he'd uttered that oath, he wouldn't tell another soul about it all. Residing on the other side of the planet hadn't helped either. Had he been nearer, he could have talked to Flash, Peter, Tank or even the master mantra maker himself, about his worries. But as it was, communicating securely across that distance was difficult at best and in his humble opinion, not worth the risk just to settle any worries he had. So he'd come up with this... using the resources already available to him in a bid to soothe his mind, ease his worries and ultimately get one step ahead of the game. This rag tag bunch of dragons here, in this disused warehouse below a computer repair shop in one of the outlying suburbs of Perth, Australia, all owed their existence to him, in one way or another. Some had just left the nursery ring of their own accord (something supposedly forbidden, but was more common than those in charge thought) drifting along with absolutely no direction, doomed to a life of being an outcast and living in abject poverty. Others, well, let's just say they'd fallen in with the wrong crowd, but had been saved in the nick of time by Yoyo himself. Numerous times he'd called on their skills, but this time might actually be the most important of all. While their official training might well be regarded as incomplete, their actual training was nothing short of comprehensive, but with an added something many dragons miss out on: imagination! It seems hard to believe really, but it's true. All the practical and theoretical matters are dealt with fantastically well in each and every nursery ring, but the young dragonlings are never really encouraged to use their powers of invention, tapping into imaginations that are some of the most innovative on the planet. For Yoyo, that always seemed a tragedy. But these youngsters knew nothing of that limitation and had always been pushed to explore, expand and apply their imagination to everything about them, in particular their work.

So it was with them all gathered round, he outlined what he needed from them. Their expressions at first were a picture, perplexed, puzzled and genuinely downright stumped. But it only took a matter of moments for the first one of them to sprout an idea. This acted as a springboard for the next, and the next, and so on. Yoyo sat watching as his assembled band of misfit dragons, already on top of the task he'd assigned them, applied everything he'd ever taught them and so much more. Pride burned fiercely inside him. Getting up to leave, he knew all along that this visit had to be a flying one (never mind the fact that he'd walked here). Just as he was about to bid them all goodbye, two thoughts forced their way into his head. A good job they did... they were important.

"Oh... before I go. You know I told you they have to be designed and adapted for fully formed, one-size-fits-all, dragon physiques?"

"YES," they all replied at once.

"Please can you modify one so that it will fit a human shaped form? I think there's a good chance we might need it. One last thing. On top of what I've just asked of you, there's a very specific mantra I'd like you to find out about."

Their ears prickled like animals sensing prey.

"What do you need?" asked one of the younger ones, full of confidence.

Yoyo smiled at the thought of being that young, standing up in front of your peers, so self assured. Nothing seemed beyond this group.

"I need something that will detect the tiniest heat source amongst a thousand square miles of snow."

"How tiny?" a different one asked, his mind already working on the problem.

"Good question," replied Yoyo. "Simply put... I don't know exactly. But a pinprick of heat in that kind of environment would suffice."

Another collective intake of breath was their only response.

"I'll leave it in your capable hands."

Nodding agreement, goodbyes were said and they all got back to work.

Leaving the building the same way as he'd entered, Yoyo hoped that what he'd just asked for would never actually be required.

15 BACK TO BACK SURPRISES

Smiling at the thought of being a taxi service for his friend, it had been a nice surprise to hear from her, that was for sure. On a normal Saturday though, they wouldn't have spoken to each other until after their respective battles had been completed. Locking his car, he walked over to the ordinary, red wooden door and thumped the brass knocker three times. A few moments passed before his sensitive hearing picked up the delicate sound of footsteps running down the stairs. With a click the door opened, and there in just her dressing gown stood Richie, yawning her head off, looking as though she'd just woken up.

"Hi Pete," she gurgled through a semi completed yawn. "Come on in."

Slipping past her, he continued up the narrow staircase and into the living room. Shaking his head, he had but one thought. 'Same old Richie.' "Mess" didn't do the room justice. Clothes, books, magazines were strewn everywhere. A tiny part of him deep within the back of his mind chuckled.

'You always fantasised about being with her, but this side of her would drive you crazy. You'd never be able to put up with it,' mocked the little voice. It was right of course, and deep down he knew however hard he tried, he would never be able to change her. She would always be... Richie, whether dragon or human.

"Make yourself at home," she stated, striding past him, heading for her bedroom. "I'm just going to get kitted up and then I'll be ready to go."

Pleased to see the plaster casts had been removed from her wrist and ankle, he noted that her other injuries appeared to be healing nicely. Briefly he wondered why she was heading that way, when most of her kit seemed to be scattered around the living room... the floor, the sofa, lying indiscriminately across her computer. Moving across to the sofa, he considered sitting down, but thought better of it after inspecting the mass of magazines and books covering the suede sofa he recalled from past visits, all the time resisting the tremendous urge he had to tidy things up. Instead, he chose to wander over to the only uncluttered part of the room, a stunning glass display cabinet full to the brim with trophies of one sort or another, all of which Richie had picked up during her lacrosse playing career. Of course most were individual awards, but, to his surprise, there were team ones as well. Wondering why they hadn't been on display at the sports club, he supposed it was just as well given what had happened recently with the bomb blast. As all this circled his brain, he heard his friend enter the room behind him. Vowing to ask about the trophies, he turned, only to be greeted by a very surprising and awkward sight. There, rifling through a huge pile of washing (at least he hoped it was a pile of washing) was Richie, dressed only in her knickers and nothing else. He didn't know where to look. As if things couldn't get any more awkward, she started talking to him about the hockey match he was due to play in later.

"So, who are you playing today Pete?"

"Ummm... Bournemouth I think," he mumbled, looking up at the ceiling, around the walls, anywhere but in the direction of his friend, who was showing off more of herself than he cared to see at the moment.

"Are they any good?" she enquired.

Swallowing nervously, his mind running away with some very powerful, and not entirely appropriate thoughts, all the time still looking away, he replied,

"Yeah... they're pretty good. Second in the league if I remember rightly."

"So tough game today then," she added, still not having found the item of clothing she was looking for.

Almost drowning in everything running through his mind, one single image came to his rescue, as if thrown and caught like a lifeline... JANICE!

"Probably," he declared, able to focus a bit more. "But they seem to be one of those teams that don't travel so well, so here's hoping."

Scattering even more clothes on the floor, Richie appeared to have at least found some of the kit she was looking for. Straightening up, she turned to walk back into the bedroom. Having noticed her turn around out of the corner of his eye, his chronic awkwardness receded somewhat, enough anyway for him to turn round fully and look at his friend. What he witnessed knocked his socks off. Having assumed that nothing else could surprise him today more than seeing his best friend semi-naked for the first time in his entire life, he found he was wrong, very wrong.

As she strode away from him, back into her bedroom, his eidetic memory grasped every last detail of what he'd just witnessed.

'It just can't be,' he thought. Moving round the sofa, with one hand he swept away enough magazines to enable him to sit down. Head in hands, he went over and over what he'd just seen, barely able to comprehend it. Impossible, and yet he'd seen it with his own eyes from only a few feet away. An underlying feeling of sadness washed over him. Of course he'd known all about the injuries she'd sustained and just how hard the doctors had worked to restore her to full health, and the toll the side effects of the *alea* had taken on her body. Given all this, the scar tissue should have come as no surprise, but it had. There was more than he could have believed possible, more than he thought anyone could have survived. But that wasn't the unbelievable part. Why had nobody else noticed what it had formed? Why had Richie not noticed? Perhaps she had, and thought nothing of it. Or perhaps, given that she was about to become fully human in only a matter of days now, she had more important things on her mind. Perhaps she refused to look at that part of her body because it was all too painful or had just chosen subconsciously to block the whole thing out. In any case, it changed everything. How, he didn't know yet. But it did.

Just then she walked back into the room, fully clothed in her lacrosse gear, kit bag in one hand, two sticks in the other. Grabbing a banana from the fruit bowl on the wooden sideboard as she passed, she turned to face him.

"Ready?" she enquired.

Nodding, his mind whirling with thoughts of what he'd seen, he followed her down the narrow staircase and out to the car on their way to a local school that had offered up their facilities on a temporary basis to the hockey and lacrosse sections of the sports club, wondering how best to proceed. Once again, the fate of the dragon kingdom might well rest with him.

16 SURPRISING RESISTANCE

Mumbling a few inaudible words as she tossed and turned, sweat pouring off her in the underground cellar, warmed by the lava, guarded by a contingent of nagas, Earth's body might well have been in the present, but her mind was most certainly stuck in the past.

Even in the pitch black, the old, wooden, two storey barn seemed to stand out. Maybe because there were no clouds, the stars and the moon all shone brightly, or perhaps it was because, for as far as you could see, the land was all flat, mainly grass, with the odd field of crops mixed in and only a very few, solitary houses dotted around the landscape. Sneaking through the wooden fence, they hurried across the grass in the direction of the barn. No lights could be seen inside. Heavy panting alongside her jolted her back to the moment.

"I'm sure they're still following us," puffed Earth, running alongside the slim, overcoated woman. "How much further?"

"Not far," replied the latest in a number of new Resistance officers that Earth had got involved with, concentrating on controlling her breathing for fear of getting a stitch.

As they ran, the woman beside her offered out her hand. Rather reluctantly she took it. A small trickle of nausea dribbled down inside her as she did so.

They were a few miles outside the town of Bourges, south of Paris, and over the last twenty minutes or so, things had gone very wrong, or very right, depending on which way you looked at it. Earth had been passing the valuable information over for nearly a month now, and had turned up to their prearranged meeting dishevelled and scared, claiming that she was being followed, which was very much part of her normal routine. Right on cue, her contact had rushed her off through the streets of Bourges at first, and then out into the open countryside in the direction of the barn, the unofficial, and temporary, home of the local Resistance.

Heavy breathing from the pair of them was the only thing that

could be heard for miles around. There was simply no other noise...
NOTHING! *After climbing through another fence and skipping around a disused chicken coop, they eventually made it to the barn. Both women looked back in the direction they'd come from, which showed no sign of any movement at all. So the Resistance officer turned and rapped on the door twice, and then three times more. Then they waited, still catching their breaths. Silently, above them, a head appeared through a tiny little gap in the wall.*

"What are you doing back so early?" it enquired, agitated.

"There was a bit of a problem. Let us in... please!"

Muffled whispers echoed from inside the barn. Neither woman could make out what was being said. And then the sound of wood on wood from behind the door made them take a step back. As it inched open, a hand poked out and beckoned them inside. Both women stepped into the darkness of the barn's interior.

Half a dozen men and women appeared in front of them, some from behind hay bales, others skulking from the shadows. Knowing it was close now, she could feel her heart beat faster and faster, only moments away from another stunning victory.

"Who's this, and what's she doing here?" a voice barked from out of the darkness.

Her contact started to reply, but Earth cut her short, having already sent the signal.

"I'm here to put a stop to your so called... operations!" smirked Earth, pulling a cigarette out of her pocket and sliding it between her lips.

Just as Earth thought about bringing her power to the fore, the female Resistance officer, whose name she'd never bothered learning, did something both surprising and remarkable. Clutching a syringe she had dragged from her coat pocket, in one swift motion she pirouetted with the speed and grace of a ballet dancer and then stabbed the needle smack bang into the back of Earth's neck. Never in her life had Earth been so surprised. Instantly she crumpled to the hay scattered floor, trying to fight off the effects of the drug, trying to access all her magic. But it was too late and unconsciousness washed over her immediately.

That's all Earth could remember, but things in and around the barn had carried on.

"Good work," announced a deep male voice from deep within the darkness. "But it's time to go. The Nazis are already closing in on our location. Allsop!"

"Yes sir," replied Allsop.

"You're in charge of her. If she shows even the slightest sign of waking up... knock her out. And none of this... it's wrong to hit a girl nonsense. Understand?"

"Yes sir."

"Good man! Let's go. Everybody out. As we practised it!"

From the back of the room, hay bales were shifted out of the way very precisely, to reveal muddied steps leading down into the darkness. Two of the men went first, followed by two women, Allsop carrying his charge, and then the rest, with the last man (a captain) making sure the hay bales were firmly back in place. It was a squeeze to say the least, with all of them having to duck down. There were no lights, there didn't need to be. It was only really wide enough for one, and it only led to one place.

Accompanied by a dozen of his finest men, they closed in on the shabby looking barn, pretty relaxed about the whole thing. Since her first operation, he'd accompanied 'Earth' as she liked to be known. On that occasion he'd been more than a little sceptical about having a woman in charge. But that had all changed with the results that had come, time after time. No other German unit had captured so many foreign spies. Their record was simply magnificent. And this operation, he knew, was just the next of many. They couldn't be beaten; in essence... they were unstoppable. Not knowing how she did it, ultimately he didn't care, he was only concerned with serving the Führer and leading his country to the victory they so deserved.

Pushing up his hat, he tugged at the collar of his uniform, proud of the pips there, disappointed by how constricted his throat always felt. Feeling the adrenaline pumping through him, his grip tightened on his trusty Luger. How much he loved that gun. A few months ago some pencil pusher had tried to insist that he swap it out for one of the new Walther things, but he wasn't having any of it. That weapon had saved his life on numerous occasions, taking many more in the process, and he wasn't giving it up for anything.

Gradually, they could feel the tunnel starting to slope upwards. Having travelled over three hundred yards, crouched down, they were now reaching the exit. A whispered voice greeted them, helping them out of their hidden burrow and into the secret enclave manned by a force of British soldiers. Pleasantries were exchanged briefly, before the small group settled down to observe the final part of the operation.

Bursting into the barn in one coordinated movement, as they had to various 'safe' houses so many times before, what awaited them this particular time was completely unexpected. The barn was empty... deserted!

'It's puzzling,' he thought. 'Has she captured or killed them all?' Both thoughts flicked through his very logical and very cruel mind. Not relaxed now, he was on edge, more so than he'd been for a long time. And quite rightly so.

As the very last Resistance members exited from the tunnel, he gave the command. All he could do now was watch and wait as his force of fifty men closed in on the barn in a concentric circle, their instructions to totally destroy every last inch of it.

Starting with a loud rap on the side of the barn, startling all those inside, instantly they all targeted their guns in that direction. Almost immediately there was another at the back of the barn this time, and then another. Quicker on the uptake than his men, but not by much, the Nazi captain lunged for the door, longing to escape what he knew was inevitable. But he didn't stand a chance. The barn was surrounded, and as the first of the grenades went off, the British commandos opened fire with everything they had. Along with the barn, the silence was shattered. Explosions littered the outside at first, and then much further in. And even with every single remnant seemingly on fire, or destroyed, still the men continued to hurl grenades into it, until every last one had been used.

In the distance hay fluttered in the air, black smoke swirled all around, accompanied by the fetid smell of death... and victory. Aware they had to move out, and quickly, with the barn obliterated and their prisoner secure, they'd completed their task. He only hoped the other operation, just west of here, running at exactly the same time, had been this successful. Now all he had to do was get his highly valued prisoner back to Britain.

'That in itself,' he thought, 'would be some achievement.'

17 LOSS

Unable to catch her breath, it felt as though the whole world was closing in around her. Tears flowed like the steady stream of rain into a gutter after a violent storm.

Moments later it passed, replaced by the heart wrenching feeling of loss: loss of a friend, loss of a future only dreamed of. It wasn't the first panic attack she'd had and she doubted it would be the last, given how her life was going. No job currently... she could cope with that, for a while, at least. But that wasn't what plagued her, haunted her dreams, both waking and sleeping alike. They were all about HIM! She missed him so badly. He was all she could think of, and it hadn't helped when he turned up out of the blue. Perhaps she'd been more spiteful than she'd meant to be, but he'd been holding things back, by his own admission. What? She didn't know. That day that the clubhouse had been destroyed changed everything. In her head she'd been over it hundreds of times. There were so many anomalies. How did they both know the bomb was really a bomb? They'd only had her vague description as a reference. How did Tank break down the office door without a sound, and without disturbing the device? What did they do after she'd left? The official account stated that they'd tried to disarm the bomb and that they were heroes. But something else had gone on, of that she was sure. What? She didn't know, but was desperate to find out. With all the free time on her hands, she had nothing else to do but search the internet for anything relevant to what had happened. Clearly it was all tied in to the global disaster. Every time she watched the television or switched on the radio, all the coverage was of the massive devastation, the clean up and the lives of those affected. The scale of the destruction in every other place was huge... catastrophic in fact. Over and over again she wondered if that's what someone had intended to happen, here in Salisbridge, and if in fact Peter and Tank really were heroes and had found some way to limit the destruction of the blast. But how? Internet searches proving fruitless up until now, she poured herself a glass of water from the chilled, clear jug always kept in the fridge, opting against anything to eat, despite growling protests from her stomach. To her, eating had seemed so inconsequential since all this had happened. Somewhere at the back of her mind, she knew she HAD to eat. And sometimes she did. But it was just very little, and very infrequently. Slumping down on the sofa with her laptop open, Janice once again started her search for any clues that might explain exactly what had happened on that fateful day.

18 POLE VAULTING DRAGONS?

For days now, he'd been tormented by his dreams. Ever since he'd seen it, he could think about nothing else, despite everything going on. What to do next? That was the question. Days of pondering had led him here in the hope that someone could make some sort of sense of what he'd witnessed.

Pulling open the door, he slid inside. Tank was away coaching rugby somewhere, of that much he was sure, which was a good thing, as he wanted the old shopkeeper all to himself. A gut feeling told him that Gee Tee's lifetime of experience would be invaluable in this matter.

Walking around the first set of bookcases that led into the shop proper, Peter felt more than a little trepidation, as on more than one occasion he'd stumbled into something resembling an action scene from a movie. Instantly his mind darted back to the ice salamander that Flash had almost single-handedly dealt with, and to the occasion he'd turned up to find the king, Tank and Gee Tee all ready to fight, and of course to the infamous giant spider and lack of clothing incident. Sweat coursed down his sides at the very thought of the last one.

"Hello little one," whispered a soft, velvety smooth voice from off to one side, momentarily startling Peter.

Returning the old shopkeeper's smile, he just about managed a "Hi," in return.

"I'm sorry to disappoint you, but your friend has the afternoon off I'm afraid."

"I know," he responded, looking the old dragon right in the eye.

"Uhhh... I see. Well perhaps we should adjourn to the workshop for a chat and some hot charcoal. Would you like to do the honours?"

All the time smiling, he nodded, knowing where everything was in the small kitchen, and just how the master mantra maker liked his hot charcoal. As he approached the kitchen, Gee Tee's voice echoed across the shop.

"Be a good dragon and see if you can find where the marshmallows are tucked away will you? And don't be stingy with them when you do."

Entering the kitchen he set the kettle to boil, and after spooning the dark charcoal into the mugs, he set about looking for the hidden treats. By the time the kettle started to whistle furiously, he still hadn't found them, having looked in all the cupboards and shelves, under the sink, rifled through the pile of dish cloths... NOTHING! Not wanting to disappoint the old dragon, particularly in light of the fact that he was here for his help, he poured the hot water on top of the tiny dark lumps of charcoal and tried to imagine just where Tank had hidden them. As he inhaled the steam from the drinks... it came to him. His friend would almost certainly play the old shopkeeper at his own cunning game. But how exactly? That was the question. Opening the massive cupboard under the sink again, a small bottle of bright pink washing up liquid at the front caught Peter's attention, but he couldn't see what that would have to do with the marshmallows. It looked as though the bright pink liquid was regularly refilled from a massive container sitting behind it, showing the same liquid, but not nearly full up.

'I wonder,' he thought, shuffling the huge container out and examining it closely. It felt the right weight, and the liquid inside sloshed about, just as it should. But there was something odd about it. Holding it in both hands, he turned it round and examined the worn label on the back. On doing so, he felt a little groove running underneath. Pressing lightly with his fingernail, he moved along the groove. A tiny 'POP' preceded a plastic door clicking open. Peeking inside to find what looked like the world's supply of marshmallows, he laughed out loud at his friend's ingenuity. Tank had done to Gee Tee, what the old shopkeeper had done to him with the Peruvian mantra ink. Scooping out a handful, he tossed them into the master mantra maker's drink, put the secret container back and headed across the shop floor and into the workshop.

Lounging back in one of the oversized chairs, Gee Tee held his bizarre glasses in one hand as he rubbed his eyes with the other. Noticing the offered drink, he flipped his glasses back on his nose and grabbed the mug for all he was worth.

"Ahhh... you found them," he said with delight, spotting the pink and white treats bobbing up and down like abandoned rubber rings in a swimming pool.

Sitting down opposite the shopkeeper, Peter looked more than a little ridiculous in the oversized chair, sipping on his drink. After a few moments of blissful silence, Gee Tee spoke up.

"What's so important that my apprentice... ahem... I mean my associate... has to be out of the way?"

Swallowing hard, Peter wondered what to say. Now that he was here, things didn't seem quite so straight forward or easy. Knowing that he had nowhere else to go other than here, he hoped the shopkeeper would be able to help him out.

"It's about Richie."

Gee Tee nodded.

"I assumed as much."

"It's all so confusing," he declared, putting his drink on the desk, before holding his head in his hands.

"I understand little one, I really do. Tank feels exactly as you do, but there's nothing you can do to change the facts of what's happened. And rightly or wrongly, the council will never be dissuaded from wiping her memory and integrating her back fully into the human world. It pains me to say it, but as a dragon, she's lost. There simply isn't anything that can be done. Nothing at all."

It wasn't in his nature to get angry, but of late he'd found a whole lot of rage bubbling away inside him. Using a series of mental exercises he'd tried to control it, tried to rationalise it, but it was hard and it didn't always work. Right at this very instant... it was there, shifting around inside him, somewhere deep down past his stomach. Having heard the words and understood the meaning, he knew the old shopkeeper was only telling the truth. But he couldn't lose his friend, not again, not like this. It was bad enough when he'd thought that she was dead, but this... this was almost worse. To have her existence torn away through no fault of her own, just because the council refused to believe that she could be trusted in the new and very permanent form she found herself in, almost defied belief. So he'd decided he would stop at nothing to prevent it. As well, this new turn of events put a whole new spin on things, hence the reason he was here.

"I understand what you're saying," he said facing the old dragon across the room from him, "but I refuse to believe that nothing can be done. But before we talk anymore about that, there's something else you need to know."

"Go on," urged the master mantra maker.

"You know all about Tim?" he asked.

"Of course. Your young lady friend's human lover, who, thanks to the side effects of the *alea* has now transformed into not just any dragon, but the 'white dragon' who will apparently save us all."

Peter was curious.

"You say that almost as if you don't believe it."

"Call me an old cynic if you like, but in my experience things like this are never quite what they seem. It's almost as if it's a little TOO easy."

Peter chuckled.

"And just why would that be funny?" asked the shopkeeper, miffed.

"Ohhh... I'm not mocking you," stammered Peter, desperate not to offend his host. "Quite the opposite in fact. It's just that what you've just said, and what I have to tell you next, will prove you're one of the wisest dragons on the planet."

Now it was the master mantra maker's turn to let out a little chuckle. His was a lot louder though, and accompanied by tiny spurts of flame licking from his nostrils and around the side of his jaw.

"Well... I do like to think of myself in that role. But enough of the buttering up. Get on with it little one, I'm keen to know."

Staring deep down into the still swirling, dark ocean of charcoal in his mug, he composed his thoughts.

"A few days ago I went to Richie's flat to pick her up. While we were waiting, she wandered around getting dressed. Anyhow, during all of this, I got to see her back. As I'm sure you're aware, it was damaged very badly in the explosion at the clubhouse. Having done a great job in healing her injuries, the doctors have always maintained there would be a large amount of scar tissue there, and on her upper arms, that nothing could be done about. Anyway, it's the first time I've seen it. And it wasn't very pleasant, I can assure you. But that wasn't the surprising thing.

Taking an enormous mouthful of his drink, he tried to overcome just how uncomfortable he was about what he had to say next.

"Well?" encouraged the master mantra maker.

"The scarring, it had a pattern, well... more of an image actually."

Looking up from his drink, straight into the old dragon's eyes, he came out with it.

"It was a dragon. An image of a dragon on her pale white back. A white dragon!"

Gee Tee, who'd been creeping ever forward in his chair, sat back and let out a sigh.

"So what do you make of all this, little one?"

Anger rolling through every atom, it spread to his arms and legs now, close to consuming him.

"Don't you see...? They've got it all wrong. Everything else fits, but it's not Tim that's the white dragon from the prophecy, it's Richie!"

"I know what I said before, but this all sounds more than a little preposterous, don't you think?" replied the old dragon softly, trying not to hurt his guest's feelings.

"I was there, I saw it. I swear to you what happened is true."

"I don't doubt what you believe, little one. Truly I don't. But it's just possible your eyes were playing tricks on you, your imagination running away, or it was a trick of the light. These are all more likely explanations."

Throwing his head back in frustration, Peter let out a feral, ungodly scream. Gee Tee jumped ever so slightly in his chair.

"WHY WON'T YOU BELIEVE ME? I'M NOT WRONG!" he yelled.

Changing from good natured to serious, the old shopkeeper's face currently looked more dangerous than Peter had ever seen it. With more than a little tension flooding into the room, the young hockey playing dragon started to shake uncontrollably, the anger within him turning to fear and despair. Tears sprinted across his face, racing to see who would be the first to throw themselves off that cliff called 'chin'. Through blurred eyes, he looked up at the shopkeeper, his friend, his hope.

"I'm not wrong. Please... help me?"

With more lifetimes of experience than any being had a right to, Gee Tee had seen his share of action, theatrics and dragons who liked to play games, all for their own selfish needs and wants. This... youngling, dragon in a boy's body, was different, and he'd known it from their very first encounter, that day he'd come into the shop and stripped down to his underpants. Even then there was something about him, something that marked him out. Sure that once again destiny was giving him a little nudge, prompting him to help the boy dragon out, though he wouldn't reveal that to anyone. But it was all so vague and unbelievable. If only he could see it for himself.

'Get the girl in here and get her to strip off. How hard could that be to arrange?' he mused.

Lifting himself out of his chair, his ancient bones almost creaking from the strain, the old shopkeeper wandered over to the, by now, quivering young dragon and lifted his chin up with the tip of his right wing.

"You have to understand youngster... it's difficult for me to fully appreciate what you're telling me, without having seen it with my own eyes. I can see that you yourself are convinced one hundred percent about what you've seen, however unlikely it might appear. But without dragging your friend in here and getting her to show me her back, there's no possible way I can judge how much merit there is to what you say. Do you think you could get her to do it?"

Considering what the shopkeeper was suggesting, he wondered what his friend would think of his unusual request. It took only moments for him to realise it was ludicrous, and something she'd never agree to. And tricking her was out of the question, as he hadn't managed to fool her in the past and was pretty sure he wasn't going to any time soon. Resigned, he shook his head disappointedly.

"No... I don't think there's any chance I could even get her here, let alone get her to show you her wounds."

Sighing simultaneously, the two racked their brains about what to do. Just as the despair in the pit of his stomach threatened to rise up and overwhelm him, the master mantra maker's face changed ever so subtly, the brow of his forehead creasing, forming tiny rough valleys across his prehistoric expression, his sullen lips rising fractionally at the ends, producing not quite a smile... but something else.

"What is it?" Peter pleaded.

"There might be another way," growled the master

mantra maker, a glint in his eye.

Peter stood bolt upright.

"Whatever it is, let's do it! I'll do anything, anything at all to prove to you I'm right."

Gee Tee snorted out the residual flame from his nostrils, making an almost pig-like "oink" in the process.

"I wouldn't be too hasty if I were you, not before you know what I have in mind."

Peter calmed down, well... a little anyway.

"A well famed dragon, both down here and in the human world up above, a certain Leonardo da Vinci, produced some very prolific mantras in his time, tending to go through phases exploring flight and art, the sun, moon and stars, and at one point... the human mind. Without doubt he was a genius, not only in his predictions of the future, but also his shaping and understanding of creating mantras.

Standing, mouth agape, hooked on every word Gee Tee said, he looked a right sight.

"Some of his mantras have endured to this very day. And one in particular may well be the answer to our little conundrum."

Shuffling past the youngster, the old shopkeeper beckoned him to follow. Weaving in and out of the ever present bookcases, looking like towering guardians, the two of them finally stood at the front door to the shop. Carefully, the master mantra maker slid out a key from between a row of raggedy scales that circled the top of his bulging belly, inserted it into the door and turned it tightly. A satisfying click echoed past Peter and back towards the bookcases. Sliding shut two silver bolts, one on the top of the door, one on the bottom, neither of which Peter had ever noticed before, Gee Tee ambled back the way he'd come, until he made a sharp left down an aisle Peter had barely noticed before now. After thirty or so yards, the two of them reached a dead end in the shape of an ancient oak bookcase, so high it strained the young dragon's neck just to look up at where he assumed the top was. And if somewhere there'd been an award for a bookcase that was the dirtiest, dustiest and most covered in spiders' webs, then this one would most certainly have been the outright winner, beating all the competition hands down. In fact, Peter was doing his best to shy away from it all, the exact opposite of Gee Tee who, much to his young charge's disgust, had thrust his hands through a mass of cobwebs and was busy shuffling tomes around. As he did so, he turned towards Peter and said,

"I'm trusting you with my most valuable secret, young one. Make no mistake, you must never, and I repeat NEVER, tell another living soul about this place. DO YOU UNDERSTAND?"

"I do," stammered Peter, suddenly wondering what on earth he'd got himself into this time.

"NOT EVEN MY APP... ASSOCIATE TANK! AGREED?" demanded the old dragon, testily. Gulping, Peter nodded, just about managing to squeak a timid, "Yes."

"Good," declared the master mantra maker, turning back to face the shelves. Continuing to move the tomes around with a speed that belied his advanced age, a few seconds later a tiny hissing sound, very much like that of escaping gas or air, filtered up from the ground. Stretching out his wing, the shopkeeper forced Peter to take two steps back. As soon as he did so, the entire bookcase started to turn on its axis, as the pair of them stood and watched in relative silence. Splitting in two, the bookcase revealed a shiny metal pole, not quite the height of the aforementioned bookcase, with the bottom of it disappearing down a very dubious looking dark hole.

Gesturing with one wing, Gee Tee urged the young dragon forward towards the pole and the darker than dark hole it descended into. Taking three very tentative steps forward, Peter peered down as far as he could... not very far at all as it turned out.

"Now follow my instructions precisely," ordered the old dragon. "Slide down the pole, careful to tuck yourself in as fully as possible. In that ridiculous form you should be fine, but under no circumstances must you stick out any of your extremities on the way down. The consequences of doing so could well be deadly."

Legs trembling, all he wanted to do was go home, but it seemed to be much too late for that, and that fate itself had other ideas entirely for him.

"One last thing. When you reach the bottom, you are to take four strides off to the side, it doesn't matter which side, but you must not, under any circumstances, move forward in any way. Wait for me... I'll be right behind you."

Tummy somersaulting, legs wobbling, hands shaking, Peter took two steps forward, leapt onto the pole, wrapping his arms and feet around it as tightly as he could, and slid effortlessly into the darkness.

Watching, the old shopkeeper waited for a moment for what he knew would happen next, and wasn't disappointed. From far below echoed up an "AAAAAHHHHhhhhhhhhhh," that just seemed to go on and on. A toothy smile lit up his satisfied face as he realised the point in the journey that his young friend had just reached. Chuckling quietly, he threw himself forward, sliding into the darkness, all the time hugging the pole as tightly as possible.

Hitting the floor hard, Peter's legs took the brunt of the impact. Both his knees hurt badly, almost as if he'd stepped off the pavement onto the road from a kerb that was much higher than normal, without paying enough attention. That was not his only issue. Currently he was covered from head to toe in so much disgusting stuff, it was all he could do to heed Gee Tee's warning and step off to the side of the by now very slippery pole. Taking four steps to the right, he started trying to brush off the worst of whatever he was covered in, but before he had the chance, the gagging reflex he'd been suppressing since about halfway down, when something from within one of the dark crevasses had either spat on him or sprayed him with pee, simply gave up. Dropping to his knees, he vomited. And not just a little.

Seconds later, announced by a whoosh of air, without any drama and with the delicacy of a butterfly, Gee Tee touched down on the other side of the pole, wrinkling his nose as he did so.

"Ahhh... Olgoi got you did he?" smirked the old dragon knowingly. "He's a one he is. Generally if it's your first time, he seems to sense it and once he does... he never seems to miss the target, if you know what I mean."

By now, Peter had finished throwing up and was brushing thick strands of webbing, a rainbow litany of coloured liquids and numerous vines and other plant material off his clothes, arms, legs, hair and face. He looked a mess, and the particular shade of green his face had turned really didn't help him out one bit. For a split second the old shopkeeper held out one of his wing tips to help, but after brief consideration withdrew it almost immediately. Staggering to his feet, somewhat disorientated, Peter choked back down the taste of sick and bile that lingered around his throat and mouth, knowing he had to at least ask the question.

"Who or what on earth is 'Olgoi'?"

A faraway look drifted across the old dragon's face as he contemplated the question for a second or two.

"Olgoi, or Olgoi-Khorkhol to give him or her their correct name, for I have no idea just how many are left, are also known as Mongolian death worms. When this vault was installed, not far off four hundred years ago now, many, many counter-measures, deceptions, traps, tricks and deadly creatures were incarcerated in, around and alongside it. At the time, four breeding pairs of Mongolian death worms were given a home in the rock and soil around the pole, roughly half way down. At that time, these creatures were rarer than rare. It was thought that only about two dozen breeding pairs were left scattered throughout the Gobi desert. Transplanting some here made sense twofold. Of course the first was as protection against anyone trying to violate the security of the vault, with the second being to try and establish some kind of breeding colony somewhere far away from their normal territory, and somewhere far safer. Whether it's succeeded is anyone's guess. I'm sure if Tank were here he'd be fascinated and would, no doubt, after only a few minutes have them eating some kind of snack out of his oversized, pudgy hands." Peter smiled at the thought of his friend doing just that.

"What you can smell on you is their poison," announced the master mantra maker casually.

As a growing look of concern spread out across Peter's face, the bile in his throat started rising again.

"Oh don't worry," urged the old dragon. "I cast a specific protection mantra on you before you disappeared into the darkness. You were never in any danger."

'Good to know,' he thought, 'good to know.'

"If anything," added the old shopkeeper, "it was their electric shock that would have harmed you. Known to kill in fact, even dragons, if memory serves me correctly."

Peter's face was a picture... and a particularly terrified one at that. As Gee Tee fiddled around in a hidden side pouch for something he'd brought with him, the young dragon thought hard about what had just been said. Knowing that the famous mantra maker had a sense of humour, albeit somewhat warped, didn't give him a clue either way. Was he kidding? Was he serious? It was just about impossible to tell.

"Ahhh... here they are." Pulling out his unlikely square plastic spectacles, the old shopkeeper delicately slipped them along his nose until they sat just so.

"Now... let me see how this place looks," he said, turning full circle, standing on the spot. "Pretty much the same as I remember, only with a bit more dust," he added, running one of his bony fingers along the rock face behind them, "but apart from that and the increase in spiders, it all looks totally familiar."

Curiosity got the better of the young dragon.

"When was the last time you were down here?"

Turning his head so far to one side that it was nearly touching his left shoulder, the master mantra maker thought about that one.

"Hmmm... let me see. What did you say the year was up above... the ones the humans use as a calendar?"

"2017," answered the hockey player, marvelling at how someone so utterly brilliant and clever could be so forgetful so often.

"Ahhh... haven't been down here since '03' then."

'A place like this is hardly likely to have changed very much in thirteen years,' Peter mused.

"Those were the days," sighed the old shopkeeper. "Everyone then was so much smarter and polite... you know what I mean. All you, you... human infiltrators. Suits, ties, hats... and as for the ladies... well, the dresses were something else. Looking that smart, they were allowed in my shop... not like the scruffy yobs of today such as you and my young associate. You wouldn't know what dressed up looked like if it jumped up and smacked you on the nose."

The master mantra maker had finally lost his marbles... well, that was the conclusion that Peter had just reached, and was frantically racking his brain for some way to extricate himself from the situation that he found himself in. And then it HIT him!

"What was the exact date you were last here?" he asked softly.

"I'VE JUST TOLD YOU CHILD! DON'T YOU LISTEN TO ANYTHING I SAY? YOU'RE AS BAD AS YOUR FRIEND! December 12th 1903, about tea time as I recall."

If nothing else, the bizarre conversation had taken his

mind off the bad taste lingering in his mouth and the back of his throat.

'So, the old shopkeeper hasn't been down here in over a century. Oh,' he thought, 'what could possibly go wrong with all those things he's so kindly pointed out...? Traps, deceptions, countermeasures, magical beasts acting as guards, and I'm here with by all accounts the oldest dragon in the world, who suffers from the kind of memory lapses that are liable to get others (me in particular) killed!

Thinking about asking Gee Tee if they could go back, he dismissed it out of hand quite quickly, instead choosing to focus on the main reason he was here... to help Richie! As well, the old shopkeeper had seemed so enthusiastic about bringing him here, here, secret here. Here, that not even Tank knew about. And besides, he told himself, it was just a matter of convincing the master mantra maker that his theory about Richie was true... and THAT was the single most important thing that in his deepest time of need, he desperately needed to focus on. So that's what he did. He threw all his concentration into one thought, and tried frightfully hard to block out everything else.

Scuttling over beside the old shopkeeper, careful not to move forward even an inch, he finally took in his surroundings. Standing on the raised rock alcove where the pole came to rest, smack bang in the middle of its semi-circular shape, an irregular rock wall curved round behind them, littered with thick webs, spiders the size of dinner plates, as well as numerous plant species, most of which he recognised as being poisonous in some way, shape or form. On either side of the alcove, carved into the rock, two eighteen foot high dragon statues, both slightly different, towered over them, casting an ominous presence. Friendly and welcoming features stood out on one dragon with its wings folded back, one arm pointing away, its long, sleek, elegant tail pointing in another direction, a disproportionately small nose sitting perfectly in the middle of its face. A rather opposite disposition hung over the other dragon. Its fangs were bared in a fearsome snarl, while one raised foot showed that its talons had raked along the floor. This one's giant wings were open and the claws on both its hands were spread wide, with what looked like blood dripping down each. Its thick, deadly-looking tail seemed more like a club, with huge spikes protruding out at almost equal intervals, and this one's nose looked like it had either been punched by a T-Rex, or it had been chasing parked cars. It reminded Peter more than a little of the evil dragon Manson. Quickly, he turned his thoughts back to Richie, hoping to forget all about evil dragons, at least for the time being. With the statues forgotten, it was then he realised that right in front of him, no more than a few yards away in the darkness, three separate passages stood there, waiting, all nearly circular in design, all dragon sized, and all apparently identical. Only really able to see the entrances, as anything further was totally obscured by the all encompassing darkness, even scrolling through all his magical types of vision did him no good whatsoever.

"NOW YOU NEED TO PAY ATTENTION," declared Gee Tee, startling Peter out of his thoughts. "This is another of the important bits. What you see before you," he said, waving his right wing theatrically, "are three identical tunnels. It's more than a little important that we choose wisely the passageway we enter, for two reasons. Only one takes us to the vault... the reason why we're here. The other two tunnels... well..." ventured the old dragon thoughtfully, "the other two in fact lead to a rather unfortunate and untimely demise."

That got Peter's attention.

"You see two of the three tunnels are in fact unending, self replicating labyrinths that once you enter, would be impossible to escape from."

Gulping, a foul tasting mouthful of bile trickled back down Peter's throat.

"The trick," stated Gee Tee, holding up one of his

fingers like the show dragon he could be at times, "is to choose the right one." With that, he squeezed his huge bulk past his young charge, and stepped up to the friendlier looking dragon of the two. What happened next nearly blew Peter's mind. Putting the tip of his finger on the dragon statue's nose, the master mantra maker then, unbelievably, spun it around. Low and behold, a new and very different nose appeared in the old one's place.

'What on earth is going on?' thought the young dragon, astonished.

Carrying on, the old dragon spun the noses around so many times that eventually they came back to the one that was there originally. In all, there were seven different noses. To add to the mystery, every time one of the noses moved round, both the dragon's arms and its tail moved, changing direction ever so slightly.

"Now," put in Gee Tee, turning to face the perplexed young dragon. "I'm only going to say this once, and with your eidetic memory, that should be more than enough. This is the key to choosing which tunnel leads to the vault. Melted, Twisted, Withered, Tiny, Flat, Scrawny, Splattered," offered up the old dragon. "You should be able to work out the rest on your own," he urged, a little smile creeping across the ancient features of his face.

More so when there was any expectation or pressure involved, Peter hated puzzles. Recalling the words, he thought carefully about each and every one of them, the number of letters each contained, their meaning, if they had any relation to any well known dragons. NOTHING! He had NOTHING!

'DAMN!' he thought, all the time being watched by the sly old shopkeeper. Then it hit him like Isaac Newton's apple. Seven noses, seven words... what else had seven? The days of the week of course. And each word started with the same letter as a corresponding day of the week.

'GOTCHA!' he thought, smiling back at the master mantra maker.

"So you've worked it out?"

"Of course," answered the young dragon confidently, going on to explain his thoughts and reasoning.

"Good," said Gee Tee, nodding his large scaly head. "So which tunnel leads us to the vault, and not a slow, withering, unpleasant death?"

"Switch the nose to the one that looks melted... since today's Monday," ordered Peter, knowing full well that he'd have to either change forms or climb up the statue to do it himself. Gee Tee did as he ordered. Ever so slightly, the friendly dragon's arm and tail changed position, with the tail pointing to the middle of the three tunnels, and the arm pointing to the one on the right. Scratching the stubble on his chin, he was sure, well... pretty sure anyway, that the old shopkeeper wouldn't let him send them down either of the wrong tunnels... still, he wanted to work it out and find the right one. More than anything, he wanted to prove his worth, something he felt he'd come up short on, on a number of occasions. It had to be the one on the right, the one where the dragon's arm was pointing. It just had to be! But judging from the smirk that still lurked across the best part of the master mantra maker's face, he was convinced there was more to it than that. Turning his head and sighing, all the time scratching the two days' worth of stubble that he found himself attached to, he caught sight of the other dragon statue, beyond the pole running down the centre of the alcove. Thinking about it for a few seconds... just to make sure you understand... he came to a conclusion. It had to be the same for both of them... didn't it?

"Perhaps you'd do the same to the rather unpleasant dragon on the other side now?" he asked.

Gee Tee slid past with all the speed of a fifty year old (dragon), skirted around the metal pole and rolled the nose on the fearsome dragon to the same position. Again the arms and the spiked tail moved ever so slightly. One hand with what looked like blood dripping down it pointed to the right tunnel, with the evil looking end of the tail pointing directly down the centre of the left passageway.

Logic, Peter thought, dictated that it should be the right tunnel as that was where both arms were pointing, while a tail each pointed down both of the other tunnels. Looking again at both of the dragon statues, he could think of no other course of action. It was a long winded process, and if you didn't know about the noses and the days of the week, you would of course only be guessing. So he piped up.

"It's the right tunnel as that's the direction that both of them are pointing in."

"Are you sure little one?" asked the old dragon, hesitantly. "Sure enough to bet our lives on it?"

Of course there was no way he could be sure, and he was most certainly not willing to bet their lives on his... best guess.

"Not entirely," he coughed up.

"Good!" exclaimed the master mantra maker. Leaning down, he whispered gently in Peter's right ear. "The eyes my boy. It's all in the eyes."

Instantly he checked the dragon statue's eyes. Both of them were looking towards the left tunnel.

'But weren't they doing that before?' he thought. As if reading his mind, the old dragon moved the nose once again through a series of rotations, and unbelievably, the eyes of the dragon did shift, almost imperceptibly. The movement was so subtle, and of course on a couple of occasions they didn't move at all, but sometimes they did and that was all he needed to know. So with the correct nose in position, Peter turned and announced,

"So it's the left tunnel we need to take?"

With a tiny nod of his head, the shopkeeper answered,

"That's correct."

Taking a step forward towards the left hand passageway, suddenly a gigantic, bony, tattered and just basically old, wing, swung round and blocked his way.

"We must walk directly to the entrance, but on no

account go any further than the first waterfall."

'Oh... things are just getting better and better,' mused the young hockey playing dragon. Choosing to walk in front of the master mantra maker, he tentatively padded his way across to the entrance of the left hand tunnel which surprisingly, to him anyway, still remained pitch black.

Standing at the cusp of the entrance, he watched as the other two tunnels faded into nothing, a wave of relief washing over him. Hoping fervently that all the action he'd seen today was behind him, he stepped into the darkness.

Letting out an almighty yawn, due mainly to the fact that he spent about ninety-nine percent of the time huddled away inside his Mantra Emporium, this was the most action Gee Tee had seen in quite some time, probably since unleashing the ice salamander, the one that young Flash had given so much in getting rid of, the one from which they were still clearing up.

Clumsily he strode past Peter and through the entrance to the remaining tunnel. All of a sudden, the entire vista before them lit up, totally taking Peter's breath away. It was the single most amazing sight he could ever remember witnessing. Trailing off into the distance as far as he could see, the tunnel was a sight to behold. Four or five yards in front of him a stream, two or three yards across, with shallow, crystal clear water disappeared over a little waterfall, which rippled, tickled, tumbled, swirled, flowed and lapped at the grassy banks on either side of it. Peter stood transfixed; never in his life had he seen water move in such a magnificent way. Abruptly, an overwhelming need to touch the water, move into it, drink from it... started to consume him. He became so distracted that he failed to notice some other key features of the enchanting and rather deadly environment he found himself in with the old dragon. You see the stunning stream, scattered with tiny weaving bends, waterfalls measured in inches and thick twisting branches looking like they'd fallen perfectly across it in places, was really something special... particularly if you looked up, something he hadn't done yet. But if he had, he'd have seen an exact copy of the stream, mirrored in every way, running along what he considered to be the ceiling of the tunnel, its water seemingly glued there, gravity somehow defying belief. Between the two impossible streams running up the curved walls of the almost circular tunnel, a stunning looking layer of perfectly cut grass interspersed with the most beautiful wild flowers complemented the running water perfectly. The flawless grass was besieged by swathes of daisies, most of which had a shield of Goldilocks buttercups surrounding them. Towers of pink and yellow snapdragons stood up proud from the river bank, protruding from the ceiling and the bowed walls of the passageway. Ironically, yellow dragon's teeth blooms were dotted about everywhere, almost splattered like paint flicked from a brush. Pink evening primrose, creeping forget-me-nots, bluebells, snowdrops, daffodils and cowslips melted seamlessly into the picture perfect landscape, if that's how it could be described. Honeysuckle and clusters of stunning red poppies beset the curled, enclosed rock walls, making it look as though it were under attack in some places. This faultless vision was set off with common spotted orchids plaguing sections of the river bank and tormenting pockets of the surrounding rock wall, almost covering it in a jacket in places, their white petals imprinted with perfect patterns of purple, looking like some kind of textbook tie-dye production. It was an idyllic scene. But still, Peter found himself focused on the running water, finding it very hard to resist. Before he could move towards it, the very same wing as before moved out in front of him, blocking his way.

"Fight it child!" the old shopkeeper ordered, referring to Peter's urge. "It wants you... wants you to touch it with any part of your body. It's part of the vault's defence system. SNAP OUT OF IT!"

Blinking furiously, the young dragon shook his head, almost as though he hadn't realised what was happening.

Figuring that his young friend needed a practical demonstration of what would have happened, the master mantra maker folded his wings back behind him, closed his hands together, held them up to his prehistoric jaw before mouthing a few words into them. Sparkling bright light shone through the gaps in his fingers momentarily, before disappearing completely. Taking one step forward, Gee Tee threw open his hands and released an exquisite looking dragonfly that he'd just created out of thin air. Transparent wings fluttered gracefully as it cut through the air, heading straight for some of the reeds that lined part of the shallow river's banks. About halfway there it seemed to become confused, almost as if it were battling to understand which way was up and which way was down. Both dragons looked on, one in fascination, the other knowing full well what was about to unfold. Having gotten a grip on gravity, or perhaps it should be reality, the striking looking insect perched precariously for a few seconds, before almost sliding down a reed towards the water. The second its body came in contact with the breathtaking liquid, it froze... INSTANTLY! Coming to rest, it looked like some kind of miniature statue erected on the surface of the river. Staggered, Peter took a step back, bumping straight into the outstretched scaled belly of the shopkeeper. It was only then that he really took in his surroundings, and the rest of the tunnel that he had little choice now but to traverse.

"It... it... it... it looks so beautiful," he mumbled.

"Beautiful but ultimately DEADLY! If you take one lesson away from today... it should be that. So much of the world we live in is nothing like we actually perceive it. And that's certainly more true at the moment with the threat we face than probably at any other time in history. REMEMBER that at all times," exclaimed the old shopkeeper, rapping Peter gently on the forehead.

Nodding, he wondered how on earth they were going to traverse the simply perfect looking vista. Eventually, when the silence between the two dragons had grown unbearably uncomfortable, the younger of the two once again piped up.

"How do we cross it?"

Stepping past him, leaning down as he did so, the master mantra maker whispered,

"Watch... and learn!"

Standing with the talons of his right foot only a few inches from the entrance side of the first tiny waterfall, the old dragon raised his head, spread his arms and wings, and in a much more powerful voice than Peter would ever have given him credit for possessing, shouted,

"SPERMA REDIMIO."

Before his slower than normal brain could grasp the rough translation, which was something along the lines of, "Seeds surround," a maelstrom of activity in front of the two dragons spun up from nothing. Flowers and their stems coiled and warped, writhed and squirmed, extended and retracted, some with their heads spinning like washing machines on full cycle. The picturesque scene ahead of the two dragons looked like a full on horror movie, particularly to any hay fever sufferers. Amongst the mayhem, vicious whirlpools, eddies, waves and what looked like treacherous currents threatened to tear the shallow streams apart, with what passed for gravity between them warping before their very eyes. It lasted seconds, ten, twelve maybe at most, but it would be engrained in Peter's consciousness forever, featuring in only his most dire nightmares. Looking on, with the brief nightmarish vision all but over, the young dragon noticed a couple of very subtle, and not so subtle, differences. The first was blatantly obvious. Across the well manicured grass two twisting and turning parallel lines, made up from tens of thousands of dark seeds, wove their way along the tunnel, climbing up the arched walls, raking across the ceiling next to the river there, crossing some of the ideally placed branches that littered the streams and waterfalls, always moving deeper into the passageway, resembling fully the outline of a path. Noticeably, the patches of earth where the dandelions had been growing still had the plants there, but instead of the bright yellow flowers, in their place stood their seeds in clusters of two hundred or so, forming stunning looking puffballs that swayed gently in the virtually non-existent breeze, puffballs that every little child and toddler has at some point picked up and blown off the stem.

"So we follow the path the seeds have marked out for us," announced the hockey player, feeling rather pleased with himself.

"We do," agreed the old dragon. "Only it's not quite as simple as all that!"

"Of course not," whispered Peter under his breath so that only he could hear, whilst at the same time slapping his forehead with the palm of his right hand, the 'thwump' sound echoing off down the tunnel in front of him.

"You see," continued the old dragon, "we do indeed need to follow the seed path, but at the same time we need to pay attention to two other things."

Listening eagerly, knowing that his life almost certainly depended upon it, Peter stood and took it all in.

"One, because of the gravity anomaly, we need to keep as low to the ground as we possibly can, while all the time staying on the grass path between the seeds. At times the gravity will try to push and pull you in the wrong direction. And two, as we move along, the seeds from those dandelion puffballs will be released into the air. On no account must you let any hit you. If even one does, there's nothing I, or anyone else on this earth can do to save you from a frighteningly painful death."

It was at this point he waited... waited for the DA NAAA, the smile, the little, "Gotcha!", or his preferred favourite... the wink from the master mantra maker, hoping to hell this was all one big wind-up. But it never came, with the old dragon being as serious as he'd ever known him to be. Feeling that he was once again in some other dragon's nightmare and that fate was confusing him with someone else, Peter couldn't help but think that it was the whole Manson thing all over again. All he wanted was a quiet, uneventful life and with that in mind he blinked his eyes furiously, hoping against hope to wake up. It wasn't to be.

Taking a step forward with one of his giant feet, the sharpened points on his talons piercing the ground beneath the finely trimmed blades of grass as he did so, Gee Tee simply stated,

"Follow me exactly. Try to step only in my footprints... and keep balanced. That's very important!"

So off they set, the old shopkeeper plodding off very tentatively, if that is at all possible, with the youngster following exactly in his footsteps (a relatively easy task given that he was in his human form, with his footprints being about a fifth the size of his friend's). It didn't take the young dragon long to figure out that the biggest problem he faced was going to be his stomach, and the urge to heave again. Coping with the odd bubble of gravity trying to either push or pull him off the path was no trouble at all... he was actually quite nimble when he chose to be, and that skill combined with just the tiniest hint of dragon strength meant that all this was really a piece of cake. Currently the seed path had nearly doubled over on itself and both dragons were effectively walking along the wall, nearly at the point it reached the ceiling again (although they felt they were the right way up) which was really freaking Peter out. Of course he understood how it all worked, but whenever he glanced up from the path... nothing was where it should be. The stream he knew to be running along the ceiling was now mere inches away from his feet, the walls were upside down, although it was impossible to tell, and just the fact that he knew made his stomach grumble and gurgle terribly. It didn't help that he continued to look back over his shoulder, he wasn't sure why, but when he did he could of course see the route they'd already taken and how, in fact, they'd traversed the tunnel's circumference once already.

Out of the blue, the master mantra maker stopped sharply. They hadn't been moving at much of a pace, but it was all Peter could do not to walk straight into him. It was then that he noticed why the old dragon had come to a halt. Just across the other side of the stream (the ceiling one), a dandelion puffball had just dispersed all its seeds into the air, which were now heading in their direction. Hairs on both Peter's arms all stood up as if a cold breeze had run along them, as all the time the tiny little seeds drifted ever closer, despite the lack of any discernible current of air. Instinctively, Peter zipped through every different type of vision he possessed, until he came to the one he thought of as bionic (he'd seen some re-runs of the Six Million Dollar Man) and very quickly zoomed in on the innocuous looking seeds of floating death that were rapidly heading their way. On close inspection he could see that despite appearing all fluffy and lovely, the way that normal dandelion seeds do, every part of those drifting menaces was in fact razor sharp, with some of the heads looking as though they were coated in a very ominous, thick, oozing liquid of some sort. Swallowing nervously, he switched back to his normal vision and tried carefully, without moving his feet, to lean round and see what his friend was up to, as it was only now that he'd realised the old dragon had been totally silent all the time they'd been standing still.

Eyes closed, Gee Tee concentrated, having of course played this game before, albeit long ago, knowing only too well that the seeds that were drifting ever closer were attracted to life of any kind and were, to some extent, almost sentient. They were using tiny funnels of flowing air to make their way every closer, intending to surround and then close in on their target. Outsmarting them long ago had been child's play looking back on it, but he knew from experience that they seemed to almost learn from one time to the next and remember how they'd been tricked previously. So far, he'd tried altering the currents of air, hoping to take the lethal seeds back down the passageway towards its entrance, but to no avail. Next he tried telepathically to alter their instructions, their target if you like. That had worked long ago, but not today. And only a few seconds ago, he'd cast a mantra that had produced a perfect replica of a sparrow, right smack bang in the middle of the seeds, something that in theory at least should have attracted all of them, in one big go. But they just ignored it and carried on floating over the shallow stream with the crystal clear running water, gliding ever closer. Up until now, he hadn't been concerned with this part of getting to the vault, but at this point he was starting to worry.

"Uhhhh... we seem to be in a bit of a sticky situation, youngster," announced the old shopkeeper.

"What do we do about the seeds?" enquired Peter, trying not to sound concerned.

"They're attracted to life, a living thing of any sort. As it stands I've tried everything I know to deflect them away from us, but nothing is having the desired effect. I'm struggling to come up with a solution."

'Blimey,' he thought to himself, 'it must be bad if Mister Know-It-All Shopkeeper doesn't have the answer.'

"Can't we just turn round and go back?" he asked gingerly.

"They'll just follow us."

"We could just run or fly as fast as we can. Surely that would work?"

"That would just pique their interest, and maybe just attract more of them. We wouldn't make it back to the alcove. Besides, to get out of here we have to make it to the vault proper, as that's the only place you can reset all the tricks, traps and deceptions and set up the way back out," whispered the old dragon, a concerned look on his face as he looked back over his shoulder.

Putting his head in his hands, shaking in despair, he wanted to say, "It's the first time I'm hearing all of this," but knew that being sarcastic to the old shopkeeper now would do more harm than good.

Pulling his hands away from his face, Peter stood almost nose to nose with the grinning old dragon leaning down, his smile clearly betraying the fact that he'd just come up with a solution to their ever impending doom.

"You... my young friend, are full of surprises," uttered the master mantra maker, lifting his head up. "If you wouldn't mind, perhaps you could just turn and face the other way for a moment, careful to stay standing still in my footprints."

Confused, he did as the old dragon asked. For his troubles, he could hear his friend suddenly become very excited.

"Ohhh... yes, this is excellent. Perfect!"

And with that, Peter could feel the old shopkeeper's hands running down his back, and along his shoulders.

"Okay. You can turn around now."

Turning round, he nearly jumped out of his skin (given that it's not really his skin in the first place... that's more than a little difficult to do, which gives you some idea of the severity of the shock he found himself in), and more importantly, out of his friend's footprints. Gee Tee was standing in front of him holding two handfuls, about six in total, of dinner plate sized spiders, which had all sneakily hitched a ride on his back, all the way from the alcove. Not able to believe what he was seeing, particularly when one or two of them started snapping at the old dragon's fingers, it was all Peter could do not to faint. It was a good job he didn't, otherwise he'd have missed Gee Tee performing the most precise throw in the world, in which one of the very bemused, very snappy spiders spun through the air, ending up in the middle of the highly toxic seeds. As the spider whipped through them, the seeds as one formed a globe like enclosure around it before pouncing without any warning at all, darting into the unsuspecting and, by now, most disturbed spider. The poor thing died instantly (even Peter didn't like this... and he harboured a real dislike for spiders) with the darts piercing its hairy flesh in almost every spot, allowing the deadly neurotoxin to perform its function.

As the spider landed on the grass with a thud, the arachnids the old shopkeeper still had hold of all looked on, instantly becoming less volatile after having seen what had happened to their friend. With the seeds all gone, Gee Tee shoved the remaining spiders into one of the hidden pouches around his waist, smiled at his young friend and very slowly headed further into the passageway on the seed path, seeking the mysterious vault.

Eventually they reached part of the tunnel where grass met rocky floor, having left both streams behind them. It was impossible for Peter to tell if they were the right way up, given all the times they'd circled the walls and floors, up to this point. Twice more, dandelion puffballs had hurled their seeds into the air at them, with Gee Tee plucking out and sacrificing spiders from his secret pouch, as before. Both times worked the same as the first, with the deadly arrow-like barbs of the seeds splintering the poor arachnids. Having reached the pure rock floor, the shopkeeper found the three remaining spiders and released them in quite a heartfelt, apologetic manner, given what he'd done to their friends, something Peter wouldn't have believed possible had he not seen it with his own eyes.

Without a word, the old shopkeeper continued on round a sharp bend in the now rocky tunnel, no more than twenty yards from where they'd exited the grass. As the passageway opened out effectively into some kind of underground courtyard, Peter let out a tiny gasp at what lay before them.

Deep within the recesses of Rome's famed dragon library, a lone, human shaped figure sat at an out of the way terminal, concentrating hard, focused on one goal and one goal only... finding out about her friend's parents. Just a single clue would have done, something so remote that it would barely have meant anything, but so far she'd found absolutely nothing. Having already scoured the library's physical shelves, delving deep into little known tomes and ancient texts, not one single record of either of Peter's parents appeared to exist. And that was odd, because they were known to have existed and Peter himself was proof of that. Whoever had wiped their information from the system had been a professional. But a professional what? So many things just didn't add up. Hacking into the library's mainframe, not at all concerned about being caught, after all, what more punishment could she possibly face, above what was already headed her way? There and then she vowed to find something, anything, that would help her friend on his quest to find the answers that so eluded him.

19 SUB-VERSION

Thick, swirling mist nestled lazily above the water's surface. Unseen wildlife occasionally sent out tiny ripples across the fluid's exterior, all of course hidden by the unnaturally dark clouds obscuring the moon on this eerily quiet night. The wooded area around the bank of the lesser known tributary was quiet... almost deathly so.

Waiting above a shallow bank, nestled between a quartet of large, gnarled trees, the group was camouflaged by brush on all sides. The stolen vehicles in which they'd made their way there had been dumped almost two miles away. By the time the authorities, or anyone else for that matter, ever worked out quite what had happened, they would all be long gone.

A delicate splash echoed out of the mist across the tributary, putting the entire group on guard. Weapons were drawn as two dark coloured nagas slithered down the bank before slipping effortlessly head first into the water in their natural forms, their vicious looking tails disappearing from view almost instantly.

Manson stood, one arm supported by his walking stick, the other wrapped around Troydenn (his father), to support him in what had become a rather frail human disguise. Caressing the top of the stick with the palm of his hand in the cloying darkness, briefly a wave of reassurance washed over him at having the weapon to hand. Not just because of the razor sharp blade that could be brought to the fore with just a single thought, but also due to the exquisite sea crystals that ran along its entire length, boosting the range, and more importantly, the potency of the wicked dark energy inside him. With little choice but to revert back to the form he totally despised, Troydenn sincerely hoped it would be the last time he'd have to take on this wretched guise, the thought of long awaited revenge keeping him focused on the challenge ahead. As a group they'd thought, planned and brainstormed long and hard about how to get across the Atlantic and back to the main power base of dragon society. Their takeover depended upon it. At this stage, with not all their assets entirely in place, it was deemed necessary to use the stolen submarine. (Using the monorail or any other part of the dragon domain presented too much of an unwarranted risk to their well conceived plan, much to the elderly dragon's disgust.) And the only way he was going to fit into the tight confines of the submarine was in his much smaller, alternative form.

From out of the darkness a sliver of light grey appeared, floating steadily in their direction. Instantly, weapons on the bank converged on the movement, but their concern dissipated as a dinghy, with two nagas swimming either side of it, rolled out of the mist.

"About time," grumbled Troydenn quietly, to no one in particular.

"It's all going to plan," whispered Manson in his father's ear, eager to put the old dragon at ease.

Slowly, the dinghy rocked up on the shallow bank while the nagas remained in the water. A man clad entirely in black let go of the oars and carefully made his way to the front of the tiny craft.

"If that's what you're bringing on board," he murmured, pointing at the pile of stacked equipment on the bank, "then we'll only be able to carry three of you and we'll have to make two trips!"

Manson withdrew his arm from around his father's shoulders and purposefully strolled forward.

"One trip will suffice," he exclaimed. "The others here will accompany us in their natural forms, at least out to the sub anyway."

Nodding, the sailor agreed, more than a little creeped out by most of the things that had gone on recently. However, he was being paid more money than he'd ever hoped to see in any single lifetime, so he just carried on regardless. Together, everyone started to load the equipment onto the dinghy, with the exception of Troydenn who just stood and peered wistfully into the darkness, thoughts of soon-to-come retribution consuming him wholeheartedly. With the dinghy loaded and Troydenn securely sitting between Manson and his female companion, the sailor shoved off from the bank, took up the oars and started rowing back out into the tributary where the waiting submarine sat in the very minimum amount of water it needed to stay afloat. All the time, five dark and fearsome shapes circled noiselessly in the water around them.

Five minutes later the equipment had been transferred, along with the passengers, and the water borne beasts had once again taken human form. With that, the submarine battened down its hatches, dropped silently through the misty haze and disappeared effortlessly beneath the surface of the murky water, on the start of its momentous journey.

20 DRAGON LORD'S HOARD

Gobsmacked at what lay before him, he could barely believe what he was seeing. Bearing in mind that in his relatively young life he'd already visited the king's private residence and the library attached to it, thumbed through some of the scrolls there and actually seen with his own eyes the fabled prophecy agreement (something so secret that most dragons don't even know that it exists,) being put into his current state by the hoard of dragon relics in front of him was quite something.

Lying there for all to see, the large, terracotta rock vault that faced them had no door, it was just out there in the open, on display for everyone.

'Well,' he mused, 'not exactly for all to see. I mean... you have to get this far, I suppose.' Nooks and crannies cut out of the walls housed the most beautiful, intricate, gaudy, powerful and frightening things he'd ever laid eyes on. From dozens of feet away he could feel the raw power of the amulets, rings, charms, wristbands and even a tiara that looked absolutely terrifying.

Shelves that ran horizontally and vertically were stuffed to the brim with spell books, layers of parchment, rolled up magical scrolls, one off mantras and thick dust covered tomes. One such shelf, overflowing with scrolls, looked like the end-on view of a neatly stacked log pile.

Rows of worn metal hooks adorned the back wall, and hanging precariously from them were dozens and dozens of leather belts, some with swords hanging off them... some stunning and bejewelled, others old, worn and rusty. There were belts with ancient pistols, one with the finest looking foil, its delicate handle looking as though it were made of glass. Further along, a rather raggedy, off-white, ancient looking canvas rucksack, huge in size, adorned with worn leather straps and golden buckles that had long since lost their shine, with cleverly disguised drawstrings and much shinier metal clasps for pockets, littering its circumference, hung across two of the hooks. Most amazingly, well to him anyway, was a gun belt with a six shooter from the old Wild West. An old, very ordinary looking rifle from the same era stood up against the wall beneath it. Mixed in with all the belts, bandoliers of all sizes hung motionless, deadly looking grenades adorning their entire length. Taking it all in, Peter stood mouth open, looking like a very well behaved dentist's patient.

Propped up in one corner stood a selection of fabulous looking wooden bows, some taller than him, made to look even taller by the line of quivers filled to the brim with arrows in front of them.

A hulking great pile of human shaped armour towered high in the other corner, looking like some kind of modern art piece. Shiny boots, bracers, chest plates, helms and gloves mingled with their rusty cousins, no distinction made, no two pieces looking as though they came from the same set, with some having a smattering of what looked like dried blood splattered indiscriminately across them. Just the thought of this sent shivers down Peter's spine and even his nowhere-to-be-seen-today tail.

Rock plinths the colour of the walls, inscribed with complex dragon runes ages old were dotted around, most with something incredible sitting upon them. One though, sat empty, looking almost sad and lonely amongst the glittering array of powerful artefacts. Huge, marble... what can only be described as bowls... sat on the floor, sprinkled between the towering plinths. Each one contained a gruesome pile of teeth, or individual scales, all different shapes, all different sizes. It was a sight to behold, and one that he would never forget for however long he lived.

Thinking about taking a step forwards and entering the vault proper, he couldn't shake the dozen or so different scenarios playing out in his head right now, of how a strikingly horrible death from out of nowhere might suddenly appear.

"Well?" exclaimed Gee Tee.

"Well what?" replied Peter.

"Don't you want to go and take a look?"

"And walk into yet another deadly trap," ventured the young dragon sarcastically.

A deep chuckle that sounded more like distant thunder reverberated from the master mantra maker.

"That's it. That's all there is. If you get this far... then you're welcome to the lot!" he announced, spreading open his wings in their entirety, indicating everything there in front of them.

'He does seem sincere,' Peter thought, waiting to be halted at any moment as he started to step forward. But to his utter amazement, he was allowed to continue onto the terracotta rock floor and up to the nearest plinth. Too nervous to actually touch anything, thinking that undoubtedly all the items were in some way booby trapped, he leaned in for a closer inspection of the items that were apparently on display. Given everything in here, what sat in front of him were no great shakes. Looking closer he tried to determine why on earth they were here. Still he had no clue. Nothing inside him could fathom out why a pair of old (very old... think Middle Ages old) just above the ankle, worn, scuffed and tattered, brown leather boots, with the tongues hanging out limply and the laces dangling untidily over each side of the stone tower, were given pride of place.

"Boots of Fleeting!" came a voice from right behind him.

Having nearly jumped, not realising the old shopkeeper could move so lightly on his feet, he turned to face the old dragon.

"Boots of what?"

"Boots of Fleeting youngling. Surely even you can't be that daft."

Determined not to rise to the bait, the young dragon raised an eyebrow and waited expectantly for an answer.

"Boots of Fleeting," started the old dragon, "were commonly, well, as commonly as can be amongst human shaped dragons, used during the Middle Ages. At one point, with the humans in their cities developing all sorts of siege weapons and whatnot, it became very inconvenient, not to say dangerous, for dragons in their natural form to travel over the populated and fortified areas generated by the creative apes. With more of our kind assuming ape form and blending in with them, some bright spark created these boots with a stunning alteration to a favourite mantra of mine. It worked a treat, and it was said that any dragon wearing Boots of Fleeting could travel leagues in just the merest of steps. That pair that you see before you are the finest example of their kind."

Leaving the boots behind, still taking in what he'd been told about them, Peter wove past one of the marble bowls full of teeth, shivering as he did so, only to stop at a tiny, foot high plinth with a hole in the middle. From out of that hole stood a cracked and twisted length of wood that slightly resembled a staff of some kind. The wood itself was rampant with knots and had most certainly seen better days. It almost looked as though it would turn to dust at the merest of touches.

'As well,' he thought, 'it just looks incredibly... ANGRY!'

"Ahhh... Merlin's staff," stated Gee Tee from the far side of the vault, his back to Peter, rifling carefully through a huge pile of parchment.

'Merlin's staff,' he thought. 'You've got to be kidding me.'

"I can assure you it is," confirmed the master mantra maker, almost as if reading the young dragon's mind, his words bouncing off the walls in the dead end they found themselves in.

Slowly and very carefully Peter walked around the plinth, examining the staff from every possible angle. It looked hopeless. If there were a thousand staffs to choose from, no matter how bad the others were, this would be the last one you would pick. But maybe that was the point. Certainly he could feel power radiating out from somewhere inside it. Letting out a short sigh he reluctantly moved on, hoping to examine as many things as possible before his time was up, knowing that this might well be his one and only chance to see the wondrous relics and artefacts kept here, given how often it was the old shopkeeper himself came to visit.

It was no good, he just couldn't resist any longer; it had been drawing him in since he first set eyes on the vault, and he just had to get a closer look. Seemingly, hovering in mid-air of its own accord, a foot or so above the plinth, situated smack bang in the middle of the vault, hissing and spluttering as it did so, was the single most beautiful thing he'd ever seen. Longer than a dagger, but not quite sword length, the blade was almost futuristic in design and could have come straight out of the latest sci-fi film at the cinema. A moving pattern of frost continually circled the blade, giving off a cold and chilly feel, whilst the whole of the weapon itself was surrounded by an eerie blue glow. Simultaneously he felt both awe and fear. Awe for whoever, or whatever, had crafted the weapon... for it was truly a masterpiece. But fear at what it could be used for. There could be no doubt that this weapon was a dragon killer, its nature almost screamed out at him. It wouldn't even need to find a dragon's weak spot, it would just carve them up regardless. Just as he was about to move on and try and put the sheer beauty, magnificence and deadliness of the weapon out of his mind, the master mantra maker called out again, still facing away, still rummaging through the parchment.

"It's a vision of true splendour isn't it?"

"DEATH wrapped up in a pretty parcel," replied Peter.

That got Gee Tee's attention.

"Who's a cynical dragon today then?" he replied sarcastically.

"Well... isn't it?"

Gee Tee lowered himself off his tiptoes and turned to face his young friend across the vault. Peter started to wonder just how wise his comments had been.

"THAT, youngster, is not just one of a kind, but is probably THE most amazing weapon you will ever come across in the whole of your dragon life."

Instantly his thoughts turned to Aviva's laminium dagger, tucked safely away in his own home. Having given his word to the king that he wouldn't tell anyone about it, particularly the old shopkeeper, he fought off the desire to mention it now, with all his self restraint.

"But it's so much more than that," continued the old dragon. "This," he said, "is my most prized possession. It's the only one of its kind, and was forged by a Chinese dragon more than two thousand years ago. Nobody's ever been able to recreate that feat, despite many having tried. It was thought to have been crafted by a master weapon smith, by the name of Fu-ts'ang. So revered was Fu-ts'ang that he was written into ancient Chinese mythology, given special responsibility for the minerals of the earth, and is sometimes known, even to this day, as the Dragon of Hidden Treasures. Hence, the weapon is known only as Fu-ts'ang. You should refer to it as if you were referring to a person. It has been claimed by some that the weapon smith's soul is encased or bound within the weapon itself, seeking out kindred spirits, eager to help those it feels worthy."

'And I bet it does magic tricks and performs at children's parties,' mused Peter, his thoughts becoming ever more sarcastic with every second that passed. But the tiny mature part of him knew not to say this out loud for two reasons. One... it was just plain rude, something he most certainly wasn't. And two... he could see how much the weapon meant to the master mantra maker, and didn't want to hurt his friend's feelings. Nodding while glancing over at the old shopkeeper, he continued his tour of the vault, determined to move on to the other main thing that had captured his attention. Carefully, he made his way to the back wall.

Before he'd even touched the magnificent belt, a faint waft of leather and associated oils filled his sensitive nostrils. Ignoring the assault on his nose, he noticed that all the bullets held in place around the entire diameter of the tan coloured belt had lost their sheen. For the most part, the same was true for the gun, a Colt .44 if he wasn't mistaken. Not the white grip of the seductive looking pistol, though, that was shiny and only a little worn. A shiver ran down his spine. He wanted to try it on... he so did.

"Can you guess who it belonged to?" asked a soft voice, floating across the chamber.

Without bothering to turn round, he racked his brain for the answer. Having always been fascinated by the Wild West era, it was only now that he realised his knowledge on the subject was more than a little limited. Moments later, it became clear that at best he'd only be taking a guess. So he gambled.

"Jesse James."

Still searching, and without breaking a sweat, the old shopkeeper nodded, grumbling a brief,

"Not bad, not bad at all."

Elated that his guess had been right, confidence and pride swelled within him, for all of a few seconds anyway.

"You're in the right era, so I suppose we should be grateful for that," stated the old dragon, stalking in Peter's direction, a loose piece of parchment flapping out precariously from his right hand. "But this belt, and the 1873 Winchester rifle you see beside it, belonged to a much maligned and misunderstood dragon, someone whose supposed infamy stretches far and wide in human history, or so I'm led to believe."

Not expecting this, he stood listening intently, eager to know who this infamous dragon was.

"His name was William H. Bonney and he was for a short time at least... one of my friends," added the old shopkeeper a little sadly.

'William, Will, Bill,' pondered Peter. 'Who on earth was...?' And then it came to him.

"Billy the Kid!" he declared.

His friend nodded in agreement.

"That's the name he came to be known by. But he was always just 'Kid' to me, always misunderstood, always fighting the good fight."

Peter had never heard of any dragons being involved in the main historical events of the Wild West. Sure there would have been dragons living in around those areas, blending in, guiding... just pretty much doing what they do now. But to find out somebody that famous, or infamous depending on your view, from that era was a dragon, he found quite shocking.

"You say that he was misunderstood and that he was fighting the good fight, but from everything I know, and yes, it's based on how the humans view history, Billy the Kid was known as a teenage outlaw, a thief and a cattle rustler, as well as a murderer."

Unceremoniously, the old shopkeeper plonked his backside on the floor and sat down, the ground protesting just a little as he did so. Gently placing the parchment on the floor next to him, he gazed over at the young dragon before him, now that they were almost at the same height.

"Kid was one of the most intriguing, loyal and courageous dragons I've ever had the pleasure to be associated with. Cool under pressure, he loved to speak Spanish, and had the most beautiful tenor voice I've ever heard, right up to the present day."

This sounded almost impossible to Peter. It was nothing like the Billy the Kid he'd read and watched films about.

"What you don't know," reflected the old dragon, "and almost certainly, what the dragon council have tried very hard to cover up and keep quiet, is that a band of dragons gone bad had virtually taken over the Wild West and were running it for their own means. At the time, there was very little in the telepathic papers about it, but dragons everywhere knew exactly what was going on. It was an unspoken secret if you like. The council, instead of going charging in like a dragon in a field of sheep, decided to fight fire with fire, so to speak, and sent in a group of their very best operatives, with a view to clearing up the mess quickly and very quietly. I'm not going to tell you who some of the others were, but rest assured, you would know their names. Anyhow, Kid was one of them. One of the best in fact. Before that mission, he'd known for some time, and let's just say we'd had a few run ins. But he came to me and explained the difficult and delicate nature of what he was doing, and pleaded for my help. Anyhow, he got it, and we became firm friends over the course of a few years. It was all supposed to have been over with almost instantly, but what the council didn't realise was that the band of renegade dragons still had help, from deep within the dragon domain itself."

Priceless, was the only way to describe the look on the young dragon's face.

"With the dragon operatives, Kid included, in their human personas, fighting tirelessly, it went on and on and on. In the process, dragons in and around the Wild West dragged Kid's reputation through the mud... very deliberately I can assure you, to make life as difficult as possible for him in hunting down those he was assigned to bring to justice. Newspapers everywhere, particularly in his supposed home town, claimed he was a disgrace, a vulgar cutthroat and the terror of New Mexico. It was all a lie, perpetrated by the dragons. Still, the public at the time, and more importantly... HISTORY all believed it to be true. Anyhow, the kid brought in dozens of dragons gone bad, lots singlehandedly, probably killing even more. But the threat continued and those he sought the most evaded him at every turn, almost knowing his next move before he made it. Eventually he was killed by a dragon in human form called Pat Garrett, who the humans had elected as their sheriff... you couldn't make it up."

Aware now of the emotion in the old shopkeeper's voice as he recounted the events, he could see exactly how hard it was for him, and just how much he'd cared about the 'Kid'.

"Eventually they were all caught of course. There was Pat Garrett himself, an attorney, William Rynerson, and some deputy named James Bell who were the ringleaders, at least in and around the area where the Kid was working. But the scale and the destructive nature of what was going on had been hugely underestimated by the dragon council who, as far as I know, went to great lengths to cover things up. What happened to the perpetrators is a mystery. Nobody knows, which in itself is intriguing. After I heard of the Kid's death, I went to great lengths to recover these items," he all but sobbed, waving his arm in the direction of the gun belt and the rifle. "I felt as if I owed him that much, after all, I did imbue them with the mantras that made them such terrific weapons."

This got Peter's attention, something which Gee Tee clearly noticed.

"The Colt .44 was keyed to the Kid's DNA, in combination with the bullets, to fire at exactly what he was looking at. I spent weeks at a time just producing enough bullets to keep him supplied. He didn't use them all the time, but I know they saved his hide on a number of occasions. As for the rifle, it has an accuracy mantra running along the length of it, something any dragon could make use of. His ranged shooting would have been out of this world."

Stretching out his hand to run his fingers along the belt and over the bullets it held, he was all but overwhelmed to be so close to something so... historical, something that had played such an important part in events. It was...

unbelievable!

Moving along, gazing at all the incredible items, his left foot clattered against a tall glass jar on the floor, just visible from behind a pile of leather armour. Curious, he picked up the jar... just. It weighed a ton, but that wasn't what piqued his interest. Inside were hundreds, if not thousands, of tiny rivets. Most amazing though, was that they appeared to be made of laminium.

"PUT THAT DOWN CHILD," chided the master mantra maker from over his left shoulder, having just got to his feet.

Surprised, the young hockey player lost his grip on the jar and watched as it arced up and away from him, spinning precariously out of control. Instantly the old shopkeeper was on it, catching it effortlessly in one hand. Before replacing it back where it had come from, he gave the youngster a... LOOK!

"COME ON," yelled Gee Tee, pushing past him. "I might as well show you the best of the rest before we get on with what we came here for."

Heading off towards the corner with the bows in, past the line of belts and bandoliers hung along the adjacent walls, Peter started to follow, full of excitement, thinking, 'Best of the rest?' As he did so, something within him felt compelled to stop, just in front of one of the swords hanging from the wall. Call it an inkling, an attraction, what you will, but he could physically do nothing but stop and look at the weapon. Carefully, he pulled it from its sheath, expecting something magnificent, riddled with gems, the perfect fighting weapon. Instead, all he found was a very ordinary, dull blunt blade, unloved and unlooked after.

"Ahhh... I should have guessed you'd find that. I forgot all about it," babbled the old dragon, having turned around to find out where his young friend had got to. "Can you guess who that sword belonged to?"

Despite the fact that he felt privileged to be here, and

could appreciate just how special this place was, Peter was starting to get a little fed up with all the guessing games. Knowing it was just the old dragon's way to show off all the artefacts and just how much smarter he was, it was just getting on his nerves now. Not normally one to pick up on such things, or if he did, never normally one to act on that instinct, the master mantra maker patted Peter on the shoulder and quietly whispered,

"Last time... I promise! And I'll tell you what, I'll even give you a clue."

Peter's face brightened.

"You've met him... that's the clue."

'It's someone I've met,' he thought, giddily, his mind racing through everyone he knew to see if any of them could possibly have a use for, or could have used that sword. None of them seemed to fit, apart from Flash of course. He could easily imagine his friend, the ex-Crimson Guard, wielding any weapon expertly, at probably any time. And then a much more plausible alternative popped into his head, and he knew he had the answer. Even in giving him the clue, the old shopkeeper had tried to cover things up a little.

"The king," he blurted out.

"Which one?" asked Gee Tee playfully.

"George... the current one."

Nodding, the old dragon added,

"Well done youngster, well done. This was in fact the very sword he used to incapacitate Troydenn when they battled in Salisbridge all those centuries ago, when he captured and returned him to the dragon domain, only then for them to decide his punishment and exile him and his followers to Antarctica."

Turning the mundane weapon over and over in his hands, marvelling once again at the history behind the object, he harked back to his favourite story from the nursery ring, not able to believe that he was holding something which had featured so heavily in it.

"Right... come on now," urged Gee Tee. "Put that back, we haven't got all day. We've been down here long enough, and there are a couple more items I've yet to show you." Turning, he stomped off towards the corner once again.

Sliding the sword gently back into his sheath, Peter turned and followed the old dragon over to where he stood with a pile of wooden bows, some much taller than he was.

"RIGHT! No more guessing games." Picking up a gorgeously smooth wooden bow, that when standing on the floor came right up to Peter's neck, he allowed the young dragon to run one finger along the not quite taut string. "Now surely even you, my young friend, will have no trouble in working out which famous English hero this longbow belonged to."

This, at least, they had covered in their history lessons, back in the Purbeck Peninsula nursery ring, all those years ago.

"ROBIN HOOD!" he cried, astounded that Gee Tee would have his bow.

"Oh yes," replied the shopkeeper. "He did, of course, have two bows, a much smaller one for hunting and this longbow which he used to fight the Sheriff of Nottingham's men. It was the stand out weapon of the time, and when issued to the army it was said a skilled military archer could fire off around twelve arrows a minute and pierce armour from more than two hundred and fifty yards away. Robin, no doubt, would have been able to easily exceed that. Normally bows were made to measure depending on your height, so we have to assume this one was made specifically for him. What a lot of people don't know is that the longbow was invented by the Welsh, to fight off the English. Elm was their preferred choice from which to make this fine weapon, while the English choose yew instead."

"What's the string made of?"

"I believe that hemp was soaked in some form of glue

for most of the bows. One thing I'd really like to know about this bow, is whether or not the wood that it's formed from came from the churchyard at Papplewick. Such trees were proven, for both humans and dragons alike, to possess medicinal, spiritual and symbolic qualities. If the wood did originate there, that would indeed make it even more special than I already believe it to be."

"Why is it so good?"

Picking it up, the old shopkeeper offered it up, along with an arrow from a nearby quiver, to the young dragon.

"See for yourself," he said mischievously.

With a hint of trepidation, Peter accepted, sure he was about to make a fool of himself (not for the first time today) but in the spirit of things, he was willing to give it a go.

Pointing to the far wall, furthest from where they were standing, the old dragon said,

"Pick one of the runes on that wall, focus intently on it, and see if you can hit it."

It was all Peter could do not to laugh.

'If I get a shot off and it goes in vaguely the right direction, it'll be an absolute miracle,' he mused.

Lifting the bow, he found it considerably more comfortable to get into position than he'd thought he would. Facing the direction Gee Tee had pointed in, he nocked the arrow, carefully pulled back the string, more worried about catching his fingers than about where the arrow would go, and focused on one particular rune on the far wall. What happened next was surreal. Without doing a thing, almost as if controlled by someone else, his vision just zoomed in, right into the rune he'd chosen. Surprised more than a little, his fingers let go of the string, the arrow shooting away at a speed he could barely see, even with his enhanced abilities. A whistling 'TWANG!!' trumpeted down his right ear. A human wouldn't have had a hope of seeing it whizz through the air. Amazingly, well, to him anyway, was the fact that the arrow hit the rune he'd been aiming for, dead on, before clattering harmlessly onto the floor.

"WOW!" he sighed.

"Wow indeed," added the shopkeeper. "Good eh?"

"More than good."

"Anyhow, one last thing," ventured the master mantra maker, snatching back the bow and placing it back on top of the pile, "before we really have to get to the reason we came down here for in the first place."

Dodging and weaving past Peter, the old dragon proceeded back down the line of swords and things dangling off hooks, his young friend dutifully following, until he stopped in front of the large canvas rucksack that he'd spotted earlier, hanging over two hooks.

Turning, the old dragon held up one finger, before adding,

"I like this, I really do. It's one more of my favourites."

It was then that he did the strangest thing. Flipping open the top of the rucksack, he gathered up a handful of nearby swords, weapons and armour, and started stuffing them into the canvas holdall.

'That's never gonna work,' was Peter's first thought, but not for very long, because before he'd even had time to finish the thought, the old shopkeeper had already managed to force more into the average looking bag than it could possibly accommodate... but it had. And the old dragon just kept on going, and going, and going. In the end, he must have put about ten or fifteen times the amount of stuff that could possibly fit into the relative space of the rucksack, and still there was no hint of anything poking out of the top. There had been no deception, he'd been checking for that, making sure his friend hadn't been trying to pull a fast one over on him.

"This, my young friend, is a 'Traveller's Bag of Capacity' and the mantra that's woven into its fabric is incredibly difficult to stabilise. Originally used by plant hunters scouring the planet for new and interesting species, the bag provides almost limitless space, as well as making sure the items placed inside are kept safe and free from harm. The plant hunting dragons found that the species they put in there would last many years and still come out in exactly the same condition they went in, in the first place. I believe there are only a few left in existence."

"A TARDIS backpack," he announced. "Cool!"

"A what?"

"Don't tell me you don't know who... oh, of course not. Never mind."

Gee Tee's scaly head frowned as he decided to move on.

"And so there it is child... the best of the rest. And now the time has come to move on to the reason we're here," announced the master mantra maker, waving the flimsy looking sheet of parchment around in his hand.

Interested and worried, Peter waited patiently to find out what his friend had come up with.

"I'll explain what I have here, and what it involves. In no way are you committed to going through with this. If you don't want to do it, then I totally understand, but as far as I know this is the only way for me to fully appreciate what you told me about your young friend Richie, and how you believe it affects the prophecy. Okay?"

Peter nodded. Gee Tee continued.

"This, youngster, is a mantra devised by the master himself... Leonardo da Vinci!"

That piqued his interest.

"Of all the mantras, artefacts, spells, hexes, runes and magical items that I've come across in my life, the ones connected with him have always been the most special. Some mantras or magical bonds that have been created seem clumsy or forced, but not his work, which is some of the finest I've ever seen. He was a true craftsdragon. You can feel the work, dedication, the love and commitment that's gone into nearly everything he's fashioned. I would so have loved to have met him, pinned him down (not literally) and picked at his brain (again, not literally) found out what drove him on, where his ideas came from, and how he designed and produced some of those amazing magical devices, spells and mantras. Not only was he far ahead of his time in the human world, but he was down here as well. Anyhow, this particular mantra of his allows two dragons to share a memory, totally and utterly."

Starting to open his mouth, the old dragon held up a finger to stop him.

"Unlike if you were just to project an image at me and I could choose to accept or reject it, this mantra will, if you're willing to give it a go, let me relive everything from that moment or moments in exact and minute detail. But before you agree, you should know that, of course, it's not quite as simple as that... it never is. Not only will I see the memory, but I'll share everything else about the events, the sounds, the smells, as well as your feelings... both the physical sensations and whatever else was running through your mind. This is something that will almost, in essence, allow me to *be* you and know everything about you at the time of the event in question. I'll know what you were thinking and it's quite possible that your deepest darkest secrets will make themselves known to me. Once it's over, I will still retain all the information, as if I've lived through that particular moment in time. It's not something to be used lightly... if ever at all. But it is the ONLY way I can think of that might convince me that what you say about the prophecy is... true!"

Blowing out a breath of air at the amount of information he had to take in, it all sounded more than a little frightening to the young dragon... having the shopkeeper inside his head, sharing all his feelings, his deepest, darkest secrets, not that he considered that he had any really, well... apart from JANICE! But time was running out, and he was committed to helping Richie, and would do ANYTHING he could to that end.

"Let's do it!" he quipped, without hesitation.

"I think we should both sit," suggested the old dragon, plopping down onto the rocky floor, the scales on his belly wobbling like a plateful of jelly.

"Here?"

"It's as good a place as any."

Sitting down opposite his friend, Peter crossed his legs, looking like a very well behaved school child.

Pushing his glasses as far up his nose as they would go, the master mantra maker studied the parchment in front of him, as his young charge focused on his breathing and tried to remain calm. Finally the old dragon looked up.

"Okay, I think I'm ready to proceed. It will take a lot of magical power to make this work, but I think we'll be alright here. Some of the objects may indeed help us out if we get stuck. Once we start, you will have to focus intently on that memory, and nothing else. No distractions, just that one memory. But know this, as with everything, there comes a risk. There's no certainty that this will work... it might well fail spectacularly, and we both might get hurt in the process. I'll ask you one last time. Are you really sure you want to do this?"

Gritting his teeth, Peter nodded, and very calmly replied,

"Yes."

"So be it!" exclaimed the old dragon. "Let us begin."

Bowing his head, in an ancient tongue Gee Tee began muttering guttural and torturous sounds, some so incomprehensible they might well have come from a wounded animal, or indeed a different planet. Closing his eyes, Peter brought forth the memory of going to give Richie a lift to the lacrosse match. Almost instantly, she was there, opening the door to her flat, yawning away, inviting him in. Watching himself slipping past her and climbing up the staircase felt weird in the extreme. And then it happened! At first it felt as though something were pushing on the back of his eyeballs, but after a split second or so, the bizarre and uncomfortable feeling encompassed his entire skull, almost as if a giant hand were squeezing it uncontrollably. Fighting off the urge to be sick, his eyelids slid closed. Still the squeezing continued. Reaching the top of the stairs in the flat, the image started to blur and fade. Redoubling his efforts, and ignoring his body's doubts, he concentrated solely on that day, that moment. It was all or nothing.

'I haven't felt this odd since I took the form of that bat, and spent the whole afternoon flying around the rafters of the shop, waiting for Tank to come back and realise exactly what I'd done to myself,' thought the master mantra maker, looking at a tiny little room, feeling as though it should be more... organised! Though he wasn't quite sure, that might not have been it at all. The sensations he was feeling were unusual to say the least, and with Peter's human body moving, talking and thinking all of its own accord, he just seemed to be a passenger, along for the ride. It was strange though. Then he found himself staring at the boy's reflection in the glass of some kind of cabinet... showing off, trophies of some sort.

'Ahhh... they must be for the sport she plays that Tank's always harping on about. La, laa, laaaaa. La something, anyway,' he mused as the body he was in started thinking there was something wrong with all the trophies and turned away. All of a sudden, he started to be overwhelmed. In his vision, he could see the young female dragon in her human form, wearing only a handkerchief by the looks of things, apparently searching for something or other. But that wasn't the problem. Flooded by feelings, deep rooted, primal feelings, he felt both dizzy and nauseous at the same time. His head swam, his vision started to fade in and out. This was all so unexpected. It was all he could do to cling on and hope for the best.

From Peter's point of view, it was all going wrong. Right now, he wished he'd never agreed to do this. It was as if he'd blocked this moment totally from his mind. But every single feeling, the wanting, the longing and the physical feelings for his friend threatened to bubble over. But worse was to come, he knew. While Richie tried to engage Peter in chit chat about his hockey match and he fought off the image of his friend semi-naked, something else popped into his imagination, a love so pure, burning so brightly, that instantly it pushed away all thoughts of his long term friend. JANICE!

As quickly as they started, the primal feelings halted. But what halted them and brought the old dragon back into the memory, was shocking.

'A HUMAN!' he thought, as events continued and his mind spun. But there was no time to dwell on that. According to the youngster, what he needed to see was about to happen, and he had to pay careful attention.

Both watched for all they were worth, one for the first time, one for the second. The moment was astonishing, and if Peter had had any doubt about what he'd told Gee Tee, it was all washed away the instant Richie turned round to go back into her bedroom. There it was, larger than life, almost more impressive than before because he knew what to look for, knew what to expect. It was the most stunning, eye catching and life changing event he thought he was ever likely to experience.

In what he thought of as a grotesque masquerade of her true beauty, the female dragon turned to go back into one of the other rooms. He was ready; he knew it was about to happen. But to be honest, deep down, he'd never really believed it. Not until that very second. As time slowed, he studied the young dragon's human shaped back. Still showing all the signs of the significant injuries she'd sustained in the bomb blast, in looking on he wondered if the *alea* had done her any favours at all. It probably had, and she was probably better off alive than dead; still, all that pain, with everything that was to come on top of it. You never really knew, and this from a dragon who cherished life, who'd done everything he could to try and cheat death and more. With the image seared into his memory, along with Peter's overpowering sense of shock, Gee Tee used his mind to negate the mantra, freeing the two of them from its powerful grasp. Gradually the images faded away, replaced slowly by a world coloured terracotta.

Reliving the shock of the whole thing again, totally disorientated Peter. He had no idea where he was, or even if he was dreaming. All he knew was that his head and the back of his eyes hurt beyond belief, and all his body wanted to do was throw up. But as quickly as it had come, the pain, the pressure and the nausea disappeared, and he found himself back on the floor of the vault, sitting opposite a very shaky and very confused looking Gee Tee.

The magic had taken its toll. Both friends sat there totally wasted, the old dragon caked in sweat, looking more dishevelled and ruffled than an Ewok in a tumble dryer. Both were breathing heavily.

Many minutes later, neither had any idea of how long it actually was, for all concept of time seemed forgotten, it was the shopkeeper who spoke up first.

"It's hard for me to say this child, and the older I get, the more often I seem to have to say it, but I'm terribly sorry. I should never have doubted you and should have believed what you said from the off. I hope you can understand why I was so hesitant, and why I needed to see it for myself. Please forgive me for not believing in you, and for putting you through that rather... uncomfortable experience."

'That's an understatement,' he thought, recounting the experience that both of them had just been through.

"Does that mean that you believe me now?" Peter asked.

Gee Tee nodded.

"When you first told me, I found your story beyond belief. But seeing first hand so to speak... I'm convinced that she's the one the prophecy refers to."

"FANTASTIC!" screamed Peter, jumping to his feet. "All we a have to do is go to the council, you can talk to them, get them to take a look at Richie, and make them see sense. Let's go!"

Ancient scales in that prehistoric face that had seen and made so much history contorted in sadness and sorrow, about as much as they could. It had been a long time since they'd done so.

"What is it?" asked the young dragon angrily, getting a sense that all wasn't right.

Gazing down at the floor, Gee Tee sighed, unable to look his friend in the eyes.

"It won't work! They'd never believe you, and as soon as I become anything to do with it, you can be damn sure they won't believe it then."

"But they have to. You said yourself, she's the one. The one the prophecy mentions, the whole reason dragons have been blending in, waiting, guiding, protecting the humans for millennia. She's it!"

A weary look had set up camp on the master mantra maker's face, but for the lack of tents.

"I'm truly sorry child. I believe you, I really do. One hundred percent. But the simple fact of the matter is, the council won't."

Again he opened his mouth to speak, and again the old shopkeeper silenced him with one long, bony finger.

"Forget about the king... because I know what you're thinking... that he'll believe us and convince them. Remember, by his own admission, he has very little, if any, real power left. Even if he could use it, I doubt he would. You have to understand, your story sounds so far-fetched, it couldn't possibly be true. But it is! You have to trust me on this. In a million years, the council will never believe you, and they won't reverse the decision about your friend. If anything, it might make things worse."

Peter was angry now. Beetroot red-in-the-face angry.

"How the hell could it get any worse?"

"They could take what you say and misinterpret it. Fear of something you don't know or understand isn't confined to humans. Dragons are just the same in that regard. Instead of granting her the human life she led as a dragon, they may consider her dangerous or a threat, and instead decide it's best to keep her down here... incarcerated!"

Closing his eyes, Peter took a series of big, deep breaths as his friend looked on, very calmly and sedately. Mind racing at the thought of losing his friend, he knew that he had to save her, he just had to. But his hope had been extinguished by the one being he thought might just clinch victory from the jaws of defeat. Hollow was how he felt... empty... a useless husk of a shell, unable to help someone he dearly loved.

"I know how you feel child."

"Oh please..." replied the young dragon, done with all of it.

"No. I mean, I *actually* know how you feel. About Richie."

Looking across at the old shopkeeper, an uncomfortable silence developed between them.

"I'm not sure what the mantra did for you, but for me it was a work of art. I could feel every sensation that you felt. For a brief time... I was you. I know how you feel about your friend, and to say the things I've just said breaks my heart. She's lucky to have someone like you to count on. So is Tank."

Feeling himself welling up, the master mantra maker's next words soon put a stop to that.

"But rest assured child, you and I WILL be having a little chat about the human girl in the not so distant future."

The menace lacing those words was enough to keep Peter's mouth firmly shut. Sitting in silence for a few minutes longer, the old dragon unsteadily got to his feet and announced,

"I do have one more item to show you before we head back."

Reluctantly Peter followed the master mantra maker

over to a set of shelves carved into the rock. Overflowing, quite literally, with trinkets and valuable of all kinds, his friend started eagerly rummaging through all the items, discarding those in his way on the floor. Precious looking amulets, bracelets and jewellery of all kinds came flying over his shoulder, landing mainly with a tinkle on the hard surface of the vault. Peter's obsession with neatness (almost bordering on OCD) nearly kicked in, but he figured the old shopkeeper would berate him if he started picking stuff up and tidying. Abruptly, something a little larger and considerably heavier than the trinkets crashed onto the rock at his feet.

'It looks incredibly like a picture frame of some sort,' he thought as he picked it up. It was then that things got off the scale weird. Turning the frame over, believing it to be empty, the sight that greeted him almost made his eyes pop out. There, framed for all to see, was... a certificate, well, more like documentation, signed by the dragon king, pronouncing Gee Tee to be a... LORD!!! His heart raced as the old dragon continued his search.

'A Lord,' he mused. 'I never even knew dragons had such things.' But there it was right in front of him, the official document, signed by the king, royal seal and all.

"Ahhh..." cried the master mantra maker, "here it is!"

Turning to find the most startled look on his young friend's face, it was then that he noticed the frame.

"Ohhh... that old pish. Forget it. It's not important."

"But, but, but you were made a... Lord!"

"You of all dragons," growled the shopkeeper, grabbing the frame and casually tossing it away, "should know that it's not shiny pieces of paper or awards that count, but your actions. If nothing else... remember that!"

Suitably chastised, he vowed to himself to find out more, any way he could.

"NOW... where were we? Oh... that's right. I've found it," exclaimed the old dragon, holding up some kind of dull, matt grey, metal band, about the diameter of a human's wrist. Tiny triangular dark indentations, which looked almost bottomless, ran around the entire circumference of the band, with one larger triangle not indented, but ever so slightly raised.

'That looks unusual,' thought Peter, 'but not worth all the fuss the old dragon's trying to make over it.' Deflated, as that's how he felt about his friend, it was as if all the hope had seeped out of him, like air from a punctured tyre.

"THIS," started the shopkeeper, "is like nothing else I've ever come across. Probably the rarest thing on the planet is the material, which certainly looks like a metal but has never actually been confirmed as such. It actually makes laminium look positively common in comparison."

That made the young dragon sit up and take notice.

"Legend describes it as being made from something that translates roughly as 'Nissix'. And the only Nissix I know that exists on the planet is this," announced the master mantra maker, holding the band up high. "Anyhow," he continued, "it's thought to be hundreds of thousands of years old, and how it was developed or conceived is a complete and utter mystery. But it does have a rather unusual and special purpose."

With that, Gee Tee stepped forward towards his friend and asked him to hold out his hand which he did, albeit rather nervously. Asking him to spread his fingers as wide as he could, reluctantly he did. Running the band over one of the young dragon's fingers, suddenly... BANG! Instantly the band constricted, changing into a perfectly fitting ring. Peter's mouth hung open in surprise. It didn't hurt. It wasn't too tight. In fact it fitted perfectly, and he could barely feel it at all.

"It is, as you can see, a ring to fit every dragon, whatever shape or form they may be in. But that's just how you put it on, not what it actually does. The lore that accompanies the ring tells of dragons being brought back to life after being mortally wounded, their so called consciousness or soul as some thought back then, being safely stored inside the ring while healers used mantras to restore their damaged bodies."

Peter stood, fascinated, taking it all in, hanging on every last word.

"How does it work?"

"There's only a very limited translation to go by, and it was a little sketchy in places. But my understanding is, once the ring is on the dragon's finger, like it is now on you, the larger triangle must be held down for... well, it wasn't entirely clear, but I think somewhere around ten seconds. After that, the dark triangles turn green to start, and then when the consciousness is fully downloaded, they glow blue. How long this takes, I have absolutely no idea. I don't know if it's almost instantaneous, or whether it takes a matter of minutes. It certainly is one of the most unusual and interesting artefacts I've ever come across. Would it work today? Who knows? There would certainly be risks... huge ones if you ask me. But who can say what a dragon about to lose their life would do?" he casually ambled on.

Peter was giddy with excitement.

"You know what this means," he started. "We can..."

Immediately the old shopkeeper held up his palm to stop the young dragon mid sentence.

"It's time to go now. I'm going over to the plinths on the far side. By running your hand over every one, starting from the bottom and working up to the top, the vault's defences will reset, and we will have a ten minute window to walk or fly back out, before it all once again comes back online."

By now, he was almost hopping up and down with urgency, desperate to tell the old dragon just how they could put the ring to good use. But the wily old shopkeeper was having none of it.

"While I do this," he declared, "I EXPECT everything in here to be put back in its rightful place." With that he turned and headed over to the stone plinths.

A shiver like a warm summer's breeze ran up both his

arms, causing the hair on them to sway just a little. It wasn't what the old dragon said, he thought to himself, but more the way he'd said it. Grabbing handfuls of scattered jewellery off the floor, he started stuffing it back into the cubby hole from which Gee Tee had taken it, all the time glancing down at the rare and ancient ring on his finger.

Standing facing the cubby hole, having put everything back, including the discarded frame with the old dragon's official 'I'm a LORD' documentation, he knew it was now or never. This could be it. It must be it. The old dragon wouldn't have shown him this if he hadn't wanted him to use it. But why all the cloak and dagger stuff, the roundabout hints, instead of just saying... "You could use it on Richie." Not knowing, he found it frustrating and hard to understand. Perhaps it was a step too far for the old dragon, perhaps he didn't want to get in trouble with the council, or perhaps the whole thing had to be his own choice. Perhaps he was the only one that could choose to save Richie. Perhaps he was the only one who could risk everything to save her life. Either way, the time had come. Swiftly, shielding his hands, he slipped the ring off and slid it carefully into his right trouser pocket, behind his thick, worn wallet. Turning round innocently enough, he was just in time to see the master mantra maker finish touching all the ancient dragon runes. As he did so, a soft hum that he hadn't noticed before tailed off, and the air in the vault became so much... lighter.

"Time to go," announced Gee Tee, strolling purposefully back towards the exit, carrying the huge, glass jar of laminium rivets under one arm.

Looking around one last time at the magnificent treasures, barely able to believe some of the things he'd seen, a tiny sliver of guilt settled uneasily inside him. Meandering back through the plinths to join his friend, guilty thoughts at the back of his mind about the ring in his pocket and whether or not the old dragon knew he'd taken it, as well as if he'd actually have the courage to use it on his friend, bubbled away at the back of his mind. Only time would tell if he'd made the right decision.

21 BE MIND-FULL OF THE RING

Sitting opposite each other, the two friends waited nervously, Peter messing with her phone, trying to take his mind off what was about to happen, Richie rifling through a magazine. Abruptly, a loud knock at the door signalled that time had finally run out. Letting out a delicate sigh, Richie got up, walked out of the living room and down the small, narrow staircase. Peter could hear her answer the door and then head back up. Standing, he waited for them to arrive.

In they marched like bouncers at a nightclub... fully suited, sunglasses, a shine to their shoes... the lot! Of the three, one was clearly in charge, and stepped forward.

"What the hell do you think you're doing? You're not supposed to be here. No one is!"

Gulping, more than a little intimidated by what he knew to be one of the most powerful and influential priests the dragon kingdom had to offer, he knew now that it was all or nothing.

"She's my friend," he pleaded. "Someone needs to watch over her... she deserves that much! That someone should be me!"

"Absolutely not," raged the priest. "Guards... remove him!"

Standing his ground, determined to fight if necessary, he tried not to show his nerves as the guards stepped towards him in their neatly pressed, dark suits.

"STOP!" shouted Richie, stepping in between the two warring factions. "There's no need for all this." Turning to look at her friend, a glum reflection plastered across her face, she tried to make everything right. "It'll be okay. I'll be fine. There's no need for you to stay. Come and see me in a few days... please?"

Touched by her words, it was a shame in some ways that he had his own agenda, and for it to work, he had to be with her.

"I'm sorry Rich... but I just have to stay. My earliest memories are of you. Of both of us in the nursery ring... playing, learning, flying... all my memories of all those things all have you in them. The thought of this happening breaks my heart. You're my best friend, my soul mate, my... dragon mate. You are now and you always have been. I won't leave... not now. Not ever!"

Richie stood agog, between Peter and the guards who were creeping ever closer. The priest, however, had heard enough.

"Bentwhistle... you know you can't be here. It simply isn't allowed."

"But why?" he asked. "What possible harm could it do? I give you my word that I won't interfere with the process. Your guards will make sure of that anyway. The council have made their decision and I know now that nothing else can be done. I've done everything in my power to try and get the council to change their sentence," (he'd written a heartfelt letter and asked for an audience to plead his case... which had been rejected out of hand), "but now it's been decreed, I want nothing more than to look after my best friend, and know that even though she'll remember nothing more of our world... just the tiniest sliver of my love for her will remain if I stay with her throughout. If nothing else, who knows, perhaps when she wakes all alone, frightened, scared and unsure, she will at least feel a little loved, and that may be of some comfort. If not to her, then it will be to me."

Everyone in the cramped room stood still. It was as tense as any standoff could get, with the guards ready to pounce, just waiting for the order. With the priest considering his words, Peter hoped he'd done enough. Richie just stared at him, tears streaming in and out of the freckles on her cheeks.

Breaking the silence, the tiny "tick tock" of the lacrosse themed clock on the wall echoed eerily around the room.

Time seemed eternal as Richie's tears dropped from her face and, in perfect detail, plummeted onto the soft carpet.

It was then that the priest made up his mind.

"You can stay," he declared, "against my better judgement. But the first sign of trouble and you won't know what's hit you. I'll make sure you never find your sorry way above ground again! Do you understand?"

Nodding, he just about managed to squeak an, "I do."

As the guards stepped back, the priest stepped forward, something of an achievement in the confined space of Richie's flat.

"Do you understand the process and what will happen, young lady?"

Richie nodded in much the same way her friend just had.

"I do."

With more compassion than Peter would have given him credit for, particularly given how he looked, the priest whispered,

"I am truly sorry about this, and if there were any other options then I would gladly have tried to explore them. What we are about to do gives me no pleasure at all. But the council have ruled and we must all follow their guidance."

Richie just nodded.

Turning towards Peter, the priest started to explain.

"Since you're staying, you can help with an important part of the ceremony. Your friend here must be standing for the mantra to take effect, but as soon as it does, she will lose consciousness and collapse. You, if you will, may stand behind her and catch her as she falls. Then you may lift her up and place her on the sofa. Are you okay with that?"

Right down to the very last detail, Peter already knew what was going to happen. Not only had he done all the research he could, but he'd coaxed the old shopkeeper into telling him every aspect of the process. Gee Tee had come up trumps and described everything in glowing detail, right down to the exact words and their inflections, the fact that Richie would have to stand throughout, and also that she would have to keep her hands placed together behind her back. The master mantra maker had known it all and had willingly passed it all on to Peter, who'd got exactly what he wanted and now, more importantly... was exactly where he wanted and needed to be.

"Thank you," he said. "I'm most grateful. I just want to make sure she's alright. She means so much to me."

"I understand," replied the priest gently. "Just so that you know, once you've placed her, unconscious, on the sofa, we will all be leaving and YOU will not be able to return for the authorised number of days. There will be dragons watching this flat."

"I know," he croaked, more emotional than he'd thought he would be. "And that's fine."

"Good, then let's start," announced the priest, proceeding to move things around in the flat so that there was as much space as possible, with the sofa tucked against the back wall, furthest from the door. Standing Richie in the centre of the room, with Peter directly behind her and the sofa directly behind him, the priest prompted the young lacrosse playing dragon to place her hands together behind her back. At this point, Peter knew it was about to start. There were so many things he wanted to say, so much so that even if he'd had days to spill it all out, there still wouldn't have been enough time. So, knowing that it wasn't over despite the council, despite the priest, despite... EVERYTHING, he leaned forward until his chin rested on her shoulder, and whispered in her ear,

"Everything will be alright... TRUST ME!"

And with that... IT STARTED!

It was complicated. According to the old shopkeeper's description, in all it would take close to an hour and would require an incredible amount of concentration, effort, focus and power. He knew the priest must be an amazing dragon to be able to carry out what he considered to be a heinous task and also knew he'd only get one chance at what he had planned, and one chance only. So... he stood and waited. And waited. Standing behind his friend, within touching distance, a blank, accepting look on his face, he waited for the split second that would be his one and only opportunity.

Continuing to chant, the priest belted out the mantra which was in Messapian, an ancient Indo-European language originating in South East Italy and thought to have died out sometime after the 1st century BC. It was, he supposed, a good job that Gee Tee had told him what language the mantra was going to be in. Although he was fluent in many traditional tongues, most of the ancient ones were well beyond his ability to pick up. Like humans, some dragons are gifted when it comes to languages, some... not so much. Most certainly he fell into the latter category. But the old shopkeeper had run through it with him, then translated it, and then... made him memorise the latter part, the part in which he would be required to act, so much so that he could now have taken over from the priest.

Picturing the words in his head, he knew the moment was fast approaching. From his peripheral vision whilst staring ahead, he could see that the guards, who at first had been incredibly suspicious of his motives, had now relaxed just a fraction. Convinced that would be enough, his biggest worry was that one of the guards would have stood off to one side, making what he had to do very difficult, maybe not impossible, but very difficult. Because of the size and shape of the room, and with the sofa behind him, the guards had little choice but to stand by the door, behind and to either side of the priest. As his brain assessed the situation, the moment approached. Calming his mind, making sure to keep his expression fixed, as it had been throughout the whole process, he delicately slipped off the innocuous looking, matt grey, metal ring he'd been wearing on his right middle finger, and in one fluid motion slipped it over the middle finger of Richie's left hand. Instantly it constricted, shrinking to fit her delicate, pale finger perfectly. This was the part he'd worried about, and had been through a couple of sleepless nights thinking that Richie herself might give the game away at this point. During one of his dreams she'd stopped the whole process and he'd subsequently been dragged off by the guards, with the ceremony starting again from scratch. Holding his breath, Richie's hand tensed for the briefest moment, but quickly relaxed again. Much to his relief, the priest and the guards hadn't registered that anything untoward had happened. Casually, he held down the slightly raised triangle on the ring, continuing for as long as he dared, all the time looking forwards over Richie's shoulder. After a count of eight, he just about caught sight of a green flicker coming from around her hands. Moving his own hands away from the ring, he listened as the priest continued. Standing there, knowing that it wouldn't be long before the mantra finished, not being able to show any outward sign that he knew... his mind raced. Would it work like the old dragon had said? Would the priest come to realise what had happened? How would Richie react to what he'd done? Just maybe she'd be better off not knowing. Time and time again he'd debated this question, but the more he thought about it, the more he thought she'd want to know. As well, he deemed that he knew her better than any other dragon, and although he couldn't tell her what he had planned, he was certain she would approve.

Less than a minute after the ring had given off its green glow, the colour along the row of glowing triangles changed to blue. Although still looking forward, he was aware of what had happened.

'So far,' he thought, 'it's all going to plan.'

Moments later, the priest uttered the final word and Richie's whole body fell back into Peter's safe hands. As he caught her, quick as a flash he tugged the ring off her middle finger and slipped it back onto his ring finger. It fitted perfectly. As gently as he could, he carried her still body over to the sofa and delicately put her down, before arranging the cushions to make her as comfortable as possible, all under the inscrutable gaze of the priest and his guards. Without the guards seeing, he pulled out Richie's phone from his back pocket and slid it carefully under the sofa. Then he leaned in and planted a soft kiss on her forehead before getting to his feet.

"It's time to leave," ordered the priest gruffly, thinking that this might be when any problems would occur.

But he couldn't have been more wrong. Squeezing past the two burly guards, Peter didn't even bother to look back, having done everything he'd planned to do. It was now out of his hands... or not, so to speak.

Leaving Richie's flat, he closed the door behind him and, looking sadder than he felt, headed off on foot into town, knowing that somewhere nearby dragons were watching his every action. All he wanted to do was act like they expected him to. Figuring walking into Salisbridge and then back home would throw them off a little, if it didn't... then so what? All he was going to do was go home, sit at his computer and... WAIT! He might have to wait for weeks, months even, or longer, he just didn't know. But what he did know was that he'd have his friend back. If he had to move the earth to do it... he'd have her back!

22 A RUDE AWAKENING

Startled awake, her fuzzy brain tried to process what exactly was going on. Trying to sit up, a sharp pain erupted across her shoulders and up the length of her neck. Then it occurred to her where she was.

'I've slept on the sofa... all night!'

Sitting up straight while stretching her neck left and right, trying hard to shake the kinks out of it, she wondered about the source of her irritation. Apart from her knotted muscles, a blaring noise was blasting out from somewhere unseen. More annoying was the fact that it was the sound of someone blowing a raspberry, over and over again, constantly getting louder and louder. Standing up, she lurched forward, the twisted muscles around both knees causing her great pain. Frantically scrabbling around on the floor, her head pounded. Reaching as far under the sofa as she could, something sleek and solid fell into her grasp.

'There,' she thought, extracting nearly her entire arm. Instantly she hit the cancel button to stop the racket coming from the alarm on her phone. 'I don't remember even setting the alarm,' she mused, 'let alone adjusting it to that awful noise.' Placing the phone on the arm of the sofa, she flopped back down on it, letting its plump cushions engulf her, all the time rubbing her neck and shoulders.

Puffing out her cheeks and blowing out a deep breath, she wondered exactly what had been going on, unable to remember a thing from the night before, no matter how hard she tried; she thought that she'd gone to work yesterday, but even that was a bit of a blur. After a few minutes of concentrated recollecting, without getting much further, she gave in, leapt up, strolled over to the curtains and pulled them wide open. The view from this particular window was stunning, one of the reasons she'd chosen this flat in the first place. In the distance she could just make out the spire of the ancient cathedral, watching over the natural wonder of the water meadows like a towering stone guardian. And this morning with the sun pouring onto it, the spire looked particularly splendid.

Abruptly a cold, biting sensation, emanating from the pit of her stomach, started to gnaw at her very being. Before she had time to contemplate what it was, a rush of emotion swept over her, almost bringing tears to her eyes. Confused and confounded, images of young children and warmly wrapped babies zipped across her consciousness as a mixture of feelings threatened to consume her. In the blink of an eye, they were gone, returned to normal, if that word could ever really be used to describe her.

Basking in the sun, she counted herself lucky to be alive on such a day and to live amongst such stunning beauty. Pulling back from the view, she decided that her muscles almost certainly needed the benefit of a long, hot shower, all the while cursing the minor blips in her memory.

As the hot, steamy water pelted her aching muscles, providing at least some relief, she focused on the day in front of her, wondering just how much training there was to be done at Cropptech. Smiling at the thought of it, she felt blessed to have a job she enjoyed so much. Life at the moment seemed just right.

23 CAPTOR CAPTURED

For her the tiniest piece of information would have done, would have resolved some of the worry, some of the angst. But not so. The nagas looking out for her in the room next door had disrupted her broken and disturbed sleep to inform her that they'd had word. At that very moment, she'd jumped to her feet, ready to join in and take her rightful place in this brave new world. But it couldn't be that simple, could it? Containing only three words, the message did little to quell the thoughts inside her.

'It has begun!'

Rolling the words over and over inside her head, she discarded the hastily arranged covers on her poor excuse for a bed, curled up into a ball, and sought the sanctuary of sleep, hoping once again not to be dragged back into the past. It wasn't to be.

Darkness faded. A brighter, whiter kind of light swam into view. A harsh pounding in her head tried to keep to a rhythmic beat, much to her annoyance. Gingerly, she sat up. Her head spun. Nausea threatened to overwhelm her. Wrestling with it momentarily, she then attempted to fight it off with just a little power from within. Strangely, nothing happened.

'That's odd,' she thought, head in hands. Concentrating on her breathing, she tried to remember what had happened. The last thing she could recall was being in that damn barn, about to unleash her power. But then the girl, that's right... that damn girl, had injected her with something, and done it so quickly she'd simply had no time to react. Rubbing her eyelids, the whole sorry mess came slinking back.

'Why didn't my troops come in and save me?' she wondered briefly. 'Of course. It was a trap, and had no doubt been a long time in the planning, given the efficiency of it. No matter. Escaping from here should be child's play, wherever here actually is.'

"Plotting and planning already?" a husky voice whispered from somewhere just the other side of the metal bars opposite her, shrouded in darkness. *"Impressive indeed. But if it's thoughts of escape, then let me assure you, you're wasting your time. We've had time to prepare. Rest assured... you're going nowhere."* And with that, the sound of footsteps echoing down a corridor, followed by a very heavy door slamming shut, brought home the reality of her situation, well... a little anyway.

Casually, while concealing her hands in case anyone else should be watching from the darkness, she wove a couple of tiny patterns with her fingers, over and over again, and then attempted to run a smidgen of her power through them. NOTHING! Once again she tried, figuring she was still a little off balance from being unconscious for all that time, and it must have been some time indeed, given just how rough she felt. Again, NOTHING, not even a sliver of her hidden ability.

'They can't know what I truly am,' she thought, *'not with all the castings the nagas laid on me. They must be guessing, trying to figure me out. It does mean that the dragons are probably involved somewhere along the line though. That will make things more than a little difficult,'* she thought, lying back on the flimsy wooden bed, the pathetic excuse for a pillow leaking feathers as her head hit it. Closing her eyes, waiting for them to come to her, she wondered what, if anything, had happened to her husband.

Unbeknown to her at the time, news of the unusual nature of both prisoners had filtered down through the dragon ranks, a tiny titbit of news really, given that World War Two was raging around them. It didn't quite reach the realm of the telepathic papers or the normal, everyday dragon in the street, but apart from that, it was pretty much out there. And so it was that Councillor Rosebloom was sitting in his luxurious office when his secretary brought him in a pile of paperwork, including news of the latest incarcerations. Normally not one to panic, break sweat, or do anything at breakneck speed, his demeanour changed in an instant on seeing the list. Shooting out of the door uncharacteristically fast, his shocked secretary only managed to catch, "I'm out for the rest of the day," from him, before he turned the corner and disappeared out of sight.

It had been over two weeks, and she hadn't told them anything they didn't already know. Over the course of that time, she'd been busy trying to figure out why her hidden abilities wouldn't work. From what she could tell, the dragons had cast a mantra of some sort across the whole building, negating or subduing her talents. There were one or two spots on her daily walk to and from the interrogation room that felt a little different... like they might be weak points in the mantra, where she could almost feel her power ready to use just beneath the surface. But with strapping great guards marching either side of her, as well as in front and behind, there was simply no opportunity to test if that were truly the case. It could of course be a dragon trap, trying to catch her out, waiting to see if she used the powers they suspected she might have. It was turning into much more of a waiting game than she'd at first intended, through no fault of her own. She was, however, bored now, and wasn't particularly renowned for her patience, despite it being evident in nearly all her operations in France. As the guards returned her to her cell from yet another round of interrogations, her mind whirled around and around, constantly looking for a way out. Any way out.

Little did she know that her way out was heading straight towards her.

A confident looking being pulled up at the little known entrance to the secret detention facility, covered in a dark cowl and cloak. At first, the guards had been reluctant to let him anywhere near the establishment, but he did have all the high level credentials and clearances, so in the end they had little option but to comply. Looking on in disbelief as the stranger marched through the dimly lit corridors, dressed all in black, looking very much how you would expect a Darth Vader from the 1940's to look, the guards were more than a little on edge.

Striding towards the prisoner's cell, projecting more confidence than he had any right to, he felt more than a little nervous about what he was doing. But he'd been given very little choice in the matter. Up until now, his involvement had been strictly behind the scenes, so much so that there was practically no chance of anyone finding out about his relationship to... the others. That's how he liked to think of them... 'the others'. Here and now though, things had got very real, very quickly. If any other dragon happened to turn up, this would all be pretty much for nothing. His escorts turned a corner, and BAM! It happened. No gradual fading off, no warning, NOTHING! Shocked didn't begin to cover how he felt. It was a good job his face was obscured for the most part. Briefly he wondered how she felt, in a place like this... without her abilities. It scared him, having his own taken away so forcefully. When he'd entered, he'd felt magnificent, in command and above these puny humans. But now... he felt so vulnerable, so afraid, so scared. Even so, he continued to walk on, the heels of his black boots clicking against the hard floor, projecting an air of confidence and authority.

A sharp turn in the corridor and then they were there, almost up against the bars. Lying curled up on the rickety bed, facing the opposite wall, he could tell she wasn't asleep.

"Release her at once," he commanded, with much more conviction than he felt. Straight away she rolled over, eyeing the stranger and the guards with suspicion.

"It's okay now. Your ordeal is over. Please come with me and we'll sort out your release."

Earth leapt to her feet, standing directly in the middle of the cell, eyeing the guards with contempt. With one finger, the hooded stranger discreetly pulled back part of his cowl, revealing only a tiny fragment of his face. Recognition blossomed in her mind. They'd only met once in their human forms, and even then it was mightily dark, but she knew who he was and that she could trust him. A wave of relief washed over her as she received a barely perceptible nod of acknowledgement.

Once the guards had finally unlocked the cell, looking none too happy about it, she followed him back through the facility, sharing a small smirk with him at the point they both regained their powers. After only a few minutes, all the formalities had been observed and the paperwork signed off. They then both climbed into his 'borrowed' jeep. Joining him in letting out a sigh of relief, she whispered a small,

"Thank you."

"You're welcome," replied Rosebloom. "But let's get as far away from here as possible. I have no idea how long the ruse will hold up. We could be discovered at any moment." She nodded her agreement as he started up the engine. Turning on the lights, they sped away towards the main road, but not before he'd given her an inkling of what lay ahead for the rest of the night.

"If we can remain undiscovered until morning, then we might just have a chance."

And they did. Remain undiscovered, that is, recovering her husband from a neighbouring concern some ninety or so miles away before the first rays of sunshine lit up the early morning sky across the country. No words were said; there was nothing to say. They were very much in love, a notion the dragon councillor clearly found... distasteful, much to Earth's amusement. Dropping them off outside the deserted railway station, he watched them leap out of the stolen jeep, hand in hand. Thanking him politely, it was all just a bit too formal, almost as if he'd passed the salt across the dining table. They realised just what he'd done, how much he'd risked, but there seemed few, if any other words to say. A whole lot remained left unsaid as they sat outside the ticket office, clutching the thick wad of money the kind councillor had left them with. She wondered what they would plan. Would they go back to France and continue where they'd left off, being a sharp thorn in the side of the British and French Resistance? Or was there something more devious and cunning, or more pressing, to do? Sensibly though, she knew not to dwell on it now, and probably shouldn't even be wondering. With the strange looking councillor having exited the station's car park at speed in what she knew to be a stolen jeep, and knowing that they were many hours away from the first train of the day turning up, they both huddled together, sharing the warmth and comfort of their bodies as well as each and every thought, on the cold wooden bench just outside the ticket office.

24 CHAIN REACTION

Things were generally quite relaxed at the Mantra Emporium. There was no dress code, no lunch hour and no official working hours. That said, the owner liked to know if his employees, or employee as was now the case, was not going to be in at all.

Pacing up and down the shop floor directly in front of the counter, staring up at the exploding volcano clock, high up on the far wall, that on every hour jettisoned real lava across a deserted section of the shop floor, Gee Tee felt frustration and worry mingle together inside him. Normally his app... Tank arrived just after 8am, ready for a full day's work. But it was nearly 10am, and there was no sign of the youngster at all. There'd been no message... he'd checked. It was very out of character. So much so, he couldn't remember the last time he'd even been a few minutes late. Considering his options, the old shopkeeper supposed he could have used that dreaded phone contraption thing, although his last experience of it left a lot to be desired. For a split second he thought about contacting the King's Guard, but dismissed that instantly. Not only would they not respond (due to Rosebloom's continual meddling) but they'd probably not take him seriously. Pretty sure Tank would have to be missing for more than a couple of hours for it to be regarded as any sort of emergency, he wondered if he might contact the child Bentwhistle telepathically, perhaps he knew where his friend was and just why he was late. That was the course of action he decided on.

Closing his eyes, he did something that he hadn't done in a very long time... he reached out with his mind, searching for the nearest telepathic node. Just as he did so, a metal on metal squeak fluttered throughout the building, from the turn of the handle on the shop's main door. Flustered, he closed down the search and stepped in front of the counter, giant wings folded across in front of him, as fast approaching footfalls headed his way.

Having run all the way... well, from the monorail station anyway, wearing the heavy backpack that contained all his rugby coaching kit, so that he could go straight to the training ground at Basingstoke after work, in all his life, not once had he ever overslept, and of course it would be on a work day, wouldn't it? He did of course have the mother of all excuses but, knowing his employer, it probably still wouldn't wash. Soon enough, he'd find out. Dust rose up around his legs as he skidded to a halt outside the Mantra Emporium's main entrance. Swallowing nervously, wondering what the old shopkeeper's reaction would be, he told himself just to 'get on with it,' before turning the handle and rushing in.

It took all his control and agility not to run straight into his employer's puffed out chest as he dashed around the final bookcase and onto the shop floor proper.

Gee Tee gazed down at him, head tilted, eyes wide open, a knowing expression on his face. Tank breathed out heavily, holding up one finger on his right hand, all the while trying to catch his breath.

"Before you start," he puffed, "I can explain... well, kind of."

All the time a neutral expression adorning his face, the old dragon shook his head.

"I overslept," declared Tank honestly. Before the master mantra maker could interject, the young dragon continued. "However, there's a really good reason why." It was only then that he realised he was still wearing his huge backpack. Extricating himself, he continued. "I've only had a couple of hours' sleep since you last saw me on Friday. I spent all of yesterday at the library in Rome, and only got back to Salisbridge a few hours ago. But it was all worth it for what I've uncovered... I think."

Looking down, the master mantra maker, that neutral expression still on his face, remained silent, something that was more than a little intimidating to Tank, who had just managed to shrug his backpack off onto the floor.

Tank waited to be berated. It never came.

"I'm not mad. Just worried. It was so unusual for you not to be here. I was concerned something untoward had happened. I was just about to try and contact young Peter in the hope that he could help me locate you."

This was not what Tank had come to expect, and a small part of him was almost sorry that it wasn't the dressing down he'd feared.

"I'm sorry," he said. "I should have got in touch, but by the time I'd woken up, I figured I could almost be here in the same time it would have taken me to contact you. It won't happen again... I promise."

Gee Tee smiled. It was more than a little disconcerting.

"So, what did you find on your European excursion?"

"Now... you're gonna laugh," breathed Tank, fiddling around with his backpack on the floor, "but I took some notes," he added, pulling out a super cool looking notebook, the front cover smattered with rugby related pictures.

Not knowing what to make of it, all the master mantra maker could do was stare.

"But there was a reason. Yes, I know I've got an eidetic memory, but I wanted to make sure I got everything all in the right order, and the information in the library was dotted about all over the place."

Stretching out his wing to indicate the way, the old dragon uttered,

"Shall we adjourn to the workshop?"

Nodding in reply, Tank shoved his backpack along the floor so that it ended up against the counter and out of the way. Carrying just his notebook, he followed his employer through the shop, eager to share with him what he'd learnt over the weekend. Taking seats on opposite sides of the room, Gee Tee lounging back in his, Tank perching on the edge of his oversized chair, looking very much like a baby in a high chair, he opened up the notebook and began flicking through its pages. Quickly skimming through his notes, he turned to face his friend.

"I started off looking for any reference at all to the nagas."

"Did you tell the staff there that's what you were looking for?" interrupted the master mantra maker.

"Let me see," replied Tank sarcastically. "There's a secret global plot that could involve any number of races, and maybe dragons at all levels, so YES, I strolled in and shouted out that I wanted any and all information pertaining to the NAGAS!"

"Sorry."

"Just let me finish... okay?"

"Sure."

"It took a while to find anything at all, and even then it was obscure. Given the resources there, I expected much more. But there seemed to be next to nothing, almost as if the library had been purged of anything to do with them. But once I'd found that first reference tucked away, I knew where to look. While I wouldn't describe what I discovered as comprehensive, it did flash up one particularly relevant fact."

"And that would be?"

"One absolutely ancient scroll had text on it that described an exchange of information between a dragon trader and a naga shaman. It took place around the 11th century, somewhere in Eastern Asia. The trader was fascinated by a metal that adorned some of the very important female nagas... specifically around their necks. From what I can make out, the shaman explained to the trader that the females were the king's concubines and that the metal in the necklaces prevented them from using their telepathic abilities."

Automatically sitting a little further forward, the mere mention of all this piqued the master mantra maker's interest.

"Anyway," continued Tank, "it turns out that the metal was also used to restrain and contain criminals in their society, disabling their abilities, turning them into outcasts." Flicking forward another half dozen pages or so, he carried on. "Here's where it gets more than a little interesting. The trader bartered, on and off, with the nagas for more than a decade, at one time spending more than three months in one go at their remote outpost. Going on to describe the metal, which he had something of an obsession with, he claimed that, as well as preventing telepathy, it was said to be... indestructible."

"Ha," snorted the old shopkeeper, "a bold claim indeed, but impossible."

Staying silent, Tank turned a few more pages until he found the one he was looking for. "During his time in the camp, he earned the shaman's trust and subsequently found out that the ore the metal is made from is a composite containing... laminium!"

That got Gee Tee's attention.

"Still think it's impossible?" challenged the young dragon, raising his eyebrows.

Blowing out a small cloud of smoke in the direction of his employee, the old shopkeeper started to say,

"Well..."

Before being interrupted by the youngster.

"It makes it a little more believable, if nothing else."

Gee Tee closed his eyes, deep in thought.

"So... go on. What else did you find?"

"There's not much more I'm afraid," answered Tank.

"So that's it!" remarked the old dragon. "A metal with the ability to block telepathic communication, which is potentially unbreakable. I admit it does kind of fit in with Flash's outline of what was going on in that cavern in Antarctica, but knowing about it does us no good at all."

Tank smiled. It wasn't just any smile. It was his... 'I know something you don't know' smile, usually reserved for a Latin name or some bizarre or ridiculous fact about a plant or animal.

"So what's the... 'not-much-more' you mentioned?" asked the master mantra maker curiously.

"After learning the metal was partly made up of laminium, the trader could think of little else. After all, as far as we know, that only boosts a being's telepathic ability. I've never come across any records of powers being blocked or altered in a negative fashion by it."

Listening intently, Gee Tee nodded his agreement.

"In his final entry the trader inadvertently made a startling discovery. While the metal was seemingly unbreakable he, in his illicit experiments (something the nagas had forbidden him to continue with, when they discovered what he was doing) had managed to use a mantra to convert the nagas' precious, unbreakable metal into pure laminium."

Gee Tee bounded out of his chair, totally astonished.

"ARE YOU SURE?"

"That's what it said. However, those were the last words recorded in the journal. It was almost as if they'd been cut off. I searched the library high and low for anything else relating to this. There was nothing. Hence the reason I overslept, and was running late."

"Yes, yes, yes... all that is of course forgiven. But a mantra, one that could change the properties of that metal, making it so vastly different. That must be something else."

"Also," added Tank, not forgetting the true purpose of their mission, "it would free Peter's grandfather and the naga king. Their chains would not only become breakable, but would boost their powers, well, Fredrick's anyway, aiding their escape. And that's what we're ultimately aiming for."

Nodding in agreement, the master mantra maker had a faraway look emblazoned across his face. Unexpectedly he turned towards his app... partner.

"We need to figure out that mantra! And for that we

need..."

"Some of the nagas' metal. I'm already one step ahead of you."

Gee Tee stood speechless.

"I think I know where there is some. It might involve a little bit of criminal activity to get our hands on it though," ventured Tank, pained at the thought of breaking the law... any law.

"Where do we start?" demanded the old shopkeeper, totally absorbed and ready to do whatever it took to get hold of that metal.

"WE DON'T! It's just me, I'm afraid," said the young dragon, shaking his head, wishing more than anything that there was another way.

25 CLIFF FACE

It had been ten days since he'd last seen her, and that meeting haunted all his thoughts and dreams. She'd turned up unannounced with her friends, Peter and Tank, in tow. It seemed odd to think of them all as dragons... Tank maybe, but Peter the hockey player seemed the most unlikely dragon of all. Anyhow, she'd stayed for an hour or so, which apparently was the most that was allowed, and only then by express permission of the king, who it turned out had some kind of relationship with Peter. On that she didn't expand. It had almost been like old times... well, except that now he was a dragon, and she was... WHAT? An ex-dragon now turned fully human who was about, by all accounts, to have her mind wiped and be expelled permanently from the dragon world. Who didn't see that coming?

'Perhaps they should write a book about it,' he mused, the warm breeze brushing gently across his scales.

Looking amazing, despite all the injuries, he was surprised that they hadn't fully healed given how long ago they'd occurred and the marvellous powers of the dragon healers. But she'd explained that it was some kind of side effect of what had happened when she'd cracked open the *alea* and whispered the shield mantra. Even having had it explained to him at least a dozen times, he still didn't fully understand it. The brief time that they chatted flew by, and then it was time for her to leave. Noticing the fear in her eyes, the regret, the sorrow at having got him involved, the tears being held forcibly in check, like characters in a television show they played their parts, her saying she'd see him again, him nodding enthusiastically, knowing full well it wasn't going to happen. And then she turned and left, gone, not coming back.

So it had been quite a surprise when Peter had turned up at his quarters earlier on in the day. Hoping she would be with him, it soon became apparent that she wasn't. Wanting to ask about her, as soon as he'd started, the hockey playing dragon shook his head in warning, confirming what he'd somehow assumed, that he was being watched in some sort of capacity. So they'd chatted about life on the surface, the destroyed clubhouse, how the hockey teams were doing, until the conversation turned to other more scaly subjects. In particular... FLYING! And that, he thought, was how he found himself balanced precariously on the edge of a stunning cliff, overlooking the mother of all drops into a roiling sea of lava so far below it was difficult to make out the bottom. Like a well worn set of tyres from a Formula One car, he too was about to 'drop off the cliff', the very thought of which scared the living daylights out of him. And standing not ten feet away was a very smiley Peter, waving and urging him on.

Right at this very moment, Peter was incredibly proud, not just of Tim, but of himself. That morning the king had got in touch, explaining that the dragons looking after Tim's welfare and training were having no luck in getting him to do anything. It seemed as though he just couldn't be bothered, despite being informed about the prophecy and his supposed role in it. This struck Peter as odd, knowing what a well rounded, hard working and motivated human being he'd been. The king had asked Peter if he wouldn't mind seeking out the newly formed dragon, with a view to seeing if a friendly face could be of some help and maybe coax some cooperation out of him. It was a request and not an order, one that Peter was more than happy to comply with. So he'd turned up nice and early at the facility where Tim was... he wanted to say staying, but in reality it was more like 'being held'. Part of him wanted to point this out to the staff there, but as usual he'd chickened out and didn't. So after security had checked with the king's private office, and having signed to take full responsibility for Tim, the two of them headed out into the big, wide, world of the dragon domain, but not before Peter had arranged the largest cloak he'd been able to find at such short notice, fastening it across Tim's shoulders, covering all his back and wings as well as a good deal of his chest, head and legs. It wouldn't do for the public at large to learn that a totally white dragon was stalking around the domain, or much would be made of the legendary prophecy, with Tim's privacy and anonymity gone forever.

As they sauntered towards the nearest monorail station, Tim could barely keep his eyes and tongue in his newly formed, oversized head. It was all so new and different. Things that Peter took for granted astounded the normally unflappable Tim. Buildings and walkways, far off ceilings, sizzling streams of lava dribbling down walls and running beneath floors. Dragons in every conceivable shape and size, walking, flying, bounding in, around and across their route. And then of course there was the... MONORAIL! Turning up at the station, unusually with no train already there, Peter pointed out the time the next one was due (10.24 and 32 seconds). Tim, convinced Peter was having him on about the 32 seconds, watched in amazement as the clock hanging over the station platform displayed 10.24 and 28 seconds, and a huge rush of air preceded the rounded silver nose of the lead monorail carriage pulling up right in front of them, exactly at the time stated. It was all the new dragon could do to remain upright.

With dragons boarding and embarking all around them, Peter guided Tim onto the carriage, the ex-human giggling uncontrollably when shown the seats with the holes in the back for tails to go through, much to the consternation of other passengers. And so they'd made their way to Purbeck Peninsula, one of Peter's favourite places and the one he thought of as his second home, having grown up in the nursery ring there.

Throughout their entire journey, dragons old and young hadn't been able to take their eyes off Tim. Those with just the faintest smidgen of white adorning their bodies were something of a rarity, but with this much white on show (his face and tail,) he proved to be something of a curiosity. It was a good job they hadn't cottoned on to exactly how white he actually was, and that Peter had thought to cover most of him up.

Having criss-crossed the highly populated urban part of Purbeck, Peter led as Tim followed on the well worn, secretive trail that led to the wonder that was Lava Falls, a little known phenomenon, only really known to locals and the nursery ring students, who were all very solemnly sworn to secrecy about its location. Excited to see what Tim's response would be, he wasn't disappointed when Tim went mad on seeing the falls themselves. Raging river rapids of lava thundered off to their right, churning and swirling, spitting and hissing, the fiery madness rumbling over the lip of the cliff they were both standing on, tumbling into the chasm of despair below, all the time producing a fine, toxic mist that washed high into the air all around them, reflecting light in almost a rainbow of colours for all to see. Like something out of a fairytale, albeit one with deadly fumes that could overcome in a matter of seconds in the wrong condition, the temperatures would almost put to shame any of the planets closer to the sun.

Both sitting down not far from the rocky, underground entrance, a long way back from the edge of the falls, Tim asked why they'd come here. Explaining that this was where he'd learnt to fly, purposefully neglecting to mention the concentric ringed structure from which young dragons took their first glided flights in the nursery ring itself, Peter hoped that this would spur the newly formed dragon into giving things a go. Unfortunately it seemed to totally backfire, with Tim becoming frightened, shaky and unsure, wanting to return back to his confined quarters. Using all his skills, Peter just about managed to turn things around, getting the white dragon to reluctantly agree to stay, although he got the impression that he could bolt at any moment. Instead of pressuring the brand new dragon into doing something he really didn't want to, they just sat and talked. Peter recalled his time in the nursery ring, recounting some of his adventures with Tank and Richie. Tim listened intently, lost in thought at the mere mention of her name. The two understood what it was to love her, albeit in very different ways.

"You love her," declared Tim, after hearing another one of Peter's endless tales.

More than a little perturbed, Peter wouldn't have wanted to have this conversation with himself in the privacy of his own home, let alone with Tim who was very obviously still in love with Richie and had quite a lot of issues of his own to deal with at the moment. Still, he considered his answer carefully, determined to let this newly fledged dragon hear the truth.

"I do," he replied after some time, "but not in the way you think."

Tim tilted his large head to one side inquisitively.

"Go on."

"For years I wanted her to notice me as a potential mate and not just her best friend. But it never happened. Not for the want of trying on my part either, I might add. I always assumed I'd get my chance. But the more I've seen of her recently, the more I know I could never compete, or be what she's looking for. She wants something more... something I just can't give her. I can't tell you what it is, or even how I know. But she does. And whatever it is that she's looking for, I truly hope she can find it. On the occasions I've seen the two of you together, she's looked happy... truly happy, which came as something of a revelation I must admit. If I'm honest, a part of me is glad. I value our friendship far too much to risk doing something stupid to mess it up. I would be devastated if something ever happened to that, so in reality nothing was ever going to happen. It was all a made up fantasy. But that's all a moot point with everything that's happened recently. I just hope she finds some small crumb of comfort and happiness with whoever she ends up with in her controlled human existence."

Tim nodded his agreement, not really sure whether he meant it or not. But he did pick up on the bitterness Peter's words carried. Clearly, he thought, the other dragon was none too happy about the turn of events leading up to Richie being banished from the dragon world and living out the rest of her days as fully human.

And so here they were, standing on the edge of Lava Falls, both as nervous as each other. Tim didn't want to jump, scared that all the theory about flight which had been drummed into him would fail to work when it most counted, while Peter was more and more convinced with every second that passed that this was a bad idea and that he could go down in history as the dragon responsible for the demise of the famed white dragon from THE prophecy. Things were more tense than the final hole of the Ryder Cup.

But somewhere deep inside Tim, a little spark of humanity jumped up and said, "To hell with it!" So he jumped. The best that could be said of it was... ungainly. Truth be told it was about the least perfect leap a dragon could make off a cliff. Both wings were for the most part still folded, and he'd fallen (for that's what had really happened) at something of an angle. It wasn't helped by a vicious updraft that had caught his right side the moment he'd cleared the edge, spinning him violently.

Looking on open mouthed, Peter was too stunned to move. At first, anyway. A mere fraction of a second later his brain started screaming "EMERGENCY!" at the top of its voice, prompting him into action. Hurling himself off the cliff, cursing the fact that he'd worn his favourite pair of light blue jeans, tears dribbled from his eyes as a howling gale blew his long 80's hair back over his shoulders and the noxious gases seared the back of his throat. Unleashing his own personalised mantra that would affect the change to his bodily form, the twisted tingling sensation in his stomach exploded into action. Shooting off like a champagne cork, the button on his jeans disappeared into the misty haze of thundering lava, as his clothes screamed at the sudden pressure they found themselves under. The contest was short lived, with the rest of his human clothes ripping at the seams before fluttering off into the smog as he arrowed into the depths, all the time watching the out of control Tim far below him.

In the meantime, Tim had gone from full blown panic, to resignation to a fiery death, to... hmmmm, I might just be getting the hang of this. Opening up his wings, which any dragon egg could have told you was a good place to start, he was currently shifting his strong, muscle laden tail back and forth, flexing it in the middle, trying desperately to control his direction. Amazed at just how easy it was to move and how much of an effect it was having, up until now he'd only really thought of the cumbersome appendage as nothing more than a complete waste of time. It was, however, starting to make some sense. And just at that point, it all went horribly wrong.

A combination of moving his tail down when it should have been up, tilting his left wing too far back behind him, and a section of rock jutting further out from the cliff that he'd failed to notice, had dire consequences for the white dragon. Catching his wing on the rock, which appeared from nowhere out of the lava driven mist, he was spun around with such speed and force that he never had a chance of controlling it. Watching from above as Tim smashed head first into the rock face, starting an ungainly slide towards the hidden depths, Peter kicked his tail out and poured everything he had into his wings, knowing that the boiling sea of molten magma was getting ever closer.

Shaking off the ringing in his ears, Tim had the presence of mind to kick off from the rock face he was currently sliding down, in an effort to get more space and free air. As he tumbled head over heels he caught sight of another dragon speeding towards him from above. Hoping it was Peter, he couldn't be entirely sure because he'd never seen the hockey playing dragon in his natural state. Belatedly he remembered to try and flap his wings. Doing so momentarily slowed down his tumble, which was both good because he could get his bearings and at least see which way was up, but bad because he'd spotted a bubbling sea of brilliant red lava looming ever closer, looking to envelop his newly created prehistoric body. Eyes bulging with fear, he let loose a terrified scream that echoed back up the chasm, assaulting Peter's ears on the way past.

Knowing it was now or never, Peter gave it all he had, the muscles in his tail and wings burning furiously from the effort he'd put in, his determination to save Tim from the hair brained scheme he'd got him caught up in fuelling his will to succeed. With the gap closing, he was almost there. But the gloopy sea of thick, bubbling lava was just too close. With only seconds to go, it looked as though they were both going for an unconventional swim. As the thought entered Peter's mind, a wonderful sight emerged directly before him. Tim had managed to get himself the right way up and currently had both wings outstretched. It was magnificent to see a completely white dragon, wings unfurled, buffeted by the wind, looking for all the world like the legend that he should be. But the momentum he'd gained on the fall down was just too much, and was about to plummet him into the lava. Instinctively, Peter knew exactly what to do. Ignoring the harmful gases scraping away at the back of his throat, he pushed on that little bit more, gaining enough ground to put himself directly beneath Tim. With the lava only yards away now, he channelled all his power into coming out of the steep dive, and sped up and away from the deadly looking sea of red. For his part, Tim had no idea what was going on. Wings spread, tail elongated, one moment he was destined for the mother of all splash downs, the next moment a weight from beneath him forced him up. It was a shock, that's for sure, but a pleasant one given the alternative. Having pulled, or pushed depending on how you looked at it, Tim out of his dive of death, Peter kicked out his tail, flapped his trembling wings, and with his head against the underside of Tim's belly, continued to push skyward. Warm air rushing over him tickled his scales, nuzzled his nostrils, making him feel... invincible. As a brand new dragon he had nothing to compare it with, but it reminded him of those 'perfect' moments you occasionally get. He'd had a few in his life... interestingly, all whilst playing hockey. Running down the wing, sunlight warming his exposed arms, the ball on the end of his stick, heading at speed towards the opposition's goal, at a mixed tournament down in Worthing, sprang to mind immediately. A diving goal line save at his home festival in Salisbridge came flooding back. Scoring the perfect goal in a cup game as time had almost run out. All were perfect moments for him, when time had seemed to stop and he'd captured and remembered the emotions and feelings of that individual instant. This, to him, felt like another one of those.

Having drawn level with the top of the cliff now, and tempting as it was to set Tim down on the rocky ground, particularly given the pain screaming from almost all his muscles, Peter sensed that his friend, for that's how he now thought of him, was just beginning to get a feel for it, and that this might be his one opportunity to get him to fly.

Rising past the top of the cliffs, Tim barely noticed as they continued over the drop and through the caustic cloud of toxic gas. Beginning to relax, feeling the air running over every contour of his prehistoric body, brushing every scale, caressing every muscle, it felt exhilarating and invigorating. It was bliss.

Unbeknown to Tim, Peter had glided silently away,

currently circling below, watching to see what would happen when the brand spanking new dragon realised he was on his own. He thought it very much like a human parent teaching their son or daughter to ride a bike. It was that kind of moment.

With a flick of his tail, the white dragon pulled up his left wing, transferred all his weight right and drifted into a lazy circle, gliding high above the cliff. Out of the corner of his eye, a shape caught his attention. Peter!

'Oh my,' he thought. 'If he's over there, then that means..."

Starting to fall away, his composure shot to ribbons, Peter stopped circling below, ready to intervene. This time though, he waited to see if Tim could turn things around without any of his help.

A graceless fall sent the brand new dragon spiralling frantically out of control; his body, which only seconds before had been elegantly circling, now clumsily twisted and turned, wings flapping out of time, only making his descent more and more awkward. Hovering effortlessly nearby, willing his friend on, Peter could remember what it was like not to have the control, the balance, the natural feel of the air surrounding your body, and how to cut and carve through it. But for him it had been long ago, way back in the nursery ring, before he'd reached the age of ten. And he was one of the later developers on the flying front. Richie, of course, had been the first of them to achieve sustained flight. Not only that, but she was performing complicated aerial acrobatics long before most of her classmates had learned to even glide. At least that's how he remembered most of it. Years later, he'd heard a handful of rumours about an illicit late night laminium ball match at the nursery ring, supposedly involving a dragon from his year group. At the time they'd sounded far-fetched, but he'd often wondered whether or not Tank was involved in some way, shape or form. His friend had of course immediately denied knowing anything about it when questioned, but there was almost something left unsaid, like a cliff hanger at the end of a great book.

Snapping out of his thoughts, he made his decision to jump in and save Tim once again. But as he surged forward, the newly formed dragon managed to unsteadily come out of his roll, spread his wings and use a handily timed updraft to swoop around and up out of danger. Smiling to himself, he watched the look of elation on Tim's face, knowing instantly exactly what his friend was feeling and that he would be totally and utterly hooked. Hockey, rugby and lacrosse had nothing on the sensation of flying. There was just no comparison. Grateful for getting this far, Peter soared forward, looking to catch up with the undulating white dragon who was now drifting up towards the cavern's ceiling. On catching up, Peter let out a huge guffaw. Tim banked round, keen to learn what was so funny. Peter pointed to Tim's head, and then to his own.

"You've got a bit of..." he chuckled.

Tim frowned, not sure what was going on. Running his hands over his face, all the while continuing to glide, he came across two large rocky protrusions embedded in his prehistoric forehead. Gingerly pulling them out, he dismissed each, tossing them into the abyss.

"What's so funny?"

"That's gonna be your new name!"

"What?"

"Cliff Face," coughed Peter, still laughing.

"Good one," replied Tim, picking up on what his friend meant.

Drifting off to explore all four corners of the gigantic cavern, their hissing, chuckling and coughing echoed out behind them.

Having lost all track of time, it was only on one of Peter's sitting out phases that he realised just how long they'd actually been there, and just how much trouble he'd be in once he eventually got Tim back. Unsurprisingly, it was difficult to tear Tim away from the falls, but the promise of another trip later on in the week eventually did the trick. As they retraced their steps, Peter marvelled at the progress Tim had made during the course of the day. Basic aerial manoeuvres were nearly well within his grasp. It wouldn't be long before he could consider full mastery of the skies, he thought, longing for his comfy bed so that he could close his weary eyes.

26 SECRET SPLICING STUPIDITY

Exhausted, that's how he felt. Deep down inside, he knew it was mainly due to his age, but it still disappointed him. In his youth, a very, very long time ago, he would have managed on little or no sleep at all. Now it was very different. Still, he'd had six hours a few nights ago and that should at least see him through until tomorrow night. Snuggled in the darkness, underneath the cosy covers of his huge dragon sized bed, he whispered a few carefully chosen words and waited for them to take hold.

'What was my app... associate thinking? Of all the things he could have done. This! Installing that blessed... what's it called? Oh, that's right. A webcam! How could he possibly think that I wouldn't find out about it? STUPID BOY!'

Rolling back the covers of his living room sized bed, the master mantra maker shook his wings and planted his feet firmly on the floor, happy to know that he wasn't being watched. The words he'd just spoken had cast a mantra which projected an image of him sleeping straight onto the lens of the webcam, allowing him to go about his sneaky business and continue his important after hours work. Disregarding his night cap, he plodded out through the door and downstairs into the workshop. Foregoing any kind of drink, not needing to be glued to the toilet any longer than he actually had to be (it was an age thing, much as in humans. Being as old as he was meant that there was nearly always an imprint of a toilet seat on his scaly old buttocks, that's how regularly he went, something that seemed to become more and more prominent with each and every day that passed.) That and the fact that it made him more grumpier than usual in the mornings, he started scrabbling around in one of the cupboards underneath the sink, the one marked 'Recycled Mantra Paper'. He'd had to be extra specially careful, particularly after Tank had caught him out with the Peruvian Mantra Ink.

'Goodness knows what else the young dragon's found out,' he thought as he rummaged. And so it was that the intricate work he'd been doing every night for months now, had to be wrapped up and hidden amongst an infernal number of old, useless scrolls. Eventually he found what he was looking for: a large, rolled up, shabby looking, piece of flimsy parchment, tied together with two pieces of ropey string. Holding it with both hands almost as if it were about to explode, he carried it over to one of the work benches, set it down and flopped into the oversized chair in front of it. Carefully, and with superb dexterity, he undid the string and removed each and every piece inside, placing them all just so on the work surface in front of him. What to him was the result of months of exhaustive experimentation and delicate work would have looked to anyone else like the aftermath of very young children sticking and gluing. But to him, the mess was exactly as it should be.

Starting some months ago, springing from an idea that had occurred to him while he'd been trying to save Flash's life at the king's private residence, the source of the idea had been all the talk of nagas and how they'd infiltrated the humans, much in the same way dragons had, the only difference being that the dragons were following their vow to protect, which almost certainly couldn't be said for those slippery serpents. Being the sneaky, off the wall maverick that he was, Gee Tee had decided something needed to be done about the naga situation. All his thoughts on the matter had centred around being able to stun the entire lot of them temporarily. Although not ideal as a permanent deterrent, it did at least seem achievable, and would buy the dragons some time, or just maybe get them out of a sticky situation.

In theory at least the idea was simple, but putting it into practice was something else altogether, not to mention dangerous, hence the reason he was doing it after dark and not giving his co-worker any clue to its existence. Having scoured his memory, the only way he could come up with to incorporate everything he needed into one mantra, was to use a method known as 'splicing', something that had been outlawed over one hundred and fifty years ago, that's how dangerous it was. But despite its illegality it was still practised, here and there anyway. Having not put his knowledge to good use in this format for many, many decades, the master mantra maker's keen mind was sure it would have no problems in completing this intricate and time consuming task. One thing he wasn't short of was confidence. So his night times at first were all about finding the right components from other mantras kicking around the Emporium, so that he could splice them into his alpha mantra. It took over a month to find what he was looking for. After that, the fun really began.

Splicing by its very nature can be dangerous in oh so many ways. Not just from the magical energy contained physically, such as in the page, scroll or tome. The power of thought can be a wonderful thing, as all dragons know. But when mantras are crafted, stray thoughts, ideas and willpower can be transferred, or can just unintentionally stick around. Either way, loose thoughts drifting around, combined with a sure supply of magical energy... not something you want to muck around with too much if you can help it. But if you want to splice, then it couldn't be avoided. Taking apart intricate details of a mantra with all these variables had proved disastrous in the past, leaving the council no choice but to officially ban such undertakings. But if you're careful, and more than a little lucky, it is possible to produce something so magical, so breathtakingly perfect, that all the risk would be considered worthwhile. This had been his goal, his aim, his obsession. Hopefully nobody knew of his out of hours exploits. Tank, of course, had always fussed over him, more so recently. Hence the reason for the webcam, he assumed, making sure that he was okay and got enough rest. Part of him felt warmed by the fact that his friend, as that's how he now thought of him, cared enough to do such a thing, but he was disappointed to have his liberty contained. It hadn't taken long to find out what it was, how it worked and just how it could be deceived, but it was a fuss to go through every night. Assuming it must be working perfectly, as the young dragon hadn't mentioned anything out of the ordinary, he was hopeful that things would stay that way, just for a little while longer. Tonight, if things went well, his dream would become a reality.

Having already gathered everything he required and retrieved the vital ingredients from their original mantras, the old dragon was ready to have a go at splicing together all the magical parts. Clearing his mind and focusing solely on the puzzle in front of him, he staved off the energy and willpower swirling around him from words, numbers, letters and symbols scattered across his desk. Very slowly, he moved the separate pieces around, this way and that, trying to find the most efficient order in which to channel the energy from the spell. So deep in concentration was he, that he missed the soft pad of footfalls slipping through the shop and into the workshop behind him.

"And there was me thinking you were fast asleep!" announced a voice from directly behind him.

Gee Tee nearly jumped out of his skin, scattering the tattered scraps of parchment everywhere as he leapt up and turned to face... TANK!

"You scared the living daylights out of me!" he yelled.

"Wouldn't have happened had you been asleep, getting the valuable rest that you so need. Would it?"

Just glaring, having been caught red handed, the master mantra maker tried to compose his thoughts.

"What on earth is it that you're doing here at this late hour?" he babbled.

"I've come to help you with the most dangerous part of your very ILLEGAL endeavour," replied the rugby playing dragon.

"How on earth...?" started the old shopkeeper, before giving up. There and then he decided he really didn't want to know how the youngster knew about the splicing. For the very first time, he started to consider that he was too old for all of this skulduggery business.

"Do you need me to catch you up?"

Jumping into another oversized chair, and then scooting over to the desk where his boss was working, Tank ventured,

"You've taken apart a series of mantras, pulling individual pieces from each, and now you plan on splicing them together to craft one almighty, life changing mantra?"

Gee Tee nodded.

"So what's the mantra for exactly? It must be something important to warrant this much sneaking about."

Smiling, the master mantra maker was secretly pleased that the young dragon still didn't know the purpose of the soon-to-be-crafted mantra.

"It will, I hope, negate whatever magic the nagas are using, and will temporarily stun them."

"Nice," said Tank nodding approvingly. "What kind of range will it have?"

Here was the bit that Gee Tee had dreaded talking to even himself about. (He talked to himself quite often in fact, like everyone else, when he thought he was alone.)

"Currently, only a very small one," announced the downcast dragon.

Tank took note of his friend's disappointment.

'No doubt he thought it was going to save the world, and it just might do that, but not if it only has a very small area of effect. I wonder if there's any way we can change all that?'

Sitting opposite each other, each keeping their own counsel, one racked his brains as to just how he'd been caught out, while the other tried hard to find the very last piece of the puzzle.

After a mind numbing few minutes of silence, Tank shouted,

"I'VE GOT IT!"

"Got what, youngster?"

"I know how we can apply it to the entire world!"

Gee Tee sat up straight in his chair, totally attentive, totally focused, ready to hear what his young employee had to say.

"We channel it through the telepathic newspaper nodes. The reach from those telepathic boosters covers nearly the entire earth's surface. What little isn't covered will almost certainly not have nagas up to no good in it."

A faint glimmer, a tiny spark burst into being, somewhere deep inside the old dragon.

"It does sound a little preposterous," he cautioned, "but it certainly has potential."

Tank decided he was going to quit there. The last line was almost certainly as much praise as he was ever likely to get. For him, it couldn't get any better than that.

"If we're going to do this, there's one more thing we'll need to make the mantra compatible with the telepathic nodes," muttered the old shopkeeper, heading for the door, urging his young friend to follow. "I seem to recall a seventeenth century dragon call to arms spell that was able to be broadcast across the entire node network, in the form of a scroll, somewhere in the shop. If we can find it, we can remove the broadcast section to add to the mantra we're splicing together. If we get it right, the mantra should work as you've suggested. Good thinking by the way." And that was it. Heading off to the far corner of the shop, leaving Tank stunned by his last words, the master mantra maker's muttering echoed throughout the bookcases.

Shaking his head clear, Tank thought about what his friend had just said. Not the compliment, but about where the mantra was located, having seen it not so long ago. Sifting through his memories, it didn't take long to find.

Without bothering to tell the old shopkeeper that he was hunting in the wrong place, Tank followed the shop counter along, past the entrance to the dead end that led to the secret vault, turned left and then right, walked to the end of the aisle, turned left again and started rifling through a shelf full of scrolls, all neatly rolled up, tied tight with different coloured ribbons. Knowing he was looking for a green one narrowed it down to six scrolls. Unfurling the second one, he could see he'd hit the jackpot.

"I'VE GOT IT!" he shouted over the bookshelves and across the shop floor.

Indecipherable spluttering and mumbling from the other side of the Emporium echoed back up the aisle as he headed back towards the workshop. Reaching the counter entrance at exactly the same time as his employer, the old dragon looked harried and harassed.

"That was the next place I was going to look," remarked the old dragon, totally straight faced, before walking past Tank and taking his place back at the table.

Following his friend back into the workshop, Tank opened out the scroll on the table in front of them.

"Hmmm... this is the right one. And I think it should do exactly what's required. Right then, let's get on and take it apart."

And they did. It took the best part of three hours to carefully dissect the words, the energy and the willpower. For the most part, Tank watched in awe as the master mantra maker lived up to his name, using a solid gold scalpel with a diamond encrusted edge to neatly carve up some of the scroll and peel away the occasional word or letter. The craftsmanship was outstanding, with the young rugby playing dragon never having seen anything quite like it. Discarding the unused part of the mantra on the workshop floor, Gee Tee sat back, his face baked in sweat, looking pale and more than a little worn out. Tank pleaded with him to rest but, stubbornly, he wouldn't hear of it. So after a huge mug of hot charcoal, well... more like a huge mug of marshmallows sprinkled with charcoal, the two of them sat side by side, about to perform a very dangerous and very illegal act. Cautiously, they laid out the pieces of the mantra they were trying to splice together, all in the order they needed to be to channel the magical energy most efficiently. In all, there were nine pieces of the puzzle. It was going to be tough. Gee Tee had already told Tank the most pieces he'd ever heard of being spliced together was seven, and that was by some ancient dragon over a thousand years ago, who was some kind of mystical mantra guru. Naturally, Tank was more than a little nervous. With the pieces laid out, the master mantra maker carefully retrieved the huge glass jar from somewhere underneath his desk. It was the one from the vault, full to the brim with glistening laminium rivets.

"Wow!" exclaimed Tank.

"Wow indeed, youngster."

"They're all laminium?"

Gee Tee nodded.

"How many are there?"

"Three or four thousand, give or take."

Not for the first time today, Tank was mesmerised, not just by the number of rivets, but by the actual amount of laminium. It was huge and must have been worth a fortune. It was probably the same in total as the amount which made up a laminium ball. That was a lot.

Fiddling about at the back of one of his desk drawers, the old shopkeeper suddenly produced a gleaming, pure silver, hand held rivet gun. More of an antique than anything else, it looked gorgeous, set off by strips of worn leather around both its grips. Inspecting it fully, he then retrieved two pairs of fine gloves, handing one pair to Tank before slipping the other pair onto his hands. As the young rugby playing dragon slid his fingers into them, he marvelled at how heavy and strong they were, despite their appearance.

"Carbon fibre weave," stated Gee Tee, noticing the

young dragon's curiosity.

Tank nodded, after which they both focused fully on what they were about to do. Gee Tee explained how, at first, all the pieces would have to be joined together with the laminium rivets. Tank would hold the pieces carefully in place while his friend did the rest. Afterwards it would be a case of checking and double checking every last line of text, to make sure that everything was right, down to the last letter and space. After that, the old shopkeeper would ignite the splicing spell, using the laminium in the rivets to bond the whole process together. If successful, it should lead to the completed mantra, the one that would stun nagas across the world when used in conjunction with the telepathic nodes. The risk, as ever, was in the igniting. If even the tiniest detail was wrong... it could lead to catastrophe. In some cases dust or even hair had got tangled up in the mantra, causing a massive failure. Dragons had died, buildings and towns had been levelled when splicing had gotten out of hand in the past, which was primarily why it had been outlawed. But they'd got this far, and both were determined to press on.

Three hours later, around about dawn, they were ready to ignite the laminium rivets. Gee Tee pleaded with Tank to leave, explaining that there was no reason for him to be present for the final part of the process. Tank felt touched at the master mantra maker's concern, but had no intention of going, wanting to see this through, having absolute faith in his friend's ability.

And so, as they both hunched over the desk in the tiny little workshop, both tired, anxious, terrified and more than a little thrilled, the masterful old shopkeeper, eyes closed, wove his magic. Rolling off his tongue, the words were almost visible, the sound of them washing over Tank felt like a warm rainstorm on a summer's day. Then, without warning, the patched up parchment in front of them burst into... LIGHT! Not just any light, but the mother of all light, blinding, white, radiant, all encompassing. Even with his eyelids firmly closed, it still seared Tank's eyes. Turning away, gaining very little relief if any, he felt around for his friend, who was standing in exactly the same place, stock still. And then as quickly as it had arrived, the light disappeared. It took a few moments to adjust, but when they did, what a sight greeted them. There on the table, where the patched up and tattered parchment had been held together with dozens and dozens of rivets, was a sparkling, golden sheet of paper with a rainbow of colours swirling about it. From an angle it looked like the floor of a garage forecourt, except it wasn't petrol that could be glimpsed, but the delicate nature of the laminium. It was magnificent. They'd been truly successful. Surely now the battle for planet earth would turn in their favour? But that could wait. Sleep beckoned, and the shop remained closed for the rest of the day after Tank departed, and after Gee Tee had placed the results of their hard work safely in the vault.

27 I'LL GIVE YOU A RING

'Difficult' somehow couldn't describe it adequately. From the outside she looked the same, behaved the same, but deep down, he knew it wasn't her. He'd arranged for them to meet for lunch today, but they weren't going to the staff restaurant. He needed somewhere a little more... out of the way. As they walked along the shiny corridor approaching the restaurant, Richie moved to dive off to her right and join the back of the long, winding queue for the hot, sumptuous looking dinners. Gently, Peter grabbed her left arm and guided her straight on, much to the amusement of several onlookers. Mere moments later, she relaxed, content to follow her friend, who had by now let go of her. A sharp left and two right hand turns later, he turned the handle on the small, glass paned door, holding it open for his friend.

'She looks surprised,' he thought. And then it occurred to him that she probably had no memory of this place, despite the fact that it was she who had introduced it to him.

"This is new," she whispered excitedly, noticing all the plant life. "An illicit trip into the dangerous wild jungles of... Salisbridge!"

Smiling as she stepped past him into the small, secluded courtyard, all he could think was,

'Same old Richie... well, almost.'

Dodging through a variety of ferns and other huge bright green plants, all of which looked as though they'd doubled in size since his last visit, they arrived at the worn old bench next to the raised flowerbed, just opposite the rectangular pond. Extending his arm, he indicated that Richie should sit. She did.

"When you said let's do lunch, I had no idea it would be romantic... like this," she teased.

"Oh... very good," he replied, slipping off his dark

backpack so that he could join her on the seat.

"So what's going on?" she asked innocently.

"Lunch," he answered, unzipping the backpack. "We always go to the restaurant. I thought we'd do something... different."

Richie smiled, trying to recall them 'always' going to the restaurant. She could remember a couple of times, but other than that her mind seemed a blank. It worried her a little. Not the actual going there with Peter, but that on a number of occasions recently she'd had trouble remembering specific things. Gazing lovingly at some of the lacrosse trophies in her glass cabinet at home a couple of nights ago, one or two of which she had absolutely no idea how she'd won, her name was carved into them, but she couldn't remember earning them, or even them being presented to her, which must have happened at some point. At that stage she wondered if it was worth her going to see a doctor about it, but as that thought popped into her head, she couldn't recall ever having been to a doctor. That in itself seemed odd, and more than a little worrying. Vowing to herself to try harder to remember, she decided to start keeping a written record of all the things that bothered her.

Meanwhile, Peter had produced a couple of lovely looking plates from his bag, two plastic bottles of mango and orange juice (her favourite), carrot and cucumber sticks wrapped in cling film, a strawberry yoghurt for each of them and a huge pile of something wrapped in tin foil. Richie took it from him reluctantly.

'How could this be better than the restaurant?' she thought.

"Go on... open it!" he urged.

Uncovering three massive sandwiches made from white doorstep bread, bright red jam leaking out from all sides, looking like something CSI might like to investigate, she managed to stammer a brief,

"Ahhh... thanks," but after a moment's hesitation, went

on to add, "but I don't really like jam."

It took all Peter's concentration not to laugh out loud, as he shook his head, having made Richie's favourite sandwiches, with the strawberry jam that was so hard to get hold of, used butter instead of spread, gone to the bakery and picked up the crusty white loaf she liked so much, while it had still been gorgeously hot.

"Sorry," announced Richie.

"Why don't you just take a bite?" he encouraged, knowing that despite the obvious differences that he knew about her, he'd been assured by the council, the priests, and more importantly by Gee Tee, that everything else would remain the same. Like her eating habits. Of course, she wasn't going to still have a hankering for charcoal, or start nibbling her way down an HB pencil mid way through a training course (at least he hoped not), but those human characteristics should still be there, something he was counting on at this very moment. Half-heartedly she took a small nibble. The look on her face was priceless; he wished he'd had his phone out to capture it. This time she took a colossal bite, chomping away, savouring every last micron.

"This is great!" she exclaimed.

Chuckling, Peter unwrapped his own sandwiches, made from the same bread but with ham and coleslaw on the inside.

Both sat back, munching away, watching tiny slivers of sunlight cut their way through the leaves of the overhanging plants, listening as occasional watery noises drifted over to them from the pond. It was really quite idyllic, and Richie was having a much better time than she had at first thought she would. They chatted casually about their mornings and their schedules for the rest of the working week.

Twenty minutes later, having finished their informal lunch and packed away everything but the drinks, they both sat back, enjoying the tranquillity of their surroundings.

"This has been great... thank you," she declared, stretching and yawning at the same time.

"You're welcome," he answered politely.

But now it was down to business, the reason he'd so meticulously planned this lunch, although Richie didn't know it yet.

"There's something I need you to do for me," he whispered, his voice dropping low, despite the fact that the windows overlooking where they were sat were all sealed shut.

Looking on willingly, she waited to hear what he had to say. Getting to his feet, he reached deep inside his right trouser pocket and pulled out a beautiful silver necklace, with an odd looking ring dangling from it. Watching the ring intently as it danced back and forth on the necklace, she was captivated as the occasional ray of sunlight sneaked through the surrounding plant life, ricocheting off it in all directions. Holding the necklace tight, Peter knelt down on the floor in front of his friend. Richie wondered what on earth was going to happen next.

"I need you to look after this for me," he remarked, dangling the necklace right in front of Richie's pale, freckly face. "It's really important!"

Up close, she could see just how unusual the ring hanging off the silver thread in front of her really was. Matt grey, it had tiny little ice blue triangles of light all the way around it, interrupted only by one slightly larger and markedly bigger grey triangle. It was mesmerising.

"I... I... I... I..." she stammered. "I... don't know what to say."

"Just say you'll do it for me. Please?"

Thinking about it for a couple of seconds, something suddenly occurred to her.

"It's not stolen or anything is it?"

Peter's stomach somersaulted as if it were trying out for the Olympic gymnastic squad, recalling how he'd taken it from Gee Tee's vault. Ignoring the uncomfortable feeling, he pressed on.

"No... nothing like that," he lied. "I just need it kept safe, and I can't think of anyone I'd rather trust with it than you."

Carefully she plucked it away from him.

"Is it valuable?"

"More than you could ever possibly know," he replied.

She thrust it back in his direction.

"If it's valuable, I can't possibly keep it."

"It's more a sentimental thing," he whispered, with more than a hint of truth about it. "Please... you'd be doing me a big favour."

Richie swallowed uncertainly.

"Okay," she eventually squeaked.

Taking the necklace, he carefully placed it around her slim neck and did up the clasp, letting the ring hang low, just out of sight below her work shirt.

'Perfect,' he thought, stepping back.

Richie twiddled with it just a little, getting used to the feel of it against her soft, pale flesh.

"Please promise me two things," he said. "First. Please don't take it off, not unless I tell you to, and guard it with your life. Okay?"

A serious look imprinted on her face, she nodded.

"Secondly," he started, "please do not, however tempted you are, put the ring on your finger. This is really important, and you need to promise me you won't do that."

"I promise," she swore, wondering exactly what she was getting herself into. "Can't you tell me any more than that?"

Moments passed as he thought hard about how to reply. Through all his soul searching and all the questions he'd asked himself since the moment he's stolen her dragon consciousness in the ring, he'd wondered what to do with it, where to keep it safe. In the end, there could only be one possible answer. She should have it, it did only really make sense, it was after all... HERS! But how to do it so that she didn't know was the million dollar question. He'd come up with all this, but part of him now needed to tell her more. Phrasing the words carefully, he continued.

"What you have there," he said solemnly, "is not only the key to your future, but the key to your past as well. That's all I can tell you I'm afraid."

Satisfied he'd said all he could, Peter stood up, and downed the rest of his drink in one go. Following his example, she joined him and finished her drink, slightly perturbed but glad to have helped out her friend, feeling more than a little odd about the whole experience though. With the tiny weight of the ring nudging her skin as she followed him back through the plants and back to an afternoon of work, she promised herself she would follow her friend's instructions implicitly.

28 PLAYING CATCH UP

It had taken every resource available to him and then some, but eventually he'd managed to pick up their trail. They were good, he had to give them that: constantly on the move, choosing out of the way places to stay, swapping vehicles non-stop, paying for everything with cash. They knew all the tricks, even avoiding CCTV cameras. He knew this because he'd backtracked where they'd been and although he knew the group had been there, CCTV footage showed not one single frame of any of them. Having already found and searched two of their safe houses, coming up a complete blank on both, a disagreement that had gotten out of hand at a gas station had been the breakthrough he'd been looking for. The owner, a distinguished middle aged gentleman, had reported the incident to the local police department. One of the station officers (a dragon, who along with most of his kind on this continent, had been briefed to be especially vigilant and on the lookout for anything suspicious or unusual) had recognised the report's significance at once and had passed it up the chain of command, pretty damn quick. It had, of course, ended up with him. Having spoken to the distressed gas station owner, it was pretty clear he was once again on the right track. Given the man's fear at seeing one of his regular customers thrown nearly eighty yards in the air, on top of the same assailant producing a stream of flame from his mouth and threatening to burn down the entire place, Flash didn't feel the slightest hint of remorse at having to wipe his short term memory.

That was two days ago, and the start of much hard work that had led him here, to this out of the way series of interconnected barns. Lying flat on his stomach, just able to see the building through the tall, sharp grass, he could feel the impossible currents and eddies of dark magic swirling in and around the structures he was looking at. Momentarily a trickle of fear ran through him. Immediately he swatted it away, in much the same way as most would with a fly around their food. His sole focus returned to what he had to do. Part of him thought about calling for assistance. Realistically that wasn't an option. The Crimson Guard, if they came at all, would simply ignore him and take over the whole operation, and that was the best scenario he could imagine, given his change in bodily circumstances. And if he called in the King's Guard, it was possible they might not be up to the task at all. NO! It was up to him, and more often than not, stealth and surprise were more than a match for a small force, even if that force was made up of magic using nagas and dragons. And it wasn't as if he were helpless... far from it.

Silently he shot up from the grass and leapt across a small gully before sprinting over one hundred yards, pulling up behind the trunk of a giant tree close to the nearest wooden structure, hoping that stealth and the protective mantras he'd shrouded himself in earlier would continue to hold up and keep him hidden. Backed up against the tree, he extended the range of his hearing, but detected nothing untoward. Taking a chance, he ran for the nearest side of the building, crouching beneath a dirtied window. Carefully, he took a peek. It was empty... as far as he could tell. On reflection, he decided to check the perimeter first.

An hour later, he'd completed his reconnoitre. There'd been no sign of movement of any sort. His mind made up, he knew now not to dally and made straight for the back door. In his mind he tossed up between breaking the glass of the wooden framed door and destroying the lock. Either way would be noisy, the glass obviously more so, but the time for stealth had long since passed. Reaching the door at a run, he unleashed the mantra he'd prepared in his mind. Brilliant bolts of yellow energy ripped from his fingertips, destroying the lock instantly. Still on the run, he used his momentum to burst through the door, throwing himself into a forward roll as he did so, quickly coming up onto one knee, having drawn the powerful looking pistol from its holster behind his back. Both hands firmly around the grip of the gun, he scanned for danger and found none, apart from the stronger presence of the dark energy he'd felt from outside. It seemed to close in around him, invisible clouds causing untold pressure, almost as if the will was being squeezed right out of him. Wanting to leave, which was probably the point of it all, he didn't, instead cutting through the dark, swirling mist that he could see with his mantra vision, concentrating on searching every nook and cranny for anything they might have overlooked, however small.

Five and a half hours later, he was done. NOTHING! That's what he'd found. Frustrated couldn't begin to describe how he felt. So close, just a step behind them, he was sure. But they were always one step ahead. Knowing he was in the right place, because he could sense the nagas had been here, with all that dark mystical energy, he asked himself the only question he could. Where on earth were they now?

Staring out of the window into the beautiful wooded landscape beyond, something in the reflection caught his eye. Turing around, he strolled over to the elegant wooden bookcase that was piled high with books on every subject. Having already searched each and every one for a clue, with nothing presenting itself, his attention now was on a tiny dot of red biro smudged onto the wood of the bookcase itself.

'Peculiar,' he thought, continuing to study it. Not able to see how ink from a pen could possibly have gotten so high up the bookcase, he closed his eyes and scrolled through the different types of vision that his dragon persona offered, albeit stuck in his ungainly body. It was only when he hit his microscopic vision that everything became clear. It looked as though someone had written on something against the bookcase, with enough pressure to leave a residual mark. Imprints of tiny letters which were, by the look of things, coordinates and a time.

'37° 31'32.28N 75° 56'42.34W at 1.15am,' he thought. 'How unlike them. I think that just might be the lead that I'm looking for.'

And with that he sprinted back through the lush vegetation to where he'd parked his hire car, just over three miles away.

It had been hard to find. At first he'd found himself going round and round in circles, following the directions of the hire car's sat nav. Deciding to leave the car and go the rest of the way on foot had proved a much better idea. Surrounded by trees, looking out over the water, the co-ordinates on his phone had led him directly to this hidden shallow bank. It was a stunning, secluded location, but the view was not what occupied Flash's mind. Meticulously, he tiptoed down the side of the bank, careful not to get caught in all the mud, all the time examining the odd shapes that had been carved into it. Most wouldn't give the muddy bank a second thought but piece by piece, his experienced and logical mind started to put it all together. Two nagas in their natural forms, a boat and a number of humans, how many, he couldn't tell. That's what all the impressions told him. All he had to do now was figure out where on earth they went.

Scrolling through his mind, he ran through the list of dragons that were in American government agencies, until he found the one he was looking for. Instantly he dialled the number on his phone and hoped to hell that a satellite had been overhead at the right time.

Twenty five minutes later he had his answer, and it scared the living daylights out of him. Then he had to spend five minutes calming down the young dragon on the other end of the phone, who'd wanted to tell all and sundry, something Flash really didn't want to happen. It was bad enough that this group had got their hands on such hardware, the last thing he needed was for them to be spooked or panicked into making a rash decision. Eventually the young dragon calmed down enough for Flash to take full responsibility, and drop the king's name into the equation.

'A submarine of all things,' he mused, climbing back into his rental car. It still didn't seem true. He'd assumed it would be some kind of boat and that he'd be able to track it down. But a submarine, that was virtually impossible to track, and God knows where it was headed. All he knew was that he had to get back to London as fast as possible and report this new twist in events to the king himself.

29 GENEROUS TO A FAULT

Sitting with the other department heads around the gorgeous oak table in the office adjacent to Garrett's, Peter admired the perfectly carpeted floor, the glistening counter of the curved, sweeping bar and the perfect lighting from the chandeliers dangling precariously from the ceiling, in this, the most opulent room in the building, which nearly always hosted the weekly management meetings.

Sitting quietly watching the head of the human resources department outline her weekly progress, he felt more than a little intimidated by all the people around the table, mainly because he was the youngest by a very long way, over a decade in fact. And while his dragon training had prepared him to talk in front of others and give speeches to groups without being nervous, he couldn't help, in these particular situations, feeling more than a little uncomfortable. Today it had been his turn to report first, something he hadn't known before entering the room. One or two minor issues with staff had come up, but nothing he wasn't already dealing with. The main area he knew Garrett and the others wanted to hear about was the laminium, so he spent nearly fifteen minutes detailing exactly how it was being stored and the security measures surrounding it. When he'd finished, the others, Garrett included, all nodded their heads in satisfaction at what they'd been told. It was a good job he didn't have to report everything about the valuable metal's security. Smiling at the thought of having to tell the rest of them about the exotic mantras he'd employed with regard to safekeeping the company's most valuable resource, if nothing else, Gee Tee's stock in trade provided him with peace of mind. Reporting first and without warning had in fact been a blessing in disguise. If he'd known, he'd probably not have slept well last night. At least this way, he'd got it out of the way and could sit back, relax (well, as much as possible in these situations) and listen to what was happening in the rest of the company.

A few minutes later, the meeting was adjourned, with everyone smiling and happy, all packing away their things.

"Peter," a soft voice called, "could you possibly stay behind for a few minutes?"

"Of course," he answered, wondering what Garrett needed him for.

Filing out one by one, the others all thanked their boss. With the last one having left, Garrett closed the door so that it was just the two of them.

"I've been looking into the request you made," he said, perching on the table. "It would seem there's a little more to it than I first thought."

'Oh no,' Peter thought, 'he's not going to help. How on earth are we going to get the sports club all back together?'

"I've brought in some geologists to look at the site, after a recommendation from the government clean up team. It would appear that the explosion from the bomb has in some way affected the ground deep below the surface, damaging a minor fault line, causing the entire area to become unstable."

Peter was truly dismayed on hearing this for the first time.

"It seems the instability can be resolved, but the cost will be considerable."

Lost for words, he desperately wanted the clubhouse rebuilt and things back to how they were, with all the sports men, women and children enjoying their chosen pastimes.

"While I do owe you a great debt and can see just how important this is to you, are you sure you wouldn't rather have a considerable sum of money, or a new house, something to set you up for the rest of your life? It will be all or nothing if I go ahead with this."

Not for a split second was he tempted. All he wanted to do was play hockey... there, and nowhere else for the rest of his life.

"I know it's a lot of money sir, I mean Al. But the sports club means so much, not just to me, but to many, many people. All I really want is for it to be back how it was, with men, women and children all enjoying their favourite sports."

Garrett nodded his approval.

"So it's set then. I'll chase up the relevant people straight away and set things in motion. I must say Peter, you are a most remarkable young man. Not just in the way you take responsibility, as you have done in this relatively new role that you've been thrust into, but in your regard for others. Most men and women would have jumped at the chance of a personal reward. But not you. Why is that?"

Thinking carefully, with Garrett watching him eagle eyed, panic started to envelop him. What was he going to say? What did Garrett want to hear? In the end, he settled for the truth.

"I love playing hockey... it's my life. There's nothing else I'd rather be doing, and I want to do it here. It's my home. I love my job. It's where my friends are. I love it here and that's a fact."

A big beaming smile encompassed Garrett's face.

"That, my young friend, is good enough for me. For the entire time I've known you, I've always thought there was something special about you. And now you've just proved it. I'll make sure that clubhouse is rebuilt, and don't you worry, it'll be better than new, you mark my words."

Gathering up his things, he shook Garrett's proffered right hand on the way out, musing on the 'bald eagle' thinking that he was special.

'If only he knew the truth,' he thought, depressing the button for the lift, his beaming smile reflecting off the shiny doors, pleased at the thought that his beloved clubhouse would at some point be back to normal.

30 EGGS-CLUSION

Remnants of the past drifted in and out of her dreams, a curse for the most part, but she'd lived with it for so long that it no longer bothered her. With a new life and a new planet on the horizon, she once again lived through something that happened long ago, almost to someone else.

After being saved by a dragon in a position of power, they made a decision, a decision to quit it all and go their own way. They hadn't exactly seen the error of their ways, but being torn apart, incarcerated and alone, each not knowing what was happening to the other, had all been too much and had made them realise just how much they wanted to be together. So they made a plan. At first they travelled throughout England and Scotland. It had been so easy, given not only their dragon training, but all the new things that had supplemented it from their previous employers. Sticking together, acting as man and wife, changing their identities and their accents, sometimes on a daily basis, they constantly moved around, never staying in the same place for more than one night. Their thieving wasn't particularly grand, and was easily achieved given their remarkable talents. Opportunistic would have been the best way to describe it. The odd safe here, a little pick pocketing there... the night's takings of a public house was a favourite. It had to be this way, small but often, so that they could avoid the attention of the dragon council and the King's Guard. And for the most part, they had, with one exception. Two of the King's Guard had nearly stumbled across them when they'd fleeced a fairground proprietor of his week's earnings in Newcastle in the north east of England. It had been a close call, after which they'd stayed on the move for the whole of the following week, choosing to sleep out in the open rather than risk a town or city. And it had worked. After eight months of a life like this, they had enough money to make their dreams come true.

Moving to the stunningly pretty town of Swanage in Dorset, she could remember the day they'd arrived, as if it were only yesterday. They had taken the hulking great monster of a steam train from Wareham, past the scenic ruins of Corfe Castle, captivated by its beauty, and only fifteen minutes or so later had pulled into the terminus, right in the centre of the fabulous seaside town. It had been a warm spring day when they'd arrived, carrying two small suitcases between them, which contained everything they owned. It hadn't taken long to find rented accommodation. Two days later, they both had jobs. Earth had taken the position of waitress at one of the seaside cafés right on the front. While slightly affronted at not having the power, position and respect that she'd come to think of as hers by right, she was at least happy, and all because of him. Things just felt so right when they were together, and although they'd had that chemistry in France when they were both hunting down French and British Resistance operatives for the nagas and the Nazis, it was different now. There was no pressure, no orders, no silly games to play. Of course there was still the fact that they were, so to speak, on the run, both war criminals wanted by humans and dragons alike. Each had done much to disguise their appearance and had quelled the magic inside them significantly. It would be a surprise if anyone at all could identify them as the perpetrators of those heinous crimes in another country.

Excitedly announcing the news of her job to her husband on returning to their rented flat, instantly he lifted her up, twirling her joyfully about the living room, adding to her news by telling her that he'd gained employment on the coveted railway, as a fireman. Both squealed in excitement.

And so it continued, for years in fact. After only a few months they moved out of their flat, choosing instead to rent a reasonably sized house. Things were perfect. They had friends, they socialised, mixed in. It was idyllic. In their mind, there was only one thing missing. And so very carefully, in a precision planned operation, they as a couple became less outgoing, attended the pubs and the social scene a lot less than they had done, instead choosing to spend all their time at home. It had been tricky, but some six months after they'd started, all their efforts were rewarded with... AN EGG!

Their ecstasy at having circumvented the many obstacles in their way was off the scale. It filled her with warmth every time she thought about it. But that was only half the story. What they had to do next was madness of a completely different order.

So, in the early hours of a weekday morning, having planned out their route both above and below ground with military forethought, they headed back to the domain of their birth with heavy hearts, constantly looking over their shoulders. After much skulking, scrabbling and concealment, they arrived in the shadows of the Purbeck Peninsula nursery ring entrance, carrying their beloved egg between them. She could remember thinking that it took an age for their knocks on the ancient wooden door to be answered. But answer them they did. Well, one lone female dragon did. And that's what they'd been hoping for. Little fuss, little attention, someone with little imagination and even less suspicion. It had seemingly all worked out fine. After half an hour the egg had been accepted, all the relevant documentation filled out (all lies of course) with a letter signed by them both, insisting that a certain dragon should not be allowed to see or interact with the youngling that was now in their charge. Both parents knew that the documentation was of the utmost importance and could never be altered, changed, infringed or ignored. The female dragon, just a girl really, processed everything quickly and efficiently, keen to get back to her brutally disturbed sleep by the look of things.

And so it was done. Of course there was much sobbing by both, but they took comfort from the fact that they were indeed nearby, vertically, rather than horizontally.

Time passed as it had before, with both Earth and her husband once again becoming more and more social, frequenting bars and events with the regularity that they once had, and although they thought about the egg often, the pain of the separation started to fade over time.

What neither knew, and only fate could conceive, was that a chance encounter late at night in one of their favourite pubs had led to them being discovered. It took a while, because few in the dragon domain now knew of their existence, with the cases against them, and whoever helped them escape custody, having long since been forgotten. But one or two in high up places continued the search, despite all this. And they were now well and truly on their radar.

31 NIGHT AT THE MUSEUM

It had been a doddle to disable the alarm system... child's play for a dragon as experienced as he was.

Slipping through the door, making sure to close it quietly behind him, he scrolled through the various visions available to him, eventually settling on infra red. Suddenly the main hall, which had been shrouded in darkness, became bright, alive, visible. With all the skills of a ninja, he padded silently around the different displays, making sure to stay in the blind spot of the security cameras. Much as he found the exhibits fascinating, now wasn't really the time for his curiosity to come out and play. Having always wanted to visit, he'd never imagined it would be under these circumstances.

His internet search about this place had gleaned much information, but not whereabouts in the museum the metal he was searching for was kept. So he had to do it the old fashioned way, and work his way through all the presentations.

Booked into a local guest house in the guise of a visiting wildlife photographer, he'd used a name other than his own, and his employer, the master mantra maker, had helped him forge a new driving licence and credit cards. Given his love of everything to do with nature, it hadn't been much of a challenge to pull off the new persona. Making a fuss of his DSLR Canon EOS 700D camera, with its variety of lenses and all the additional equipment that went with it, was more than enough to convince the guest house owners, along with all the staff. Normally he only ever used the camera to capture rugby pictures, be it from one of the other teams playing at the sports club, or some action or other from one of his coaching courses. Over the last few years, he'd developed a keen interest in photography and could often be found chained to his computer, manipulating some of the images he'd captured with various forms of software, late into the night. All this had helped him with his cunning cover.

Crawling beneath a display case of ancient coins, Tank hoped he was getting close in narrowing down the search. It had been more than fifteen minutes now since he'd first entered but it felt more like fifteen hours. Both his body and mind screamed at him to leave, get out, go. Every atom of him knew that it was wrong being here like this, but he just had to get his hands on that metal, so many lives depended on it. For him, it was the key to everything.

Sneaking past the end of a flint weapon display, he rolled across the open space in front of him with more agility than most would have given him credit for, especially just by looking at him. Coming up in front of a tall, singular exhibit, a smile stretched across his face as he realised he'd found the treasure he'd been searching for. Quickly he checked out the case the metal was contained in. It looked as though it was hooked up to a separate alarm, something he knew would only take him a few seconds to defeat. Abruptly a loud CRASH of something heavy falling from somewhere further down the hall echoed back up towards him.

'Someone or something else is here,' he thought. Oddly he'd felt all night like he was being watched, but try as he might he could find nothing to prove his gut feeling, up until now that is. He needed the metal inside the case, and he needed it NOW! On planning his illicit visit, he'd been determined not to leave a trace of having been there and especially not do any damage to the much cherished museum. But things had changed now and he needed to get his hands on that metal and scarper. This was not the time for niceties, particularly given that he had no idea who, or what, he was facing. Reluctantly, he slammed his large gloved fist through the plate glass of the display case, causing alarms to blare and the lights to flicker on. Grabbing the long, warped bar of metal, he pulled it out. As he did so, waves of intense emotion assaulted his very being, threatening to overwhelm him. Struggling to stay standing, continually fighting against dropping the valuable prize he had gone through all this for, out of the corner of his eye he glimpsed three bulky shapes much further up the main hall, all heading straight for him now that the lights had come on. Gripping the metal for all he was worth, instinctively he conjured up a mantra that filled the air with a high pitched whine.

'Darkness, at the moment,' he thought, 'is my friend and I want it back.'

Out of nowhere there was a large POP, followed by another, and then another as the bulbs in all the lights started exploding, one by one, the tinkling of glass drifting to the floor echoing across the vastness of the building, as darkness once again consumed it. Having made a mental note of where each attacker was before the lights went out, Tank decided on a course of action. Whether it would succeed or not was entirely dependent on whether or not they were dragons. If they were, he was already doomed. As the last vestige of light disappeared and full on darkness took hold, Tank sprinted, not away from his attackers, but across their path towards him. Careful to put as little weight as he could in his steps and with his infra red vision restored, he leapt for all he was worth towards a display case full of ancient skulls and bones. Part of him was dismayed that he would momentarily be landing on top of it, while the rest of him focused on what he had to do. For a brief moment he was surrounded, one attacker to his left closing in on his previous position, two to his right, backing up their friend. Casting all thoughts aside, he landed on the exhibit with cat-like-grace and, bending his knees, pushed off for all he was worth, sailing high over the head of one of his attackers, landing half way up the stairs that led to the first floor displays. Glancing over his shoulder, he was glad to see the three of them still searching around the tall, singular display. Quietly, he belted the rest of the way up the stairs, searching for anything that looked vaguely like an exit. Laid out in much the same way as the ground floor, with row upon row of glass display cases and the odd standalone exhibit, there was one noticeable difference: glass for walls, providing a stunning view off in the distance of the, by now, sleeping village. Darting down the length of the displays, Tank hoped for a fire exit or some other means of escape. But he was out of luck. There wasn't one, at least... not yet. It looked as though some building work was about to take place in a cordoned off area right at the end. In a few weeks' time no doubt, there would be what he was looking for, but right now he was aware that time had just about run out, not only because he'd picked up on the three strangers' distant whispers, but also because the police or someone else must surely be on their way, responding to the alarm he'd set off. Shaking off that muzzy feeling from his head, trying hard to push away all the negativity flowing through him from the metal, as that's what it felt like, he knew there was only one course of action and it broke his heart on realising that he'd have to do it. Behind him, footsteps came rushing up the stairs.

'Damn,' he thought, taking two steps back. With seemingly no other option, he sprinted forwards, crossing his arms in front of his face as he hit the glass, reinforcing his very being with the same mantra he'd used in THAT rugby match. A huge SMASH of epic proportions, followed by the sound of rushing air washing over him, startled him momentarily. He'd known when he jumped that he'd have no time to revert back to his natural form, not that it had ever really been an option. Even at this time of night, there would have been too many people about to take the risk. With the ground rushing up at him fast, he wondered what kind of damage he'd incur if he weren't a dragon. A long stay in hospital was all that he could come up with as he bent his knees, preparing for impact. Even with the mantra it hurt, as he carried his momentum forward into a roll, choosing his left shoulder to take the brunt of the collision. Stumbling to his feet, he looked back up at the hole he'd made in the glass above, just able to make out two gruff faces looking back out at him. It was time to leave, and so he sprinted across the road leading up the hill to the museum, cut between two giant trees, hurdled a barbed wire fence into a farmer's field, all in the pitch black, thanks to his infra red vision. Halfway across the field he threw himself to the ground, the soft squelch of something big and runny thumping against his stomach.

'Oh great,' he thought, catching the smell of what it was. Turning his head towards the road that ran parallel to the field, he could just make out two officers in a police car speeding up the road, the blue flashing lights casting an eerie reflection out across the field. As soon as the car had passed he took off as fast as he could, the cow pat running like a river down his front. He ignored it.

Ten minutes later he was back in the village, lurking in the shadows, having run all the way. During his run back, he'd made up his mind to leave. First though, he wanted his stuff back. Luckily his room on the first floor had a balcony, the very reason he'd chosen this particular guest house. That was how he'd slipped out unnoticed earlier. Sneaking up the driveway, around the side of the building and into the garden, he tucked the precious metal behind the drain pipe's base before shinning up it to the balcony. Quickly and quietly he gathered up his things, unlocked the door to his room and then headed back towards the balcony, not before leaving sixty pounds in crisp twenty pound notes on the dresser. Leaping back down onto the lush grass in one clean go, he retrieved the metal and headed for the nearest entrance to the dragon domain, a wishing well at the back of a magnificent stately home, only a short walk away.

With the metal tucked away in his giant backpack and his camera dangling around his thick neck, he watched rock face after rock face whizz by from the comfort of the monorail carriage he was in. Able to take a breath now, something he didn't seem to have done since he'd left the museum, sadness ran through him at having caused so much damage. Racking his brain to think of a way to make it up to them, the only option he could come up with was an anonymous donation. Vowing to do just that later on in the week, he wondered if the strange piece of metal would unlock the clues to the puzzle they were trying to solve. With all his heart he hoped so.

32 STASH CRASHED

Russian dragons had been squirreling it away for some time now. Previously it had been stored secretly beneath the Kremlin, but an order had come in out of the blue to move it to a new location. Strange really, but fortuitous at the same time. If that much laminium had been in the Kremlin when the bomb there had gone off, there would have been nothing left of Moscow or the surrounding countryside for at least thirty miles in every direction. It would have made Nagasaki look like a drop in the ocean.

Currently the valuable stash of the incredibly rare and impossibly hard to extract metal which the Russians had built up over a number of decades, was on its way to its fourth safe storage facility in the same number of weeks. Disguised as a beat up old ambulance well past its best, the inside was state of the art, temperature controlled, lead lined, all surrounded by a carbon fibre/titanium mono filament wall which was impossible to break into without the handheld computer tablet (one of a kind) to access the security lock. In all... very well protected indeed. Unfortunately, not everyone was aware of this.

They'd had their instructions, only a few hours earlier as it happened, and were aware of the danger, but there was nothing they wouldn't do for their king. Told it wouldn't be long now before he was back, and they could exact their revenge, they would, as a race, of that there could be no doubt. So they powered on down the hill on the perfectly straight, snow covered road, heading for the all important intersection.

"Take it easy," observed Vlass, gazing across at the speedometer from the passenger side of the cab.

"Easy for you to say," replied Slodge from the driver's seat. "It wasn't me that forgot to warm the engine up, which incidentally has now led to us being a tad behind schedule."

"Alright, alright. You know what I mean. And you know full well that some of that snow on the road is ice. All it takes is one slip and..." he let his words trail off. They both knew what he meant. One way or another, they would be dead. Worse still, they would have put their monarch's life in jeopardy as well.

Easing his foot off the accelerator just a touch, Slodge kept his eyes glued to the road in front of him out of the windscreen. Perspiration poured from every part of him, ironic really given that they were in one of the coldest parts of Russia, which even in the summer was still much colder than most countries' harshest winters.

Five miles later, they crested the brow of the biggest hill they'd seen so far. With the dazzling sunlight cutting through the bright blue sky like a knife through butter, shining straight into their cab, the two of them could just make out a small town in the distance. Old and decrepit buildings, most wooden, some brick, lay strewn about in an awkward pattern. The centre seemed to be built around the intersection of the road they were on and another thick set trunk route. A bar, a café and a convenience store all merged together in this confined space. Off to one side, a building of some sort had recently been demolished. On the ground where it had once been, there now stood a mobile crane, a huge yellow beast, metal feet deployed either side of it, with two thick built men encased in its glass cabin, one talking urgently on a phone, the other wielding the various controls. One or two locals scuttled along the main street, most sensibly staying inside.

"There it is," announced Vlass.

Slodge gazed across to his left. There in the distance, trundling down the hill to their west, was the beat up old ambulance, their target, their mission. Slodge applied the brakes. They locked, forcing the massive truck into a slide. Lifting his foot, he then applied pressure again, this time with a little less force. The truck started to slow. Vlass exhaled a sigh of relief.

Heading down the hill into the next dreary town, the driver looked on, trying to stay focused. It looked identical to the last one, and the one before that, and the one before that. Monotony was by far the worst part of this job. It was only really the pay that made it bearable, he thought, chomping down on a bar of sickly milk chocolate that one of his friends had bought him back from a regular trip to Austria. Slowing down a little more, he took in everything in front of him, after all, he was a careful driver. The gentle slope led into town; traffic was coming from either side approaching the intersection ahead. Knowing it didn't matter too much as he had right of way, and any traffic (he could see a huge truck approaching from his right) would have to stop and give way to him, he continued on, chomping on his chocolate, fiddling with the radio, trying to pick up anything remotely listenable.

Slodge slowed down even more, trying hard to gauge things just right, knowing that he had to give the impression that he was going to stop and give the ambulance the chance to escape.

Stuffing the last of the chocolate into his mouth all in one go, his eyes caught sight of the café. It occurred to him that he hadn't had a hot meal in over two days, and that perhaps now was a good time to stop. But he'd had orders, ones that he was pretty sure he should obey to the letter if he wanted to see any of that well earned pay he was so looking forward to spending. In an instant, he decided against stopping. It was a shame, he really should have done. It might have saved his life. That thought of food, in that instant, was enough to distract him, just momentarily. A second earlier and he might have been able to brake in time to avoid the truck. As it was, he was too late.

Instantly he slammed on the brakes, which under normal circumstances would have been fine. But the brakes locked up, sending him into the mother of all uncontrollable skids. All he could do was look on.

'He's speeding up,' was the first thing that ran through the ambulance driver's head, the second being the truck itself.

The impact was stomach churning, no matter where you were. In the ambulance, in the truck, walking along the street, or inside one of the businesses, it was horrific. Instantly, the driver of the ambulance died. Vlass and Slodge, despite being heavily strapped in, had significant injuries, not that they really mattered. It would be relatively easy for them to recover after the incident and just slip off into obscurity.

With the wreckage of the two vehicles scattered across the intersection, smoke poured from radiators and engines as bizarre things started to happen. Out from between a set of ramshackle old buildings, a brand new low loader appeared, turning up on the highway away from the intersection at first, before reversing back towards it. From in and around some of the other buildings, masked men approached, wading into the wreckage, not bothering to check on casualties, only interested in the back of the ambulance. The bright yellow crane thrummed into action, its operator swinging the extended arm right round until it lay directly above the shattered ambulance. Immediately the masked men got to work, securing the back of the ambulance to the crane's giant arm. Ninety seconds later it was done. One of the men indicated it was ready to go, so the crane operator raised the huge arm, pulling the undamaged back half of the ambulance free from the gushing black smoke of the two vehicles, carefully swinging his load around in a tight semi circle, letting it hover directly over the back of the perfectly positioned low loader. Meanwhile, the masked men made their way to either side of the truck's cab. Vloss and Slodge were relieved to see them. They'd had some idea of what would happen, but needless to say, hadn't been filled in on all the details. They knew getting away wouldn't be a problem, but just needed a little bit of time to apply the perfect spells and heal before fleeing. Knowing it was best not to struggle in the wreckage that they found themselves trapped in, they both thought it was great that their cohorts were about to free them from the smoke choked cab, and give them the opportunity that they needed. Two of the masked men ripped the driver's door off the cab, leaving it dangling precariously, attached only at the bottom. Slodge smiled, trying to indicate that his leg had been ensnared in the wreckage. To his utter amazement, both masked men whipped out silenced guns from behind their backs and poured half a dozen shots into each of the nagas disguised as humans. Casually, they walked back to the low loader, which had now been joined by a nondescript four by four.

Carefully, the crane operator lowered its load onto the base of the vehicle. He must have been good at his job, because it barely made a sound. All but one of the masked men began to release the load from the crane and started strapping the still burning cargo to the low loader. Making sure to douse the bodies of the two dead nagas, the remaining masked man finished pouring petrol into the cab of the truck. One or two pedestrians looked on, with most having ducked back inside either the bar or the café.

Inside the crane, the man with the phone shot the crane operator and retrieved the vast sum of cash that he'd passed him some time before, then proceeded to place a small explosive device, set on a five minute timer, in the footwell, before taking his place in the four by four. With a rumble, the low loader's engines roared to life, putrid black smoke coughing out of its engine. The last masked man tossed an identical explosive device into the cab containing the two dead nagas, before sprinting off towards the by now moving four by four. Catching up just in time, he leapt majestically into the open back door, swinging inside and closing the door behind him, all in one slick move. Overtaking the low loader, the four by four led the way east up the hill, the route the ambulance would have taken had it continued straight on its journey. Five minutes later, two massive explosions ripped through the town, peppering the main street with shrapnel and throwing two towering plumes of thick black smoke far up into the atmosphere. Onlookers and customers all had the sense to retreat to their houses, something that saved their lives. For the most part their town had gone, along with a very large supply of LAMINIUM!

33 TABLES TURNED

It was getting to him and he was rattled. It was more than he could take. For some time he'd suspected that he was being followed, but the last few days had confirmed it. Racking his brains as to why anyone would want to follow him, he'd had precious little sleep over the last few nights worrying about it. In the end, he could come up with only one answer. THE DAGGER! Aviva's dagger... it had to be! How anyone could possibly have found out about it, he had no idea. As far as he knew, only he, Richie and the king himself knew about it. Richie really didn't count, because having had her memory wiped, she would of course remember absolutely nothing. And he couldn't believe for one minute that the king had revealed its existence to anyone. It was a mystery, but it was also the only logical answer as to why anyone would be tailing him. So in his mind there seemed to be only one solution and he was about to do exactly what the king had expressly told him not to do. But he couldn't think of any other way, or of anywhere safer for the dagger to be.

So here he was, skulking down Camelot Arcade, with the very valuable object wrapped in an old cloth taped to the small of his back. With all his might, he tried to act normally, to be casually going about his business, but if the profusion with which he was sweating was anything to go by, he was having little, if any, success.

Turning the door handle, he slipped inside, but not before scanning the street behind him. It was deserted. He expected nothing less. Letting out a huge sigh, not aware up until then that he'd been holding his breath, he marched off towards the front counter, weaving in and out of the bookshelves and aisles. Every time he visited, he would swear the aisles and shelves were in different places... not by very much, but he was convinced that was the case. He'd quizzed the shopkeeper about just that at least twice who on both occasions had very seriously told him that he was talking rubbish. But the more Peter thought about it as he headed into yet another dead end, the more he was sure he was right. After doubling back for the second time, eventually he caught sight of the counter. Walking swiftly towards it, he purposely stamped his feet, trying hard to make his presence known, not wanting to startle the old dragon.

"Good day, youngster," whispered a silky smooth voice directly in Peter's left ear.

So shocked was he, that he nearly lost his footing. The old dragon hadn't made a sound before he'd spoken, of that he was sure.

"Hi," he replied, visibly shaken.

"Sorry if I surprised you little one. It wasn't my intention."

"It's okay."

"Why don't you come through to the workshop. I'm pretty sure that's where my app... Tank, is."

And with that the master mantra maker stalked off through the raised slab of the front desk, towards the workshop. Peter followed, mouth open, his tongue hanging out. As they walked, or more like plodded in Gee Tee's case, Peter noticed the weirdest thing. The old dragon didn't make a sound. Not his footsteps, his wings brushing against the counter as he passed, or even opening the glass encased door to the workshop. It was all done in total silence. AMAZING!

On entering the workshop, a thickset head with hair cut short appeared from beneath one of the desks.

"Well?" it said. "Did it work?"

"Let's see what your young friend thinks."

"PETER!" yelled Tank, banging his head sharply as he jumped up.

Both friends took a step back after embracing briefly.

"What are you doing here?" asked Tank excitedly.

"I have a favour to ask," answered the young hockey

playing dragon.

"What... AGAIN?" exclaimed Gee Tee, just teasing.

Peter nodded. And then something occurred to him.

"What was it you wanted to know whether it worked?"

"Well," said Tank, "the big Kahuna here has been testing out an old stealth mantra that we found buried away in the loft."

"Ahhhhh," exclaimed Peter. "That's why he made no noise walking into the workshop and how he was able to sneak up on me in the store."

Tank nodded, all the time a big Cheshire cat grin spread out across his face.

"What did you think?" the master mantra maker enquired.

"It certainly seemed to do the trick, but it was incredibly spooky to watch you walk and know that you're there, right in front of me, but not able to hear you at all. Just really weird. Like those fully electric cars above ground that make no noise at all. I mean, you can see them moving, but in total silence. It's just wrong on so many levels. At some point they're going to have to add some kind of noise to them so that pedestrians know they're coming."

"A resounding success," exclaimed the old shopkeeper sarcastically. Tank gave him a look.

"Come on, let's all sit down," suggested the giant rugby player. Gee Tee didn't need to be told again, and quickly slouched into one of the oversized chairs. Tank followed. Peter remained standing, fiddling about with something behind his back.

"You alright Pete?" Tank asked.

Nodding before pulling out from behind his back the reason he was here, wrapped in a dirty old cloth, he then proceeded to sit down, the object placed firmly in his lap. Sitting comfortably, he began.

"As you know," he said, nodding in Tank's direction, "for some time now, I've been convinced I'm being followed. Over the last few days, I think I can safely say that I have been. With this in mind, the only reason I can think that anyone would want to follow me, is because of this," he said, holding up the object wrapped in the dirty old cloth. "I was rather hoping that you could put it somewhere safe for me," he uttered, looking directly at the old shopkeeper.

"We don't really have anywhere secure I'm afraid Pete. I mean the shop itself is protected, don't get me wrong, but if the item that you're holding is that valuable, then maybe you should think about a bank vault or something like that. Everything you can see here is just scattered about. I doubt the defences would do much to deter serious dragons from gaining entry," offered Tank.

Silence wrapped them all up for the next few seconds, with Peter wondering what would happen next, and just whether or not he'd just dropped the old shopkeeper right in it.

"What is it that's so important you'd come here?" Gee Tee asked, a tiny glint in his eye.

Peter found himself thinking of the king's words. They cut right through him. But still, he carried on.

"It would take an awful long time to explain the exact story behind it, most of which I don't know anyway. But suffice to say, Fredric, my grandfather, left me this a very long time ago. It only came to light recently when the king, who'd been keeping a whole trunk full of stuff safe for me, delivered the trunk and its contents safely into my hands. I think when you see it, you'll know what it is and recognise not only its beauty, but its value as well."

Carefully, Peter unwound the cloth, his other hand taking all the weight of the object. Instantly the old shopkeeper scooted forward in his chair, which had tiny little wheels on it, much like a human office chair. Not wanting to be left out, Tank did the same. Gathered as close as they could, almost looking over the object, Peter pulled away the last part of the cloth, like a magician on his big finale, and waited.

Simultaneously Tank and Gee Tee gasped. The atmosphere in the room was electric.

"It can't be. It just can't be!" declared the old shopkeeper.

Tank simply stared, his eyes wider than Peter would have thought possible. In one swift move, the master mantra maker held out his hands. Again, Peter thought about the king's words. But he could think of no other alternative, and gently placed the dagger in the old shopkeeper's palm. Turning the dagger over and over in his hands, the shop owner was transfixed by the light reflecting off the perfectly cut jewels.

"Of all the things..." whispered the old dragon. "I've spent my entire life seeking out that which is rare in the extreme. I've seen, and possess, some of the most amazing artefacts and relics ever to reside on this wondrous planet. This however," he said, letting out a breath, "must be considered right up there with the best of them. I assume it is what Tank and I think it is?"

"Aviva's dagger," answered Peter, nodding.

Both shop workers shook their heads, flabbergasted. After a long silence, Tank finally cut in.

"How long have you had it?"

"The king gave me the contents of the trunk on the day we visited his private residence, when we first met Flash, and Gee Tee saved his life."

Tank had a faraway look in his eyes. That day was of great significance to him, and not just because of meeting the ex-Crimson Guard for the first time. It was the day he'd stood up to his boss, the day he'd had his say. And things hadn't been the same since. Feeling a sense of freedom, of mutual respect, of cooperation, things had changed a great deal for the better since that day.

"It doesn't feel as powerful as I would have expected," declared the master mantra maker, weaving the blade through the air. "Somehow I thought I'd be overwhelmed by the sheer force of its power."

Not sure whether the old shopkeeper was just fishing, or actually knew, Peter decided to 'fess up anyway.

"It has a mantra designed to contain its power cast on it, currently."

"Indeed," sighed Gee Tee knowingly.

"And yet I can still feel it," observed Tank.

"Whispering, calling," added Peter.

"Yeah," replied Tank, nodding in agreement. "It feels charming, seductive somehow, almost as if it wants me to... UNLEASH IT!"

On seeing its effect on his friend, the master mantra maker handed the dagger back to Peter, who for the most part seemed unaffected by its very nature, whether due to prolonged exposure, or something in his underlying dragon make up.

"Would you not be better asking the king to look after it for you? I'm sure he has access to some amazing security facilities, much better than anything we have here," remarked Tank, slightly more clearheaded now Peter had the weapon.

Before Peter could answer, the shopkeeper butted in.

"There's something you need to know, app... Tank. Something I've been keeping from you, and something that your young friend here knows."

"Peruvian mantra ink all over again!" quipped Tank, cuttingly.

"I've been meaning to explain... honest! It's just with everything going on around here, and with the urgency with which we've been working lately, it's totally slipped my mind."

"Come on then... out with it!"

Gee Tee and Peter shared a quick look.

"There's a hidden vault beneath the shop."

Tank eyed both of them suspiciously.

"I know every square inch of this shop, as well as all the mantras used in its containment, protection and structural reinforcement. There's not one single part I don't know, and I would know if there were some kind of vault anywhere in its vicinity."

Turning his prehistoric head in Peter's direction, the master mantra maker urged him on.

"There is Tank, I've seen it."

Tank eyed his friend with a mixture of suspicion and disbelief.

"I would know Peter," he said with determined conviction.

"It has the most wonderful things in it," continued the hockey playing dragon. "Legendary things that just can't be possible. But they are. Merlin's staff, Robin Hood's bow, Billy the Kid's pistols, it's just out of this world. And there are other weapons too. Magical knives, fantastic swords, foils, rifles... you name it, it's there! That's not to mention all the amulets, rings and charms. Wall to wall shelves full of spell books, tomes, scrolls and one off mantras. Piles of armour higher than I am tall, full to the brim with shiny chest pieces, helms, bracers, boots... it's all there."

At first Tank had been more than a little sceptical, but Peter's enthusiasm and detail were more than enough to convince him of the vault's existence. Silently he cursed himself for not realising it had been there all along. Over the course of his employment he thought he'd mapped out the whole shop and its surroundings so carefully, but in essence all he'd really done was fail. Part of him felt embarrassed, ashamed. He tried to push it to one side.

"So just why is it so secure?" asked the young rugby player, determined to find out more.

"Ohhhh... you just have to see it. There are all these security measures, Mongolian death worms, self replicating tunnels, freezing water, gravity anomalies and deadly flying seeds. It's all there. There's no way anyone who didn't know what to do, could gain access. It's just impossible!"

"Whoa, whoa, hold your horses child," interrupted the old shopkeeper. "The vault's good... in fact, better than good. But to say it's impenetrable is very dangerous indeed. There's no doubt it's one of the best around, but nothing, I repeat nothing, is impenetrable."

Peter felt suitably chastised, while his friend felt... curious. He wanted to see it now, had to in fact. Recognising the look on his former apprentice's face, the old shopkeeper could hardly blame him for it. Tank found himself harbouring a slight resentment for not having been told about the vault in the first place, as well as a burning curiosity to find out more.

"Are you sure, young Peter, that you really want to place that very special piece of history in my vault? You are of course very welcome to do so, but know that you would be the only other person to have anything in there. Everything else belongs to me. And understand this. As I've just said, nothing, I repeat nothing, is impenetrable. The safeguards as you've seen are beyond belief, and I judge them to be possibly the best in the kingdom. But that's not to say they can't be defeated. I want you to understand the risks. This is a very special dagger, and in the wrong hands could no doubt change the course of history."

For his part, Peter thought hard about whether this was indeed the right thing to do. Sensing it was, not just because he couldn't think of anywhere safer, but there was something else, a kind of gut feeling, something he rarely got, but whenever he did, following it usually turned out to be the right thing to do.

"If it's okay, I would very much like to store the dagger in your vault."

Gee Tee nodded an acknowledgement, small sizzling slivers of flame licking the outside of his nostrils as he did so.

"Very well," announced the shopkeeper. "Why don't you take Tank and go and put the blade in the vault? I would place it on the empty rock plinth, that way it will benefit from a little extra protection."

Wondering briefly about the 'extra' protection mentioned, Peter had little chance to dwell on it as Tank bounded up to him, unable to remember the last time he'd seen his friend this excited. And then it all came back to him. How dangerous traversing the vault was, how many close encounters they'd had, and that was with the master mantra maker there. Surely he should come along?

Sensing Peter's reticence, almost as if reading his mind, the old shopkeeper spoke up.

"You'll be alright; I've cast the mantras on both of you. Take your time, go slowly and remember each and every detail from your last trip. Everything will be okay. Don't forget to take some of the spiders with you."

Nodding, ill at ease, and with Tank like an excitable puppy beside him, Peter wrapped up the dagger before signalling for his friend to follow him, which he duly did. Leading them both down the dusty dead end of oak bookshelves, towering high, almost out of sight, Tank's first thought was that there must be some kind of mistake, but as he stood behind his friend, watching him move the web encrusted tomes this way and that, he marvelled at the ingenuity of it all.

'So simple, and yet so utterly complex,' he thought.

Slipping what he thought was the last one into place, Peter took a step back as a loud hiss of escaping air whistled past his ears and the tiniest of clicks set in motion the circular bookcases splitting in two, revealing a shiny metal pole. Smiling at what was to come next, he had to contain his laughter.

'If nothing else, I'm going to have some fun with Tank,' he thought, turning to face him.

"Remember, don't touch anything, and always do as I do."

With that he turned, took a running leap at the pole, which he managed to grab first time, and shouted "GERONIMO!" at the top of his voice, as he slid into the darkness.

Tank didn't know what awaited him in the black void, but had already committed himself to finding out.

'Oh well,' he thought, 'here goes nothing,' and with that followed his friend's example, right down to the "GERONIMO!"

Across the world phones rang, emails arrived, text messages were received. Innocuous looking for the most part, but in reality, far from it. All the communications had one thing in common. Three words were used in each. *Rare, requisition* and *relinquish.* Innocent enough you might think, but not if the recipients were waiting for those very three words. In this case... THEY WERE! Nagas across the globe, most disguised as humans, some as dragons, were all being made aware that something was imminent. Something was coming, a storm of change. All were now on alert, ready to act at a moment's notice.

34 SUB-MISSION

A few hours ago, that's when the partying had finished. Clearing up the beautiful little town would begin early in the morning. But now, for the most part, Swanage slept on a warm summer's night.

The bay was the surface of a pizza, the boats and yachts the mouth watering toppings. All aboard had stayed up long into the night. All now slept.

Only a few hundred yards beyond the bay, in the much deeper water, a dark shape silently broke the almost mill pond still surface, creating barely a ripple. By now, the epic submarine's powerful engines were resting, the state of the art craft anchored to the seabed in what would be regarded as quite a minimal amount of water. Noiselessly, hatches opened aboard the dark metallic sea monster. Eclectic shadows scuttled to and fro. A small dinghy with an advanced electric motor appeared from somewhere. Carefully, it was lowered into the sea. More dark shapes, some moving faster than others, transferred aboard the smaller vessel. Its complement complete, it sped off towards the bay, heading directly for the town itself, the gigantic sea monster that had spat it out swallowed up once again by the ocean.

Cautiously, giving the vessels in the bay as wide a berth as possible, the dinghy found its way to the tiny slipway in the very centre of town, adjacent to huge three storey guest houses and fabulous fish and chip shops.

Two nagas in their peculiar human forms were first to step off the boat, followed quickly by Manson, leaving the female sitting next to the old dragon Troydenn. Strolling purposefully up the slippery, cobbled slope, Manson's head darted this way and that, constantly on the lookout for danger. From out of the arched doorway of the nearest guest house, a figure emerged and tentatively made its way forward, past the bins overflowing with fish and chip wrappings and around the plump seagulls, still squabbling over the remnants of what had previously been someone's meal. Both nagas tensed, ready to spring. Before they had a chance, the low light provided reassurance that the figure was a familiar one. Manson clasped the figure's hand tightly.

"Rosebloom!" he whispered, aware that the windows of the surrounding houses and flats were all open wide on this hot summer's night.

The traitorous councillor, currently in his human form, still sporting a ridiculously long pony tail, grasped his co-conspirator's hand.

"Good to see you," he replied quietly. "There's nobody about. We have people keeping watch. We've secured one of the entrances, here and down below. and are ready to go."

Manson nodded.

"Great work," he uttered softly.

"Your father would be very proud," commented another voice from behind them, much too loud for Manson's liking.

"Thank you," ventured Rosebloom. "It's my honour, like it was my father's, to help and serve."

Manson turned to face his serious looking father.

"We need to be quiet," he hissed, pointing up to some of the open windows around them all, "and we need to move swiftly and silently." The ancient dragon's face took on a look of thunder at being told what to do, but at least he had the common sense not to pick a fight in response, not here anyway. No doubt that would be something to look forward to later.

With the woman joining them, Rosebloom led them past the fish and chip shops, across the main road, up a steep, narrow road, into a rundown ground floor flat. Off in the distance, the delicate sound of the dinghy's electric motor faded into nothing. A disguised being in human form held open the front door while they all filed past.

Following Rosebloom through a deserted kitchen into a crowded open plan living room, a disjointed group of beings all rose to their feet as the submarine cohorts arrived. Quick, impromptu introductions were made by Rosebloom, something that Manson and Troydenn both seemed unimpressed with.

"Who's that?" exclaimed Troydenn, pointing at a seemingly middle aged human lying on the floor off to one side, his throat cut.

"The current occupant of the flat," answered the traitorous councillor nonchalantly. "I thought I'd secured his cooperation, but he had second thoughts at the last minute... something I'm assuming he's rather regretting at this very moment."

Manson stormed right up into Rosebloom's face.

"YOU ASSURED US IT HAD ALL BEEN PLANNED TO PERFECTION," he growled.

"I... I... I... I... It has been," stammered the, by now, very nervous Councillor.

"If this is your idea of 'planned to perfection', it makes me wonder what else there is that can go wrong," raged Manson. "WE CAN'T AFFORD ANY SLIP UPS!"

"The... the... there... wo... wo... won't be. It's all sorted."

"Hmmmmmphf!" snorted Manson.

"I'm sure our good councillor here has everything under control," remarked Troydenn softly, patting Rosebloom gently on the shoulder. "In that, I don't doubt he's just like his father. And I'm particularly sure he hasn't forgotten what those misbegotten, lying, cheating, thieving dragons did to his dear father, after all."

"I most certainly haven't," fumed the treacherous councillor, simmering with anger.

"Good," replied Troydenn, "because it's almost time for payback... for us all!"

Manson looked on like a pent up raging bull. Timidly nodding, whilst still shaking, Rosebloom ordered the guards to pull back the dark green sofa that smelt deeply of cigarette smoke, to reveal a set of wooden steps disappearing off into the dark, rectangular hole.

"And this is your idea of easy, is it?" sneered Manson, wondering how on earth they were going to get Troydenn all the way into the dragon domain down a stairwell.

"It's only four flights," responded the quivering councillor, "and then there's a freight elevator we can use. The previous incumbent used it to transfer fresh fish into the domain. The elevator can easily take us all."

"I hope so for your sake!" spat Manson, stomping off down the steps into the darkness.

"Don't worry about him," reassured Troydenn, all the time watched by the woman. "He's just keen to get on with the next phase. As soon as we start that, he'll be much better tempered."

The woman and the councillor both very much doubted that.

35 REUNITED

Having reported in, he'd been told to get some rest. Although that sounded nice, it wasn't what he needed, particularly since he'd been away for so long. There was something more important, more primal, that required his time. So hoping for a little luck, he'd set out... and a short monorail hop and a quick walk led him to Camelot Arcade. Striding boldly forward towards the Mantra Emporium, something familiar begged for his attention. Stopping right in the middle of the deserted walkway, he screwed up his face, trying to seek out just what was wrong. Extending his senses, he searched further, deeper. But he could find nothing, no beings, no mantras... NOTHING! But his feeling of unease was off the scale bad. Looking around, he switched through his different visions, still having no luck. About to give up when it hit him, like one of Tank's brutal rugby tackles... that smell! It was the same smell he'd experienced when tracking across America, the same smell that haunted his Antarctic dreams... NAGAS! And they'd been here, recently. Sprinting the rest of the way, he darted through the door, ready for any eventuality.

He was in luck, and needn't have worried.

"FLASH!" shouted Peter and Tank simultaneously from the front of the shop, on seeing their friend.

Concerned about his findings outside, Flash strode across the shop floor to greet his friends.

"Hi guys," he said casually.

From out of nowhere, a huge scaled beast rose up, off to one side.

"Little one," exclaimed Gee Tee. "It's so good to see you. How have you been?"

Flash smiled for what seemed like the first time in ages. How anyone could refer to him as 'little one' was quite beyond him, but it always felt just right when the old shopkeeper did. Anyone else might be offered an insight into his rarely seen temper, but not the master mantra maker.

"Busy," replied Flash. "How are things here?" he asked, all innocent.

"Just about the same as when you left," replied the old dragon. "Why don't we adjourn to the workshop, and we'll tell you all about it."

"Sounds great," quipped Flash, being squeezed in a great big hug by Tank and Peter as he headed towards the shop counter.

"Peter and I will get some hot charcoal on the go, unless of course you want something a bit... STRONGER!" suggested Tank to his boss.

Not entirely sure about the amount of sarcasm that laced his words, the master mantra maker narrowed his eyes in the direction of his former apprentice, before replying.

"Hot charcoal will be great." With that, he led Flash on through to the workshop.

Peter followed Tank through to the small, well, not quite a kitchen, more like a cupboard, to help make the dragon's favourite drink. Flash and Gee Tee both flopped down into a couple of oversized chairs. Before Flash had a chance to say anything, the old shopkeeper came out with it.

"Something's bothering you. What is it?"

"What makes you think that?" replied the ex-Crimson Guard.

"Because when you came flying in, you were in combat mode... ready to fight. Am I wrong?"

Flash swallowed, annoyed at being caught out, supposing he shouldn't have been, because there was so much more to the old dragon than any of them knew, that was for sure. The more he hung around him, the more that always seemed to be the case. Looking around to make sure Tank and Peter were still out of the way, he leaned forward, his chair scooting closer to the master mantra maker as he did so.

"You're not wrong. When I was outside, I sensed something, something unusual, something I've sensed before, and something that I've been hunting in North America."

"Over the past couple of weeks, something odd's been going on. I'm not sure what exactly, but I do know the shields protecting this place have been tested on a number of occasions, mainly late at night it would seem. At first I thought it might be dragonlings up to some mischief, but the more it's happened, the more I'm convinced that it's something else. I've tried to set traps for whoever's doing it, but much to my surprise they've managed to circumvent them. Whoever it is, they're good, I'll give them that."

Flash nodded, scratching his stubbly chin in thought.

"I think perhaps you should let me take a look at those shields and see if there's anything I can do to reinforce them. At the very least I can check to see if there are any weak points."

"That would be much appreciated. Thank you."

"And just why do the shields need checking?" asked Tank from the doorway, where he stood with Peter, both holding gigantic mugs of steaming hot charcoal.

Gee Tee and Flash looked guiltier than children sneaking a peek at their Christmas presents.

"Perhaps you'd better come and sit down," suggested the old dragon.

They did so, doling out the drinks on the way. Gee Tee then explained what had been going on, with Flash offering up his thoughts on things. When they'd finished, and before Tank could chastise the master mantra maker for not telling him before now, Peter cut in.

"There's something else you should know, something that might be related to all this."

This got everyone's attention, because it wasn't often the young hockey playing dragon spoke up.

"Over the last few weeks, I keep thinking I'm being

watched, followed sometimes. I know it sounds stupid and I don't have any defining evidence to back it up, but I'm sure it's happening. Sometimes it's when I'm walking, often when I'm in the car. I honestly don't think I'm wrong about this."

Of course the old shopkeeper and Tank already knew about this, but it was news to Flash, who ran through everything he'd heard. It all sounded like nagas. They were, after all, masters of disguise, it had been claimed even more so than dragons. Despite the fact that his friends would almost certainly ask, he'd been determined not to reveal what he'd been doing in his time away, even though they were probably able to guess. But everything he'd heard led him to believe these dragons could well be in danger, and that was something that changed everything. Only answering to the king himself, he knew he had a responsibility to protect the information that he'd gleaned. But also, he knew the king trusted these dragons not only with his life, but with the fate of the kingdom. Feeling more than a little uneasy about his decision, but given the situation they all found themselves in, he couldn't think of anyone else on the entire planet, with the exception of the monarch himself, that he trusted implicitly, so he swore them all to secrecy and told them. All of it. On learning about the sub, they were all absolutely flabbergasted and had a gazillion questions, pretty much as he had himself. Where were they going? What were they up to? Did the missiles on the submarine pose a threat? Who made up the group? Was there any way to destroy the submarine? What would happen if the humans found out that one of their most advanced weapons was missing? All these and more were questions that Flash had considered time and again, and he didn't have the answers. The king didn't have the answers. Whatever was going on was deadly serious, more so now with a nuclear submarine in play.

With the four of them sitting around speculating on each and every question the missing submarine posed, time trickled into the early evening. It was only when Gee Tee gave a massive yawn that they noticed quite how long they'd been brainstorming for. Tank tried to rush the master mantra maker off to bed, but he insisted on staying while Flash checked the building's shields. Flash agreed that it would be good to have his opinion, much to Tank's dismay. But before they got on to checking the shields, the ex-Crimson Guard had a little bit of training for the two young dragons.

"There are of course numerous ways of telling if you're being followed, the most common of which is an expanded web, which I'm sure you both know how to cast. However, the mantra itself is more than a little unreliable, particularly if your pursuer is a magic user. The spell itself is limited by height, and while a human would struggle to defeat something thirty feet high, it would offer little resistance to other beings, most notably dragons. It does have its uses though," offered Flash, the others all watching intently. "Adding *'lentesco'* to the main body of the mantra gives it a whole new dimension, especially in a confined space. Let me demonstrate."

Indicating with his index finger for Peter to get up, Flash moved out through the doorway beyond the counter. Closing his eyes, he put all his energy and belief into casting the expanded web mantra on the doorway through which he'd just walked. Moments later he opened his eyes and instructed Peter to walk towards him through the doorway. Tank and Gee Tee watched, fascinated.

Peter knew what was going to happen. Well, he didn't, but he knew whatever it was, it would end up with him being hugely embarrassed somehow. How right he was. Walking through the door as if nothing were there (he couldn't see anything, it looked totally normal, despite him knowing otherwise), he abruptly felt as though he'd walked into a bath full of treacle. An invisible sticky mass clung to his face, arms, legs, midriff... everything. Instinctively he tried to raise his arm to pull the stickiness off his face. But that just made things worse; he got more and more tangled and more and more entwined. Frustrated, he tried to spin away... a fatal mistake. It was almost as if he were cocooned in stickiness now, a human shaped, dragon caterpillar, waiting to emerge.

A suppressed giggle covered by a cough from the old shopkeeper was how it started. That in turn started Tank off, who guffawed with laughter. Flash just shook his head at his trapped friend, a huge smile woven across his face. Peter would have shaken his head at the predicament he found himself in, but he couldn't move... not even an inch. Every single part of him was fully immobile. Of course he could see the funny side and tried to laugh. But the stickiness that had enveloped his face prevented him from doing so.

"So you see," said Flash from behind Peter's back, "by adding the *'lentesco'* to the main body of the spell, the web becomes tacky, acting as an adhesive to whoever walks through it. I'm afraid it's only effective on magic users, and of course in time they would almost certainly be able to break free from its confinement. But not easily, or quickly, thus making this a good gambit to buy yourself some time in a confined space."

Tank and his boss clapped. Peter didn't. Closing his eyes, Flash silently cancelled the mantra, allowing the previously captured dragon to drop clumsily to his knees. Offering out his hand, Flash pulled his friend up to his feet.

"Sorry," he said, "but I knew you'd be a good sport about it."

"Not to worry," replied Peter. "It was worth it to see how well the mantra works." On this they all agreed.

Despite the fact that it was well into the evening now and Gee Tee looked more than a little fatigued, Flash continued to share his knowledge on all things spy craft, in an effort to help his friends stay safe. Over the course of the next couple of hours, they learned all sorts of new and wonderful mantras. Scale detection nets, perfect for the ceiling of any cavern to catch out dragons in their natural form. Shadow concealment mantras to blend seamlessly into any darkened area and disappear almost for good. Clothes changing mantras: walk around a corner in one colour, reappear in something completely different, guaranteed to fool all but the most experienced onlooker. Rapid aging mantras for when a quick escape isn't always the first choice: age rapidly and with the right accessories, i.e. a walking stick, glasses, scarf etc, and appear to be totally harmless and innocent. All number of perception pullers, where anyone who's looking in your direction gets their focus pulled away on to another target, which makes it doubly difficult to maintain focus, even for the most determined agent of chaos. Crackle tail: casting a tripwire that if activated will attach itself to the being and give off a sound and light show worthy of bonfire night. Anyone trying to be subtle will be lit up like a Christmas tree and flee in the opposite direction in no time at all. But Gee Tee could add another that even Flash, the ex-Crimson Guard, hadn't heard of.

"This," announced the old dragon, "is called 'sand trap'. Lay it down in front of you on ground that you know your shadow must walk on. It is of course keyed to magical beings and once they set foot in it, every step they take is like walking in deep, soft sand. It will feel like they're sinking up to their knees in it and however hard they try, they won't be able to shake off that feeling. The harder and faster they move, the deeper they will sink. It lasts for about twenty four hours, so it's great to use to get away, or even turn the tables on said pursuer."

Flash was impressed, and that took something extraordinary. It was a trick he would add to his repertoire straight away.

36 SANDY SABOTAGE

'You cowardly, cowardly, cowardly bucket of custard,' he thought to himself as the fine drizzle matted his hair, having just decided it was time to go home. He'd tried... he really had. But it was no good, he just couldn't do it, not after last time. Having planned it all out beforehand, how it would go, what he would say and how it would all be resolved in the happiest of endings... but he'd bottled it, lost any courage he might have had. It was all he could do not to cry.

Standing at the end of her street, sheltering outside someone else's house using one of the giant trees as a makeshift umbrella, for over forty-five minutes, only a few moments ago he'd given up and told himself it was time to head home. It had all seemed like such a good idea, but not being able to go through with even getting as far as the door made him feel like such a fool. He missed her so much, even with everything else going on in his life. Everything felt in motion at the moment, like a tornado ploughing across the landscape, constantly turning up new things, changing the view, and not just for the better. But at the back of his mind, she was always there. Janice, the diminutive bar worker, beautiful, caring and kind, with those melting eyes and her drop dead gorgeous pout. He missed everything about her, the seductive whisper of her voice, the warmth of her hands, the smell of apples in her hair. It should have come as no surprise that he couldn't pluck up the courage to at least knock on the door, after all, this was the third time in as many weeks that it had happened. His darkened mood led him to wonder if she'd moved on with her life, found someone else, someone more suited, someone not a dragon. A tiny part of him hoped she had and that someone could make her happy and give her the life she deserved, but most of him hoped it wasn't the case, despite the fact he couldn't see how on earth they were ever supposed to get back together, especially after his last visit to her house, in which she'd made her feelings abundantly clear.

Running his fingers through his tousled, damp hair, he was surprised at the amount of moisture there. He supposed he shouldn't have been, given that it had been raining on and off ever since he'd left his house. Needless to say, he wasn't looking forward to getting back. His home seemed so empty, mirroring the feelings inside him.

Expertly skipping around half a dozen badly damaged paving stones and the puddles they had inadvertently created, he recognised the single, run down shop on the road. Selling new and old guitars, he'd stopped to gaze in its window on both his previous visits, but not tonight, not in the cold and wet. However, as he trudged past he spotted something in the angled side window that led into the doorway and showed the scene directly behind him. Just for a moment, he'd spotted someone across the other side of the road, dressed very darkly, clinging to the shadows. Forcing himself to continue on in the same stride, he knew that anything unusual on his part would give things away to his pursuer.

Mind racing, fearing what might happen, a host of questions popped into his head. Who was it? What did they want? Were they human, dragon, naga or something else? His thoughts then turned to what he could do. Unable to phone Richie... what good would she be, now that she was no longer a dragon? Tank might be of some use, but he was pretty sure the big fella was on a coaching course somewhere else. And as for Flash, he could be just about anywhere in the world, and would almost certainly be doing something ever so important. And then it hit him. Flash... that was the key... the spy craft that he'd run through at the Mantra Emporium. Perhaps he could use some of the knowledge that had been passed on that evening. So stopping at a junction and waiting for a car to pass before crossing to the other side, a huge smile wiggled across his face for the first time in days, all thoughts of Janice momentarily lost.

For the next few minutes, he continued walking back the way he'd come, glad that at least he'd gotten Aviva's dagger to the vault some time ago, before twice catching a fleeting glimpse of whoever was tailing him, both times in the wing mirrors of parked cars. Mind whirring as he walked, running through all the possibilities and permutations, until one stuck out. Instantly he knew just what he had to do.

At the next junction he turned left, veering off from the quickest way home. Not wanting to go into the city centre itself, he'd decided on the outskirts... there was a little alley that ran along the river, past the back of a couple of pubs and then out into one of the main car parks, across which he could walk, leaving him only a few minutes from home. Knowing the alley was scarcely used and that it was something of a risk in the dark, late at night, given that it was especially secluded, it was the perfect place for the sand trap mantra that Gee Tee had taught them in the shop. More confident now, he picked up the pace, striding purposefully through the damp, the wind having picked up enough to almost have dried his hair. Cutting through a children's park, past the renowned arts centre, he cut down two small side streets and then turned sharply into the darkened alleyway. On facing the all encompassing blackness ahead, he almost paused, barely able to see the pinprick of light that represented the end of his short journey. Striding on, all the time looking down at the floor, searching for just the right place, the mantra in his head was ready to be deployed. And then he saw it, three paces in front of him, as far as he could see in the dark. A metal drain cover. He knew just what to do. Whoever was following him would want to skip over the cover and avoid making any noise, and since it was quite big and took up most of the alley, they would almost certainly have to land just the other side of it. So he made a big play of walking onto the cover, which obediently made a suitable ringing noise that echoed back down the alleyway. As he was on top of it, he cast the mantra onto the ground directly beyond it and then walked on, desperate to turn around and see if his pursuer was there, but knowing that it was best not to. Lightening his footsteps to see if he could hear anything from behind, he listened intently, not really expecting very much. In the distance, he could just make out the light from the street lamp, signalling that he'd nearly reached the end of the alley. It was then that he heard it. More of a squeak than a yell, he turned without thinking, looking back on the path he'd already trodden. In the darkness he could just make out the shape of a man, a man trying hard to walk. I say walk, it looked as though he was wading in treacle, bringing both his legs up as high as his hips, almost as if he were climbing a stile. Confusion gripped Peter. Part of him wanted to laugh it was so funny, but another, much angrier part wanted to confront whoever it was and find out exactly why they'd been following him. In the end he turned around and jogged off, settling for just knowing his pursuer would be stuck like that for the best part of a day, happy that he'd managed to get himself out of a fix, with of course a little help from the master mantra maker's magic.

37 WELSH HIDEAWAY

Another day passed and still no word. No more than she'd previously had from the nagas guarding her. Deep down, she knew it would take time, even if everything ran smoothly. And if it didn't, then the timetable could be anything. She missed him. It seemed like an age since they'd last been together. Part of her worried, worried that he might have changed his mind about her, found someone else. But she knew deep down that was an impossibility. They were bound together in love and in deeds that they'd done. It was meant to be. Rolling her legs back onto the bed she knew that she needed to rest; she had to be strong and full of energy for when he arrived, knowing that her skills might well be needed. As soon as her eyes closed she was asleep, thoughts once again drifting back to a previous time that seemed almost like someone else's life.

Narrowly escaping the King's Guard in Swanage had caused them both a great deal of soul searching and heartache. The idyllic life they'd shared had been shattered, torn viciously away from them. Looking back it was almost inevitable in the end, but that didn't take away the hurt and bitterness they both felt. Knowing that they were further away from their precious egg was what really cut deep, despite the fact that they had agreed never to go near it, or the dragon that hatched from it, ever again.

After weeks spent sleeping rough and avoiding any kind of built up area, both of them finally agreed on what needed to be done. They'd hidden a good deal of the money that they'd stolen after escaping prison, and having retrieved the large sum only a few days earlier, were now on their way to a much more secluded destination. They could have chosen to go anywhere on the planet, but both had agreed that there was as much chance of a dragon encounter there as there would be if they stayed within the borders of Great Britain, somewhere both regarded as their home, despite the traitorous crimes they'd both committed during their time in France. So they'd decided on somewhere remote, out of the way, somewhere the dragons would hopefully never think to look. Somewhere they could live together on their own, enjoying their time together for the rest of their lives.

With the money that they'd stolen, they purchased a tiny little cottage about two miles north of Llansanffraid on the west coast of Wales, overlooking the sea on one side, surrounded by rolling green countryside on the other. It was idyllic. They would pop into town every week, tending to keep themselves to themselves. To start with, the locals were a little suspicious, but their perfect accents (claiming to have come from Aberdaron, further to the north, in the hope that no one would be able to prove otherwise) helped them seamlessly blend in over a period of months, which slowly turned into years.

One harsh winter's day, they popped into town to stock up on some essentials, walking there like they always did, the cold weather attacking their heat favouring bodies. It was painful, no matter how many layers they wore. They were after all dragons, and all dragons have an affinity for the heat and despise the cold. Nevertheless, they endured. On arriving in town, they made straight for the shop, sliding across the icy road and treacherous path on the way. Having purchased bread, eggs, milk, potatoes, onions and carrots, they thanked the shopkeeper and his wife, opened the door and walked out into the street. At that exact moment a car approaching from the west, going a little too fast, lost control on the icy surface of the road and mounted the pavement on their side of the street. Earth, surprisingly, was quite slow on the uptake. Her husband wasn't. Instinctively, he pushed her back into the shop doorway, causing her to slip and fall. By then, he'd made another decision. Fifteen feet in front of him, the daughter of the shop owners was playing with a skipping rope. Aged seven or eight, she was oblivious to the approaching danger of the out of control car. Given everything they'd done in their previous lives, it was unnatural for him to even think of saving the girl. But he'd changed since being here, since living the life he'd always dreamed of, with the woman he loved. Impulsively he acted, selflessly and with the courage of many men. Earth could only sit and watch in horror, mouth open in shock as events unfolded.

Springing towards the girl, whose face twisted in torment as he approached at speed, she dropped the skipping rope just as he reached her, mouth hanging open, too scared to even scream. Grasping her tightly, he hurled her up into his arms. And then the car was upon them. With no other option, he jumped for all he was worth. As the car careered into the wall next to where the little girl had been standing, he twisted in mid-air, using his body to protect the helpless child. A loud CRUNCH accompanied the first impact, his hip taking the full force of the windscreen, immediately followed by the THUD of his back smashing fully into the bonnet of the car. With the youngster cradled safely from danger, he ignored the mind numbing pain of the collisions and concentrated on continuing his roll, slowing his speed and delivering her back to her parents in one piece. Bouncing off the vehicle, he tucked in, threw all his weight to his right and hit the ground with a bone shattering THUMP, taking the full force of the icy street on his right shoulder. Rolling over so that the child was on top of him, he lay prone, unable to move, in the middle of the chilling street. It had all happened so fast, in a matter of seconds really. Having managed to regain her feet after being thrown into the doorway, Earth hadn't realised what was happening until it was much too late. She could have used her abilities; the magic, as always, bubbled away inside her, just beneath the surface. But she'd been too slow to react and now he lay there, damaged and broken for all to see.

Now it was all over, the child's body remembered to scream. And scream it did, at the top of its voice, waiting for her parents' warm, safe embrace. Steam poured from the car's radiator as it sat embedded in the wall of the house next to the shop. Carrots, potatoes and onions rolled around the pavement. Cracked eggs, a puddle of milk and broken glass covered the shop doorway. The jingle of the bell floated across the air as the shop owners raced out onto the street, narrowly avoiding the mess from the dropped shopping. The still screaming young girl raced into her parents' arms. Earth side-stepped them and dashed over to her husband. Pedestrians from all around came rushing over to join her.

Eyes closed, he looked as though he was fighting some sort of battle to remain conscious, if she was any judge. Aware of all those around her, she pleaded with him to wake up. But to no avail.

Kneeling over him, she cradled his head in her hands, able to feel exactly what he was doing. She had a sense of just how bad his wounds were: broken ribs, shattered pelvis, damage to his internal organs. Desperate to lend him her strength, she knew that it was too much of a risk given the gathered crowd. Already there was talk of an ambulance on the way, pretty much the last thing the two of them needed, given exactly how hard they'd tried to keep a low profile. More than a few minutes passed before a loud breath startled the crowd into moving back. Opening his eyes, and despite Earth's protestations, he sat up. A loud murmur whispered around the crowd.

"I should sit still if I were you," announced one onlooker. "There's an ambulance on the way."

Turning to his wife, they both shared the same thought. They had to get out of here, back to the safety of their cottage. With the damaged car hissing, spluttering and steaming away behind them, gingerly he rose to his feet. The gathered crowd were dumbstruck.

"I'm alright... really," he mumbled. "Just a few bruises, nothing too serious. Not enough to require an ambulance anyway. I think we'll just wander on back home. A couple of days' rest and I'm sure I'll be as good as new."

Nobody wanted to argue. So with his arm around Earth's shoulder, they turned as one and headed in the direction of their home. From out of nowhere, the shopkeepers stepped out in front of them.

"What you did was so brave. Thank you very much," said the girl's mother, clutching the young child close to her.

"You're welcome," replied Earth's husband, trying hard to force even the faintest semblance of a smile onto his face.

"If there's anything you ever need, just ask," declared the girl's father, handing them a bag full of all the things they'd just lost.

Earth and her husband nodded, before heading back up the street, turning the corner and disappearing off into the distance, eager to get back to their cottage.

They couldn't have known it at the time, but their good

deed was about to cost them dear. In a house across the other side of the road, an old woman had seen everything. Regarded as a nosy neighbour by all of the insular community, it was something that didn't really bother her. She too kept herself to herself, not mixing with others unless she really had to. And her reason wasn't too far removed from that of Earth and her husband's reason. You see, she was a dragon, one that had been cast out for nothing more than a minor transgression, at least that's how she saw it. But having witnessed the events of the last ten minutes or so, she was sure that she'd been privy to something important, something the dragon world would want to know about... something that could be traded for the end of her exile. So she set about contacting the relevant dragons, with a view to bargaining for her return.

38 THE ELEMENT OF SURPRISE

About ten minutes, that's how long it took to walk from Camelot Arcade to the nearest monorail station. It seemed a lot longer, probably because all the two of them had done was muck about. Tank constantly tried to trip Flash up (something that hadn't happened yet, despite his best efforts) while the ex-Crimson Guard kept knocking his meaty friend's rugby kit bag (something so big, you could probably have fitted a couple of small adults in it) off his shoulders. Childish didn't begin to describe it. But they were happy and their laughter echoed throughout the surrounding tunnels, streets, roads and paths that they crossed, much to the consternation of the dragons around them. On their way to the charity sports day in Salisbridge, with Tank due to play, Flash was keen and excited about watching and meeting up with Peter and Richie much later on, having some thrilling news to tell them all... at least it was thrilling to him, and he hoped it would be to them. It would ultimately mean that he'd get to see much more of the unconventional trio he was so proud to call his friends. Recently he'd decided, and it flew in the face of pretty much everything he believed in, to follow Tank's example and take up playing rugby. For some time now he'd marvelled at his friends' passion for their respective sports, finding it unfathomable at first. It made no sense at all. But the more time he spent in their company (something he enjoyed immensely) the more he felt compelled to join them. Deciding which sport to try hadn't been easy, but listening to Tank talk, animatedly, time and again about the coaching he did and the games he played in, narrowed down the difficult choice. So later on that night, in whatever setting they found themselves, he planned to announce his decision, in the hope that they would approve. Backslapping, hair ruffling and high jinks all continued, even on the monorail, with disapproving looks the order of the day from all the other commuters.

Mere minutes later they arrived, announced by the customary whoosh of the carriage doors. Joining the throng of dragons heading out onto the platform and wading up the stairs, both friends continued their antics. It was a shame really. If they'd been paying more attention to their surroundings, they might just have recognised the danger earlier, saving themselves a whole world of pain.

Reaching the top of the stairs, that's when he noticed it, but by then they were both being dragged across the plaza by the crowd of dragon passengers. It felt to him as though someone were scratching his brain... at first anyway. With everything that was going on, it was hard to make head or tail of the strange sensation. And then a feeling of total and utter dread washed over him, along with the sense of something very, very familiar. Instantly his body exploded into action, every nerve ending, every cell, ready and waiting to burst. Across the plaza in front of them, the crowd had stopped, some even backing away. Flash's mind had just worked out what he'd sensed... NAGAS!

'Here, now?' he thought, perplexed. Gripping Tank by the elbow as they fought their way to the front of the crowd, Flash was determined to find out what was going on and confront it head on, whilst at the same time protecting his friend. Ducking beneath the wings of two retreating dragons, all the time pulling Tank with him, Flash rose up to his full height, ready to act. But the sight that greeted him was the very last thing he expected. Automatically, his mind raced through the options open to him.

Bumped and bruised from being dragged through the crowd by his friend, Tank stood agog at what lay before them, and what the crowd in the plaza all seemed to be trying to escape from. It looked a little like a flare going off, sitting there all alone, brilliant green smoke pouring forth, like something akin to an industrial chimney. There was, however, more to the object at the middle of the mass. A shimmering, deep blackness, swirling hypnotically at the very centre, was what caught Tank's eye. There and then he knew he had only a matter of moments to react.

In less than a heartbeat, Flash's mind reached a decision, his body flying into action. Releasing his grip on Tank, he sprinted for all he was worth towards what he knew to be a highly unstable heavy element, having seen them before, many times, commonly used by terrorist groups throughout the domain. I say commonly... perhaps not so much. Decades generally pass before one of these so called terrorist groups raises their heads above the parapet, and then are normally swiftly dealt with by the dragon authorities... usually the Crimson Guards. The weapons in question come in all shapes and sizes, all with very different properties and effects, ranging from concussion and sonic blast waves to deadly area of effect explosions, able to inflict the kind of death and carnage only ever seen in a dragon's worst nightmare. Midway through his run, all his mind could think was,

'This one looks wayyyyyyy more dangerous than any of the others I've dealt with in the past.'

For all he was worth, he kept moving, enhanced by his magic.

'Oh my,' thought Tank, frozen in place, watching helplessly as his friend bombed on towards the lethal heavy element that seemed primed and ready to go off. If there was one thing he'd learned from his very temperamental boss, it was to stay as far away as possible from the materials that combined to make those things work. With that singular thought in mind, he wondered what on earth Flash thought he was doing, heading towards it at top speed.

It was nearly impossible to see the swirling dark mass at the centre now. Flash knew that he had only moments before it happened and hadn't, however, figured out what he was going to do, if in fact he reached the device before it detonated.

'Helpless' wasn't in Tank's dictionary. And so although he was too far away to do very much, there was one thing he knew for certain he could do that might make a difference to his friend.

High above, shrouded in the shadows, he looked on, waiting for them all to die. It was delicious, poetic, deserving. As he watched, the crowd backed away, some at least realising what was about to happen. But that wasn't what caught his attention. Two human shapes, one very much from his past, pushed their way to the front of the ever fearful mass of dragons.

'What in the hell...?' he thought, watching the shape he didn't recognise race forward towards all his very hard and valuable work.

Within a few yards, Flash swept the sickly green gas away from his face, his mind having reached the only logical conclusion it could: erect a shield and hope it would stop whatever the hell that thing was about to unleash. Deep inside, he knew it wouldn't be enough.

Dropping to his knees, ignoring the pain from the

impact, Tank closed his eyes, searching for his magic, and his... friend. The connection was instant and just what he needed. Opening himself right up, he delved deep inside, finding his well of magical energy. Without a thought for his own safety, he sent it all off to his friend.

What they thought they could achieve, he had no idea. As he watched Tank drop to his knees and the stranger dive head first into the putrid, green smoke, his confidence shattered like a mirror being dropped from a great height.

Answering the mantra Flash had just cast in his mind, the shield sprang forth all around him, powered by the magic that was his birthright. Deep down, his mind continued to whisper that it wouldn't be enough. He really didn't need reminding. Just as he bounded into the flying leap that would put him right on top of the device, a leap that every rugby player in the world would be proud of, a sudden influx of magic wove itself all around him.

'TANK,' was all he could think, recognising the very flavour of what had been offered up, as he channelled all the magic into the shield that encased him.

For the device... the time had come! Swirling, dark, negative energy transformed into a pinprick of light on the blackest of black backgrounds. With energy fit to burst, it fulfilled the very purpose it had been created for.

Flash, and moreover his shield, hit the device just as the explosion initiated. Most of his magic took the brunt of the blast, deflecting and absorbing the deadly kinetic energy in equal measures. He though, was tossed high in the air, a rag doll flung by an out of control toddler.

Dissipated by whatever Flash had done, the shock wave knocked Tank to the floor with the force of a tempestuous hurricane. Before the blackness took him, he realised that they were all meant to have died.

"NO, NO, NO!" he screeched to no one in particular. 'They've ruined it. Totally ruined it. They're all supposed to have died, annihilated by the blast wave, bits of dragon splattered across the monorail plaza. But those two have transformed everything,' he thought, looking down at the ocean of unconscious dragon bodies. Knowing he'd get into trouble for this, it was supposed to have been a demonstration of his power and fealty towards his new master, to signify the beginning of a new age.

'DAMN!' Sweeping down in a tight spiral from his concealed, overlooking perch, he was determined to make them suffer for his failure, particularly his former classmate and the stranger.

Seemingly from out of nowhere, a refreshing breeze whipped along the enclosed tunnels and plaza attached to the monorail station, dispersing any and all remnants of the foul smelling, noxious green gas.

39 ALWAYS IN MOTION

Double locking all the doors and checking all the building's shields, he was now firmly ensconced in his workshop. The unusual and, to him, unsettling events of the previous weeks had him worried, more worried in fact than he'd been in centuries. And there weren't many beings on the planet that could claim that. So after Tank and Flash had left, off to some charity sporting event on the surface somewhere, he'd settled down, his course of action decided some time ago.

From out of one of the scaly pouches lining his belly, he pulled an old scroll that looked like it might disintegrate at any second if touched. Carefully unfurling the ribbon that bound it, he stretched it out on the table, using an inkwell and a mantra pen to hold it in place. The writing was all Japanese, something he found quite foreign despite all his training and language skills. Clearing his mind, focusing solely on the writing, well... more like symbols, in front of him, he closed his eyes and let the meaning of the mantra coalesce at the forefront of his imagination.

'It really is a work of genius,' he mused. There could be no better description of this particular mantra. The combination of words, letters, symbols, meaning, desire, willpower and magic was nothing short of astounding, with just a hint of madness. No dragon in their right mind would have thought to combine all these elements in the way he had. Dangerous didn't begin to cover it.

Throughout the ages dragons, as well as other races, had all sought to look into the future. Difficult at best, seemingly impossible at worst, vast amounts of time, resources and magic had been wasted on this most prized pursuit, across many thousands of years.

Over the centuries, it was something he'd become obsessed with. Not as much as prolonging the dragon life span, but still, enough that he was probably the foremost expert on the planet. The scrolls that sat in front of him were the only artefacts that showed even the faintest glimmer of hope at all in catching the merest glimpse into the future.

From out of the desk's top drawer he started to retrieve the eclectic mix of ingredients he needed to combine with the ancient, far eastern scroll. A handful of pine needles, half a dozen walnuts, a carefully procured vial of king cobra venom, a sliver of magnesium and the tears of a mermaid. It had taken him over two years to procure everything, with the mermaid's tears being particularly hard to acquire. But once he had, over two decades ago, he'd kept them all together in frozen storage, waiting for the right moment, knowing that he might only get one shot. Removing them from storage two days ago, defrosting them if you will, now, in his workshop, mind focused fully on his task, he began to add each and every item, piece by piece, to the huge mortar that sat on the desk, its accompanying pestle lying next to it, looking lonelier than a tramp at a ball. It took the best part of an hour. By the end, the whole experience had taken its toll on the old shopkeeper, so much so that he found himself wishing for his bed and the sleep that had so recently eluded him. It wasn't really an option and so he had to make do with a giant cup of coffee and half a dozen HB pencils to nibble on. After half an hour resting in one of the oversized chairs, contemplating what he was about to do, he was ready.

Finding his second wind, he gathered his thoughts and returned to the desk with the outstretched mantra and the giant mortar on it. Gripping the pestle for all he was worth, he began to grind the ingredients down, eventually achieving a slimy looking paste for his trouble.

'There's no turning back now,' he mused, the gooey globules dripping off the pestle into the mortar. Running his eyes over the scroll one last time, and feeling the weight of history and the hopes of hundreds of other dragons on his shoulders, he took a long, deep breath, savouring the hot, fiery feeling rolling around inside his stomach and carefully recited exactly what was on the scroll, reinforcing it with every ounce of willpower he had. Leaning over the mucky mixture, the wily old dragon started to exhale slowly, a snaking stream of fire shooting out from between his jaws. The ingredients started to bubble and pop, wispy layers of foul smelling steam rising into the air, washing across his shiny scales, the very first tendrils disappearing up into the dark recesses of his nostrils. Closing his eyes while continuing to blow out a consistent stream of fire, the master mantra maker started to inhale the rising gas through his nose. Immediately his head started to spin, slowly at first, quickly becoming much faster. He knew it to be part of the experience and wasn't unaccustomed to it. But he didn't like it at all. Blurred images, impossible to make out, blinked in and out of his mind. Trying to stay relaxed, knowing that it was part of the key to things, he fought off the feeling of unease that threatened to consume him. It wasn't easy though. With seconds blending into minutes, and minutes blending into who knows what, the old shopkeeper continued to heat up the crazy concoction, all the time the odour from it pervading his very being.

Abruptly the blinking started to become less frequent, each of the out of focus images staying there just that tiny bit longer. Screwing up his eyes despite the fact that they were already closed, he hoped that would help make the difference.

'Thirsty,' he thought, 'so thirsty.' Just as this thought left him, the image in front of him flittered into clarity. Sweat dribbled down the side of his prehistoric face, as the sound of his crackling flame interrupted occasionally by the popping of the slimy paste reverberated off the walls around him. Despite the image being in focus, it was hard to make out exactly what was going on. It looked a lot like dragons marching.

'But marching where?' was all that he could think. Suddenly the scene changed to a faraway shot of a square or plaza, somewhere here in the dragon domain. The beings were tiny little dots, the vantage point was so far away. It was tough to make out what was going on. Just as he'd given up on making any sense of this one, the view seemed to zoom right in. An icy chill ran up his back as he recognised the tall piles off to one side. Dragon corpses! Still it continued to zoom in. Dragons captured by the look of things, two human shapes being tortured. For a split second he glimpsed the face of one of the tortured human shapes. Panic raced through him at the very thought of what he'd seen. He needed more... more information. So he delved deeper, deeper into whatever he was doing, desperate to know more about the future. Hazy pictures slid by, most of which he couldn't make out. Once or twice he thought he recognised the odd thing. The council building seemed to feature, along with outlying parts of London, as well as somewhere cold and snowy on the surface of the planet. It all made little or no sense. By now he was exhausted, caked in sweat, bathed in horrid fumes from the mortar. But still he had to go on, push himself further, he just had to. It was all too much. Fatigue threatened to overtake him. Resigned to failure, his flame burnt out with a whimpering crackle. Before he could open his eyes, the image of the square or plaza whipped back in front of him. It was all he could do to look, having seen the last face he'd expected to be there. This time though, instead of focusing in, the image seemed to turn around and started to fly out across the rooftops, away from the action and off to a seemingly insignificant part of the underground dragon city. His eyes wrinkled in concentration as he hung on for all he was worth, hoping with all his heart to see something of value. He did, and not just one thing either. The first thing he noticed was a very specific lava formation called the runny nose, because the rock formation that it flowed out of looked like a giant nose. It was famous throughout the kingdom. So now he knew where things were taking place. But before the image drifted off into nothingness, it showed one last titbit that took his breath away, blowing his mind like nothing else ever had.

'It can't be... can it?' he thought, shaking off the effects of the smoke inhalation. Taking a long slurp of his by now cold coffee, he knew he had to act, and now. Time was ticking away, and although he didn't know when things would happen, he assumed it would be soon. So, banishing tiredness and fighting back the effects of age that constantly threatened to overwhelm him, he pushed his square framed glasses to the top of his nose and headed down into the vault to tool up, in the hope that it would be enough. As he got up to do just that, he caught sight of the replica ring they had made for the king. It was of little use now, as the vote the king had been concerned about had been overturned. But something deep within him felt compelled to pick it up and put it in one of the many pouches around his belly. He did as the compulsion demanded and secreted it away on his person.

40 STICK IT TO 'EM!

Pulling the handbrake tight, Richie turned off the ignition and gazed out at the sight in front of her. The city council had done an astounding job in such a short space of time. Of course the rugby pitch had already been there, with the men's section of the sports club having already made use of it. But to have created two grass lacrosse pitches and one grass hockey pitch, just for today's fundraiser, was above and beyond the call of duty. And more remarkable still was the fact that the surface of all the pitches looked stunning. Grabbing her kit bag and sticks from the back seat, she locked her car and headed off through the throng of people towards the temporary portacabins that she knew to be the changing rooms. As she snaked in and out of the crowd, friends and acquaintances nodded and said hi to her; most she recognised, some she didn't. Following some bright yellow signs that said 'Lacrosse Ladies' Changing' eventually she walked up a set of steps and into the changing rooms, the last one of her team to turn up.

"Glad you could make it," commented one.

"Nice of you to join us," declared the next.

"What time do you call this?"

And so it went on. And do you know what? She loved every second of it. After all, that's part of what being in a team is all about.

Outside, the place was filling up. Cars were streaming in now, newcomers having to use the overflow car park. Families walked in on foot, all happy to pay the entrance fee, all supporting the efforts of everyone involved in the fundraising event.

No one could remember exactly whose idea it had been, given that it had occurred late on a Saturday evening around a table in a restaurant, smack bang in the middle of Salisbridge. Of course copious amounts of alcohol had been consumed as committee and club members from all sections had met up in what was almost their usual high spirited Saturday night, just not in the normal place, not after it had been destroyed so violently and abruptly by THAT bomb. Most could barely believe what had happened and were still in a constant state of confusion about why they and their clubhouse had been targeted. But given the events across the world, most counted themselves fortunate that people hadn't lost their lives on that fateful day. Salisbridge was most certainly in mourning for its clubhouse, but also for those around the world who had lost their lives in such tragic circumstances. So the idea had come about to hold an event that would raise some funds not only for the sports club, and for the teams' use of alternative facilities in the area to continue to play their selected sports, but also to go towards those who had lost loved ones and in particular their homes, in some of the hardest hit areas. A late night drunken idea had taken off immediately, with all parties agreeing on something they did best... play sport!

So here it was, the 'SUPER SPORT, SUPER DAY OUT!' Of course the council had chipped in, allowing the use of their sports fields on the other side of town from the giant crater that now filled the spot where their beloved clubhouse had stood. They'd even prepared four pitches (two lacrosse, one hockey, one rugby) working overtime to get them all ready, and to the highest possible standard. Temporary cabins had been loaned to them free of charge, along with many portable loos. Over the last couple of weeks, the local paper had been promoting it free of charge, along with nearly all the city's traders. And of course word of mouth about just how good it was going to be had spread like wildfire. Fairground attractions, stalls, shops, bands and entertainers had all pledged their time and abilities for free to such a good cause. Every player in each of the respective sports had spent weeks since the idea had first taken off collecting sponsorship, many individuals reaching totals of several thousands of pounds from the kind hearted people of the city, as well as their opponents pledging to do the same. At this very moment, the atmosphere was buzzing and felt more like a carnival then a sporting event.

Many thousands of people had crowded in, so much so that a whole new field had to be found for the stream of cars flooding back on to the main road, as far as the eye could see. Volunteers from the different sports sections manned the gate, all staggered at just how many people had turned up to see the three different sports, hockey, lacrosse and rugby, all played simultaneously on four different pitches.

As the ever increasing noise outside assaulted her ears, Richie's thoughts turned to her friends. Picturing Tank in one of the other changing rooms, quietly scheming about how his second team could beat the first team that they were playing against, she imagined him sitting calmly, back against the wall, clothes hung up perfectly on their assigned peg, even though it was only a friendly game, knowing him well enough to be sure beyond any doubt that he and his friends would want to put one over on the supposedly better team in, of course, a fair and controlled manner. She had no doubt that the adrenaline would be coursing through his veins now, in much the same way as it pumped furiously around her body right at this very moment. Undoubtedly Peter was already here, she assumed, but as a spectator only, as the hockey match was a mixed affair, with a team made up from the men's and the ladies' first XIs. Remembering that Peter had mentioned Tank would be bringing Flash along as well, she could only recall meeting him on a couple of occasions and didn't know him that well, but he seemed very nice, and as far as she was concerned... the more the merrier.

"Well?" asked the team captain.
The rugby player cancelled the call on his phone.

"He's not picking up. It just rings out, with no option to even leave a voice message."

"That's really odd," piped up someone else. "He's nearly always the first one here. I do hope nothing's happened to him."

Trying not to let his disappointment show too much, the captain was well aware of just how much more of a formidable team they were with Tank in their side, and knew exactly how much the hulking monster of a rugby player wanted to win this match. They'd talked about it only a few days ago, agreeing on a strategy and some very simple and straightforward plays. But for him not to turn up now was something of a letdown to say the least. His mind echoed the sentiments that his fellow player had just expressed... he hoped nothing bad had happened to him.

Janice snaked through the crowd, following them this way and that, almost carried on by a will other than her own. Sunglasses and a baseball cap provided her anonymity. For the last week or so, she'd been undecided on whether or not to attend. Even that morning, she still hadn't known. But in the end, the desire to be here had outweighed any doubts that she'd had. So here she was, mingling with all the other spectators, ready to watch all the fabulous sport on offer. At least, that's what she told herself. Inside though, she knew it was nothing to do with that. She needed to see him, even if it was from just a distance, and she knew that he'd be here. The team sheets with the names of the players competing today had been listed on the website for a week now, and two names stood out: Tank in the rugby match, and the one and only Richie Rump in the lacrosse match. If she hadn't known before that he'd be here, those two names only confirmed it.

With the matches not quite ready to start, she found herself beside the rugby pitch, right next to the second team warming up. Trying to look casual and not too interested, she attempted to see where Tank was, assuming that Peter wouldn't be that far away. Beside her, the team captain was talking to one of his players.

"Any sign of him?"

"No. None at all I'm afraid."

"Damn. I can't believe he's not here. It's so unlike him."

"Perhaps he's just stuck in the traffic."

"Unlikely. Tank's normally the first one here. If we've all made it and he hasn't, something somewhere is very, very wrong."

"What are we gonna do?"

"We'll just have to start the match without him and hope to hell that he turns up at some point."

With that, both players turned away and trotted over to the main group that were warming up.

'How odd,' thought Janice, 'Tank not turning up. That is unusual. I suppose I'd better check the lacrosse pitch to see if Richie's there.'

Shoving her way back through the crowd and away from the rugby pitch, the diminutive bar worker continued to look out for the love of her life.

Richie, by now fully kitted up, her stick in one hand, a ball in the other, led her team into the corridor, out through the main door into the blazing sunshine, down some rickety old steps and headed through the crowds straight towards the pitch. The last team member locked the changing room door. Adults clapped and children waved enthusiastically as the team wove through the crowds, a smile on everyone's face.

Almost ready to start, the teams for all three of the other matches had nearly finished warming up. The idea had been for all four games to kick off at the same time, allowing spectators to drift between matches and get a good look at all the sports and the teams involved. Given just how many people had turned up, the moving about bit might prove more than a little difficult.

Oddly, the ladies' lacrosse team opposition hadn't turned out on the pitch yet. Realising this, Richie asked one of her players to go and check if there was a problem. She knew that they were here, as they'd been in the adjacent changing room. After a few minutes, the messenger came sprinting back to inform her captain that one of the opposition's cars hadn't yet arrived, so they were currently four players short. Richie nodded, understanding that such things happened, with the high volume of traffic in and around where they were no doubt only compounding things.

"Go back and tell them we'll wait," she declared. "We're not in any hurry, and after all it's supposed to be more like an exhibition match, rather than anything too serious. I'm sure the crowd would much prefer to see us take on a full team, rather than one depleted through no fault of their own."

Richie informed the rest of the team and the officials about the slight delay as her teammate sprinted back towards the makeshift changing rooms to deliver the message.

Around them, whistles blew to signal the start of the other matches. As one, the lacrosse girls stopped, taking in the spectacle of all the sport on offer.

A bright, clean rugby ball spun high up in the air, over to their left. It was impossible to see which team had kicked it, let alone which player, with the scale of the crowds around the pitch. Looking on, Richie was sure that Tank would be having a great time, totally immersed in the fever pitch atmosphere of the game.

Off to the right, the men and women playing mixed hockey stood out in their bright orange and bright blue tops, respectively. Full pelt was the best description of the game from what little Richie could see, with both the men and women struggling to fully control the ball on the slightly more uneven surface than they were used to. Richie smiled at that. Peter had confided in her that he'd often wondered what it would have been like to play hockey on a grass pitch, as it had been all the time in the not so distant past. Sometimes he'd drive past a beautiful grass pitch at a school or something and be slightly envious of those playing on it. By the looks of things, playing on grass was a lot more random and a lot more dangerous than on Astroturf, something the Salisbridge men and ladies were just finding out, no matter how well cut it had been. Hoping that Peter was watching from somewhere amongst the crowd, drawing his own conclusions about the surface, she looked forward to catching up with him later.

Like giraffes in a zoo, giant lacrosse sticks rose into the air above the crowds on the men's pitch right next door, a tangled, corded head on the end instead of ears, eyes and a gargantuan tongue. Watching in fascination at the appearance of the long sticks, she knew there could be no more than four of them on the field of play at any one time, and that's how many she counted. It was a facet of the men's game that had always intrigued her. Of course, she'd had a go many a time and was constantly astounded at how far it was possible to throw the ball. Playing a match with one of those would be totally different from anything she was used to, but the possibilities of how to change the game tactically rolled round and round inside her mind. So many options.

A shout jolted her back to reality, just in time to see a bright orange ball heading for her face. Instinctively her lightning reactions took over, catching the ball in the head of her stick.

"SORRY!" came a shout from Ali, one of her teammates.

Smiling, with a flick of her wrist, she sent the ball hurtling back to where it had come from, with just a touch more speed.

With the sun bathing her limber body, surrounded by her friends, she continued to warm up, stretching her arms, legs, back and ankles before joining in with the other players, cradling the ball while all the time twisting and turning her stick, passing to her team mates before moving on towards goal. Emma and Joey, the two other forwards, were already there, firing shot after shot at the very agile Harriet, the Salisbridge goalie, looking menacing in her black as night helmet and facemask with matching gloves, throat and chest protector. Even her gum shield was black. All of that, combined with her oversized stick, made for something very intimidating. Richie scooped up one of the practice balls from the ground, turned her stick from side to side, weaving her body back and forth, all the time cradling the ball. Harriet watched intently, as did the other two forwards. With little drawback, Richie powered her shot forward. A few of the spectators let out a gasp, realising the speed of the shot. The first thing poor Harriet knew was the sound of the ball hitting the post and bouncing into the back of the netting. She gave Richie one of her looks (not that anyone would have been able to see with all that protection around her face) glad that the awe inspiring super striker was on her side.

After a few more minutes of warming up (well, mainly Harriet's back in Richie's case, from all the bending down and retrieving the ball from the back of her net) they were greeted by the sight of their opposition heading out towards the pitch, all twelve of them by the look of it.

'Hurray,' she thought, 'a few minutes' warm up for them and then we can get underway.'

As their smiling opposition jogged past them, eager to reach the other end of the pitch and warm up, one turned and looked menacingly in her direction, standing out like a black cloud in a clear blue sky on a summer's day, pretty much like this one. Recognition blossomed into life inside Richie's head, sending a cold chill down her spine and goose bumps up her arms.

'What the hell is she doing here?' was her only thought.

Unable to remember the woman's name, Richie always thought of her as either 'Attitude' or 'Hulk' given her muscular physique. (Richie always did this with her opponents. During warm up, which she regularly watched with intent, she normally picked out names for them all for her to apply during the match itself. Cocky, Hairy, Freckles, Ginger, Blondie, Big Gloves, Fancy Trainers... all those and more she'd used on more than one occasion.) Attitude/Hulk normally played for Bristol Fire Foxes, but for some reason had appeared today and seemed to be turning out for the Avalon Avengers, a very friendly up and coming team from Somerset. Richie's reaction to the player could be put down to their meetings over the course of several seasons, where there had been many run ins between the two of them, with the Salisbridge captain almost always coming out on top. But Richie considered this woman her nemesis, if indeed such a thing existed, particularly given the physicality of her game. She could remember coming off after games against her, literally covered in cuts and bruises, aching from head to toe, just from the beating she'd taken at the hands of this woman. Right now she hoped there'd be none of that, after all it was a friendly and all about raising money not just for the sports club, but also for the poor people who'd been affected by the devastating attacks across the world. Pushing it all out of her mind, she gathered the team and started giving them their customary talk, remembering to be clear about precisely what manner the game should be played in, given that it was in fact a friendly and that lots of spectators who'd never even seen the sport would be watching, with the aim being to show them everything good about the sport. Everyone agreed, and with a mighty cheer, left the aforementioned huddle to take up their positions on the field of play, with the Avalon Avengers doing exactly the same thing.

Some of the crowds from the other matches had

started to take an interest now that the ladies' lacrosse looked as though it were about to start, with a twisting line of onlookers filing their way around the circumference of the pitch, carefully avoiding the space at the back of the substitution area where players that have been sent off sit out their two minute penalty. Everybody's intention was undoubtedly that this particular area wouldn't be called into use this afternoon.

With all the practice balls off the pitch, Richie strolled up to the centre line, ready for the draw, having already indicated to the umpire that Salisbridge were ready to play. Standing facing her opponent, all thoughts of anything but the match had been wiped from her head as the umpire, sporting his usual attire, placed the ball between the back of their crosses. Without a hint of emotion, he said,

"Ready."

Both women remained completely motionless, focused, waiting for the inevitable whistle. It seemed to take an age, there in the glorious sunlight. Not for the first time that day, Richie felt the tiny weight of the necklace with the ring on it that Peter had given to her some time ago. For some reason it seemed to be charged, almost burning her skin... but in a good way. Nearly drifting off into thoughts of what it all meant, she was abruptly shaken out of it by the shrill, piercing sound of the umpire's whistle. One thought above all others registered in her brain: 'PLAY!' And so she did.

Channelling all her might into raising her stick as she had done countless times before, she watched as the ball zipped high into the air, over her left shoulder and back into her own half. Instinct took over, her feet moving her body into the nearest free space, all the time mindful of where her teammates were, and just what she could do to help them out. Currently Angela, one of the Salisbridge defenders, had the ball nestled in the crosse of her stick, having just feinted one way and then sprinted the other way around the outside of her attacker. Richie slowed her run a little, intent on heading out wide on the left, as that was the direction Angela was now running in and it looked as though that was the place to be. Just as she was about to turn, a sharp, almighty pain tore across the lower half of her back, forcing her to close her eyes and drop to her knees in agony. Aware of what was going on around her and that the match was still continuing, she staggered to her feet, wheeling around, trying to find out exactly what had happened. It didn't take long to figure things out. Attitude was standing not six feet away, an ominous looking grin chiselled into her dour, plain face. A thesaurus of expletives sprang forth in Richie's mind as her mouth opened automatically, but by then her brain had the presence to stop anything from spouting out. Shocked, open mouthed and wide-eyed, she watched Attitude turn around and run back, just catching Angela out of the corner of her eye, zipping past her, out wide on the left.

'Damn,' she thought, hoping against hope that what had happened was just a sporting accident. Pushing the pain to one side, she stumbled off towards the goal they were attacking, hoping to give her side at least one more option.

Harriet, the Salisbridge goalie, had seen it all. Well, she hadn't as it turned out, but she was sure she knew exactly what had happened. Just as Richie had checked her run and was turning to move outside, the strapping great defender who she recognised from another club they played against, must have hit her teammate hard with the end of her stick, right in the base of her spine.

'That,' she thought, 'is just *not* what today is all about.'

While Richie hobbled as quickly as she could to catch up with play, Angela had just played a beautiful one-two with Joey, one of the other forwards in her side, and was in the process of lobbing the ball to Emma who stood expectantly some way back, behind the goal.

Still deeply disappointed that the officials had missed what felt like an assault, Richie darted around to the right of the goal, careful to stay well back from the goal circle. Emma, having caught the ball, zipped in and out of the player trying to block her off, all the time looking for someone to pass to. Richie knew that Emma was trying to pick her out, hoping she'd make one of her normal runs. And so she did... well, at least she tried to. Her right foot pushed off, but suddenly as if from nowhere, a weight had appeared on her left foot as she tried to move... resulting in a screaming pain down the inside of her left knee. Once again she buckled over, landing hard on the lush, freshly cut grass. This time a whistle accompanied her fall. Staying down, vaguely aware of the whispered voices all around her, it wasn't until a gentle hand came down on her shoulder, followed by some comforting words, that she opened her eyes.

"Rich... take your time. Are you okay?"

Fissures of pain streaked up the inside of her knee, on even the slightest lateral movement.

'At least it distracts me from the pain in my back,' thought the beautiful former dragon, trying hard to find some kind of relief as she rolled up into a sitting position.

By now, half the team had gathered around her, concerned by her injury, knowing there was no way she would go down unless genuinely hurt.

"What did she do?" spat Sue, one of the team's midfielders, angrily.

"Deliberately stepped on her foot to stop her from moving off," replied Joey, before their captain could say a word.

"She's an evil one, she is," offered up Ali.

"Why is it she's playing for them now?" asked Jan, up from the back. "Last time I heard, she was still playing for the Fire Foxes."

"Who cares?" muttered Poppy into the gathered group. "Let's just kick their arses back to next week, and make them scamper back to Somerset with their tails between their legs."

"That's not really the attitude... is it?" exclaimed Richie, getting to her feet with a little help from Emma. "We need to show everyone watching what this sport is all about. Don't forget that!"

The group crowded around her looked suitably chastised.

Planting her left foot down, Richie ignored the pain that flooded up and around her knee. At exactly the same time, something primal and frightening flittered around her subconscious. Murky and dark, it fought to be unleashed, even through an overwhelming sense that she was above all of this. Sweeping it to one side, almost as if she'd been trained to do just that, the comforting voice of Emma cut in.

"Do you think it's wise to continue?"

"Wise or not... we're done!" announced the bullish ex-dragon, who'd had more than enough of this bully, even though only a few minutes of the match had passed.

Sue passed Richie's stick back to her, while the others took up their previous positions. Determined, but visibly shaken, Richie too took up her position, all the time eyeing Attitude, wondering what the hell was going on.

For the next ten minutes or so, the crowd were treated to a smorgasbord of smashing lacrosse... just how the game should be. Action changed from end to end, with both defences putting outstanding pressure on the passers, leading to fabulous interceptions, which in turn led to relentlessly quick transitions, turning defence into attack in the blink of an eye. Nobody, however, had scored yet. Both keepers had made astonishing saves. The Avalon Avengers goalie had made two brilliant saves, one with her hand, that she tipped over the crossbar, the other she caught in her crosse. Harriet, the Salisbridge keeper, had used her feet to good effect, making what most would consider to be a mind-blowing save, to keep her team level at 0-0.

During all this time, Richie had touched the ball

perhaps three times, and when she had received it, she'd moved it on quicker than a schoolteacher leaving for their summer holidays. Constantly aware of Attitude, all the time looking over her shoulder, getting deeper and deeper, further away from the opposition's goal, she'd figured out that her nemesis would only follow her so far, before letting her wander off. So she hung back, unsure of what to do, nursing the ever increasing pain that continued to shoot up the inside of her left knee.

When the ball next went out of bounds on the sideline, Emma and Sue called over to their captain and friend, to check that she was okay. She told them she was. But it wasn't so much the injury that was causing Richie to hang back and not help her team. It was fear. This was the first time she could ever remember being afraid on the lacrosse pitch... or anywhere else come to think of it, and she didn't care for it very much. Every second, deep inside her head she pictured Attitude's sneering face closing in on her, intent on doing her some more harm. Even though she was well back from the opposition's goal, she was constantly aware of where the big defender was. Abruptly, she knelt down on the gorgeous green grass, rubbing the side of her wounded knee carefully. But it was all an act. She could move, even take the pain. But the feelings inside her were something else. Images of the past flooded her mind, reminding her of how fearless and inventive she was, being the one that dragged her team, Salisbridge, out of trouble and on to winning, singlehandedly on more than one occasion. It was hard for her to understand why she felt this way. Something was different. Just as she thought this, the ring she wore on the chain around her neck, the one that Peter had given her to look after, seemed to burn her skin. Leaning forward, allowing the chain to swing away beneath her top, she was surprised to find the burning sensation still there. Taking a peek, she could see the ring was away from her skin, and there were no marks or obvious signs of burning.

'What the hell is going on?' she thought.

But that would have to wait, as the familiar sound of something small and lightning fast whistling through the air towards her, tickled her senses. Automatically she rose to her feet, turning instantly, the head on her stick a submarine's periscope searching for anything out of the ordinary, seeking the danger. Off to her right, the spinning orange ball zipped over her head. With just one hand on her stick, she thrust it out as high as she could, ignoring the spark of pain this caused in her knee. Having captured the ball perfectly she trotted off, not at full speed, but a fast jog, nagged by the unusual sensation, for her at least, of needing to get rid of the ball to a teammate... fast!

Unfortunately for her, there wasn't a single obvious pass on. Her teammates were doing their best, dodging, weaving, cutting inside and out, but none seemed to be able to get free of their marker at the moment. Richie's vision pulled back from her teammates, aware that Attitude was coming out of defence to meet her. Sweat scampered down her spine, her heart rate increased, it felt as though her boots had turned to lead, while all the time a wanting-to-run-away feeling nibbled at the insides of her stomach. In a panic, she threw the ball towards Rachel, one of the Salisbridge midfielders who'd raced up to support play. Unsurprisingly it was a rubbish pass, nowhere near her teammate, and had now allowed the Avalon Avengers to break quickly. About to turn around and head back in the hope that she could help in some way, it was then a hulking great form swung into view. Attitude!

"All your silky skills deserted you today, Tinkerbell?" she all but grunted.

Richie was frozen in terror, unable to speak or even move. It was such a strange and unfamiliar sensation; she had no idea what to do to get rid of it, if indeed she even could. Leaning right up into Richie's face, her nemesis's cloying breath washed over each and every one of the ex-dragon's freckles.

"None of your friends will be able to save you today. Before the day is out, you'll be visiting your city's fancy new hospital." And with that, she turned and plodded back towards her own goal.

Shaking inside and out, Richie wanted nothing more than to see the game end and be able to return to the comfort and safety of her home. Abruptly a shrill whistle forced her thoughts back to the here and now. Looking around, she could see one of the officials signalling for a goal. All the while she'd been caught up with Attitude, her teammates had been defending desperately but to no avail and had conceded a rather cheap goal from a lucky bouncing shot that had cannoned in off the post, leaving goalie Harriet with absolutely no chance.

As Salisbridge made their way back up the pitch, ready once again for the draw, a few of the players could be seen huddling together and their captain had a fair idea she was the subject of their discussions. Sue left the small group and sprinted over to Richie.

"Nobody's going to blame you for going off. If you're injured, you're injured," she stated.

Wanting to go off, more than anything, her comrades' faces caused a swell of emotion to spill out inside her. These were her friends, her teammates. They'd won together, lost together, drunk and dined together. She knew their families, their boyfriends, husbands, children. Tied together in victory and defeat, she was supposed to be their leader, the one they looked to for inspiration, the one they looked up to. And here she was, about to throw in the towel because of one single opposing player. It was all so confusing. But deep down inside her, something primordial, something ingrained in her very DNA screamed at her not to leave the pitch. And against her better judgement, she didn't. Instead, she stepped forward, determined to use her talent to gain control of the draw.

Aligning their sticks, placing the ball between them, the

umpire gave a stern "Ready," which drifted across the silent pitch before, seconds later, blowing his whistle loudly. Turning her fear into anger and choosing that to fuel her muscles, Richie's stick powered into action, shooting the ball high above her head, almost exactly as she'd planned. Salisbridge gained possession with a ground ball pick up by midfielder Rachel. Quickly she propelled the ball out wide right to Ali, who caught the ball running full tilt, making this the fastest transition of the game for the home side. Emma had lost her marker and was swinging around behind the goal on the right hand side, with Joey out wide on the left, while Poppy and Sue had almost caught up with play. Ali sidestepped the defender, cutting in and then pulling back at the last moment, darting around the outside, using her momentum and the defender's flat footedness to her advantage. Adjusting her hands along a different part of the shaft, her stick twisted and turned, almost as if it had a life of its own, so much so that the ball itself must have been almost dizzy. Spotting Emma's raised stick behind the goal and off to one side, bending her run perfectly, Ali cast the ball into the path of the onrushing Emma.

Richie's experience told her to hold back, that and the fact that fear still threatened to consume her. Keeping one eye on what Attitude was doing, so far that threatening presence was content with being the extra player over at the back, hoping to double up on any attacker coming through, sure that she'd already done enough to take the former dragon out of the match. It was borderline, that's for sure. Richie was terrified, so much so that if she'd had to think about what was going on, almost certainly she would have frozen up or taken herself off the pitch with her injury. But her response was instinctive, a reaction to all the games she'd played, stimulated by all her accumulated knowledge and shared experiences. For the briefest time, her body almost didn't belong to her but to someone else, her spirit watching her actions from somewhere high above. And precisely at this very second, her body screamed,

"RUN! Run for all you're worth." And she did, directly towards the goal.

Emma snared the ball out of the air perfectly, continuing on her speeding arc, looking for what she'd seen hundreds of times before, hoping against hope that her teammate would be there. Sure enough, she was!

Sprinting at full speed now, Richie's trajectory was taking her towards the goalie's left hand post, stick raised in the air, waiting to capture the ball that would be spinning her way at any second. Emma, not one to disappoint, flung the ball as hard as she could, knowing before it had left her stick that her teammate wouldn't have to move the head of her stick even an inch, that's how perfect the pass was. Moving so fast it was just a blur, Richie recognised the slight change in the weight of her stick before anything else, at which point her body took over. By now she was closing in on goal, defenders (one of which was Attitude... although Richie was so consumed by it all, she had no idea which one) closing in on all sides, hoping to block her shot. Her body rolled with her gut feeling, as the rest of her looked on. Ducking underneath the closest defender, her movement was sublime as she cut inside and, with all the strength she could muster, let loose a low bounce shot that hit the exquisitely trimmed turf just in front of their goalie and leapt up past her outstretched boot, smashing into the taut netting behind her that she'd been guarding. Screams of jubilation echoed all around as friendly arms and faces engulfed her, all offering congratulations. Wheeling away with the others to head back to the opposite end of the pitch, a quick glance over her shoulder noticed the dark and foreboding expression etched into Attitude's face. It was only then that she started to realise just how much trouble she was in.

With the score being 1-1 now, the action came thick and fast, with adrenaline pumping for everyone on the pitch, including the officials. Transitions, when they came, were lightning fast with both teams leaving holes in their defence that their opponents continued to try and exploit. The Avengers went through a period of trying to constantly force Salisbridge out of bounds wide, which worked to a degree, but left a great deal of space behind, something the Salisbridge ladies took full advantage of with some mighty risky passes. But as the whistle blew to signal half time and the women headed off for the agreed ten minute break, it was only thanks to some more stunning saves by each keeper that the score had remained level.

Both teams filed off the pitch on the same side, but at opposite ends. For the sweat drenched players, taking on fluid was the first priority, and Richie was no different. As the cool contents of the water bottle worked its way down inside her throat, she could just make out Attitude glaring in her direction from the heart of the Somerset players. Turning away, the ex-dragon poured some of the water across the front of her curly hair, encouraging it to spill down on to her face and then run down the front of her neck and cleavage. A firm hand on her shoulder jolted her.

"You alright Rich?" questioned the accented voice of Harriet the goalkeeper.

"Uhh... yeah," she replied, panting. "Just worn out... you know."

Harriet nodded, understandingly.

Most of the team had taken to sitting down on the lush grass, stretching and flexing their tired and well worked muscles. Richie joined them, pulling her legs in close to her chest, all the time taking small sips from her water bottle. An aura of expectation hung over the team, waiting for their leader to speak. But try as she might, she just couldn't find any words for them. Still badly shaken up from her painful encounters with Attitude, she wanted nothing more than to leave and go home. In her life, she couldn't recall having ever been intimidated on or off the lacrosse pitch, and it was having a profound effect on her. More so, her silence was having a profound effect on the rest of the team.

"I think if your injury's that bad, that you should go off," announced Rachel.

One or two of her teammates nodded their agreement. Richie just clutched her legs tighter to her chest.

"My guess though, is that's not what's bothering you," exclaimed Emma, the closest of all of Richie's friends on the lacrosse team.

"So, what's up then?" asked Poppy politely.

"It's that girl, isn't it?" stated Sue.

Remaining silent, for the first time in a very long time their captain was unsure of what to say or do, so very unlike her. The team all looked at one another in the bizarre situation they found themselves in, insomuch as Richie had always been larger than life and full of an inexhaustible amount of energy and enthusiasm. Now... it was almost as if the life had been well and truly sucked out of her, leaving a husk in her place.

"Why has she got it in for you?" asked Jan, softly.

"I don't know," came the mumbled reply from their captain, her head still buried somewhere between her knees.

All of them were almost ashen as they sat surrounding their distraught captain, nearly half of the interlude having come and gone. It seemed that only now were they realising the degree to which they'd previously relied on the ex-dragon, not only for her stunning goals, her thankless running and her tactical knowhow, but also for the way she acted as a role model for each and every one of them. Only now could they sneak a glimpse into the real woman and see that they were not so different, that she had her fears and worries just like the rest of them. For the first time in what seemed like forever, the whole team could see Richie for who she truly was, and not the happy go lucky, super talented, score a goal from almost anywhere talisman that they'd so often thought her to be. On many occasions she'd saved them, dragged them by the scruff of their necks to victory, inspired and amazed them. Now it was their turn to save her, and by God they would.

Standing up, Emma spoke first.

"Rich! You're not here alone. You're part of a team, out there with all of us. I might be the one speaking, but I think everyone here agrees... we're all in this together. So many times you've carried us through matches, when either we weren't good enough, or we were playing teams who were so much better. But amazingly we won, and at times... that's been solely down to you. Speaking for myself, I recognise those as times that I haven't performed, haven't been at my best, despite giving my all. But to know that I can count on you and the others around me always encourages me to be more than I am, try harder than I would alone, punch above my weight. Others, including yourself, have lifted me up when I've been down, encouraged rather than criticised when I've lost the ball, and always, always, believed in me. And I don't think it's possible to ever express my gratitude in the way that I would wish or that you all deserve. So you see... we're all in this together. Your problems... even off the pitch, are our problems. And I for one won't see anyone here bullied, intimidated or downright hurt. We all play the game as it should be played... it's something that makes me so proud to be part of THIS team. Hard but fair, strong but just, no hint of cheating, always obeying the official's decisions, even when we know they are wrong. This, I believe, is how all sport should be played... not just ours!"

Every single player, including Richie, who had now lifted her head up from her legs, sat open mouthed, incredulous at what Emma was saying. More importantly, they all wholeheartedly agreed with every last word.

"YOU," observed Emma, pointing at Richie for emphasis, "have given so much to all of us, we could play for another twenty years as a team and still not be in a position to repay you. But here and now, we can and WILL help you. This isn't your problem... it's OUR problem. And if someone tries to hurt YOU, or anyone else on this pitch deliberately, then they can damn well answer to me! I for one would follow you almost anywhere, and certainly into battle on any lacrosse pitch, against any opposition the world has to offer. You're my friend, my teammate, my... CAPTAIN!"

The words carried more power than most nation states as they surged through the invigorated group of players. Optimism replaced apprehension, worry washed away by togetherness. Richie stood, her knee throbbing, as she embraced Emma in one gigantic hug. Only moments earlier, the ex-dragon had felt the most alone she ever had, but that had all changed with Emma's startling speech. Now she felt alive, rejuvenated, part of a team and much loved.

As one, the whole team stood and enveloped Richie and Emma, the two women at the centre of their improvised huddle. Off to one side, the official's whistle blew to indicate that it was nearly time for the match to resume. Before the group broke up, Richie whispered her heartfelt thanks to them all, before telling them what they were going to do.

Returning to their places on the field, a pensive mixture of fear and excitement rocked Richie's world. Mistakenly, she'd looked across at Attitude only seconds before, to see that familiar evil glower directed against her. The words of the team and in particular, her friend Emma, from only moments before, echoed throughout her head. Knowing she was safe amongst friends, and about to do what she considered herself born to do, hope and happiness flared up inside her. The opposing centre (whom she thought of as Pony Tail) joined her and the umpire for the draw. All thoughts of the outside world were forgotten now. No spectators, no other games going on around them, no sky, no clouds... nothing! Only the battle about to commence.

And only WINNING! Fairly, of course, because otherwise there'd be no point at all. Who in their right mind would want to win any other way than fairly? Not her, that was for certain, and not her teammates either, the very thought of which made her chest swell with pride.

Placing the ball between the two sticks, the umpire said, "Ready," whilst backing away, and then blew his whistle to restart the match. Richie's tense muscles blasted into overdrive, flinging the ball far overhead in the very direction she'd wanted. As a team, Salisbridge surged forward, just as Sue seized the ball out of the air, already dashing at full speed into the opposition's half. The Avengers didn't know what hit them. There had been some fast attacks before, but nothing as quick and aggressive as this. Sue moved the ball quickly through the air to Joey who, after an audacious dummy, in turn played it straight down the line to Emma, again on one of her arcing runs.

Drifting outside, Richie feigned to go down the line and then cut inside and was now rushing with every ounce of energy in her body, powering towards the goal on almost exactly the same line that she'd scored from in the first half. Taking in the scene in a slow motion, high definition moment, Richie was rewarded by the terrified looks imprinted on the faces of the defenders before her, Attitude included.

Towards the end of her supposed arc, Emma drew back her stick slightly, as if to make that same throw towards her captain and friend. Lunging in desperation, the defender chasing her tried despairingly to block the pass, but ended up instead crashing to the floor for her valiant efforts. The defenders in front of her reacted in almost the same way, throwing themselves between the two Salisbridge players. Not Attitude though, she stood her ground, front foot forward, looking as menacing as ever. It was then that Richie slammed the brakes on, dried mud and dust mushrooming up from the bottom of her shoes, so quickly had she drawn to a halt. Attitude's look of menace transformed immediately to one of confusion. Smiling as she watched Emma continue on her arcing run, Richie could barely contain her delight as her friend drew the goalie slightly, before flinging the ball across to Joey who'd sneaked in on the other post and, taking the ball first time, smashed it into the back of the net. The Avalon Avengers looked as though a hurricane had whirled down the centre of the pitch to devastating effect.

High fives all round for Salisbridge, followed by raucous cheering from the crowd, put a smile on each one of the girls' faces, including their captain, as once again they took their positions for the restart.

Salisbridge scored two more goals in quick succession, one for Emma and another for Richie. Attitude's disappointment was there for all to see, especially when her named nemesis scored. But the rest of the Avengers seemed to be coping with it all right, given that the match was for charity and they themselves had all raised sponsorship money to play in it.

It was at about this point that Richie started to feel like her old self again... well, almost. Something inside her seemed very different, but try as she might she couldn't put her finger on exactly what it was. She felt like a jigsaw puzzle with the very last piece missing, albeit an outside piece, one that made very little difference to the overall picture. At least that's the closest way she could get to explaining it. But beneath all the confusion, a bubbling concoction of anxiety and vulnerability trickled around her relatively new (not that she had any idea of that) body, masked at the moment by the flood of adrenaline from the thrill and excitement of the lacrosse that she loved so much, and which had become such an integral part of her life (both before and after her recent change in bodily circumstances).

After many more transitions (sloppy passes being intercepted from both teams seemed to have been a common theme for the past ten minutes or so) the match entered its final eight minutes. Currently the Avengers had the ball and were passing it around the goal circle, with the home side defending for their lives, working hard to pressure all the passers. The Somerset side were looking to exploit any holes in the Salisbridge defence, but the home team had made some defensive adjustments over the last few minutes and the holes that had been there had now disappeared.

Angela closed down her player behind the goal, giving her no room at all, weaving this way and that with her, keeping her stick in line with that of her attacker's. But the Avengers player, Fancy Trainers as Richie had named her within her head, had more than a modicum of calm about her. She didn't panic but continued to duck and weave, turn and dodge, all the time the ball cradled in the head of her stick, looking for the perfect pass to one of her teammates. Harriet darted back and forth in front of goal, trying to cover whichever side the Avengers player moved behind. Jan, Angela and Tina all stuck with their players, getting their bodies in front, staying tight on the woman adjacent to the ball, hoping to slow the flow of momentum by the ball carrier.

Fancy Trainers dropped her shoulder, twisted one way and then quickly turned back the other. Angela moved with her, but her foot slipped on the well crafted turf, allowing her opponent a slight advantage which she duly took, flinging the ball out wide left to the attacker who Richie thought of as Pony Tail, who had managed to just get in front of Salisbridge's Poppy. Both teams were in full swing now, totally absorbed in the match. To each and every one of them nothing else existed, each pumped full of adrenaline, each totally focused and immersed in their roles, with the sole purpose of winning the match.

Pony Tail charged towards goal, stick cradling the ball, its twisting and turning motion like the gears on a child's bike. Ali left her player, drawn towards the ball at speed.

Giving it all she had, the Avengers player pulled back the head of her stick. But Ali had made up an incredible amount of ground, so much so that nobody would have believed it had they not seen it for themselves, and was able to make a beautiful check and come away with the ball. The Avengers were stunned, along with most of the home side. Not Sue though, who was off to the left, waving her stick frantically in the air, hoping her teammate would spot her. She did, and let fly with an inch perfect pass that Sue was able to snare on the run.

Peeling away from the position she'd taken up on the right, Richie was now heading in field to try and help Sue. Joey had continued her run down the left flank in front of Sue, but was being marked one to one by an Avengers defender who Richie thought of as Whippet. Meanwhile, Emma had crossed paths with Richie on a diagonal run, dragging her marker out wide right to where her captain had just come from, creating a great big hole for her friend to run into. Glancing up, Sue spotted Richie dashing towards her. With footfalls coming up fast behind her, Sue thrust out her stick, sending the ball on a trajectory towards her captain. Seizing the ball out of the warm air, Richie spun sharply, changing her direction and heading straight towards the opposition's goal, grasping her stick with just her right hand, although comfortable on the run with either. It would have been hard to find a better demonstration of stick handling on the entire planet at that precise moment.

Swarming all over the Avengers, the Salisbridge team's midfielders were breaking their necks to catch up with play, in the hope of scoring another goal. Turning her head, Richie hoped to catch sight of that elusive run from one of her teammates, one that she could pick out and then thread the eye of the needle, one that would almost certainly lead to a goal. But at the moment, it just wasn't on. So with little option, she kept hold of the ball, jinking and turning, ducking and dodging.

Sue had come inside from her left position, after her storming run up the outside and pinpoint accurate pass to Richie, and although slightly behind play, she had a pretty clear view of what was going on. And what she saw bothered her... A LOT! The Avengers' huge, muscular defender had murder in her eyes, the object of her rage being Richie, at least that's the way it looked to Sue. Not knowing what else to do, she pushed her burning legs as fast as they would move and beyond, hoping at the very least to warn her captain, who seemed momentarily distracted, looking around for that perfect pass.

Having slowed her run, Richie turned and cut inside, running in an arc right in front of the goal, but some way out, thinking about the possibility of a shot, as currently no obvious pass presented itself. In the past, despite the difficulty, she had scored from just this kind of range. As this thought flickered in and then out of her consciousness, her internal sense of danger sprang from nothing into a high pitched screaming voice, warning her of an impending threat. Tilting her head right, she could just make out Attitude charging at full speed towards her, stick in an almost horizontal position, about to make contact. The only thing she had time to think was, 'This is going to hurt.' But to her surprise, and that of the hulking great defender, Sue quite literally flew between the two of them, taking the full force of Attitude's stick on her right arm, a sickening sound echoing around the pitch from the contact. Immediately she hit the ground, shrieking out in pain as she did so. Instantly Richie was at her side, her stick with the ball still cradled in it discarded on the turf beside her.

Abruptly the official's shrill whistle rang out across the pitch, louder and sharper than it had sounded at any other point in the match. Storming across the pitch towards the villain of the piece, Attitude, the umpire pulled out a yellow card, held it out in front of her face, said the words, "Illegal contact," and signalled with his arm towards the penalty area, to which she duly trudged off to serve her two minute suspension.

Most of the Salisbridge team, with the exception of Harriet the goalie and Angela the defender, had gathered around Sue, who was now at least sitting up on the pristine turf, nursing her injured arm. Suddenly, making a big fuss, a stern looking woman in a black uniform came barging through.

"St John's ambulance... let me through please. Clear the way!"

Both sets of players surrounding Sue all took a step back. Richie stayed where she was, right by Sue's side, as the woman placed her medical kit on the ground and started to carefully take a look at the damaged arm. Immediately it became clear that Sue would take no further part in the match, and judging from the dark purple colour that was rapidly spreading from the site of the impact, a trip to hospital looked inevitable. As indeed it was! Sue was led off to the waiting ambulance, with Jan promising to pack up her sticks and the rest of her kit and meet her there. Richie tried to accompany her friend on the walk across to the ambulance, but the stern looking woman waved her away, telling her in no uncertain terms to get back to her match. So reluctantly she did, wandering back to find her stick and the ball, as well as an... argument! Joey, the Salisbridge winger, was currently being restrained by Emma and Poppy, all the while telling the Avengers left on the pitch exactly what she thought about their new player. And although Emma and Poppy were trying to make peace (after all, this was a friendly match, being played for charity) they couldn't help but echo her sentiments. Richie intervened by stepping between Joey and their opponents.

"What's going on?" she asked.

"THAT," spat Joey, "was nothing short of deliberate. And everyone here knows it."

Quiet, impossibly so, that was a fitting description of

the entire Avengers team. They had all seen quite clearly what had happened, with some now in a state of shock, and others unsure of how to deal with the situation. Normally you stuck by your teammates, but this was something else altogether.

The matter was settled by the Salisbridge captain who, like everybody else, knew that the attack was meant for her, and was very much premeditated.

"Enough!" she ordered. "We have a game to play, in front of all these wonderful spectators, and I for one want to show them what our sport is all about. Passion, power, aggression, agility, all channelled in the right way... into playing our beloved sport. But let's not forget fairness, sporting behaviour, teamwork and just the sheer exhilaration of actually playing. Let them see us all having fun. I for one don't turn up and do this because I have to and it's a chore. I play because I want to, because the thrill I get is like nothing else." At this point something deep within her subconscious tickled her brain, wriggling just outside her reach, elusive but there, promising something more, something else, something... forgotten! "I love playing this sport, as I'm pretty sure all of you do. Let's show everybody how it should be played, and let's damn well enjoy it!"

With the Avengers all nodding in agreement, echoing every sentiment that Richie had just expressed, Joey pulled free of her teammates and headed out towards the wing. Richie picked up her stick with the ball still lodged inside it, and everybody else took up their positions.

With the award of a free position, both teams stood ready to start, both a player down, with Sue heading off to hospital in the ambulance, Salisbridge not having any substitutes, and Attitude for the Avengers being consigned to the penalty area for the next two minutes. Turning to look at Emma, Richie gave her friend a very crafty wink, something Emma returned, unseen to everyone but Richie. They'd practised this over and over. Now it was time to see if it worked. The umpire blew his whistle. Richie took off towards the outside of the right post of the goal, legs moving as fast as they could, stick turning all the time. Emma crossed behind her friend, already a touch in front of the opponent marking her. The Avengers keeper stepped forward to narrow the angle. Just before she reached the goal circle, Richie swivelled round and, on the move, flicked the ball back across the front edge of the goal circle. Wrong footed for a split second, the Avengers' goalie had absolutely no chance as Emma swept up the ball and hurled it into the bottom left corner of the goal. Perfect!

Once again the team all rejoiced, much more muted this time though, due to Sue's injury. The match quickly resumed, with the Avengers controlling the draw and immediately going on the offensive. Richie watched, frustrated, as the opponents she liked to think of as Pony Tail and Rake combined a wicked one-two, resulting in Pony Tail getting a fabulous shot off. It looked like Harriet had saved the best for last though, instantly stretching out her leg, turning the ball just around the post with the tip of her boot, brushing the sweat away from around the chin strap of her helmet with her gloved hand (not easy at the best of times) as she leapt back up, ready for another onslaught. However, Salisbridge had gained possession, but a poor pass from Angela saw the ball that was meant for Joey out wide on the left, travel into the crowd, out of bounds. With a little over three minutes left, the umpire blew his whistle and signalled to Attitude that she could once again take to the field. As she jogged back towards the Avengers' goal, she turned towards Richie, an ominous snarl scrawled across her face.

With the clock ticking down, Salisbridge were on the back foot. Although leading 5-1, they were all determined not to concede another goal and if at all possible, regain possession and score at least one more themselves. To this end, they were all defending valiantly, marking tightly, throwing themselves into check after check, desperate to retrieve the ball. In the end, the one Richie thought of as Rake became ever more impatient, shooting from an almost ridiculous distance, never really standing a chance of beating a goalkeeper of Harriet's quality from that far out.

Knowing that there was still just time for one more attack, Harriet's oversized stick propelled the ball out near the touchline on the right to Poppy, who on capturing the ball took off at full pelt, leaving the tired and weary Avengers player who was supposedly marking her, well behind. Both teams knew this was the last play of the game, something that spurred the home team on, while at the same time drained their opposition, despite the Avengers now having a one player advantage. With superior numbers on this attack, picking a pass was relatively simple for Poppy, and after having laid it off to Rachel in the centre of the pitch, continued on with her run.

Rachel moved forward quickly, not quite at a sprint but certainly fast enough to show that she was aware of the time counting down. By now, and with both the delay at the start of the match, half time, and the time it had taken to deal with Sue's injury, all the other matches had long since finished, with most of the spectators and players crowding around what now seemed like a very tiny lacrosse pitch.

With the Somerset team having almost given up, Rachel, like Poppy before her, had more than a couple of options, but very single-mindedly knew what she was looking for. And then she saw it. Richie was making a sweeping run in from the right, her body language screaming for the ball. This was the pass that Rachel had been looking for, this was the one that would gain them the goal. Mechanically she cast the ball to the onrushing Richie, its target. But as if from nowhere, up popped Emma's stick, her route intersecting that of her captain's.

With a flourish, she plucked the ball out of the air, all in one graceful move and at top speed headed towards the goal circle. Only two players remained between her and the ideal end to the game. Their goalie and Richie's nemesis... Attitude.

By now, Emma's body had decided on a course of action. Feinting left but cutting back right, she drew her stick back a touch before unleashing a rip-roaring shot that was heading straight for the bottom left corner of the goal as she looked at it. The shot was so good that she was already wheeling away, raising her stick aloft in celebration.

If Emma had been watching, she would have seen something absolutely amazing happen, probably in fact the best piece of skill in the game so far. Attitude the defender managed to intercept the speeding shot, her reactions akin to a Greek god.

A collective intake of breath from almost all those watching at once, was Emma's first clue that all had not gone to plan. The lack of applause for the would-be goal just confirmed it.

Richie slowed to a halt, hanging a little back from Emma, who had just stolen the goal scoring opportunity away from her. She didn't begrudge the young forward her moment of glory, quite the opposite in fact. In Richie's opinion Emma deserved the man of the match award for her outstanding performance on and off the pitch, especially after her rousing speech at half time. As captain, she was just grateful to make it to the end of the game without anyone else getting hurt, and knowing that they'd put on a valiant display of lacrosse for everyone who'd turned out to watch and support this great event. Watching in admiration as Emma unleashed her shot, she'd just taken half a step in her teammate's direction to congratulate her, when it happened. Richie stood gobsmacked. The take was out of this world, and one that she herself could only have dreamt of. How the ball hadn't gone flying into the back of the net, she had no idea. But she had no time to dwell on that particular thought now, because Attitude was only a few yards away, ball firmly cradled in the crosse of her stick, eyes firmly focused on Richie, stomping very angrily towards her.

Fear welled up inside her. Proper, overwhelming, can't move a muscle fear. It felt like a completely new experience, which in itself seemed odd. Her mind screamed out at her to react but, momentarily, her body wouldn't obey, it was so afraid. In what seemed like a faraway place, the ring around her neck burned her flesh, almost as if trying to get her attention.

One word resounded through her head. 'REVENGE!' She knew what she had to do, and she didn't give a stuff about the consequences as she approached the woman who'd ruined it all.

The world had slowed, with the whole field caught up in a scene from a slow motion, high definition, action replay. Emma had stopped running, reeling in her stick, realising what had just happened. Richie stood frozen to the spot, too terrified to move. Attitude advanced menacingly towards the Salisbridge captain, raging anger swirling in her eyes.

Many hundreds looked on, aware in the back of their minds, even though they had no knowledge of this wonderful game, that a turning point had been reached. Something was about to unfold. Expectation engulfed the crowd.

Attitude's grimace transformed into the tiniest of grins as she put everything into powering the ball. It was a shot, certainly not a pass, just in front of her own goal, just aimed at a person rather than the netting between two sticks. That was some achievement. Also, probably the hardest and fastest one she'd ever let fly. A warm glow spread throughout her as something deep within was finally satisfied.

The ex-dragon saw what was coming from only three or so yards away. She had no chance... NONE! Still caught up in the slow motion replay, she looked on as the perfectly formed, spinning ball exploded out of Attitude's stick, heading directly towards her right eye. Images zipped through her mind. Feelings as well. She was aware of the ring, continuing to burn the skin beneath her top. Briefly, she knew solace, but we're talking about units of time only usually reserved for Grand Prix teams. And then every fibre, nerve ending... atom, exploded into action, like an Olympic sprinter out of the blocks. By now the orange ball had covered over half the distance, looking more like an out of control, raging sun, than something used to play this totally addictive, adrenaline filled, all consuming sport. But angles had been calculated, power transferred, agility and strength maximised, almost as if her old self (not that she knew any different) had stirred from somewhere deep inside, unlocking exactly what she required, exactly when needed. In a whirling blur, her stick came up, well... more round actually, stopping directly in front of her face, the ball cannoning into the pocket of her stick, the leathers and nylon cord being stretched to their limits, straining to contain such power, and stopping only a fraction short of the surface of Richie's right eyeball. If the take that Attitude had made only moments before had been good (and it had been) then a whole new scale of brilliance was needed to describe this. 'Godlike' and 'out of this world' were but a couple of ways to express accurately what had just happened.

Quite appropriately, in the blink of an eye, it was all over. The sharp shrill of the umpire's whistle reverberated across the playing fields as the enormous crowd let out a collective sigh of relief, nearly all not having realised they'd been holding their breath. Then the applause broke out, ringing all around them. It seemed almost inappropriate.

There was still the matter of the standoff between Richie, who hadn't moved a muscle since catching the ball, and Attitude who stood close by, dumbfounded at being confounded. The umpire strode over purposefully. Players from both sides crowded around the two of them. Thrusting out a red card in front of him, towards Attitude, the umpire muttered, "You're done," before turning around and striding back. The spectators started flooding towards their cars, and for those on foot, the exit. Players from all the other games trudged back to their designated changing rooms, leaving two ladies lacrosse teams (minus Sue) on the field of play, angry and very much determined to find some answers. But before they could, Tina, the Salisbridge defender stepped forward, ripped Attitude's stick from her hand, threw it off to one side and pronounced,

"That... was ASSAULT! I'm a police officer, and you're coming with me."

The gathered players had been stunned before, but this was something else entirely. Before any of them could gather their thoughts, the Avengers' captain, the woman who Richie thought of as Pony Tail, stepped forward.

"I don't know what your game is, but you can be damn sure it's not lacrosse. I've never been so disgusted in my entire life. YOU will NEVER play for us again. EVER!"

Echoing their captain's sentiments, the rest of the team pitched in, the Salisbridge players all nodding their agreement.

Tina grabbed Attitude by the arm, with a view to doing who knows what. But Richie stepped forward, at the same time dropping her stick carefully to the ground, afraid of her rising temper.

"Hang on a minute," cried the ex-dragon. "I want to know what's going on!"

Tina released her grip, momentarily at least. Richie stormed forward, invading her tormentor's personal space, right up close.

"What's this all about?" she spat, jabbing a finger right in the middle of Attitude's chest.

"Like you don't know," snarled her opponent.

"I don't," replied Richie, genuinely surprised.

Both teams gathered round, with Richie and Attitude smack bang in the middle of the circle, all the players waiting for an explanation, along with the ex-dragon.

"You did it! YOU! You ruined our lives. And all for what? Just so that you could have some petty sort of vengeance," cried Attitude.

By now Richie had taken a couple of breaths, most of the anger inside her having drifted away. She was calm, focused and determined to get to the bottom of what was going on.

"I have absolutely no idea what you're talking about," answered the Salisbridge captain. "Why don't you enlighten us all?"

Attitude swallowed visibly, seeming to take in her situation for the first time. Surrounded by two teams of really... 'disappointed off' (see what I did there?), angry lacrosse players, with no place to run, and no place to hide.

"It all started two weeks after we played you last year," she uttered.

"When you say 'WE', you mean Bristol Fire Foxes (Attitude's former club)?"

"Yes."

"And...?"

"We beat you in the last minute of a very niggly game, something you were most upset about," announced Attitude smugly.

Richie could vaguely remember the game and her feelings associated with it, but it did all seem a bit of a blur, that and a lot of other things from her past.

"Anyhow, a little under two weeks after the match, my brother, who at the time was living with my parents, had a job interview at Cropptech, here in Salisbridge."

'Wow,' thought Richie. 'I didn't see that coming. I wonder where this is all going?'

"After spending the whole day here, he returned home

to inform us that he hadn't been successful. When we asked him why, he told us it was the fault of the woman in the training department, who plays lacrosse. That is you, isn't it?"

Richie mumbled a "Yes," as her mind recounted what she'd just been told. She'd never been involved in any interviews... why would she? And as for being asked about her opinion on new staff, that had never happened either. This was all most odd.

"So you see," continued Attitude, "you ruined our lives. My brother had been back living with my parents for over three years, putting great pressure and strain on them, both physically and financially, eventually leading to my father having to go into hospital not long after the job interview. So there, there it is... the reason I despise you, and your petty... hatefulness."

Richie moved across to Emma and whispered something in her ear, causing the young forward to sprint off in the direction of the temporary changing rooms. Turning back to face Attitude, Richie rubbed her chin in front of what was, by now, a very expectant audience.

"I've never had anything to do with interviewing people... NEVER! As you so rightly pointed out, I work in the TRAINING department. And as for the match... yes I was frustrated, but only for a few hours. After that, just like every other match... the frustrations are forgotten. And just so you know... I would never do what you've just accused me of. Not in a million years!" exclaimed Richie, a little undercurrent of anger running through her voice.

Emma pushed through the throng of players, holding out Richie's mobile phone. Richie took it and thrust it in Attitude's direction.

"PHONE HIM!" she ordered. "I want to hear all about this interview."

"Uhhhh... I'm not sure I'll be able to get hold of him," she replied nervously.

"YOU WILL get hold of him. Because if you don't,

things are going to go very badly for you, very quickly," threatened Richie.

Attitude took the phone and dialled the number. Richie leant over and hit the speaker button. The ring tone echoed around the circle of players. Three rings later, a voice answered.

"Hello?"

"Hi Jeff, it's me... Lynn."

"Hi sis," replied Jeff.

"Ummm... I'm going to ask something a little bit strange now, but can you just do it without arguing please? It's really important."

"Okay," replied Jeff.

"You remember that interview you had last year with Cropptech? Could you just tell me about it again?"

"Uhhh... okay. Sure."

"You told me it was the fault of the lacrosse playing woman in the training department. What exactly did she say to you?"

There was a very long pause. It was clear the line hadn't gone dead and that someone was still there, but it was all a little too quiet. Something wasn't quite right, a fact that everybody there had noticed.

"Well?" demanded Attitude.

"I... uh... uh... uh... didn't actually see that woman," stuttered Jeff.

"What do you mean you didn't see her? You came home and told us it was her fault you didn't get the job. How can you not have seen her?"

"Uhhh... well, it was this Manson fella. I spent most of the day with him, and right at the very end he told me he would have loved to have offered me the job, but that some lacrosse playing woman in the training department had put a stop to the whole thing. He sounded really genuine, and devastated that he couldn't take me on."

As soon as Jeff had uttered the word 'MANSON', the ring around Richie's neck felt as though it had turned to

299

lava and was burning its way through her pale flesh. So much so, that she couldn't help but look down to make sure that wasn't the case... and it wasn't, so she tried her best to ignore the strange feeling, but that wasn't the only one she was having. Currently, her skin felt as though it were crawling and her legs seemed a little weak. Strangely, that word conjured up images of Peter, but she wasn't sure why. Something just out of reach in her mind constantly slipped away as she tried to grab hold of it, wriggling and squirming, both wanting to be noticed and to conceal itself. In the end she gave up the chase, but it continued to nag at her and would do so for many hours to come.

"Oh Jeff," said Attitude, barely holding it together, "that's not what you told me."

"I know," replied Jeff. "Sorry."

Rubbing her eyes, barely containing tears, Attitude, or Lynn as they now knew her to be, said,

"I've got to go. I'll give you a call later."

"Okay," whispered Jeff. "Is everything alright?"

"Yeah, yeah. I'll call you later. Bye."

Lynn cancelled the call and handed the phone back to Richie, all the time not able to look her in the eye.

"I'm sorry," she said as she did so.

"Not good enough," piped up Tina, once again grabbing her arm.

Richie stepped in.

"Just leave it. It's not worth it."

"You don't want to press charges?"

"No," stated Richie, deflated. "All I want is a shower, and to forget all about today."

And with that, it was all over. Well nearly. The Avengers told Attitude in no uncertain terms that she would never play for them again, that she would have to find her own way back to Somerset, and then threw all her stuff out of the changing room. The disgraced lacrosse player was last seen walking into town, still dressed in her kit, looking very sad and lonely indeed.

Both teams made their way to the local pub to join up with the other teams that had played that afternoon, where refreshments and food had been put on. It had been an extraordinary day, and Richie was just looking forward to hooking up with her friends Peter, Tank and Flash.

41 SHAKE, RATTLE AND... ROLL

Somehow it seemed quieter than usual, something that given the prisoners' unchanging circumstances was unlikely at best, impossibly bad at worst. Inadequate lighting flickered, hissed and spluttered as the fast flowing, ice cold stream gurgled, guzzled, groaned and grumbled. Something extraordinary seemed to radiate from it.

And then there was the old dragon. Which one? The one punished the most by this harsh environment, if that were at all possible, the one transfixed in his natural form... Bag O' Bones!

Despite the freezer-like prison having an air of being quieter, the old dragon's wheezing, spluttering, moaning and hacking cough had grown worse over the last week or so. Even though there was no visible way to track the passage of time, Fredric had always been able to ascertain the passing of minutes, hours and weeks with astonishing accuracy, even without his dragon magic. By his estimate it had been eleven days, six hours and about forty minutes since that lowlife jailer had last appeared, inflicting devastating beatings on both dragons, while leaving the naga king to watch in silence. A little over three days later, Bag O' Bones, as both Fredric and the naga king had come to think of him, had started to sound much, much worse. Gradual at first, now the noises he made almost seemed too much for any one being to bear. Fredric glanced over to his fellow prisoner. For some time now he'd thought of them as comrades in arms, despite their clear differences and beliefs, bringing to mind that old dragon saying, 'My enemy's enemy is my friend.' Just as he did so, the naga king imperceptibly nodded back, a movement so small that unless you knew what to look for, you wouldn't have noticed a thing.

It had been more than sixteen hours or so since their last telepathic communication, in which both had expressed their concern about not only the odd feeling of emptiness and change around the icy hellhole, but about the deteriorating condition of the suffering, ancient dragon guard nearby. Contact between both prisoners had grown a little more frequent, with short bursts preferred to longer periods of fruitless trying. A few important words or a well thought out question seemed to work much better than what had been going on before. Each of them worked out what they wanted to say, long before the toll taking exchanges took place, leading to things being smoother and quicker, as well as them being able to 'exchange' more often. Fredric found it somewhat frustrating, mostly because there was so much that he wanted to ask. The only thing he'd learnt so far that he considered of any real value, regarded the chains that bound the three of them in place. Supposedly they were unbreakable, and were able to constrain and retain both magical and physical powers to one degree or another. According to the naga king, no being in his race's history had ever escaped from them. Fredric was, he considered, ever the optimist, but this information hit him hard. Always assuming that eventually he'd break free, given enough time and provided he wasn't murdered by one of his captors before the opportunity presented itself, for the naga king to reveal this meant real trouble and sapped the life, and some of the hope, from him. Over the past few hours he'd considered all possibilities, almost recovered as he was from the jailer's beating. The only smidgen of hope that he'd come up with was that if the chains weren't too long, just maybe he could reach what they were attached to, release them, free the naga king and make their escape with them still on. In fact, before now he'd tried to dig his way into the solid wall of ice surrounding them, and had received many beatings just for his token efforts. But that was when the jailer frequented their prison far more often. Perhaps now, given the infrequency of the visits, any of which might be the last, it was worth making another attempt. He vowed to ask the naga king his opinion the next time they communicated.

A noticeable vibration throughout the entire icy cavern shook him out of his reverie. Bag O' Bones was shaking violently, the tiny scarps of skin hanging from his broken wings flapping around furiously. It far exceeded any of the normal (if that's what they could be called) bouts of shivering, which they all suffered from at some point. This was something different. And all he could do was watch helplessly.

Starting to flail about, the ancient dragon's talons, hands and head all waved around as if he were suffering from some kind of fit. And then he did... but of the coughing kind. It sounded disgusting, Fredric thought as he watched and listened. Abruptly it ended with a disturbing sound, just like that of a baby's rattle. More troubled than Fredric had ever seen him, the naga king looked over. Both turned back towards Bag O' Bones. Silence had overtaken him... FOREVER! With one final shudder, the tortured, ancient being toppled onto one side, rolled as far as the length of chain restraining him would allow, and was fortunate enough, finally, to leave the pain and sorrow of this unforgiving hellhole. Fredric promised himself he would remember, and that the dragon's pain and everything he'd gone through would someday count for something.

42 LOST PUPPY LOOKING FOR A LEAD

Perched on a high bar stool, nursing a cool diet Pepsi that reminded her of him, loneliness threatened to consume Janice, despite the crowded nature of the very popular pub. Having had no joy at finding Peter during all of the sports matches, she had reluctantly tagged along to the after match drinks and food that had been laid on at one of the nearest pubs. It wasn't odd for her to be there, at least she didn't think so; after all, she knew almost all the sports men and women, even if it was just to say hello to. Besides, most of the other bar workers from the sports club were there, as well as the manager himself. So it wasn't odd in any way, shape or form. What was peculiar though, was that Tank had still failed to turn up. It was practically the talk of the rugby section. From what she could gather from one of the very friendly rugby players (Hook, his name was, if she remembered correctly) the second XI had lost to the first, albeit by quite a narrow margin. The talk was that if Tank had been there, he would have been the difference between victory and defeat. His team were most disappointed, and more than a little concerned for his out of character no show.

Taking the smallest slurp of her drink in the world (microbes would have downed more in one go), she wondered if Tank's absence was in any way related to the fact that Peter hadn't turned up. At first, she thought that she'd just missed him. It wouldn't have been an unreasonable assumption, not given the crowd of thousands that had turned up to support such a good cause. But on arriving at the pub, she'd bumped into Richie on her way to the toilets. 'Uncomfortable' would have been the very best that could be said about their encounter. After an awkward pause that lasted way too long, and with Richie just wanting to scoot past her in a very narrow corridor, Janice decided that she at least had to ask. So she had. She'd asked the young lacrosse player if Peter had turned up to watch, or was at least here in the pub. The answer had troubled her more than a little. Richie, despite clearly not wanting to engage Janice in conversation at all, had gone on to explain how Peter was supposed to have been there, and how unusual it was for him not to have been. That, combined with the missing-in-action Tank, led her to be concerned for both of them. Janice figured if Richie was more than a little anxious, then there was indeed something to worry about. After the painful conversation, Janice had done something that only a few hours ago would have seemed impossible for her to even contemplate. She'd phoned Peter. First on his mobile, and then, after no response and no option to even leave a message, at home. Getting through to his home answer phone, she even left a message asking him to call her back on her mobile as soon as possible, that's how worried she was. That was over ninety minutes ago, and still he hadn't returned her call. So here she was, afternoon dragging into evening, clinging onto her best hope of finding out what had happened to him and his friend, by hanging around the remaining sports players that still resided in the very noisy pub. A sense of real foreboding hung over her.

43 A CAPTIVE AUDIENCE

It had all happened so suddenly, it was hard to make sense of it really. Having just stepped off the monorail at Salisbridge station with Tim (both in their human forms, with Tim having had intensive training over the last week or so about how to hold his complex alter ego together) they'd come back from a tour of the Purbeck Peninsula nursery ring, when all of a sudden they'd been surrounded by strange dark shapes, both dragon and human alike. Armed with lethal looking, dark coloured swords, it was blatantly obvious to everyone on and off the monorail that they had little choice but to comply with their demands. There were simply too many of them to do anything else. Marched from the station to the market square like lambs to the slaughter, nothing could have possibly prepared the two of them for what awaited them there. It was like something from a nightmare, but no nightmare on earth could possibly have been that bad. Off to one side, a group of very ordinary dragons lay surrounded by this new enemy. But that wasn't what turned theirs and the other detainees' stomachs. In the far corner of the square, a towering pile of butchered dragon bodies stood higher than most two storey houses. The sight made them tremble with fear, and they both started to gag as the smell of death wafted in their direction. As their group was marched across the market place, Peter knew things were as bad as they could get and that fate had conspired to put him in the wrong place at the wrong time, once again caught up in an unimaginable horror that couldn't possibly get any worse. How wrong he'd been! As the prisoners from the monorail were guided into the middle of another group of guards, Peter watched, fascinated by a structure that was being constructed at the far end of the massive square, some kind of metal monstrosity that required almost as many beings to build it, as were guarding the captives off to one side. As they continued walking and were about to enter the guarded area, two terrifyingly huge swords dropped down in front of both him and Tim, simultaneously.

"Not you two," barked the guard. "You two... over there!" he said, nodding his giant scaly head off to the left.

Terrified out of their minds, Peter and Tim headed off in the direction that had been indicated, hemmed in by their captors. Abruptly the crackling, spluttering and hissing of dragon flame caused them to look over their shoulders at the massive structure being built. Whatever it was, it was big. Strong as well, observed Peter. Taking his eyes off the construction effort, he'd turned round just in time to see his surrounding captors all part in front of him, like a pair of stage curtains. He'd thought this nightmare couldn't get any worse, but now knew just how wrong he'd been. Instantly his body started to shake of its own volition. His mind used all its conscious will to command his form not to urinate (which it really wanted to do right now) and to try and curb the shaking.

"Ahhhhhhh... if it isn't my young friend!" boomed a loud, terrifying voice from in front of him. It was a voice that featured regularly in his nightmares, a voice that he'd told himself had gone forever and he would never hear again, a voice he'd encountered on that cold, winter's night. A voice belonging to a being who had very nearly killed him.

Manson stood surrounded by an entourage of dragon, naga and human shapes. Terrified as he was, Peter's brain had the capacity to recognise that some of the human shapes with him were actually nagas.

'This is it then,' he thought, 'the big play.'

"How nice of you to join us," announced the most frightening voice in the world.

He knew this was it. The end. There was no possible escape, and out of the corner of his eye he could just make out a heap of executed dragons. Sure he was next, Manson would get exactly what he wanted, exactly what he didn't get last time, on that cold, chilly night, just above where they now stood.

"I have to admit to being more than a little disappointed that you and this entire place," he said opening his arms wide, grandstanding, "weren't wiped from the face of this planet with my little bomb. It seems, BENTWHISTLE, that your luck knows no bounds. Rest assured, this time though, your luck's run out. There's not even the tiniest sliver left."

The smallest fraction of his brain smirked a little at the way in which Manson always seemed to be able to make the word Bentwhistle sound like something someone else's cat was doing in your garden right now.

By now Peter had resigned himself to his fate, a painful death at the hands of the being he hated the most on this planet. With that in mind, strangely, his body calmed down, allowing him to take everything in for almost the first time. As well as the guards in all their various forms, there appeared to be more important beings surrounding his nemesis, he judged. A woman stood at the far end of the line, clad fully in skin tight black, the look in her eyes pure evil. Peter thought he knew danger when he saw it. She might as well have had a massive red neon sign above her, with that very word written on it, and was to be avoided at all costs he knew. Next to her was a wizened old man who, by Peter's guess, had to be a dragon as well. He looked frail and weak, sitting as he was on a bench made of rock. Moving on, a sight that just made him angry, angrier than he could ever remember feeling, greeted him. A reasonably small, light green dragon stood, looking more than a little cocky. A white shape like a delicate rose blossomed across his stomach. A dragon Peter recognised, one he'd dealt with and one who'd not only betrayed him, but the king as well.

'ROSEBLOOM!' he thought, dark images of what he'd like to do to the so called councillor rising within him.

Noticeably he still had that ridiculous looking, long, dark mane of hair rolling down the back of his head, currently tied into a ponytail, but he seemed to have lost the jewel piercings and the crazy wrap around glasses since their last meeting. On noticing Peter's interest, the councillor smirked in a very superior way. And that left Manson. Only it didn't, and Peter wasn't the least bit surprised to see his former classmate lurking behind Manson's right shoulder, skulking in the shadows, trying not to be noticed.

'CASEY!' he thought, his anger almost erupting. So many things ran through his mind. Normally a calm, kind, friendly being, an overwhelming instinct to KILL bubbled up inside him, something so sinister and primal he hadn't even been aware of its existence until now. But all dragons had it, some just controlled it better than others.

As Manson slowly strode forward towards him, his heart raced, the tap, tap, tapping of his cane against the rock getting steadily louder. Mouth dry, almost frightened out of his mind, he wasn't prepared for what happened next. Ignoring Peter, Manson walked straight up to Tim, grabbed him by the chin and started tilting his head from side to side.

"So this is it?" he enquired loudly, glancing back over his shoulder.

"It is!" replied the vicious looking woman that Peter considered death on legs.

"Hmmmmm," muttered Manson. "Doesn't look much... does it?"

"It's him Sire! Apparently he's still learning to be a dragon."

Manson burst into a cackling, raucous laugh that bounced and echoed around the furthest reaches of the market place.

"Ohhhh... it's just too easy!" he yelled to no one in particular.

Turning back to the newly confirmed dragon, looking him straight in the eyes, with menace in his voice, he declared,

"Some saviour you're going to be. You'll be lucky to see out the day!"

'Oh crap!' thought Peter. 'He knows... but how is that even possible?' Of course, it was obvious now, even to him. ROSEBLOOM! Once again, dark deeds crested his thoughts as he considered how he could punish the traitorous councillor, should the opportunity arise.

A stinging pain in his face followed by the most horrendous crunching sound snapped him back to reality, quite literally. Blood and tiny fragments of bone exploded out in front of him. For a split second, it seemed as though it had happened to someone else and he was just an unwitting onlooker. But not so. Manson had caught him square on the nose with a whole-hearted punch, his nose not so much broken, as mashed.

As blood trickled down his face, running onto his lips and into his mouth, a silver metallic tang ran over his tongue. Briefly, he wondered why it tasted the way it did? And did other beings' blood taste the same, or different? Mind wavering, thinking about blacking out, what came next almost made him wish he had. A vicelike grip grabbed him around the throat, before a sinister, evil, twisted looking face with a manic grin ground across it, appeared within his vision. Manson!

"Alright me old mucker?" barked the deranged dark dragon, sounding to Peter like some awful impression of a very dubious pirate. "I've missed seeing me old friend."

Off the scale, that's how bad the pain at the front of Peter's face was now, the grip around his throat so tight that he couldn't pull in a fresh breath. He hadn't known it, but he'd started turning blue. As he looked at the face he hated so much, the edges of what he could see started to go all cloudlike and fluffy. Before he passed out, he just managed to hear words that would have made him tremble, had he stayed conscious.

"We're all going to pay your mate the king a little visit.

Won't that be nice?!"

All that had happened some time ago. How long? He didn't know for sure. But hours at least. Slowing, trying to catch a decent breath, a hurtful shove by something sharp, right in the middle of his back, brought tears to his eyes.

"NO STOPPING! MOVE!"

Stumbling slightly, he regained his balance, barely able to shuffle along in the three being wide line that he found himself in the middle of, marching through a ghostly, underground, urban area. Not one hundred percent sure, he thought it was the outskirts of London somewhere. At least, that was his best guess from what little he'd seen.

Swallowing hard, something stuck in his throat. Coughing violently, he hacked up a huge mouthful of blood from somewhere inside him. Pain blossomed around what remained of his nose. It was all he could do to remain upright. Desperately he began searching within himself for the tiniest trace of magic; all he needed was a trickle. That would be enough to repair his damaged face. But try as he might, he just couldn't find any. It felt as if it were swirling and writhing just beneath the surface, but the surface of what, he just didn't know. Perhaps it had something to do with the manacles around his wrists behind his back, which felt as though they were constantly burning him.

Taking a sneaky glance over his left shoulder, he could just make out Tim, surrounded by guards, marching unhappily along with everyone else, yet looking relatively unharmed. Just then his foot clipped an uneven piece of rock jutting up from the walkway they were on. Stumbling, he barely managed to keep himself upright. Quickly he resumed his previous pace, eager not to feel the pain in his back once again, that he knew the guards weren't shy about dishing out. Keeping his eyes on the guard in front of him, all the time watching the floor for any obstacles, he found himself carried on by the self styled army, getting ever nearer to the seat of power. Deep within himself, he hoped the king was safe, and that he had some kind of plan to thwart the oncoming threat.

44 PULLED INTO THE ABYSS

As the leader of this squad, he supposed it was his duty to go and investigate; after all, he was constantly telling the others he would chip in, do his bit, whatever the task, nothing was too menial. But with the noises coming from the other side of the door, none of the others wanted to even take a look. They were too terrified of the being in there. And rightly so, as far as he was concerned. She was a dangerous beast, of that he had no doubt. But they'd been assigned to protect her, and protect her they would. He assumed, as he opened the door to the room, that meant even from herself. Watching from the doorway, he felt uncomfortable just looking. Lying on the bed, she twisted and turned, writhing this way and that, all the time babbling, as that was the only word to describe it, babbling about dragons coming for her. Clearly asleep, for the briefest of moments he thought about waking her up, but decided against it. Knowing he wasn't brave enough for that, so closing the door back up without even a hint of a noise, he left Earth to her own accord, somewhere far off in the distant past.

On an ordinary night, mere days after the incident in which her husband had saved the shopkeeper's daughter from a head on collision with the out of control car, the couple slept soundly in their elusive, out of the way hideaway, unaware that fate was about to catch up with them.

Swarming out of the cave into the darkness, some five miles or so from their target, their human shaped bodies were entirely shrouded in black. Under normal circumstances they would have exited the dragon world nearer and not had so far to travel on foot, but this was the nearest exit, entrance, call it what you will, to their target, for some considerable distance.

Fifteen in all, it was nothing short of overkill to capture two renegade dragons, especially given the fifteen's training. They were members of the elite Crimson Guard, the specialist force answerable only to the king himself. And they were here in the icy cold of West Wales to bring to justice the two rogue dragons who'd hindered the war effort so much, as well as escaping from high security dragon containment facilities. Their superiors had no idea how they'd accomplished such a thing (insider help hadn't been discounted) and was one of the many questions they were eager to ask the pair. Limited information regarding the fugitives implied new and unusual talents, something they neither understood or tolerated. Hence the reason the fifteen troops had been dispatched. The group, as one, continued to march silently along the windswept shore, closing in on the unsuspecting couple.

At around two miles out, the group split into three units of five, with a view to outflanking them and cutting off any pre-planned escape they might have. Their leader, known only as 'One' (they all had numbered designations) continued with his group along the beach, using the soft sand to mask their approach. Both of the other groups cut inland at different points, circling around the countryside to the other side of the cottage that was their target, using their infra red vision to see where they were headed. A mile from their target, all three groups ran across variants on a theme. Several sets of interconnected web traps formed a barrier to their progress. While appearing to have been constructed with great care and cunning, they were no match for each of the team's considerable talents. Both the inland teams reported their situation to One. He gave both the go to continue their assault. Simultaneously the teams began to take down the traps, silently pitying the two targets for their rather simplistic approach to security. Unbeknown to them, the traps were much more than at first they appeared.

*A mile away, two sets of eyes shot open at exactly the same time.
"We've been discovered," they both whispered.*

*With not a moment to spare, they leapt out of bed, quickly
pulling on a set of clothes each, eager to be protected from the bitter
cold outside. Gloves, boots, and hats followed, and while this was a
little time consuming, they both knew the bitter weather had the
potential to be as deadly as their attackers. Grabbing a small
backpack from a secluded, secret cubbyhole, there for just such an
occasion, containing money, jewels to sell, weapons and some chocolate,
they opened the back door and silently slipped out into the darkness.
Using touch telepathy for fear of being discovered, the two discussed
how they would proceed, while swiftly traversing the landscape towards
the beach, all the time holding hands.*

*"We should make a run for it," he said, sending a calm
reassurance across their link.*

*"NO!" Earth replied. "We stand and fight. Give them exactly
what they came here for. I'm tired of running, and more than a little
disappointed at being discovered here and once again having to give up
everything we've worked so hard for."*

"But..." he started.

She wasn't having any of it.

*"NO MORE! We take them on here. Teach them a lesson.
Make the cost of them finding us hurt them dearly. So there are three
groups... so what! A maximum of three each, that's only nine at
most. I don't think we should have any trouble taking care of nine,
do you?"*

*Annoyed because he let her question go unanswered, she could feel
him trying hard to shake off the devastation he felt at having to give
up this place. It seemed inevitable that their discovery was almost
certainly linked to the rather unfortunate accident last week. If only
he'd done nothing, or stayed inside the shop a few seconds longer.
Fate, in their bitter experience, had a way of knocking you back
down flat, just as you thought everything was going along so well.*

*'It has been so long since I last used it,' she could hear him think
to himself, forgetting about the physical link to his wife.*

'Are you afraid you won't remember how to?' she questioned.

'It's not that. It's just that I thought this was all behind us. The running, fighting, the taking lives. All I wanted was for us to be left alone.'

Remaining quiet, she abruptly tugged him to a halt. Crouched motionless on a sandy path, masked on either side by tall, wavy grass, some five or so yards above the beach, tears streamed from their eyes as the wind howled viciously around them. With their combined power, their senses extended further, with their physical connection acting as a conduit now, channelling each of their abilities together, making them stronger than the sum of their parts. The five (surprise ran through them at that discovery) dragons were starting to ascend the slope towards their position. With one ancient word, channelled magic cloaked their heat signature, making them all but invisible to their opponents. Before they both rolled to different sides of the path into the long grass, their last words through their physical bridge were to divide up exactly how they were going to launch their attack. Conjuring up her familiar as she hid amongst the long grass, a huge thick serpent with two mighty heads, looking like any dragon's worst nightmare flickered into life. She watched as it slithered off into the darkness, waiting to do her bidding.

Padding along stealthily, the dragon elite ignored the blustery gale they found themselves caught up in, despite the shivers it sent splintering through their false human forms. One had dropped to the back of the group, bringing up the rear. Unable to see how just two of them could possibly outflank them, his briefing had stressed how dangerous these two were, and he was determined not to take any unnecessary risks. Cresting the rise, he could just make out the cottage in the distance, showing up as a dark, cold oblong over the shoulders of his troops in front of him. And then without warning, it happened! At first, he thought they'd been struck by lightning because that was the sound that accompanied the blistering surge of magic that had landed amongst them. But he was a professional and trained by the best, and so his survival instincts kicked in instantly, despite the terrible pain behind his eyes from the almost blinding assault. Switching his vision back to normal, an array of attacking mantras from which to choose leapt to the front of his brain as he rolled up onto his feet, after having dived for cover off to one side of the well travelled path.

Others in his group hadn't fared so well. Three, the dragon in front, had taken a huge hit to his back, from the force of whatever had exploded amongst them, falling flat on his face, ears ringing, pain surging down his legs and up his neck. Spitting out the mouthful of sand he'd taken in, his powerful arms pushed himself up, only to be greeted by a dark shadow with a menacing smile standing out in the electrically charged air. Giving everything he had, his reactions were out of this world, but they simply weren't good enough. The shadow (he could just make out it was a woman now) let crackling bolts of bright blue, zigzagging lightning rip from her fingertips. On contact with his body the lightning surged across his skin, burning, flaying and destroying. Like nothing the well trained dragon had ever experienced, the pain was off the scale. In the blink of an eye, he was dead.

In but a few seconds, Earth had unleashed her power to considerable effect. To her, it was rapture. The feeling was like nothing else. Here and now, she had many beings' lives quite literally in her hands. The power which accompanied that feeling was a rush like no other. Determined to make them pay, she sought out her next victim.

At exactly the same time, Earth's partner in crime had been dealing with Two, who'd been thrown off the path by the force of the explosion, straight into his onrushing enemy. All Two really needed was a split second to get his thoughts together, but his opponent had other ideas. A swift kick to his right knee sent the Crimson Guard flying to the ground, a substantial CRACK the reward for such a well executed attack. Pushing the pain away, the guard tried to focus, but the dark shadow of Earth's husband was on him in an instant. First, a swift, sharp blow to the nose with the side of his hand. Thick red blood spurted everywhere as the guard started to choke. Reaching behind him to the side pocket of the backpack he wore, Earth's husband whipped out a deadly blade that had been secreted there, and plunged it with all his might into his opponent's heart.

With two of the group dead in only a matter of a few seconds, the odds on the survival of the rest had shortened considerably, despite their leader being back on his feet and ready to join the melee. Four and Five were now both back in the game, with Four looking in desperate need of hospital treatment. Blood flowed freely from a hole in his left thigh, while a massive gash over his right eye left a huge, bloodied sheet of skin flapping about in the frozen wind. Nevertheless, he remained upright, determined to play his part.

The three Crimson Guards approached the two rogue dragons head on in the darkness, on the narrow sandy path. With a vicious snarl on her face and the pent up anger and frustration of having been on the run for years, Earth forced her magic to produce a humungous ball of electricity which she carried in both hands. Blue and purple lightning coursed from the inside to the outer shell, making it look like a child's giant plasma ball. But this one was deadly and her opponents realised it, all simultaneously taking a step back. Bringing her hands round to one side, she thrust the ball in the direction of the three stunned dragons, who immediately all dived for cover, each missing the fatal ball by the merest fraction.

With the ball having disappeared over the edge of the rise, One and Five jumped to their feet to once again confront their attackers. Four remained motionless, face down in the long grass. Without a moment to lose, One released an onslaught of bright green filaments in the direction of the husband and wife team. Earth cartwheeled off to the right, but her husband wasn't so lucky, being caught by two of the writhing green tentacles, one piercing his upper right arm, the other holing his stomach. Earth screamed in rage as her husband doubled over in agony. Five, in the meantime, had snuck off to the right, into the grass and, under cover of darkness, launched a blistering attack of poisoned bees at the still raging Earth, assuming that her all consuming anger had given him the distraction and opening that he needed. But as soon as the toxic bees got to within striking range, they sizzled and burnt, crumbled and fried from the invisible shield that the deranged woman in front of them had managed to erect around herself. Still trying to figure out how the hell she'd got a shield up so quickly, Five didn't see the movement in the grass behind him until it was much too late. From out of nowhere the two headed serpent with a body the thickness of the largest human thigh, slithered in behind the distracted dragon, biting both his legs in quick succession before starting to wrap itself around his lower left leg. Five howled in agony as the shiny dark serpent twisted up his torso.

One kept up his onslaught on the male protagonist, determined to even the odds in his favour. With no time to contact the other groups, he knew they must have realised something was wrong by now and be on their way here. All he had to do was buy himself enough time and the odds would become overwhelmingly in his favour. And there would be hell to pay.

Both the inland groups had contacted each other as

soon as it became apparent that their leader couldn't be reached. A hasty decision was made to reach their leader's group with all speed. So ten dark shapes now rushed as fast as they could towards the last known position of their colleagues, all thoughts of stealth forgotten. Speed, each of them knew, was the key.

Earth couldn't bear to hear her husband in so much pain. It turned her blood to fire, stoking her rage even more, if that were at all possible. With her serpent peppering the stricken dragon in the long grass with ever more poison, she darted left towards her husband, taking a flying leap, landing directly in front of him. Diverting all her magic towards her shield, she extended it out, cutting off the flying tendrils of bright green, dangerous magic. Exhausted, her husband slumped to the ground. Knowing that time was of the essence, she turned to face a very confident dragon, one she assumed must be their leader.

'Not for much longer,' she thought to herself.

"You will desist and come..." he said, before his voice trailed off.

Desperately, he clutched at his throat, scrabbling at it with his gloved black hands, but the invisible force around it could not be wrestled away.

"I'd give you a message for your precious dragon council," screamed Earth, "but on reflection, I think your broken bodies might do the trick just as well. What do you think? Cat got your tongue?"

One fought with everything he had, drew on every last resource of magic within him, trying to launch a counterattack, but the oxygen had been forced out of him and his vision was fading fast. In his mind he tried to lash out and unleash a deadly telepathic assault, but he just didn't have the strength.

Turning to her husband, while still choking the life from the dragon force's leader, she urged him to get to his feet and run.

"But I can't leave you here to face such numbers," he babbled.

"GO!" she ordered. "I'll be right behind you, after I've cooked up a little surprise for them."

Seeing little use in arguing, hunched over, he trotted past the upright, blue in the face body of One and headed north, not towards the beach, but the cliff side path. It would be harder work for him but there was more cover, and it would be more difficult for anyone to track him, especially compared with the sandy beach.

One's limp body fell to the ground with a THUMP. Earth revelled in the sick satisfaction of knowing just how much he'd suffered in his last moments. In her mind, she'd planned to conjure up some bombs and booby trap the dragon bodies, knowing full well the other groups would want to recover them. But she'd underestimated them. They were here, almost upon her, and she didn't have nearly enough time to execute her terrible plan. Glancing over her shoulder, she just managed to make out her husband staggering up the rise of the cliff top path, hundreds of yards in the distance. Spinning round, she took in her attackers, sprinting across the undergrowth, any hint of subtlety long gone. Fuelled by rage, she called forth everything she had, lighting up the scenery around her like a bonfire night celebration. Hoping to draw all ten of them to her, giving her husband half a chance to escape, the Crimson Guard were more disciplined than that. Six of them headed her way, while four sprinted off after him. Silently she cursed, but there was little she could do to help him at the moment; she just hoped he could hold on until she could reach him.

They came at her all at once, no holds barred. Streaks of blue tinged flame rocketed out from one dragon, brilliant bright purple bolts of crackling energy ignited the air from another. One of the six had conjured up a golden lattice of pure energy, which hovered steadily in the air, all the time moving towards the, by now, raging mad Earth. This all happened in the blink of an eye, as the other three of the six designated to take Earth out, closed in for some hand to hand combat, determined to take her alive and present her to the dragon council.

So many thoughts whizzed through her mind, primarily, how the hell she could catch up with, and save, the love of her life. Instinct and common sense fought off the battle lust that she felt, telling her she had to deal with the six in front of her, and fast. By the look of things, they were all professional and experienced. This was going to be no easy task. Searching her mind for something, anything, that *might get her out of this hole, her search didn't include anything dragon related. There seemed little point. Clearly her attackers would be able to defend themselves against anything they already knew about, so it had to be something different, something that the nagas had taught her in all the time she'd spent with them.*

Off to one side, the Crimson Guard stood still, his eyes closed, concentrating with all his might on the golden net hovering in the air, getting ever closer to his target's position, totally unaware of the tiniest of movements in the long grass beside him. That is until a bite, causing him the most unbelievable amount of pain, made him lose focus and drop to the ground. The sizzling golden trap disintegrated into nothingness, with the overwhelming odds having just turned a little in favour of the rogue dragons.

Earth's husband pulled up, dropping to his knees as he did so, wanting to vomit, but fighting against the urge. Instead, he coughed violently, globules of blood spewing out across the stony path that he found himself on. Knowing they were behind him, he was conscious that he had only moments to act. Before now, he'd never been afraid of dying. Many situations across the years had seen him close to death. In each and every one of those, he'd always faced his destiny with the typical arrogance that was probably a trademark of his old self. But over the years, he'd changed. Whether it was him, or because of her, or just the fact that they were together, he didn't know. But that arrogance was long gone, replaced with love, and regret. He didn't want to lose her; he didn't want to die. For the very first time he was afraid, not only for him, but for her as well. Staggering to his feet, all the while clutching his belly wound, he moved as quickly as he could into the breeze, the salty sea air a constant reminder of what he'd just lost.

Out of the corner of her eye, she glimpsed her serpent taking down another of the hopeless dragons. A twisted smile writhed across her face. Not just because of what she'd just seen, but because she had it. The answer. And now she intended to use it. With the streaks of fire and purple bolts being deflected harmlessly away by her cleverly designed personal shield, she lowered her head to face the attackers who were almost upon her, twisting her finger in a very intricate fashion, putting all her rage, willpower and temper behind but one thought. BOOM! A solid ring of sound erupted out from her. All the Crimson Guards were thrown back, with the closest one smashing his head on a huge chunk of rock jutting up out of the path. The other two charging dragons had fared little better. One twisted his ankle, while the other was out cold, both of his arms twisted in unnatural positions where he lay. Both the Crimson Guard's who'd been casting spells stumbled to their feet, blood streaming from their ears and noses. All around, the 'thud', 'thud', 'thud', of birds dropping to the ground, dead, could be heard. In the sea, fish floated to the surface in nearly a half mile radius, while crabs stayed buried beneath the sand, never to move again. Earth strolled purposefully forward, heading straight for the two spell casters, stopping briefly on the way to break the neck of the unconscious dragon, which she accomplished with the ease of a trained professional. It clearly wasn't her first time.

Ignoring the pain they were in, the two Crimson Guards concentrated on channelling their power. But it was too little, too late. Earth was upon them, gouging the first one's eyes out in an instant, his howling screams carried off into the distance by the squally gusts. The second one, despite the severity of his injuries, lunged forward, swivelled and kicked Earth's feet from under her. Falling brutally to the ground, the wind having been knocked out of her, for a moment she was completely at his mercy. Knowing this was his chance and despite decades of training, his anger tore through him, controlling his every action. Leaping upon her, he rained down a torrent of punches into her face and chest, watching as her cheeks erupted in a shower of blood and bone. She tried to mutter some words, but they only came out as a gurgle of blood. With all consuming rage defining his actions, he'd decided what needed to be done.

'To hell with the council and their judgement,' he thought, still hammering blows into the seemingly helpless Earth. 'She deserves to die,' he decided. And so calling forth every last ounce of power within him, he let rip. Purple bolts surged out of him, so lightning fast they looked like one long continuous stream. Her beaten body started to convulse and writhe with the pain, making him look like some demonic rodeo rider on the cold, dark, evil winter's night. Thoughts of justice and righteousness consumed the guard, knowing that for once he'd become judge, council and the king all at once. It was then that two huge mouths slithered up from nowhere and clamped themselves around his head, causing him to scream out in pain, all thoughts of his previous target forgotten. Rolling off Earth, hoping to shrug off the giant beast, he'd not counted on its teeth having firmly dug into his skull. He tried to get to his feet, but as he got to his knees, powerful muscles wrapped themselves around both his legs, squeezing as hard as they could. Tumbling onto the hard ground, all the time rolling, both his hands searched in the darkness for the beast's eyes, hoping to jab a finger or two into them. But it was no good, he couldn't find them and the pain was stopping him thinking. By now the evil looking snake had wrapped its entire twenty yard body around the guard, literally crushing the life out of him. As his vision went dark for the final time, and he expelled his last breath, he smiled, knowing that at least that witch of a rogue dragon would never harm anyone ever again.

A sharp, metallic tang filled her throat and lungs. For all intents and purposes she'd died. But the single thought within her hadn't been told about that. All it cared about was him. And it knew that to keep him safe, this broken and battered body it was concealed in had to get up, get going, and fight. The thought urged the body to roll over and expel its contents. It did. Whacking great mouthfuls of blood were coughed up onto the sand beside it. Casting aside the pain it felt, Earth's body lurched to its feet and, avoiding the mass of dead bodies surrounding it, started to jog in the direction she'd last seen her husband.

'He has to be alright, he just has to,' she thought, over and over again as she followed in his footsteps.

Having never had his wife's skills with familiars, they were, for him, out of the question. But that didn't mean he needed to concede defeat. Resting behind a craggy rock on the cliff's edge, needing to catch his breath and focus his thoughts, the cold wind whipped at his face, keeping unconsciousness at bay. All his eyes wanted to do were close and stay that way. But as with his wife, one singular thought pushed him on. HER. He needed to fight and stay strong for her. They would be together again, he was sure of it. It was meant to be. Over the harsh screaming of the wind, his enhanced senses could just make out noises... no, words. With a great effort he lifted his head up against the rock he had his back to, all the time panting heavily, aware of the precarious drop to his left. The cliff path had mainly headed up, and the rock that he was sitting behind lay at its highest point, some hundred yards above the beach, somewhere below him in the darkness. With a fall like that, he'd definitely be done for, and there would be no time to revert back to his dragon form, even if he had the energy to do so, which of course he didn't. Weary and mindful of his enemies approaching, he grabbed a handful of large stones from the ground around him. Ignoring the blood seeping from his stomach wound, he channelled his magic into the stones. One by one, they turned the darkest shade of black known to man. Holding tightly onto what had now become something of an arsenal, he reached out behind him, searching for his ever elusive pursuers.

All the time scratching at her face like some mad, delusional witch, she wobbled up the cliff top path, at times using the fauna around her to pull her up just that little bit further. Sensing them, and of course him, she could tell he was hurt, but not too badly. But they were closing in on his position. She had to move, move faster. But the pain was out of this world, with her face feeling like it had been torn off. Spitting out yet another mouthful of blood, she caught her breath next to a thorny little bush, just for a few seconds, before once again pressing on, knowing time was of the essence.

Eyes firmly closed, he stretched out with his mind... and found them. Now within fifty yards of his position, two were together, two were on their own, wading through the surrounding undergrowth, clear of the path, no doubt fearful of a trap. Taking a breath and then exhaling slowly, he threw a stone up over the rock he was sitting behind, high up into the air, satisfied with the trajectory it was on. Leaning his chin on his chest, he grabbed another stone and waited for the mayhem to begin.

Eight was stationed directly behind Nine as they moved through the scrub on top of the cliff. Abruptly Nine's closed fist sprang up into the air. They both stopped stock still, tense and on the lookout for danger from every possible angle. They were good, that's for sure. But neither noticed the solid, dark object dropping upon them from directly above as the wind had cancelled out any sound that might have given them a clue. And then it was too late. BOOOOOOMMMMM!!! The explosion tore the earth apart right in between them both. Fire and intense heat scorched the surrounding area, with stones acting as projectiles, peppering the two Crimson Guards with holes, while the kinetic force tossed their ragged bodies yards into the air, both finally landing face down, suffering massive trauma. Just outside the blast radius the two remaining guards looked on in disbelief, a tiny trickle of terror running through each. Both reaching the same conclusion at pretty much the same time, they were sitting ducks for whatever had just taken out two of their team. They had to act now. And so, in unison, they did, taking off, heedless of the risks, at full pelt towards the rock which they knew was sheltering their target.

About to throw the next stone that he'd prepared, he realised just a fraction too late that they'd done the last thing they were supposed to. By the time he'd reacted, they were too close to use the stones. He was on his own. Leaping to his feet, ignoring the blossoming pain in his stomach, he prepared to meet them.

Cresting the rise of the adjacent cliff top just in time to see the explosion go off and bits of dragon guard go everywhere, she smiled at the ingenuity of her husband, the feeling of pride soon turned to horror as she watched the two remaining guards break cover and head towards her husband at a sprint. Thrusting out her right arm, she tried to aim her magic somewhere in the guard's path, a series of terrifying electrical charges leaping from her not quite instantaneously. The surrounding air crackled and hummed, filled with electricity, but she was too far away and her desperate efforts were very wide of the mark. Starting to run, her momentum was helped by the slight down slope, but by now the dragons clad only in black had disappeared behind the craggy old rock.

On him in an instant, he blocked an oncoming blow by the first one, surprised at how his body remembered to fight, almost on its own. The second came in, snapping a low kick towards his left leg. Jumping and turning both at the same time, he aimed a well placed kick towards the guard's knee. But he didn't fall for it, instead opting to somersault back out of range. Closing him down, both Crimson Guards knew he had nowhere to go. His back was to the rock that had provided him with cover. To his left, there was a sheer drop into the darkness, with the beach and a quick death waiting. Knowing that if he could get them to commit to an attack, he just might be able to use their momentum to his advantage and force them over the cliff, he put on his best demeaning sneer, almost as if to say, "Bring it on." But these two knew what had happened to the others and recognised a serious threat when they saw it. And so with the coordination and teamwork that comes only with years of experience, they moved as one, launching themselves at him simultaneously. Ducking his head to one side, he let rip with the most powerful punch he could under the circumstances. It wasn't enough. The first Crimson Guard had got well within his defences, while the second had countermanded his punch. After that, it was all over. A head butt struck him first. It wasn't full on, as he'd pulled back his head, but it was a powerful glancing blow, enough to momentarily stun him, making his head ring like a church bell. While blocking the punch, the second guard spun slightly on his heel and then planted the sole of his other foot straight through Earth's husband's knee, causing him to bellow in pain, as the CRACK of snapping bones rose above the gale.

Hurrying down the rise, crashing through bracken, the wind whipping her hair into a Medusa-like appearance, the sound of a loud CRACK resounding over the wind forced her into running faster. Pride in her husband's work and the thought of yet another dragon badly wounded sent a jolt of excitement through her. During the years that they'd been living in the cottage, she'd missed the thrill of the fight. Often she'd thought about it, those that she'd betrayed, captured, tortured, killed. Not a hint of remorse had ever shown its face, in fact quite the opposite. It thrilled her to think about the power she'd held over others. She missed it. Now... she was making the most of it, living off it, letting it course through her veins, powering her on to something greater.

Spent, he dropped unceremoniously to the ground, the two guards looking like ninjas towering over him in their all black outfits. Instinctively he curled up into a ball, willing his mind to conjure up something in the way of protection as the kicks from each of them smashed into him. It was, however, not going to happen. The pain from his gut wound alone was almost enough to make him black out, and that combined with his fractured knee cap and the onslaught he was now taking left him vulnerable, defenceless, incapable. Leaning down, the first dragon guard grabbed him by the neck, forced his hands away from his face and then hit him with a wild punch, bursting the skin above his right eye, sending blood and bone fragments hurtling up against the craggy rock they all found themselves in front of. Just as another punch was incoming, a bewitching, insane figure, lit up with magic, powered by rage, came flying round from the other side of the rock, forked electricity sizzling from each of her fingertips, death to all written in her eyes.

His good eye caught sight of her. She looked magnificent. He'd never been prouder. Alright, she looked as though she'd been in a fight, but just how many dragons had she destroyed this night? After she put these two mutts out of their misery, he looked forward to finding out.

Both Crimson Guards were horrified at what had just skidded to a halt in front of them. Neither had experienced nightmares, but if they had it would be hard to imagine anything worse than that which stood before them. Automatically their training took over. Ignoring the wounded enemy on the ground, the first threw all the magic he had at her, while the second instantly erected a makeshift shield to protect them both.

Despite the run down nature of her personal shield, the magic thrown at her only tickled. Both dragons were nothing more than insects to her now, able to bite, scratch and sting, but nothing more than that. With her hair dancing around to its own beat in the wind, and spying her battered and beaten up husband curled up in a ball on the ground, right by the cliff's edge, a despairing madness overwhelmed her. She wanted to punish them for what they'd done, make them pay, torture them for days on end before deliciously removing their still beating hearts. Unfortunately she didn't have the luxury of any of that and so instead decided to get it over with. It can only be described as hell being unleashed. Electricity, primarily, with fire, ice and just a hint of pure poison whooshed from her hands, totally filling the gap between her and the two dragons. It ripped apart the childlike shield one of them had erected and then caught both in the chest, forcing them to stagger back towards the pitch black drop behind them. From the floor, he looked up into her eyes, smiling at the power she wielded, proud that she was his. Out of the corner of her eye, she could see him smiling at how well she was doing. It brought forth memories of their early days together, days that were amazing, like no other. Days that would come again, now that they were reunited, standing together against their common enemy.

Unsurprisingly, a wave of tiredness washed over her; she was, after all, using nearly everything she had to continue the onslaught of magic that was burning from her hands. In an instant, she decided to finish it.

Both Crimson Guards pushed back with all they had, but to little effect. In a sense, they were resigned to their fate, which would be the same as the rest of the team. So when a surge of power from the demonic witch they were fighting pushed them ever closer to the cliff edge, only a blink of an eye from going over, the more experienced of the two switched his focus, knowing that he'd be meeting his doom a few seconds sooner than intended. Reaching out, he clamped onto the injured rogue dragon curled up into a ball on the ground. Despite knowing that death was but a moment or two away, his action was rewarded by the looks on both his opponent's faces, as he, the other member of his team and the injured rogue dragon slipped slowly over the edge of the cliff.

It hadn't seemed possible. One second he was there, the next he was slipping away in slow motion, his look of pride exchanged for one of terror. The magic ceased as she sprang towards the cliff edge. Reaching over, her mind raced for any and all mantras or spells that would save him. But it was too late. With a muffled CRUNCH, the three bodies hit the rocks below all at the same time. Wailing and screaming she punched the ground repeatedly, the craggy rock... herself. But it was no good. He was dead. Gone forever. She lay against the rock for many minutes... who knew how long? A long time. Tears streamed as she screamed herself hoarse, magic crackled and fizzed, sizzled, bubbled and flew. Eventually she passed out, her bloodied body resting against the rock.

A few hours later, dawn broke. Sunlight streamed onto her broken body, the wind having died down. Sitting up, she licked her cracked lips. Everything hurt, but nothing more than her broken heart. It was hard to find the will to go on, but she knew that she had to; it was what he would have wanted. There was also the tiny matter of... REVENGE. That's right, she had to get back at those dragons, repay everything they'd done to her with interest. Deciding to bide her time, she would wait patiently and then rip their world apart, just as they had done to her. A sparkle from only a hand's width away caught her attention. Sun glinted off the broken remains of a bright green bottle. Pulling the massive shard from the sand, she held it up to the light, gazing at her reflection as she did so. Although difficult to tell in the warped green of the bottle, she could just make out her face and see just how badly it had been ruined. Massive, bright purple lines crisscrossed her once perfect complexion, making her face look like one giant spider's web. In that instant she knew that because magic had been used, she'd be stuck with it forever.

'Yet another reason to rain down hell upon those dumb dragons and their oh so perfect world,' she thought, scrambling to her feet. Deciding to head back to the cottage to quickly gather some fresh clothes, she didn't even bother looking over the edge of the cliff to see what lay there. Her future had already been decided.

45 TORTUOUS TROUBLING TURN

Even though on some level he'd been half expecting and watching out for it, it still came as something of a surprise when it actually happened. As far as he could ascertain, it had started with a number of different minor calls for the King's Guard to respond to, all within London, all within an hour of each other. Not totally uncommon, there were always enough dragons available to cover almost any eventuality. But on reflection, it had been a huge mistake, because something in the order of half the fighting force assigned to the council building had gone out to assist in one form or another. It didn't take long to realise that something out of the ordinary was going on. It happened so quickly, and could have been no coincidence. Contact was lost, not just with one team (unusual in itself) but with two, three, four, five teams. The list went on. In the end, no more teams were dispatched. Not a single dragon from any of those teams had returned or been heard from.

That had been just over six hours ago. And since then, things had gotten worse. Strange and mysterious mantras were popping into effect throughout the elegant and modern building. Far advanced from anything the humans were capable of creating, the computer system had developed a number of fatal flaws and had been shut down, its power supply having to be destroyed. Throughout the building, emergency seals and doors randomly opened and closed, occasionally cutting off important intersections within the structure itself, making it very difficult to mount a strategic defence against whatever was coming. Last but not least, the council chamber and everything within it could not be accessed. Dragon masters were currently working on a way to negate whatever mantra had taken over the room, but at the moment, with very little luck.

The king, his immediate staff and the councillors that

remained had all been asked to withdraw back into the king's private residence, by the highest ranking officer left in charge. Not knowing whether it was a good plan or not, the king could see no alternative, given that they had no idea what was happening around them in the city itself. So, he'd agreed to Captain Amelia Battlehard's request and here they sat, cut off, with no information feeding through to them. King's Guards were scattered throughout the failing council building, guarding the overhanging walkway that joined the king's private residence, clustered around the entrance to the stunning ancient wonder of a building, waiting for what seemed like an inevitable attack. As the guard captain with them issued orders to those in the adjoining building telepathically, the king wondered if there was any way out of this for them all and what other options were available to him. No communications, no tactical information on what they were facing, no defending dragon army, no one coming to their rescue, no real way out, no hope! It all looked rather bleak.

46 CURRYING FAVOUR

It had been an odd kind of day, with one of the most bizarre games of lacrosse she'd ever taken part in, followed by the no show of Peter and Tank at the pub. Perhaps that was nothing unusual in itself, but they'd both let down their respective teams in different ways, as Tank had been due to play, with Peter supposed to have been supporting. Richie couldn't ever remember that happening before. That said though, she did appreciate her memory recently had not been that... reliable, but still... something tickled the recesses of her very being, almost whispering to her to remain alert, on guard. Her instinct was to listen, and listen carefully. Despite not really wanting to, she'd got caught up in the after match hubbub, and much to her surprise, had just walked into the favourite Indian restaurant of the hockey, lacrosse and rugby playing sections of the sports club, located almost smack bang in the centre of Salisbridge. Holding the door for the rest of the eclectic group she found herself with, she smiled politely as two of the hockey men squeezed past, then three of her lacrosse teammates, followed by two of the rugby men, and Janice, all thanking her. Janice's forced, "Thanks," stung. Despite trying her best to convince the gorgeous looking bar worker that she had nothing to worry about with regards to Peter, and that they were very much only friends, albeit best friends, things still tended to be on the frozen side of frosty whenever they were in a confined space together. Richie couldn't think of anything else she could say or do to convince Peter's squeeze (or ex-squeeze, who knew) that she was anything but supportive of their relationship. Letting the door swing closed, the ex-dragon followed the rest of the group up the main aisle of the restaurant to their normal table on the raised part of the seating area, right at the back of the room. As the smartly dressed waiter showed them to their seats, she slipped into one of the high backed chairs in between two of the rugby players, ignoring a sharp twinge of pain in her knee from the earlier lacrosse match. Slipping off her brown leather flying jacket to give to the waiter, one of its arms dragged across the front of her neck, rubbing roughly against the necklace holding the ring that Peter had given her. As it did so, a burning sensation seared into her collarbone, not for the first time today, or indeed at all. Strangely, the shimmering blue triangles lining the circumference of the ring appeared to be glowing slightly brighter today, at least she thought so. On both the other occasions she'd thought this had happened other than today, Richie had told herself repeatedly that she'd been... MISTAKEN. On one of the occasions she'd been in the ladies' toilet, and had found herself having a conversation in the mirror to deny that the necklace was doing anything out of the ordinary. But now, with it having happened on three very different days... she simply didn't know what to think. Peter had given her the ring and made her promise two things. One... to guard it with her life, telling her it held the key not only to her future, but to her past as well. And two... not to put it on her finger at any cost. At the time, she couldn't ever remember seeing him more serious. It was all very mysterious... but what did it mean?

With the group all seated, a different waiter took their drinks order and promptly disappeared towards the small bar at the front of the restaurant. The banter, and it was banter being mid evening on a Saturday, with lots of beers and the like having already been consumed by everyone with the possible exception of Richie and Janice, turned to the respective sports played by everyone. Hockey and lacrosse players ganged up on the rugby boys (except Richie, who was still considering the day's events in her mind) goading them about how slow their sport was, supposedly. Poppadoms arrived without having to be ordered, along with two glasses of water and a table full of beer. As the friends mulled over their selection of food from the worn, tattered, plastic menus, talk turned to the missing Peter and Tank.

"So Richie, what's up with the big man today? Never known him to miss training, let alone a match."

The whole group quietened significantly (no mean feat considering how many drinks they'd all had) and listened to what the lacrosse captain had to say.

"Not really sure what I can tell you Hook. I'm as surprised as you are. I've tried phoning both Tank and Peter to find out why they didn't show, as I'm sure Janice has with Peter, but with no luck," she ventured, trying not to look in Janice's direction. "It's unusual for sure, and I've no explanation. As well, I confess to being more than a little worried."

"I've phoned and left messages, but heard nothing so far," added Janice.

"In my experience, these things always appear worse than they actually are. I'm sure there's a perfectly logical explanation. We can't see what it is at the moment, but I'm sure in a couple of days when everything becomes clear, we'll all be laughing about this," slurred Angela, one of Richie's lacrosse teammates.

"Maybe," whispered Richie, as the waiter arrived to take their food order.

With the overpowering sound of Indian music in the background, on top of the noise from the throng of overly enthusiastic Saturday night patrons, Richie found it hard to concentrate. She was worried, and not just a little. For a while now things seemed to have been... not so much wrong, just not right! Unable to put her finger on what it was exactly, the one thing that was clear to her was the importance of her relationship with Peter and Tank. In fact, it probably went beyond important. Pivotal, instrumental, significant, key... but key to what? Recalling memories of the three of them together, things were a little hazy, fuzzy around the edges even, but even though she couldn't remember clearly, deep down inside her, her soul stirred. Just the thought of her friends sent a tingle down her back and goose bumps up both arms. Threatening to overpower her, the nagging sensation she'd been feeling all day was starting to get worse. Unfortunately for her, the only people in the world she trusted enough to confide in about it were missing and the cause of her angst. Sitting in this aromatic restaurant with teammates and friends... she felt truly lost and alone. All this and more whistled through her head as she fingered the ring which the necklace traversed. Glancing up and down the table, she felt disconnected from the group she sat with. They all looked so happy and bubbly. For the most part it was a lie, she knew, or at least an exaggeration, the alcohol enhancing the mood of everyone... well, almost. A fleeting look at the far end of the table showed Janice, looking utterly miserable. In fact, she thought, Janice looked how she, Richie, felt. Perhaps the two of them had more in common than they ever dared to admit.

As the evening continued to pass, for what felt like an age to the lacrosse captain, more beer arrived, accompanied by starters and then main courses. Richie barely touched any of hers. It just didn't seem important. By now the nagging sensation had almost turned into a compulsion, but a compulsion to do what? She could almost feel the blood pumping through her veins, her heart beat so wildly. Having spent the last forty minutes or so twiddling with the ring, it seemed the most natural thing in the world to take the necklace off and place the ring in the palm of her hand. It was dull, matt grey, with beautiful blue, tiny little triangles running around the outside of it. In fact she had barely registered that she was now holding it. If she had, then maybe her promise to Peter would have swum to the surface of her thoughts.

As the others drank and ate merrily, all apart from Janice who continued to stare glumly into the bottom of her half empty glass of water, Richie held the outside of the ring with the thumb and index finger of her left hand,

and, as if it were the most natural thing in the world, slipped it on the ring finger of her right hand. Instinctively, she depressed the raised grey triangle. THE WORLD EXPLODED! Richie's chair shot back, tossing her to the floor with a resounding THUMP, causing the entire restaurant to look round, as rugby, hockey and lacrosse players all jumped up from their chairs to go to her aid. Curled up in the foetal position on the sticky, patterned carpet, she just about managed to bark out, "STAY BACK!", before being overwhelmed by the images coursing through her mind. The phrase 'life flashing before your eyes' could have been invented for just this moment.

As her friends stood around her not knowing what to do, beautiful blue triangles on the ring shifted and glowed fiercely.

"We need to help her," urged one of the hockey players, taking a step forward.

An arm built like a tree trunk sprang out in front of him.

"Not so fast. You heard what she said," growled Hook. "She said to stay back, and that's what we're all gonna do. Understand?"

Fuelled by more than a little Dutch courage, the hockey player stood face to face with the strapping rugby player. Well... not exactly face to face, more like face to... sternum.

"Clearly she's in pain. We need to help her," he slurred.

"Listen sonny, you've no idea who you're dealing with here. If she says stay back... then you stay back. If she says, 'Dance like Take That,' then you say, 'Which one do you want me to be?' For the time being, we watch over her, take care of her and most importantly, do exactly what she asks. Do you understand?"

As the hockey player averted his gaze from Hook's angry scowl, he just about managed to whisper,

"Sure, whatever you think's best."

By now, Richie was constantly moaning and wailing, all the time rolled up into a tight ball on the floor next to the table.

All looking at one another, the friends tried to gauge if they were doing the right thing. Each and every one of them, except perhaps the hockey player, knew all about Richie. Knew that she wasn't one to be messed with, knew to have her approval and friendship was something to be cherished. And knew, above all, that if you were going to trust anyone with your life... it would have to be her. That's just how it was.

Images of massive eggs, dragons hatching and the feeling of warmth pervaded her every thought. She tried to block them out, tried to pull the ring off her finger... but she just couldn't. Dragon and human shapes walked side by side. There appeared to be a school. No... she knew what it was called: nursery ring. That was it... nursery ring. How did she know what it was called? After all, only the images continued to assault her mind, no words... nothing. A feeling of warmth instantly washed over her, as if somehow she'd been transported to a tropical island at the hottest point of the day. She wanted nothing more than to rip her clothes off, that's how hot it was, but she was totally paralysed. Just as she thought it might be wearing off, a kind of weightlessness took over, causing her to feel sick. Really, really sick. Before she could actually be sick, she realised what was happening. She was FLYING! And had wings and... SCALES. As the sun shone down from the bright blue sky, her body basked in its warmth. It was the best feeling she'd ever experienced. Except, now... she had started to remember. The images changed, starting to come thicker and faster. Her breathing increased, sweat poured from every part of her and her heart felt as if it were going to come crashing out through her chest.

For the most part, the other customers in the restaurant had gone back to their meals. This was mainly down to the fact that Hook had told them to in no uncertain terms. He was not somebody you wanted to get on the wrong side of.

One of the waiters, a youngster of no more than eighteen, approached the group tentatively. They all recognised him as one of the hockey club's outstanding talents, called Taibul, who always attended training and played for the most part in the second XI.

"Would you like us to call an ambulance for your friend?" he managed to stutter, all the time wary of Hook's presence.

"Not at the moment... thanks," replied one of the lacrosse girls politely.

Taibul wandered carefully back towards the kitchen, making sure not to look back. Emma, one of Richie's closest friends on the lacrosse team, leaned across to Hook and whispered,

"How long can we leave her like this? At some point, someone's bound to call either an ambulance or the police. And who's to say it's not the right thing to do? She looks in a massive amount of pain."

Before Hook could respond, Janice interjected.

"I was watching her as it happened. She'd been fiddling with the ring that had been on the necklace. She took it off the necklace and after a little more fiddling, slipped it on her finger. The instant she did so... that was what happened."

"You're saying it's the ring causing all this?" replied Emma, incredulous.

"I'm just telling you what happened."

"Whatever it is," interrupted Hook, "we give her the time she needs. I don't know her as well as Tank and the hockey player... what's his name... Peter. But I know her character. I've seen some of the things she's done and I'd trust her with my life. And I can't say that about too many people."

Others in the group nodded their agreement with what Hook had just said.

Pieces of the puzzle were starting to fall back into

place. A world with... DRAGONS! Not only that... but she was one of them, at least, that's what it was starting to look like. Hair caked in sweat, distantly, she was aware of her surroundings, the group of people, the restaurant, the diners, but it all seemed so far away that it might as well have been on another planet. More images flashed through her head. Her home, her work at Cropptech, a threat, from not too long ago. A relationship. No a taboo. An explosion, saved by the skin of her teeth. And a loss. A loss of something so familiar. And then the priests. In her house. It all merged into one now. How the priests had removed her memories, her past. Now she remembered it all. Who she was. Who she really was. She was a dragon, and not just any dragon. It all came flooding back to her, along with a torrent of righteous anger. Rage and fury at how unjustly she'd been treated. Anger at not being trusted. And then something else shimmered into existence. Something... familiar. It was like a scene from a film. An open air bazaar, a place she knew well, flittered into view. Dragons lay dead in huge pyres, round and about. Other dragons had been rounded up and sat surrounded by deadly looking guards with murderous intent in their eyes. Smack bang in the middle of the bazaar, a crude form of gallows had been erected. A steel frame, hastily put together, overshadowed everything else. What she saw filled her with dread. Using everything she had, she tried desperately to push the depiction from her mind. Blinking her eyes, desperate for it to be over, desperate to return to the reality of the restaurant, an overwhelming sense of doom flooded through her. Still the vision invaded her. Swinging from the makeshift gallows, two male human forms could just be seen, naked but for their underwear, swinging gently backwards and forwards. Blood dripped off their bare torsos, forming eye catching puddles of bright red below on the cobbles. Huge cuts and scars adorned them from head to toe, front to back. Their faces looked as though an elephant had sat on them. They were barely recognisable. But recognise them she did. They were her friends. At first she was sure that it was Peter and Tank she was looking at. But the images, in their own way, became clearer, sharper and, well, just kind of zoomed in. When they did, it was clear who was hanging from the ugly, dark, steel frame. Tank dangled from the left side of the monstrosity, looking like a gruesome, oversized, human, horror dolly. On the right as she viewed the fearsome scene, Flash, friend and ex-Crimson Guard, swung precariously, barely conscious. Off to one side, a dragon Richie knew cracked a vicious looking magical whip, inflicting yet another deep cut to Tank. CASEY! One time tormentor of Peter, and a former nursery ring class mate of all three of them.

Without warning, the images of her friends being tortured started to fade, but not before she caught the briefest glimpse of Tim, being dragged off into the shadows somewhere.

'Tim,' she thought, barely able to contain the tears that threatened to flood out of her. She'd had no memory of her relationship with Tim. And yet he'd meant so much to her. Momentarily, her resolve wavered just a little as she thought about not going through with what she had planned, leaving the dragon domain to deal with their own problems. But wish as she might that she could, she knew deep down that she simply had to go. After all, she was a dragon, despite what they'd done to her. Above all though, her friends were in dire trouble and anyone who knew her well would know that she'd lay down her own life for her friends in the blink of an eye. With a dragon's strength of purpose, Richie called forth information on the nearest access point to the dragon world. Very different images flooded into her mind. A church, two high street shops, a takeaway pizza outlet, a children's park, a disabled toilet and...

'Yes,' she thought, 'that's the one.' Closing her eyes, to her relief, it just went dark. No unwanted pictures, images, or thoughts. In the restaurant around her, she could just make out the clang of cutlery over a chain of whispered voices. Sensing the group of friends watching over her, she knew she had a lot to thank them for... lesser people might well have called the authorities in some way, shape or form. But what must they think? A good question, but one that she really didn't have time for at the moment. If everything she'd seen was true, then time really was of the essence. Uncurling, she slowly sat up, her brown curly hair matted with sweat. Audible sighs of relief resounded around the small group.

"You okay Richie?" whispered Hook, with more tenderness than his hulking great frame would have implied.

"I'm fine guys... really. Thanks to all of you for... looking out for me."

"What happened?" asked Emma.

Richie jumped to her feet, albeit looking more than a little shaky.

"I don't have time to explain now. But I will at some point. I'm sorry."

The group looked heartbroken after all they'd done. Across the restaurant, Richie caught a glimpse of Taibul, a familiar face from the hockey club, and beckoned him over with her right index finger. Obligingly he came straight away. The others made way for him.

"I need a torch Taibul, and a... knife. A really, really big knife. Perhaps the biggest that you have. Do you think you can help me?"

Nodding enthusiastically, the young lad turned and headed off towards the kitchen. Again, it was Hook who spoke up.

"What's going on Richie?"

The lacrosse playing dragon, as that what she now was despite the human form she was stuck in, turned to face the man mountain of a rugby player.

"There's something I have to do. And I need to do it

now. I know things seem a little odd, but I'll try and explain later. I promise."

Hook paused, not sure how to respond.

"This has something to do with Peter and Tank doesn't it?" demanded Janice.

Richie turned to face the cute blonde, her expression wavering.

"I really can't say any more... I'm sorry."

Janice shook her head in frustration.

"You can be as sorry as you like, but I'm coming with you."

"I'm really sorry Janice, but this is something I have to do alone."

"Then you'll be needing that knife to stop me," replied the young bar worker, steely eyed.

'I really don't have time for all this,' thought Richie, watching Taibul argue with some of the kitchen staff through the small window in the kitchen door.

"Is this about Tank and Peter?" asked Hook.

"Are they in trouble?" enquired Emma.

"I really don't have time for all this!" exclaimed Richie, frustrated. Trying to walk through the group towards the kitchen doors, she was surprised when a large hand grabbed her bicep. Stopping, she gazed up at Hook. Her expression could have turned most to stone, but he wasn't perturbed.

"They're our friends as well. There's nothing I wouldn't do for the big man. Whatever's going on... you need our help."

Richie tried to wriggle free of his vice-like grip, but he was simply too strong.

"You of all people should know how a group working together can achieve more than any one individual. If I've heard Peter tell me about hockey and teamwork and how it was you who got him into it all, once, then I've heard it a thousand times. He believes it with a passion. And I believe it because he believes it," muttered Janice, her voice starting to wobble.

Richie stared at the other woman, incredulous.

"She's right Richie," added Hook, easing his grip on her arm. "If they're in trouble, then I'm coming as well."

The others in the group all agreed with Hook, apart from the hockey player who'd wanted to call the ambulance, slurring something about having to get home and look after his sick mum, clearly too drunk to know exactly what was going on. One of the lacrosse girls opted out, with Simon the rugby player declining to help as well.

Taibul returned holding a powerful torch, and the mother of all kitchen knives, bigger and sharper than any of them had ever seen.

"Uhhhh... we're going to need more knives and flashlights if you have them. Please..."

Smiling enthusiastically, the young lad darted back off in the direction of the kitchen. Hook asked what the others were all thinking.

"How much trouble are they in?"

"And we want the truth," demanded Janice.

Over the last few minutes, Richie had gained a new respect for the young girl. Turning to them all, and with her most serious voice, she said,

"The truth is... they're in planet changing trouble."

If anyone else had said this, then it would have been taken with a pinch of salt. But it was Richie, and she was deadly serious. Each and every one of them were more than a little taken aback.

"I'm not going to lie to you. I'd prefer to go alone, but I think you may be right... they, and I, might well need your help. But where we're going... it's dangerous... deadly so. If you want to tag along then I'm not going to stop you, and I'll do all I can to keep you safe. But it may not be enough. Peter and Tank are in grave danger, but there's more, so much more, that I can't even begin to explain. You'll have to just trust me. I'll repeat again, I would much rather go alone."

Nodding, they all once again expressed that they wanted to accompany her, albeit without the kind of enthusiasm that they'd shown before. With that, Taibul returned, carrying with him what looked like half the kitchen. In seconds, he'd distributed the few torches and all of the knives to the rather reluctant members of the group. He stood there holding a spare knife.

"Thanks Taibul, but I don't think we'll be needing that one," ventured Richie, slipping her torch onto her belt.

"It's not for you. It's for me. I'm coming with you."

Richie was blown away.

"I'm really sorry, you can't."

"Peter's my friend. One of the few I really have. My confidence at hockey, the reason I've stayed in the second team and progressed so well... it's all down to him. If he's in trouble, then I want to help. No, I need to help. PLEASE!"

Shaking her head in disbelief, Richie agreed that he could tag along. The beaming smile he shot her way troubled her deeply.

With the team all gathered, Richie turned and glared out of the front window of the restaurant. About fifty yards away, lit by a couple of street lights, she could just make out the Poultry Cross, the centrepiece of the old market place which was hundreds of years old, and their key to gaining access to the dragon domain. This was their destination.

"Okay," she stated, not at all happy. It wasn't so much taking them into the below ground dragon world that had her worried; after all, the dragons would just wipe their memories. It was the danger. If what she'd seen was going on, there was no telling exactly what they would be walking into. Turning to the very dangerous looking group, she thought of one more thing to say.

"Just one more thing before we go. You are all to do exactly as I say. Do you understand? No thinking about it, no arguments... exactly what I say... first time. However odd the instruction might seem."

They all nodded eagerly, more due to the serious look on Richie's face than anything else.

Grabbing her jacket that along with all the others had been returned, she slipped the ferocious looking knife into the inside pocket, turning to the others, all of whom were concealing their not so makeshift weapons in the same way. Leaving all the cash she had as payment, she turned to the others.

"Let's go."

As one, they strode past the other diners, all of whom weren't sure what to make of the very unusual happenings of the last half hour. About halfway to the door, Richie stopped at a table of diners, none of whom she knew. One of the two women seated was chewing some gum. Richie looked at her, all businesslike. The restaurant held its breath. Holding out the palm of her hand, Richie ordered,

"Your gum... GIVE!" Obligingly, the woman immediately spat the gum into Richie's hand. Without a word, she turned, squeezed past one of the waiters and continued on towards the exit. Another of the waiters held the front door open for them. Nodding to Taibul, he wished him, "Good luck," as he exited. Crossing the road in front of the restaurant, Richie told them all to wait. As the group stood still, the lacrosse captain sauntered over the ancient, uneven cobbles towards the Poultry Cross, all the time weaving as though she were a little the worse for wear. Her friends had no idea what was going on. Just before she reached the ancient monument, she staggered theatrically and veered sharply to one side, where she crashed into the base of a long, thin, blue pole, with a CCTV camera designed to keep an eye on the Poultry Cross atop it. In the blink of an eye, she shimmied thirty feet up the pole until she was behind the camera and, clinging on precariously with one arm at the top, she reached around and stuck the aforementioned gum right across the lens. At the same time as she released her grip, she kicked off the pole, her friends looking on, stunned, as she performed a perfect back flip and landed unharmed at its base.

Beckoning them over as she skulked into the shadows of one of the city's most recognisable features, the friends gathered round her as she stood up on the shiny, worn stone that formed a circular seat around the monument. Reaching up with both hands, she ran them along the centuries old stone, looking for two particular points. Finding an indentation shaped like an upside down tankard, she felt a finger sized groove, which she ran her longest digit along. As soon as she'd finished she turned around, jumped back down, and stood facing one of the stone pillars that formed part of the outside of the Poultry Cross. Each and every one of the friends were perplexed, but they didn't have long to wait for the answer to their unvoiced questions. In total silence, a triangular section of stone floor exactly in front of where Richie now stood, appeared to drop down and then slide back out of sight, revealing a set of worn, curved, stone steps. Without looking back, Richie stepped down, followed tentatively by the others. As soon as they'd all cleared the entrance, Richie whispered for them to all turn on their torches. They did so straight away, as the stone above them glided back into place, blocking out every last bit of light from the street lamps above. Following one another down the tightly wound spiral of worn stone steps with just the torches that they'd been given for light, the stale smell of the air they breathed became almost overpowering. Nobody said a word. They moved like this for some time, nearly an hour in fact, by which time they were nearly all panting like overworked sheep dogs, dripping in sweat. When they started, the air had felt cold, but was now something akin to a sauna, and of course there was no way they could remove their jackets and coats in such a confined space.

"Go careful now," Richie whispered, "we're just about

to stop." Other than feet on steps, it was the first sound they'd heard since starting out. Janice nearly dropped her torch in surprise. They stopped, all except Richie grateful to catch their breath. It was impossible to see exactly what she was doing, but again it looked to the others as though she was scrabbling around trying to find some sort of concealed switch or contact. In a matter of moments, bright light flooded through a gap large enough to act as an exit. Richie slid through, closely followed by the others. If they'd thought it was stifling inside the stairwell, the wave of hot air that greeted them was like opening the door to a furnace. Emma nearly passed out, indeed she might have if not for Hook seeing her discomfort and removing her jacket in double quick time. Only then did the friends take in the scene around them.

Exiting from a solid stone wall that had to be a hundred feet tall, it was hard to see the ceiling or roof of the... cavern, at least they thought it was a cavern they were in. Rounded houses carved into the surrounding rock sat either side of where they stood, giant in size, disappearing off into the distance. They weren't just any houses though. The lip of the window on the house next to them came up to about the height of Hook's head. Made of rock, the front door must have been about three times Hook's size, and he was by far the biggest of the group. They couldn't help but wonder who these houses belonged to, where on earth they were and why lava flowed freely down the walls and along tiny rivulets in the middle of the street. All fought back the desire to ask the troubled looking Richie.

"Jackets off. Lose the torches, and if you have a knife... keep it handy," ordered the lacrosse captain, tossing her jacket to the ground, followed closely by the others.

"We're heading to the main bazaar which is about two thousand yards directly in front of us," she whispered. "We need to make sure we're not seen. I can't begin to stress how important this is. So we're going to go slow. I'm going to lead. Hook, you bring up the rear. Everyone else... pay attention. If I hold my fist up like this," Richie held up a closed fist, "then we all stop... dead still. Understand?"

They all nodded their agreement.

"I can't answer all your questions now, but all I can say is that if you think this blows your mind, you haven't seen anything yet. But remember, all of our lives depend on stealth. Do not, and I repeat do not, get separated. If you see anything that looks like a danger, whisper a warning to me. Okay?"

Again, they all nodded.

"Good. Let's move out."

With that, Richie, all the time crouching, moved along the building they were beside and headed straight across the next intersection, the rest of the gang following in her footsteps. Three side alleys (each about the width of a one way street) and four more significant thoroughfares later, the group hugged the side of a dusty orange bungalow with a walled off garden, that housed a chicken coop with over fifty chickens in it. The noise and smell were overpowering, the heat, stifling. Richie leaned against the wall and took a moment to compose herself. They were closing in on the bazaar, and had yet to see any dragons. Her vision, prophecy, call it what you will, was starting to look spot on. Quite a significant part of her had hoped she was wrong, that they'd have walked out from the staircase and been instantly surrounded by dragons and carted off to appear before the council. At least that way she'd have known that everything in the underground world was okay. But this... the deserted houses, the eerie quiet (apart from the occasional animal) worried her no end. Although not as much as how she was going to take on what had appeared in her vision as nothing short of a small army. Although her memory had returned for the most part, she was still stuck in the form of a human, with human strength and stamina. How she was supposed to go up against even one dragon with just a knife was frankly beyond even her. Sucking in a breath, she crouched, and checking across the street and to her left, tiptoed around the corner... straight into a humungous wall of scales. The impact left her ears ringing, but she had the presence of mind to plunge the vicious looking knife straight into the rather stunned looking dragon that stood before her. It was a great strike, having put all her power and strength behind it. Unfortunately for her, all that happened was that the reflective silver blade crumpled on impact. Standing, shell shocked, waiting for the worst, as the audible gasps and sighs of surprise from behind her got louder, it was then that it got even weirder.

"Whoa... little one," whispered the silky smooth voice of the dragon in front of her.

Momentarily she was frozen by shock, something which in itself surprised her, as though it were her first time. Nothing had ever even phased her before, let alone induced paralysing terror. Her friends were the same, but for them it was understandable. The only dragons they'd ever seen were either in books, on the television or in video games. To see a real one standing only a few feet away, living and breathing, was a reality altering experience, that's for sure. Looking over her shoulder, she could see her friends' wits just about starting to regain control over their petrified bodies. Two, Hook and Taibul, were both starting to raise their weapons, clearly intent on attacking. Knowing their situation was hopeless she immediately raised her closed fist, drawing things to an end. Both friends reacted instantly, standing where they were, grateful not to have to go up against the giant, prehistoric beast.

Something inside her stirred. Questions filtered to the surface. Why hadn't the dragon attacked? It could surely have taken them down in just a handful of seconds. As well, it looked kind of odd. Not like any she'd pictured in the vision she'd had. Those that looked in control of the situation there, the ones who had clearly chosen to side with Casey and were torturing her friends all had very peculiar markings/tattoos on their bodies. She couldn't recall exactly what they were, but knew that each dragon had exactly the same thing. Briefly, she wondered if she might not bargain with the beast; perhaps it could be bought or persuaded just to let them go, but the very thought seemed as futile as the strike she'd made with her borrowed knife.

Shuffling back slightly, the dragon leaned down, bringing its head level with Richie's face. A resonance of familiarity rang through her mind. Sifting through her newly gained memories, trying to match them with what she knew was a very unusual looking dragon, her heart pounded with the seriousness of the situation. For a start, the strange beast carried an enormous dragon sized rucksack on its back, the dimensions of a small car. As well, it looked... old. In all her dragon memories she recalled, every dragon looked... well, young. Not even middle aged. And then, there were the... GLASSES! Square plastic framed glasses...

'How odd,' she thought, 'a dragon wearing glasses.' Something about those set alarm bells ringing (in a good way) throughout her subconscious. Before she could hit the nail on the head, a flimsy looking wing that had seen better days, enveloped her tightly.

"Oh it's so good to see you, little one," stuttered the old dragon. "I thought for a moment that I'd been mistaken, or gone to the wrong place."

As the two of them stood nose to nose, it just started to dawn on the old dragon that the human shape in front of him was having a hard time remembering who he was.

"Ahhhh... you don't remember."

Summoning up all of the courage she possessed, Richie managed to stammer,

"I know I have nothing to fear... you're, you're a... friend."

"Good, little one, good," rumbled the dragon, smiling.

And then it came to her.

"Gee Tee."

"Exactly," roared the old shopkeeper, his scaly belly wobbling like Santa's belly when his sleigh hits turbulence.

"I'm so sorry. My head, it's still kind of... fuzzy."

"That's alright my dear. It's the ring. It'll do that to you, for a while at least."

Shuffling forward, she hugged as much of the old dragon as she could reach, as the group of friends behind her looked on, astonished.

"Much as this is very nice my dear," ventured the master mantra maker, looking at the group over Richie's shoulder, I don't think we really have time for all this. Perhaps now would be a good time for introductions, before one or all of your comrades pass out."

"Uhhh... sure," sighed the young lacrosse player, finally able to gather her wits. "Everyone, this, this is... Gee Tee. He's, he's my... friend."

The group's expressions were priceless.

"And this, Gee Tee, is..." Richie moved over to each one, pointing them out with their respective names.

Plodding over, the old dragon reached over to each of them, offering out his hand as Richie introduced them in what must have been one of the most bizarre encounters in the history of the planet. Each human grasped the outstretched hand and shook it gently. With the introductions done, the subject moved on to more pressing matters.

"How did you know where to find us?" asked Richie.

Gee Tee pondered the question thoughtfully.

"Odd things have been going on for some time now. Weeks in fact. Tank thought my comments were just the continued ramblings of an old dragon, but anyway, things started to come to a head when a group of very serious beings tried to break into the Emporium two nights ago. Of course they didn't succeed, but they were very well equipped and they only failed by the skin of their teeth. I'd already instigated every mantra that I'd acquired over the past five hundred years or so to protect the premises, but it very nearly wasn't enough. I knew I had to take matters further. And there seemed like only one thing to do. The Japanese dragons of old developed a mantra that could... see into the future. As it happens, it wasn't very reliable and, as we both know, the future itself is always in flux, very much on the move. But this mantra was different to the ones we're always hearing about. So with a copy of it tucked away in my personal vault for safekeeping... I tried it out. I was sceptical at first, as the dark images started to consume my mind. But on seeing my app... friend, Tank, strung up from some kind of metal gallows, I knew that I was on the right track.

"In the bazaar, here," added Richie.

"Precisely," nodded the old dragon. "Anyhow, I continued with the mantra, trying to piece together exactly what was happening. And that's how I stumbled across you and your merry little gang. I saw you sneaking down here and knew that if I left straight away, that I could intercept you before you reached the bazaar."

"To what end?"

"I'm not exactly sure. But I'm way too old to take on a band of mass murdering dragons all by myself. And while you and a group of humans wouldn't be my first choice as help, you are all that I have."

"Thanks for the ringing endorsement," pitched in Richie, her voice laden with sarcasm.

"Don't be like that, little one."

Richie could hear one of her friends stifle a bit of laughter at her being called 'little one'. She thought it was Hook, and made a note of it for... later!

"Anyhow, I figured if we're all in this together, the least I could do was to... even up the odds a little," announced the master mantra maker, sliding the gigantic canvas backpack off and gently lowering it to the ground in front of them all.

This got Richie's full attention.

"Would you like to see?" asked the old dragon, a

playful smile on his face, sensing full well how keen Richie really was.

"If it's not too much trouble," replied the lacrosse captain, grinning from ear to ear at the thought of whatever mischief the old shopkeeper was about to introduce them to.

Gee Tee turned and beckoned to Hook. As the strapping rugby player made his way nervously forward, the old dragon bent down and retrieved something large out of the backpack. Hook pulled up next to Richie and was rather surprised when the old shopkeeper offered him what looked like some kind of rusty old jetpack. Hanging off the right hand side was a flimsy looking holster holding a metallic gun, which had an oversized barrel, making it look more like a rifle than a pistol. It was in fact a cross between the two, and not dissimilar to a modern day jet washer.

"Put it on, put it on," urged the old dragon. Not wanting to offend something three times his height and weight, Hook slipped his arms through the straps and shrugged it into place, unable to believe how heavy it actually was, as the old shopkeeper had used just one finger to pick it up out of the backpack and hand it to him. Richie frowned on noticing the worn label running down one side of the main compartment. It had obviously once read 'WATER', but the word was now barely visible.

"What are we going to do... give them all a shower?"

"Now, now, little one," admonished the master mantra maker, waving his index finger at her. "That's not the attitude is it? Besides, that's not just any water. It's Romanian heavy water."

Hook looked more than a little unsure.

"Here's what you do," ventured the old dragon, as he moved to the back of where Hook was standing. "Draw the gun, adjust the flow regulator and arm the backpack," he said, slipping the rifle-like object from the other side of the pack, on which he turned a small, silver knob totally clockwise, and then flicked an ancient looking switch hidden right underneath, causing the whole thing to hum gently.

"Now, just point and shoot," he gestured to Hook.

Reluctantly the gentle giant pointed the end of the rifle in the direction the dragon had gesticulated and pulled the trigger. Sluggishly, a great big squirt of gloopy looking liquid jumped out and hit the house about twenty yards away. It did nothing but cling to the wall.

"There you go, what did I tell you?"

"That's great," sighed Richie, "but what exactly is it supposed to do?"

"Ahhhh... for that, you'll need a dragon my dear. But let's just say that they won't like it, and it WILL have the desired effect."

Shrugging her shoulders, Richie raised her eyebrows theatrically. Given his track record, she remained more than a little sceptical about what use, if any, the heavy water was going to be. Still, Hook seemed to be enjoying practising with the weapon.

One by one, the master mantra maker beckoned the rest of the friends forward, all except Janice. The others all received bandoliers that strapped across their chests, all holding different types of grenades. Some were smoke grenades that made it almost impossible to see, some were electrical grenades that caused shock and momentary paralysis. Gee Tee explained how to arm the five second fuses on them, and how best to throw them at their intended target. Next, Janice was asked to step forward. Tentatively, she did so. Noticing the worry in her face, the old shopkeeper did his best to buoy her spirits.

"Hmmmm... I know all about YOU!" he remarked menacingly, recalling the trip inside Peter's mind.

Instantly, Janice took two steps back, as the old dragon leaned forward and put his ancient reptilian head right in her face. Tiny little flames sizzled and danced from inside his nostrils.

"You must be something special to capture the heart of a dragon," he whispered so that no one else could hear. "I know why you're here and will tell you only this. It will be hard to find a more honest, loyal, brave and trustworthy being. Tread carefully, little one, he thinks the world of you."

Janice's heart raced, and she had to remind herself to breathe. He'd almost confirmed what she thought she knew from the events of the night so far. All she could think was... 'He's a dragon!'

Pulling his face slowly back from hers, the master mantra maker declared,

"It'll be okay... honest. There's nothing to worry about... well, there is actually. But I've saved the best for last, well, almost." Reaching deep inside the backpack, the old shopkeeper pulled out the most mesmerising thing the whole group of them had ever seen. It gleamed from almost impossible angles, so shiny was the metal it was made from. Its design was so sleek and unusual that it looked like something from far in the future. However, those features weren't what made it stand out. Surrounding the blade of the knife/sword, as that was the only way to describe it due to its significant length, was a kind of moving frost that circled continuously. It gave off an eerie, light blue glow while spluttering and hissing ever so slightly. It looked AWESOME! Gee Tee held it out for Janice, encouraging her to take it as everyone else looked on, slack jawed. Taking a deep breath, the petite blonde stepped forward and grabbed the surprisingly comfortable hilt. Waving it around a few times, she created a kind of blue trail across the air in front of her, much as a child would do with a sparkler on bonfire night. All she could think was how light and natural it felt in her hand. Looking on, the old shopkeeper seemed pleased with his selection.

"This," he announced, "is my pride and joy. It's the only one of its kind, and was forged by a Chinese dragon more than two thousand years ago. Nobody's ever been able to recreate that feat, despite many having tried. It is thought to have been crafted by a master weapon smith by the name of Fu-ts'ang. So revered was Fu-ts'ang that he was written into ancient Chinese mythology, having special responsibility for the minerals of the earth and is sometimes known, even to this day, as the Dragon of Hidden Treasures. Hence the weapon is known only as Fu-ts'ang. You should refer to it as if you were referring to a person. Do you understand child?"

Swallowing involuntarily, Janice just about managed to mumble,

"Yes... sir."

"Ohhhh... 'sir'," said the master mantra maker, turning to Richie. "I like her, she can stay."

Janice blushed fiercely.

"Now listen carefully, child. It's a serious responsibility you bear. This weapon will cut its way through just about anything: metal, stone, even with the necessary intent behind it... dragon. Probably not fatally, but you could in theory remove a dragon's tail, rendering it off balance and relatively defenceless. But here, today, that's not your main purpose. I will now demonstrate. Little one," the old shopkeeper whispered, referring of course to Richie, "please would you go and stand in front of us, with your back turned."

Striding forward ten paces, Richie turned to face the other way, having heard about the master mantra maker's demonstrations she was far from keen to have anything to do with one. It was bad enough that he made her idiot friend participate on a regular basis. Abruptly her thoughts turned to Tank, hoping they were in time to save him, if that were even possible. Before she knew it, a strange sensation dripped down her back. Just as she was about to turn round to find out what was going on, she experienced the most painful sensation she'd ever felt in her entire life. Worse still, she was paralysed.

Whilst Richie had been facing the other way, Gee Tee

had gotten Hook to fire a burst of heavy water at her, as he sneaked up behind her and touched Fu-ts'ang to a trailing part of the heavy water covering her. Immediately her whole body froze. As it did so, he turned and addressed the group of humans.

"Combined with the heavy water, Fu-ts'ang will freeze almost anything it comes into contact with... including either dragons or humans. If you can cover enough dragons, it would be possible to freeze many at once. You, my dear, may be the difference between success and failure," he continued, moving his gaze across to Janice.

"Cool," whispered Emma under her breath.

"'Rockin'," stated Hook, gazing lovingly at the trigger of the heavy water rifle.

"And now, I really must defrost our friend, before her anger gets the better of her." With a simple wave of his hand and a few muttered words, a jet of fire surrounded Richie, enveloping her in a cloud of steam that released her from her stasis.

"That was fun," she remarked with heavy sarcasm.

"Ahh, but now you see how we even up the odds a little."

Nodding her head, she could see how the old dragon was right. Before, as a group, they hadn't stood a chance. But now there was at least an outside possibility that they might be able to take on the aggressors in whatever action was being played out. She was starting to have a good feeling about it all, apart from the fact that she had nothing to fight with. Feeling naked, defenceless and incomplete, she needn't have worried though. Giving the inert backpack a little tug, almost as if reading her thoughts, the old dragon made it known that there were other things left inside.

"Did you think I'd forgotten about you?"

Richie should have known better. So she showered him with her best smile, the one that any film star on the planet would have been proud of, the same one that had melted hearts both above and below ground. Radiating a smile back at her as he reached into the rustic looking canvas bag, adorned with leather straps and buckles, something wrapped in an old cloth came out in the shopkeeper's hands. Suddenly Richie wasn't feeling so happy. It looked distinctly like she'd wound up with the booby prize.

"Why don't you wait and see what it is before you pull that face?" scoffed Gee Tee, trying not to laugh. "You of all beings should know not to judge a book by its cover."

Knowing he was right, briefly she wondered what on earth could be better than Fu-ts'ang? Reaching out to take the mysterious object from the old shopkeeper's hand, sheer raw power overtook her. It was akin to someone removing the kryptonite from Superman, Bruce Wayne donning his Batman outfit, and Green Lantern slipping on his ring, suddenly having all that power back. It was overwhelming, seductive, magical. Gripping the object and soaking up its power at the same time, Richie unwound the ropey old cloth and couldn't believe her eyes at what lay inside.

"Ahh... Peter's dagger."

"You know?"

"He's shown it to me."

"I was safeguarding it for him. And while I promised him with my life that I would keep it locked away, I think he of all beings would want you to have it here and now. In fact, I'm sure of it."

Slowly, Richie curled her fingers around the gold coloured, solid laminium, jewelled hilt. It felt intoxicating. Raw, unashamed power coursed through her as she sliced the dagger through the air in front of her. It felt as if there were no resistance at all, almost as if it were carving the atoms of the air itself apart.

"How do you feel?" asked the dragon, seriously.

"Strong, powerful... invincible," responded the young lacrosse captain, a keen glint in her eye, all the time wielding the dagger through the air in front of her.

"It should compensate for part of what you've lost. Remember though, don't let any other dragon get hold of it. If you do... well, I think you know the consequences."

She did. To let another dragon, one of the enemy, take that weapon would mean DEATH, and almost certainly not just for her. While enhancing her beyond belief and restoring almost all her dragon powers, albeit whilst still stuck in human form, the dagger was a huge responsibility. She would guard it with her life and intended to steal life from those that got in her way.

"I think it's time we made a move," exclaimed Gee Tee. "First of all we're going to make our way to the southernmost point of the bazaar because I believe that to be where we will all get the best view of exactly what's going on. After that, we'll have to improvise. I trust you, little one, to form a plan with the weapons we have at our disposal."

Nodding her agreement, Richie knew there was something she had to do before they left. Closing her eyes, she focused hard on two things. One... the dagger, and by that I mean drawing power, energy, magic, whatever you will from it. Secondly... her injured knee. With the dagger's power throbbing and humming, eager to be of use, she guided it down through her body, letting it loose around her injury. Instantly coalescing, she could almost feel it knitting and weaving the tendon on the inside of her knee back together. For a moment it felt glorious, intense and refreshing. And then it was done, her knee healed, as strong and perfect as it had been before. All this had been done in a fraction of a second. Having recalled how to do it, she marvelled at just how easy it had been.

"Good," said the shopkeeper, bringing Richie back from inside herself. "One last thing. When things kick off, it will be frantic. At that point, I'll do everything in my power to help. I've prepared a little surprise in the form of a mantra that I hope will slow them all down, almost as if they were wading through treacle. That should help to buy us some time. The only problem is, I don't know how long I'll be able to cast it for. I'm not as young as I once was, but I'll do my best."

Again Richie nodded, knowing better than to question the old dragon. Meanwhile, the others just looked at each other, not knowing what on earth was going on, or even what a mantra was. They were placing their trust, and their lives, in Richie's hands.

Strapping on the backpack and spreading his wings open, Gee Tee said,

"Lead the way, little one," to Richie. Instead of being offended, she smiled, and with a renewed vigour slipped off into the alleyway opposite, heading for the bazaar... to save her friends.

Flash, his thick, longer than normal, blonde hair matted to his skull, took the unerring pain, boxed it up and slid it into a compartmentalised part of his brain, just as he'd been taught to do in the Crimson Guards. Of course, he yelled, screamed and writhed about, but really it was just for show. He could take this and a little more, even stuck in this inconvenient form, he thought, dangling precariously from the hastily put together frame, Tank swinging next to him. Glancing briefly at his friend through his very swollen eyes, anger and pity fought amongst themselves at what was happening. A huge amount of flesh had been flayed off his friend's body, and his face looked as though it had lost a fight with an oncoming train. But still, Flash sensed there was more to the tough looking rugby player. A well of untapped strength, an instinct for survival sat beneath the surface, he was sure. All he had to do now was figure a way out of this mess. Off to his left the other Salisbridge dragons, having been rounded up, most of them taken by surprise, took up about a quarter of the square, all bound by restraints and all surrounded by deadly looking guards, just waiting for an excuse to kill. In fact, they already had. Dragons had already tried to rush the guards and escape. They'd been killed instantly by the magically enhanced bastard swords that all the guards carried. The rest were... shocked. Shocked at the brutality, shocked at the surprise of it all. Seven hours ago they were all going about their daily business: feeding livestock, washing, cleaning, working. But in almost an instant that had changed, and now they found themselves fearing for their very lives, for their very existence, and for the entire dragon domain, if what they'd seen was true.

SMASH! Another flick from the evil looking, magical whip struck him across the belly, its brilliant crackling line of multi-coloured energy snapping, hissing and whining, almost splitting the air in two before burning the flesh of his taut six pack of a stomach in a straight line. Screaming in pain, he let himself react as any normal being would. At the moment the only advantage he had over his assailants was the fact that they seemingly had no idea of his past, no idea what he was capable of. Only strung up here because of his friendship with Peter and Tank, something he was immensely proud of and grateful for, it was also, he realised, something he'd die to protect and something he was determined to prolong. He needed a plan, and he needed one quickly.

It didn't take long to reach the periphery of the crowded square. Currently they were concealed behind the wreckage of what had been the bazaar stalls. Nearly all had been overturned, broken or simply destroyed, their wares littering the cobbled square, not just where they were, but as far as the eye could see. Gee Tee had cast a protective mantra over all of them on the way, one that would help conceal their very essence from the enemy, until they were spotted that is. Once that happened, the mantra would fail and their presence would become clear.

Slithering forward on her stomach, Richie peeped out through the debris strewn around her, just in time to see Flash catch another strike from the whip. Each and every one of them heard the sound of it searing flesh from his broken body, followed by his desperate howl. Anger flared from Richie's very core. Murderous intent stoked the adrenaline that flowed through her, threatening to engulf her entire being. The soft touch of a dragon wing stroked her back gently, followed by a series of very wise words.

"Save your anger child. Now is not the time. I know how you feel; it seeps through me that those two are up there. But if we are to stand a chance, we must be prepared. Look around. Unless we're ready, we'll end up like that. Is that what you want?"

From her prone position, Richie looked around, nostrils flaring. Staring into those big, square glasses had a soothing effect, enough to take some of the anger away, at least. With the red mist clearing, at least temporarily, she started to formulate a plan. It didn't take long.

"Here's what we're going to do," she said. And with that, she set about trusting and tasking each and every one of the humans with saving dragon civilisation as she knew it.

Once everyone had been briefed, they all set their watches to count down and moved stealthily into their assigned positions. Now there was no turning back. It was quite literally do or die!

For a while now, something else had been eating away inside her. She knew where Tank and Flash were, quite clearly being able to see them subjected to massive amount of pain. But where on earth was Peter? He was, of course, missing as well, but try as she might, from where they were, she could see no sign of him. She hadn't mentioned this to the others, but off to one side of where the dragons were being kept prisoner, there were bodies. Dragon bodies. Not able to see well enough to make out any, she didn't think her friend was there, but if not there, then where exactly was he?

Blood trickled down his stomach, pooled a little, and then continued flowing down his strong, muscular legs. It seemed odd to him that it was red, given that he wasn't unaccustomed to watching his own blood flow. Some of the missions he'd been on... well, let's just say that he'd lost a serious amount of blood along the way, though nearly all of it had been green, because nearly all of it had been in his natural form, if such a thing even existed for him now. Wondering, if he survived, whether these wounds would heal or become a permanent feature like the scar that sat just below his left eye, again he pushed away the pain. As he did so, he caught the briefest glimpse of movement through what were now slits in his vision. As soon as he'd glimpsed it, it had vanished. His high vantage point afforded him a fantastic view of the surrounding houses, shops and streets. Certain he hadn't been mistaken about what he'd just seen, what did it mean? A rogue dragon, one his captors had missed when rounding up all the others? Or was it more than that? A rescue mission, a full on attack? He knew not. But what he did know was that he needed to be ready. Pretty sure he could break out of the restraints holding him to the frame of the metal monstrosity, he hadn't done so before because he was seriously outnumbered and, by the look of things, he'd be killed before he hit the ground. Now though, just maybe something was in the offing. Maybe he had a chance, a chance to at least save his friend, even if it meant sacrificing his own life. Once again, he was back in the game.

Thirty seconds remained. Thirty seconds until all hell broke loose. Thirty seconds of life remaining. At least that's how she looked at it. After that she was dead. But she had a chance. She could fight, fight for her life, and those of her friends. What had she been thinking... bringing humans here, to fight... against... DRAGONS?! It was too late now though. Too late to change things. But she could fight for them. Fight for all of them. Turning her head slightly, taking in the old shopkeeper, he looked surprisingly calm and clear headed. He'd been the voice of reason ever since they'd encountered him. Richie gave a slight chuckle at that... Gee Tee, the voice of reason. It would have made Tank laugh anyway. Turning back towards her friend, hanging limply, about to be struck again by that blasted energy whip, rage consumed her. She felt it build up. She tried to dam it. Immediately the dam sprang leaks. Fury rushed through her limbs. Glancing at her watch, she knew the dam only had to last a few more seconds. After that... well, she'd see exactly how tough these bullies actually were.

Janice lay on her belly, trying not to choke on the sand and dust all around her. Situated on the rooftop of a shop that looked out over the bazaar, Hook had helped her get up here unnoticed, and she'd spent what seemed like an age crawling towards the edge. About at eye height to Tank and Flash, the roof was behind them, so there was no chance of them spotting her. Currently, they were the only ones that could have. Knowing not to peek over the edge, it had been made quite clear to her that was forbidden for now, and in fact the very thought terrified every bone in her body. She was to wait. Wait until it all kicked off. And then, she was to act, to free the other dragons and do as much damage as she could. Although terrified, strangely she felt more alive than she could ever remember. Her life up until now had been so safe, so secure, so... dull. And then she'd met Peter, someone like her... so safe, so secure. At least that's what it had seemed like at first. But she knew deep down that there was more to it than that. She didn't know what and to be honest, if she'd had a million guesses, she'd never have guessed THIS! But she loved him. Not just a little, but all consuming, all or nothing, the do or die kind of love. Having never known this kind of love before, it was totally intoxicating. So she was determined to give her best, her all. Determined to see him again.

Hook had, as Richie had asked, stationed himself in an alleyway running parallel to the bazaar, not far from the menacing looking dragons guarding the prisoners, roughly in the direction Janice was facing from the roof that she found herself on. Well concealed, he had no concerns about being spotted. In the short time that he'd had the heavy water jet pack on his back (that's what he thought its name should be, as it didn't have an official one) he'd become reasonably proficient at picking out targets with it. Gee Tee had assured him that it was impossible for the pack to run out of water, as its insides had been imbued with a replenishing mantra, whatever that was. It was good enough for Hook though, and every opportunity that he'd had, he'd been practising with it. Near or far, he'd been picking targets and had experimented with firing at them, and was quite comfortable with his accuracy, and had even found a setting on the rifle part of his newly gained equipment that changed the single stream jet of water to something more akin to a shower.

'That,' he thought, 'would be perfect for a group of dragons.' Checking his watch, there were only a few seconds to go.

It was time. Emma the lacrosse player, her friend and teammate Angela, Sam the hockey player and Taibul had circled around the square so that they were on the opposite side to Richie and Gee Tee. About three hundred and fifty yards behind the market place, tucked away in the back yard of a small house (small by the standards of the others they'd seen) in the middle of the Salisbridge urban sprawl. And they'd just found what they'd been searching for: a metal bin. At least, that's what it looked like. It could have been used for something else by the dragons, but for their purposes it seemed ideal. They'd been asked, no, ordered, to come over to this area and to make as much noise as possible with what they'd been given, and then to head away from the bazaar at speed, circling back around in a wide arc to their original positions. They were under no circumstances to engage a dragon. Bizarrely, the group were more excited than worried now.

"What exactly are we going to do?" asked Emma.

Taibul, normally very shy and introverted, whispered,

"We'll put a smoke and electrical grenade in the bin, throw on the lid, stick this heavy rock on top, and run like hell. And perhaps for good measure, leave another smoke grenade next to the bin, just in case."

They all nodded. So Taibul pulled the pins from his grenades, and with Angela ready to shove the lid on the bin, tossed them in. Angela slammed the lid on and stepped back. Sam carefully placed the large rock on top of the lid before joining the others. Emma, waiting patiently, pulled the pin on her smoke grenade and lobbed it towards the bin. All of them turned, and as fast as they could, sprinted off in the opposite direction to where all the dragons were situated.

A split second later, the pair of grenades in the bin went off. The noise was unbelievable. If that didn't get their attention, then nothing would.

Strung out over Casey's right shoulder, his long fingers delicately gripped the dull silver, reflective handle of the deadly looking whip, ready to strike again at one of the captives. Just as he was wondering which one he should hurt this time, the loudest of booms resounded from somewhere off to his right. Everyone in the square turned their heads in that direction, alert. Pointing to two of his trusty lieutenants, he signalled with his hand.

"You two... check it out. Bring back whoever's out there."

"YES SIR," they both barked back in response, quickly taking flight in that direction.

The sound was the signal, and Hook had already started drizzling a light mist over the nearest dragons guarding a group of prisoners. Careful not to hit any of the captives, he knew that their plan depended heavily on releasing them to join in the fight. Aiming again, he fired.

As the boom echoed throughout the enclave, Richie gave Gee Tee one last look as he'd just finished muttering the last word of the mantra that would slow down all their enemies. Standing staring at the bazaar, the master mantra maker had the utmost conviction etched onto his face. Grabbing Aviva's laminium dagger, Richie unleashed all her dammed anger and took off towards her friends, using the dagger's precious metal to enhance her speed.

Flash braced himself for the next strike of the whip, hoping it was for him. That way, Tank at least got some sort of respite. But just as he'd inhaled a deep breath... BOOM! A massive sound very much like an explosion shattered the quiet of the square from somewhere off to his left.

'This is it,' he thought. 'Time to act.' Tensed, coiling up all his energy ready to strike, he hoped that whatever was going on, there was more to it than just a loud noise. Moments later, he had his answer. He wasn't disappointed, but he was surprised. There on the edge of the bazaar, over a hundred yards away, directly in his eye line, was Gee Tee and by the look of things, the old shopkeeper was casting some sort of mantra. Even more surprising, and he had to blink to make sure that he wasn't seeing things this time, right next to him, up popped Richie, something glinting in her hand, sprinting with the speed of a... DRAGON, towards the action. As rescues went, this seemed the most bizarre in the history of everything. But he wasn't complaining and figured that his rather unique skill set might be required sooner rather than later.

'Oh well,' he thought, 'here goes nothing.' Releasing his pent up energy, the binders holding him snapped, and he fell ever so slowly towards the ground.

Forehead caked in sweat from the strain of the effort, it was one thing casting the mantra, but another thing entirely holding it in place over such a large area. But somewhere inside, Gee Tee smiled. This rated right up there with some of the crazy stunts that he'd participated in during his long life. And the best thing of all... they actually had a chance. Since this had started, something inside him had whispered that he was making a mistake, a fatal mistake, his last mistake. And deep down, he'd accepted it. But he had to at least try, he owed... Tank that much. He'd thought that throwing his lot in with a bunch of ragtag humans and one rather damaged dragon was a sign of desperation. But as the mayhem started, he weighed up the odds, finding them much more in favour of winning than not. Watching as the very thick, immovable air parted in front of the speeding blur that was Richie, in his mind, he wished her good luck.

Casey faced the direction from which the massive boom had emanated, his danger sense racing into

372

overdrive. For some reason, he could barely move, with his spindly brown arms feeling lead like, and his legs feeling as though they were rooted to the ground. Having trouble turning his overly orange head, the long bony protrusions upon his cranial ridge remaining firmly facing one direction, from the corner of his eye, a momentary glance caught sight of movement heading his way from the opposite direction. Fighting with all his strength to turn around and face the threat head on, he'd turned almost halfway when he recognised what was speeding towards him. Well, not what, but who. Panic stricken, he nearly swallowed his tongue. Unable to believe she was here, sure she'd been expelled from the dragon world for good, her memories wiped forever. If there was one being that he feared more than Manson, it was her.

'Why can't I raise this blasted whip over my head?' was the thought that ran through his mind as she skidded to a halt in front of him.

Feeding off the energy from the dagger was pure ecstasy. Her speed was exhilarating. And then she focused on what had been done. What had been done to her friends anyway. In the distance her ex-classmate turned in her direction, but not fast enough.

'Gee Tee,' she thought, 'is clearly weaving his magic, and weaving it well.'

It was time. At least that's what Janice told herself. Shaking ever so slightly, her right hand clutched Fu-ts'ang tightly, as everything kicked off around her. Stomach flipping over and over, and a continued weakness assaulting her legs, it didn't help that she knew everyone was counting on her. Despite not wanting to, she took a deep breath and popped her head up above the parapet, just enough to see what was going on. The scene before her was both awe inspiring and terrifying in equal measure, and looked like something out of a Hollywood blockbuster. Watching as the spray of heavy water from Hook's backpack settled gently over the dragons guarding the prisoners, nerves threatened to consume her as the thick liquid dribbled across their wings and down their legs. In slow motion, the prisoners watched everything unfold nervously. It was time for her to act, she knew, so with a promise to herself to see her beloved Peter again, she ran, jumped off the roof and landed softly on the cobbles behind the guards. Clutching Fu-ts'ang for all she was worth, she crept towards them, all the time aware of the captives watching her.

As Flash hit the floor hard, the pain escaped his mind and tore through his body. Rolling instinctively, he managed to just about get to his feet. In a split second he took in everything around him. Not thinking it could get any weirder, suddenly it just had, with one of Tank's rugby playing friends' heads poking over the wall of the bazaar, shooting some kind of liquid by the look of things from a very strange rifle. He watched as... JANICE of all people leapt from the roof of a building behind the dragons guarding the prisoners. JANICE!! Sweet little... JANICE!! Of one thing he was bloody sure... she was most definitely not a dragon, and most certainly was a human. What in the hell was going on? Humans saving dragons?! The world had turned on its head, and he had a pretty good idea who was behind it all. That damned shopkeeper almost certainly had a hand in it, and as he watched Richie slice a very seductive looking dagger across the chest of the torturing dragon with the whip, he came to the conclusion that she was almost certainly up to her neck in it too.

'Time to act,' he thought. 'But what to do?'

Gee Tee was spent, drained of every last ounce of energy, having tried his best, realistically he'd done more than he could have hoped to do. Collapsing to his knees, too exhausted to even stand, he knew that he'd given them all the best chance he could. It was impossible for him to do any more. Now it was down to them, they had to make all his effort count for something. Slumping to the floor, he caught sight of Tank, head flopped in front of him, still as death itself, swinging back and forth. As his eyelids fluttered, one last thought consumed him.

'Please, please, please don't let us have been too late.'

Hook adjusted the pressure on the rifle, before changing his aim towards the guards furthest away, wondering where the hell Janice was. Although the plan was a little sketchy, he was pretty sure she should have been on the scene by now, and the bazaar should have been full of huge dragon sized lollies. With a limited view of events he supposed she could have been crouching down somewhere making her way towards the action, but still... time was running out. For their part, the guards had murderous looks in their eyes, some even drawing deadly looking, black swords from their scabbards.

Janice had tiptoed up to the nearest dragon guard, all the time being watched by the captives. Things were in full swing now, with Richie battling the evil looking dragon with the energy whip. Looking down at the guard's thick, scaly tail, the young bar worker noticed some of the scales glistening more than others, the thick heavy water standing out in the bright light. As she reached out with Fu-ts'ang, the guard started to turn around. Janice looked up, terrified, into huge, snarling jaws. Without thinking, she dived forward, touched Fu-ts'ang against the heavy water on the dragon's tail and then rolled away across the cobbles. Before the guard could react, solid ice began to form across the whole of his body, starting at his tail before working its way up to his head. And it wasn't just him; three of the other guards, to which the same water was connected, also found themselves frozen in place. Janice smiled to herself. It had worked. She'd done it! Only then did she realise a huge, dark shadow had enveloped her, blocking out the bright light that she'd only just got used to. Looking up into the almost alien face of another guard, she watched helplessly as he drew his sword and raised it above his head to strike.

Flash looked around, trying to decide on a course of action. For the most part, things seemed to be under control, or so it appeared. Not unfamiliar with the organised chaos of conflict, having fought in three hardcore dragon versus dragon battles, he was fully aware that events can change in a split second, and how taking a moment or two to try and grasp the overall picture can pay huge dividends. The most obvious thing for him to do was to try and get Tank down from where he was hanging as his friend looked drained of life. But it would take a while, and was it the right thing to do? Taking a step forward with a view to doing just that, an eerily familiar sensation tickled his neck, something he'd felt many times before, usually in hardened battle, and it nearly always meant danger. Turning, expecting to find an imminent attack, instead he glimpsed what was going on fifty yards or so away. Watching intrigued as Janice pressed something against a dragon's tail, he was amazed to see what happened next. But then he recognised the danger... a dragon guard was coming up behind her from one of the alleyways. Guessing it was one of the dragons who'd been dispatched to check out the loud boom, finding it was a diversion and then coming back, what was patently obvious was that Janice only had mere seconds to live.

Anger, magic and power stirred deep inside him as he shot off in her direction like an arrow being fired from a bow.

Richie slashed the dagger wildly across his bulging underbelly. The look on Casey's face gave her a certain satisfaction. Not only surprise, but fear as well. She could always tell when he was afraid, and he was afraid now. As she whipped the dagger round to strike again... it happened! Gee Tee's slowing mantra that everyone had been encased in ceased. In all honesty, she was surprised he'd lasted this long, unable to imagine how much effort it had required to hold the mantra over such an area. Even in her past, full on dragon life, she probably wouldn't even have attempted to cast such a thing. As this thought shot through her brain, Casey suddenly became alert, fast and understood what had gone on. Instantly Richie threw herself backwards as the magical whip came screaming through the air only inches away from where her neck had been. Her back flip wasn't perfect. Clumsily, she crashed to the cobbles, landing hard on her right shoulder. Pain exploded within it, but she knew better than to dwell on it. Movement, movement was the key. Staying flat, she rolled across to one side and came up on one knee. Casey was in the process of pulling the whip back over his shoulder again, and so she lunged forward and sliced the laminium dagger through the sinew of his left wing. A very unflattering squeak spluttered out of the injured dragon's mouth as she once again shot back out of range of the deadly looking whip, in two giant bounds. By cutting the sinew in his wings, she'd left him with little option but to fight, knowing that now escape was all but impossible for him (as there was simply no way he could take to the air), the chances were he'd become more desperate and infinitely more deadly. Slowly, the pair circled each other, Richie holding out the jewelled dagger in front of her, while Casey's whip dragged across the cobbles behind him.

Both dragons had murder in their eyes.

As he brought down the sword to cleave Janice in two, the sneer on the dragon guard's face was all encompassing. Her entire life didn't flash by, a grinning skeleton with a scythe didn't appear, and there were no last regrets. Mainly because a speeding blur picked her up and lobbed her onto the relative safety of the roof of the nearest single storey building. As the guard's matt black sword clanged off the cobbles, the blur resolved itself into... FLASH! Missing one human target made the guard angry. Really angry. And he sure as hell wasn't going to miss another. Using all the agility he had, he was on Flash in an instant. The ex-Crimson Guard was defenceless, or so it looked. But then again, he had been in the Crimson Guards, and being defenceless wasn't something they'd ever been accused of, well, not by anyone still alive that is. Swinging his blade towards Flash's head, the guard put all the strength he had into the attack. Rolling forward, Flash tucked in and sprang up, putting all his energy into the jump, popping up inside his opponent's defences, at about head height. As he reached the apex of his jump, he stuck out his index and middle fingers and with as much power as he could muster, jabbed them both into the guard's left eyeball. A squelch, followed by the guard's enraged howl, echoed off every corner of the bazaar and got every being within the confines of the square looking in their direction. With his enemy distracted for a moment, Flash rolled across to the edge of the bazaar and scooped up the juiciest lemon from a group of them littering the floor near an overturned stall. Determined to press home his advantage, he swiftly crept round the back of the flailing guard, and having ripped the lemon in half, jumped onto the guard's tail and sprinted up it. Knowing exactly where his target was, he reached around the tormented dragon's head and pulled the lemon back onto the dragon's one remaining good eye. Feeling it impact, he squeezed the lemon for all he was worth. In his wildest dreams, he couldn't have imagined his efforts being so well rewarded. The sound was surreal. It was so... alien, like nothing he'd ever heard. Somersaulting back to the ground, he kicked the guard in the back for good measure, sending him off in the direction of one of the houses on the edge of the square, effectively rendering him out of the fight and of little danger to anyone. Turning back to size up the chaos, Flash swallowed awkwardly as he did so, noticing a large contingent of guards having left their prisoners bound, sitting on the ground, now heading his way, as if to avenge their comrade.

'Things,' he thought, 'are about to get interesting.'

Having taken the longest route back they could, inasmuch as they figured they might be needed for the battle that ensued in the huge square. They were right. Peeking out of the shadows of an alleyway that opened out onto the square, they were all absolutely terrified as they watched monsters from nightmares breathe fire, wield swords and batter each other out of the way. Arriving just in time to see Flash spirit Janice to safety, nearly all their hearts skipped a beat, the ex Crimson Guard's save had been so close. But now it was Flash's turn to be in trouble, and despite his bravado it looked as though his time was about to be up. With courage he didn't know he had, the young waiter amongst them spoke up.

"We have to act... NOW!" It brought them all to their senses.

"Whhhaaatttt can weeee doooo?" stuttered Angela, petrified.

"The grenades," offered up Emma. "A concerted attack from all of us at the same time on that group might just work."

All agreeing, in unison they tore grenades from the bandoliers they wore.

"After three," said Emma. "One... two... three," and together the four of them let fly with their weapons.

Janice had barely taken a breath since her rescue. It was only when Flash had engaged the guard in combat that she'd realised exactly what had happened and who had saved her. Tears streamed down her face. And now as she watched, a whole gang of dragons headed his way, by the look of things, determined to tear him limb from limb. But that wasn't going to happen, not if she had anything to do with it. Thinking about the best way to help Peter's friend, it took her only a fraction of a second to realise that either jumping down next to him and joining the fight, or throwing him Fu-ts'ang was little more than futile. But what caught her eye, behind the onrushing guards, were the prisoners they'd left unattended. They were the answer, and perhaps the salvation of everyone.

Standing up, she wobbled slightly, her legs full of anxiety, like the rest of her. Facing the building next to her, she knew that if she could make the jump across the alleyway and onto its roof, she could leap down unhindered and land almost amongst the unattended detainees. The jump must have been nearly ten feet though. Gripping Fu-ts'ang tight, she ran. As the front of her trainer reached the edge of the roof, she launched herself for all she was worth. Amazingly, she cleared the chasm with ease. Landing with too much momentum, she crashed carelessly to the ground. Surprisingly, she didn't mind. On her feet in an instant and with the group of prisoners watching her every move, she climbed down the front of the building. With a quick look from side to side to make sure there was no immediate danger, she sprinted across to the group and started to cut off their restraints with Fu-ts'ang. As the first prisoner's bonds clanged to the floor, she looked up into the dragon's eyes, not knowing what to expect. She got more of a surprise than she bargained for. A loud chortle assaulted her ears, followed by words that would always stay with her.

"For such a pretty human, you have a mean attitude and an even meaner sword. Keep up the good work, little one." And off he shot to join in the battle. Janice was stunned, that is until the growls of the other dragons brought her back to reality. They, too, wanted to join the battle and this was their chance. Janice had no intention of depriving them of their wish. One by one, she set them free.

Well, he'd given it a good go. At least that's what Flash thought. Counting eight, even in the good old days, in his true dragon form, before the unspeakable encounter with those bloody nagas, he might still have struggled with that many. Alright, maybe not. His record, from what he could remember, was fourteen... in one go, anyway. Crouching low, making as small a target as possible, he looked at what he faced. Having already taken out three of them, he'd killed the first unwitting one with the splintered end of a wooden pole off a broken market stall, finding the watery crunch which had signalled the end of that first guard's life, incredibly satisfying. After that, the next two had been relatively easy. It hadn't been hard to steal the first guard's dark coloured sword and dispatch the overeager attackers. But now, for the first time today, he felt as though he were in trouble. The rest had backed off and he could see in their eyes exactly what they were about to do. They were going to rush him. As it stood, there was no way he could take five, not at once. Maybe if they all came one at a time, but even then it was unlikely that he would make it through them all. For several seconds he'd been searching for options, but he could find none that made any sense. Hoping that he hadn't consigned Janice and the others to a fiery fate, he positioned himself in classic Roman battle stance, the blade of the dark sword running alongside his head, inches from his right ear, and chose which two of the guards would be joining him in oblivion.

All five charged. Flash didn't take his eyes off any of them. And then something beautiful happened. Objects dropped out of nowhere, amongst them. Objects that his perfect memory, perfectly recalled. He smiled. The onrushing guards could make no sense at all of what they were seeing. As the air crackled around them, that was the least of their worries.

Taibul, Emma, Sam and Angela each found themselves another grenade, and in the kind of teamwork usually reserved for their respective sports, each pulled back their arms and, with a flick of their wrists, launched the ticking time bombs once more into the path of Flash's assailants.

The first grenade to go off scattered a huge electrical arc across the cobbles around the guards' feet. Two of the five tumbled to the floor. Flash didn't know where the help was coming from, but figured that his best course of action was to hold his ground. He couldn't have been more right. Almost immediately after the first, four more electrical grenades erupted amongst the group of guards, spitting sizzling bolts of crackling energy in all directions. All but one of the guards was hit, with the remaining lone dragon continuing on towards his target: Flash! Stumbling, the others fell, nearly all suffering in one way or another. As the aroma of scorched scales wafted delicately across the battleground that had once been the revered bazaar, the four dragon guards extricated themselves from the tangled muddle that the grenades had caused, and watched as their comrade reached his target. Once on their feet, they'd taken no more than a step in Flash's direction, when four more grenades landed in between them. Panic zipped across their faces.

The lone dragon couldn't quite understand where his friends were. Only an instant ago they'd been beside him. And then, it was just him. He didn't care though. This human, this... abomination... that stood before him was just inhaling its last breath. Marvelling from a distance at the luck this thing had somehow found to defeat the first guard and then dispatching the other two, with one of their own swords of all things, he was no doubt a practised warrior. But practised against humans, and had just gotten lucky. Now luck wasn't going to save him, he thought as he flew into range of the human. Now, it was time to die and he was looking forward to skewering this thing like a stuffed pig; perhaps after all was said and done, he'd feast on its entrails.

Casey was done with all this, he'd decided. For his entire tenure in the nursery ring, he'd been thwarted by the female dragon now before him, stuck in her human form. But only seconds ago she'd sliced through part of his wing. It hurt. It hurt beyond measure. But there was more to it than that. In his peripheral vision, he'd been taking stock of everything that had been going on. Up until this DNA challenged protagonist had arrived, everything had been going very nearly to plan. But since her arrival, other things had happened all around the cobbled square. Guards were being defeated, some, he'd seen out of the corner of his eye, even frozen. Tank's new friend, who felt... unusual, not quite a dragon, but not quite a human, had escaped and was terrorising a group of guards... what on earth was going on with that? And the dragon prisoners that had been rounded up from this godforsaken city, were being freed right at this very moment. With things having taken a turn for the worse, he'd just decided to cut his losses, run and take his chances with Manson, when that no good, smart arse, thinks she's better than anyone else... dragon, had sliced right through his wing, preventing him from taking to the air.

'Typical,' he thought. 'These things always happen to me. Never to Theobald or... Fisher!" A smidgen of sick tried to force its way up his oesophagus at the thought of what had happened to his friend. If he could go back, he'd never have agreed to take part. But it was too late. His friend was dead and he was up to his neck in it. That, and the... conspiracy. He just wanted to go, take off. Leave. But that opportunity had been cruelly snatched away from him. And the dragon responsible waved her dagger around in front of him, supposedly toying with him. She was about to find out what it meant to mess with a real dragon.

Exploding simultaneously, a crescendo of electricity scattered about the entire area, rendering the guards perfectly still. Taibul, Emma, Angela and Sam were unsure about what to do next, not knowing how long their targets would remain immobile. They didn't know if using any more of the electrical grenades would harm the dragons. It wasn't as if they could just waltz right up to the guards and either incarcerate or even kill them. All they seemed to have done was buy Flash a little more time. Time he was using, even now, to reacquaint himself with his primary skill set.

A semi-circular stream of fire erupted from between the lone guard's jaws, Flash the intended target. Smiling to himself as he bounded off to one side of his enemy's attack, Flash had but one thought. 'Amateur!' Rising up, he planted two feet firmly on the cobbles, ready to go again. Having seen the guard's telltale inhalation of breath for what it really was, he knew exactly what was heading his way, long before his opponent had even opened his mouth. Dancing out of the way was as easy as any game played by dragonlings in the nursery ring, but much as he was glad his training was serving him well, giving him an edge and making the fight easier than perhaps it would have been for some, he felt a sense of urgency niggle at him. He had to dispatch this one quickly, because who knew what might happen next in the ensuing mayhem? Also, he could just make out Tank, hanging limply like a broken, useless limb. The sooner things here were at an end, the sooner he could help his friend and they could all find some answers.

While he'd been exhaling flame at Flash, the guard had drawn his vicious looking bastard sword that hung from his side. It now sat firmly in his left hand as he leapt forward and tried to take Flash's head off with one giant swipe of it. Leaning back just below the blade's edge as it shot past, Flash regained his balance and pivoted on his right foot, throwing nearly all his weight into a controlled turn. As he did so, he brought his left foot up and, adding a little of his dragon power, performed a roundhouse kick that punched a foot sized hole in the guard's wing membrane, as well as crushing more than a few delicate bones, judging by the sound of the CRUNCH it made on impact. The guard, who'd been about to unleash another round of flame from his mouth, started to gurgle and choke. Flash seized the moment. Wrestling the guard's sword out of his hand, Flash brought the hilt up underneath the dragon's jaw with all his might to the sound of a rapturous THUMP, and as he toppled forward, slid the blade of the sword into the dragon's weak spot, much to the guard's surprise. He died looking... perplexed.

Immobile after the electrical discharges, the guards on the ground had gone from being statues to vibrating like the strings on a guitar. They weren't quite ready to continue their attack, but the friends figured it was only a matter of seconds now. In agreement, they all drew more grenades and prepared to throw them. As they drew back their arms, the need to do so disappeared.

Two of the prisoner dragons freed by Janice dropped out of the air, skidding to a halt on the shiny cobbles, right in the middle of the trembling guards, whose resistance to the grenades' output was just about complete. But it was too late for them, needing but seconds to break the spell the electricity had cast over their muscles and once again join the fight. It wasn't to be. The first freed prisoner, a silver and yellow flecked dragon, slim and sleek like some kind of record breaking car, opened his jaws wide, leant forward and in an instant, bit right through the first guard's throat. A thin spray of light green liquid arced into the air, splattering all the surrounding stone. Under normal circumstances, this kind of attack would have been met with complete and utter disgust, contempt and revulsion. But these were far from normal circumstances. Also, only a few truly saw what happened, and most were too busy fighting for their lives to dwell on something that may well have helped them survive the rest of the day.

A little less specific with her targets, the next freed prisoner landed amongst the quivering guards and began ripping at them with the talons on her feet, all the time blinding them with a purple and blue tinged streak of flame from between her jaws. Scales lay strewn across the ground, while the aroma of freshly burnt dragon floated lazily on what little breeze there was. Blood lust threatened to overcome both attackers, who considered that they were only really defending their homes, their friends, their way of life.

Watching both dragons rip into the two guards that only a short time ago had been their captors, Flash was unsure of what to make of the intensity of the violence.

On one level he understood: the need for revenge and to protect one's way of life was almost coded into every being's DNA. But the change from enlightened being to savage had taken mere moments. To be honest... he thought it would take longer, be harder. Oh not for him, after all, he had been trained for a very long time in nearly every form of violence that existed. But he was trained so that dragons like the two in front of him didn't have to be, so that they could live, quiet, happy, productive lives without the burden of worrying about plots, conspiracies and terrorism. It was a crying shame, he thought, sensing movement behind him. Turning, ready to strike, he was relieved to see Janice accompanied by a dragon protector. In her right hand she held the most wicked looking weapon he'd ever seen. He'd thought the one Richie had turned up with was awesome, almost something from the history books, but this, this looked so... futuristic! Sparkling with an almost light blue tint, the blade seemed to be constantly moving, with the cold turning the vapour in the air around it into... mist. Not a being in the world would not be fearful of it. It sent shivers down his spine, up his arms, and he knew that if he'd had his tail back, it would be positively shaking.

Wrapping her arms around him, delighted to see a friendly, human face, Janice gave him the biggest hug ever.

"I'm so glad you're okay," gushed the blonde haired braveheart. "Oh... thanks for the save by the way. If you hadn't turned up I'd be... I'd be..." It was only now the nervous energy and adrenaline had started to fade away that she could see exactly what had happened, and just how close a call it had all been. Sharp reality hit her like the powerful left hook of a title fight boxer. She could barely speak, everything felt so overwhelming. Flash put his arms around her to comfort her.

"It's nearly over. Everything's going to be alright. And by the way, it's me who should be thanking you... and the others. You saved us, not the other way round." In the hope that it would cheer her up, he offered up his best smile. As he did so, the tiniest voice inside him screamed a warning as loud as it could.

Feigning an attack with a burst of fire from his jaws, Casey wove one of his fingers like he'd been shown and added as much conviction to the mantra as he dared. An invisible ball of solid air hit his nemesis... Richie, full on, just as she was rolling out of the way of the fiery breath that never materialised. So powerful was the impact that it tossed her thirty feet back along the ground, battered and out of breath. This pleased him no end. To gain so much from so little. What he'd picked up in the last few months had given him more power than anything he'd learned over the course of the rest of his life. He was going to enjoy this, going to enjoy squeezing the dying breaths from her misshapen, flawed body. Stalking after her as she tried to shake off what had just happened, brilliant red blood flowed down her arms, running into the gaps between the cobbles as she tried to push herself off her elbows and back up to her feet. Having never seen her look so weak and pathetic, that feeling alone provoked a deeply satisfied grin, and a sense of wellbeing in the universe deep within him. He'd never felt this good, and he'd never won. Never beaten her. Today was different. Today he'd beaten her... in more ways than one.

Summoning nearly all the energy he had left, Tank barely managed to hold open his left eye; his right, for some reason, wouldn't respond. The sight that greeted him was astonishing. Dragons fought dragons, on the ground and in the air. A battle raged on below him and around him. Twisting his neck just slightly, he tried to see how Flash was holding up. Pain starburst across his shoulders, down his arms and ignited his back. Rallying against it, only just holding his own, he was surprised to see the space next to him where Flash had been, was empty. His heart sank. Questions flitted throughout his mind. Where was he? Was he dead? If there was a battle, were they being rescued? If so, who was doing the rescuing? All of these and more bombarded his cognitive functions all at once. With his damaged eye barely giving him any sort of view at all, he scanned his surroundings for clues that might give him some sort of answer, just before the darkness took him.

From the relative safety of the darkened alleyway, the four friends viewed the almost mythical scene. To be honest, they weren't sure what to do next. All around them, dragons collided and tumbled together in the air, fighting for grip and their very lives. On the ground, it was little different. The prisoners that Janice had released were more than holding their own against the remaining guards. It was superheated chaos, with elongated streams of rainbow coloured flame shooting every which way, interrupted by the very occasional fireball exploding around and about. For the time being, truth seemed much stranger than fiction.

Staggering to her feet, more than a little disorientated, Richie wished the ringing in her ears would stop so that she could catch her breath. Trying hard to inhale, the pain was monstrous, not only that, but she couldn't stand up straight. A couple of fractured ribs, at least, that's what she figured. Clutching Aviva's laminium dagger, she snarled, and in her half prone position, stepped forward to meet the now grinning Casey, determined to wipe that smug smile off his face, if it was the last thing she ever did.

One of the freed dragon prisoners was fighting tooth and claw with a former captor. Heads butted, talons raked, jaws angled trying to get a decent bite. It was evenly matched, that is until the free dragon's right foot slipped on some previous victim's bright green dragon blood. Taking immediate advantage, the guard brought his gigantic tail round, catching the freed dragon right beneath the jaw, in a bone shattering impact. Landing with a crunching THUD, the freed dragon flew over ten yards in the air. Nonchalantly, the guard strolled on over, towering menacingly above his helpless victim.

"Pathetic dragon," he spat, preparing to dispatch his adversary. "You and your like have had your day. We're taking over and you won't be around to see it. But rest assured, I'll make sure your friends follow you straight to hell."

And with that his chest puffed up as he pulled in a huge breath, ready to unleash a devastating final burst of flame from between his mighty jaws.

Just a few yards away, ducked behind a rustic coloured stone wall, Hook watched the entire event play out. He knowing what was about to happen, as he'd already seen the same kind of thing more than a few times in the preceding minutes. Aware that he had to stop it, and with little regard for himself, he turned the intricate dial on the heavy water rifle he held to full, flicked the switch on the backpack to increase the power and, in one swift move, belted around the corner, rifle held out in front of him in both hands as he skidded to a halt in front of the ever expanding guard.

As the guard prepared to let loose the natural flaming devastation from within him, he'd shut his eyes to savour the moment, knowing that nothing could stop him from destroying the pitiful being splayed out on the ground in front of him. And so he did what comes naturally to all dragons. With fire already moving up from his belly and into his throat, awaiting the opening of those huge jaws, at the same time he opened his eyes and his mouth. To say he was surprised to see a human figure standing right in front of him holding some sort of projectile weapon, was something of an understatement. What happened next was even more baffling.

Hook fired his rifle as soon as the dragon's mouth opened. He was, by now, more than proficient with the strange looking weapon and hit his intended target with ease. The first few flickers of flame licked around the side of the guard's open jaw, but the heavy water quickly negated the mighty heat that had built up inside the prehistoric beast. Hook hadn't developed a plan; his only thought had been to stop the guard killing the innocent dragon. Not sure what to do next, he just continued shooting the heavy water down the dragon's gaping throat. In turn, the heavy water slowed the dragon, practically to a standstill. Although his mind registered everything that was going on, he felt bewildered, slow, stagnant. His arms and wings felt unresponsive and he was unable to force his prodigious jaws closed. All the time, the thick, cloying liquid dribbled down his throat.

Unsteadily, the prone dragon that the halted attack had been intended for, got to his feet. Not an especially big beast, perhaps a foot or two taller than Hook when standing, he'd been injured badly but was still able to offer the rugged rugby player a wink as they stood side by side. Witnessing his enemy rise to his feet without being able to do anything about it, the guard was frantic. Well, at least on the inside anyway. On the outside, he resembled some sort of stone dragon water feature that had gone badly wrong, with the water being sucked back in, rather than propelled out as it should be. Hook's rifle had been pumping the heavy water into the dragon at quite a rate, and it was obvious that saturation point must be close. With the freed dragon standing next to him, keeping a close eye on proceedings, all the while checking his injuries, Hook began to see water sloshing about at the back of the dragon's throat. He'd filled him up... quite literally.

'What am I to do next?' he thought.

As the guard's belly bulged like an overinflated football and heavy water sloshed out of his mouth, trickling rapidly down his chin, the freed dragon standing next to Hook held out his arm and said,

"You can stop now. I'll finish this."

Releasing the pressure on the trigger of his rifle, the strapping rugby player kept his finger hovering above it, just in case he was needed again. Stepping forward towards the statue-like guard whose eyes and nose were bulging in much the same way as his belly, without any ceremony or fuss the freed dragon pulled back his head and did exactly what the guard had been about to do to him, only moments before. He let rip with the mother of all flames, the heat from which Hook could feel radiating off him from where he was, over ten feet away. Concentrated on the guard's belly, despite supposedly being immune to heat or fire, the intense stream of flame lit up the guard's scales, forcing them to glow brightly. Whether that was the result of the intense heat radiating out of the freed dragon's jaws, or the fact that the guard's belly was bursting with heavy water, wasn't apparent. What was apparent, however, was the fact that something had to give, any second now! Glowing the brightest red possible, the remaining scales that had been holding the bursting belly in place disintegrated simultaneously. SPLAT! The guard's stomach exploded with such vigour that soft tissue and organs shot off in all directions, some landing on the roofs of houses over fifty yards away. Hook dropped to his knees, at the same time turning to face the other way. It was a good job he had. An array of the dead dragon's scales sat buried in the metal on one side of the ancient backpack. Letting out a sigh of relief, the strapping rugby player turned to look at the freed dragon beside him. He shouldn't have been surprised. He really shouldn't have. But he was. The ecstatic looking dragon was just swallowing what looked like a large organ of some description, his jaws, cheeks and stomach covered in thick green blood. A long tongue darted out, licking the glistening scales down both sides of his mouth and the underside of his jaw clean. Turning to look at the rather stunned human, deadpan, he ventured,

"Hmmmm... Saturday night. Can't beat a takeaway."

And with that, he smiled, before turning and limping back off towards the action. Tears of laughter rolled down Hook's cheeks.

Casey pulled in a massive breath. Richie stood her ground, worried about being fooled again. This time it wasn't a feint. A scorching line of flame hurtled towards the ragged looking lacrosse captain. As was her prerogative, she met it full on. Holding the laminium dagger out in front of her, she siphoned off some of its power and used it to form a shield in the shape of a hemisphere. Sizzling orange, yellow and blue tinged flame bounced off the barrier, deflecting harmlessly away. Casey's smile disappeared instantly. Lunging forward, all thoughts of battle tactics out of the window, the evil ex-classmate of hers was determined to exact revenge for every wrong he considered he'd been on the end of. In a million years, she wouldn't have expected him to do that. Momentarily stunned, she was caught off guard. Swiping at him as he rushed her, a thin line of blood along the end of his jaw gave her the briefest feeling of satisfaction. Unfortunately, he'd breached her defences and hit her at speed, butting her up in the air. Tumbling head over heels, she landed hard on her back, the laminium dagger clinking to the ground many yards away. As he wiped the blood from his jaw with his hand, the smile returned to Casey's face. It was nearly over.

Turning into a cacophony, the tiny voice in Flash's head screamed that something somewhere was very, very wrong. Turning in a circle, it instantly became obvious what it was. The last time he'd looked, Richie had been more than holding her own, but he watched helplessly as the dragon torturer butted his friend into the air, praying silently for her to right herself as she dropped to the floor. She didn't, instead landing badly. She was in trouble. And he knew with every fibre of his being that he couldn't possibly get to her in time. What to do now?

Standing next to Flash, Janice turned with him, horrified at what she witnessed. Richie crashed onto the cobbles... HARD! She couldn't believe that anyone could get up from that, but knew if anyone could, it would be Richie. For a long time she'd found herself jealous of the young lacrosse player. Jealous of the relationship she had with her... boyfriend (currently that was too strong a word, but that's how she felt about him), her lover... PETER! But recently, she'd found herself admiring, believing in her. Tonight for instance, she hadn't particularly wanted to go out, and was worried out of her mind about Peter. It was so unlike him not to turn up and to be out of touch for so long, and on seeing the young lacrosse captain at the pub, Janice knew that she shared that worry. She also knew that Richie would leave no stone unturned in finding both Tank and Peter. She'd been right, and had followed her on the most unbelievable, the most incredible, the most downright dangerous quest, in just being there, trusting this awesome young woman with her life. Tears streamed down Janice's face as she watched, clutching Fu-ts'ang for all she was worth.

It came down to this. All his training, with every weapon imaginable, was for the most part irrelevant if you didn't choose the right weapon for the job in the first place. But sometimes, sometimes you just had to improvise with what was available. Mind racing through every possibility, one by one they were erased from the list of things that might work. All this happened in less than a hundredth of a second. That's how it worked in the Crimson Guards, and despite his rather sticky DNA position, Flash still considered himself affiliated with the elite troop.

As the last of the tears plummeted to the floor, Hook turned to see where he and his loaned backpack could next be of use. It was then that he spotted her, crashing desperately to the ground. Hairs on his arms stood to attention as his mouth ran dry, knowing he had to act. But he was over one hundred yards away, and she probably only had a few seconds at most. Instinctively, he twisted the dial on the rifle to the narrowest setting for the jet of water, flicked the switch to full power, while at the same time in his mind figuring out the trajectory he needed to hit the approaching dragon. It didn't seem possible, but he had to at least try. Standing tall, he aimed and fired, having calculated the trajectory spot on, with the water travelling as far as it could from where he was. However, it wasn't far enough. It must have dropped about thirty yards short of his intended target, the evil dragon with the whip who was now almost on top of Richie. Despair swallowed him up. There was simply no way he could run thirty yards with the backpack on, aim and fire in the time Richie had remaining. Frozen in place, the rifle dropped to his side as he watched the inevitable. Grief ripped his heart out. After all the violence he'd seen in the last hour, it couldn't end like this... COULD IT?

Flash knew exactly what Casey was going to do. It was

exactly what he would have done if their roles had been reversed. With Richie immobile on her back, the dragon was going to line up his whip with her neck, and then... BAM! He would separate her head from the rest of her body, and was just moving in position to do so right now. Feeling sick to his core, in all his time, all his missions, he'd never felt under so much pressure. But he'd been taught to thrive on pressure, to embrace it, and... TO USE IT! He did as he'd been taught.

It was unlikely to work. There was, at best, only an outside chance, but it was the only chance he had. Swivelling on one foot, he reached out to Janice who was standing next to him and snatched the space age looking weapon from her, much to her surprise. Before he'd done so, he'd had no idea about its past, about its name. But as soon as he came into contact with it, it called out to him, sang to him even. Startled briefly, his professionalism meant that he was still fully focused on what needed to be done. But this was indeed a turn up for the books. In only a fraction of a second, the dagger had passed on its name and much of its history, and its... PURPOSE! In Flash, Fu-ts'ang recognised a kindred spirit, another who was stuck in a form anything but natural. Pulling back his arm, the one which grasped Fu-ts'ang firmly... the pair of them formed a bond which was hard to describe, so much information had been exchanged between them. Fu-ts'ang knew Flash's darkest secrets, and vice versa. At first Flash felt... violated. But that thought, that feeling, had disappeared before he'd even had a chance to contemplate what it meant. Panic and despair turned to hope. To camaraderie. To teamwork. Knowing it meant a lot to his friends, having watched them play their respective sports on a few occasions, he was full of awe at the spectacle of it all. He planned to join them at the first available opportunity, should one ever present itself again, but he hadn't told them yet. He was determined to though, and soon. Aiming for all he was worth, he put all his commitment, strength and willpower behind the throw, brought his arm forward, and released Fu-ts'ang on the start of his journey.

Casey looked on in disgust at the pathetic form of his former classmate, prone on the ground, his face a mask of smug contentment at the thought of what he was about to do. Taking a few steps to one side, so that his right arm was directly in line with Richie's neck, he knew he'd take great satisfaction from watching her head bounce away along the cobbles any second now. Tightening his grip on the whip, a whistling sound moving ever closer grabbed his attention. Glancing back over his left shoulder to see the unidentified human, who'd been hanging up next to Tank, tossing a mist enshrouded weapon vaguely in his direction, he let out a small chuckle, before turning back to the task at hand. Even a pathetic human could see that the throw in question was way off target, he thought. With nothing to worry about, and no one in range to thwart his deadly plan, he set about the task before him, vowing that the human and his friends would be next on his 'to do' list.

'Damn,' thought Flash, as Fu-ts'ang left his grip. His aim was off. Not by much, but it was off. In the distance, he caught sight of the dragon, turning, taking a look, and then turning back towards his unfinished business. Good. Just as he should do. All he needed to do now, was... REMEMBER!

All the time, Fu-ts'ang whistled through the air, parting it with ease, set to pass off to one side of where Richie lay, unmoving.

Racking his eidetic memory, Flash contemplated the plan that had changed on the run, much the way the best plans nearly always do. He'd intended to throw the weapon to hit the dragon, with a view to buying himself some time to get there. But as he wrestled it from Janice's sweaty hands, he knew it wouldn't work. And if he'd needed confirmation, he got it from Fu-ts'ang. Grasping his plan instantly, the weapon had worked out the flaw in it almost as quickly. Despite the dagger's power and magic, it was more than likely Casey could either get out of its path, or block it with a mantra of some kind. At the time, overwhelming despair and panic had threatened to consume him at the thought of letting down his friend. But Fu-ts'ang had other ideas. With their bond formed, the weapon showed him a glimpse of his past training, performed a long time ago. In it, Flash recognised himself, albeit younger, using his mind to control deadly looking laminium boomerangs across some kind of obstacle course. At the time, it looked ominously like the future of weaponry, supposedly. But like many of these things, the inventions had fallen by the wayside, outmoded, outdated, inaccurate, dangerous and well... just useless. But in showing him this picture of his past, Flash was sure Fu-ts'ang was actually showing him how to control the flight of the futuristic weapon. All he had to do was remember. And just like the flicking of a switch... it was there. He could recall it all. It was all about the song... replicating the song. Flash had at first thought Fu-ts'ang was singing to him, and he wasn't far off. What he could actually hear was the weapon's natural sound, the sound of its very soul. We all have it: dragons, humans, animals... perhaps not inanimate objects. And absolutely not cutlery. But Fu-ts'ang was beyond special, and most certainly had a soul. And the sound of that soul was the key to controlling its movement.

Continuing on his journey, Fu-ts'ang was wary of his surroundings, and aware of how far he would miss his intended target, unless...

Flash had the answer, with the pitch of the song being the key. If he sang the song in his head, but changed the pitch, the lethal looking weapon would change direction.

How much would depend entirely on how drastically the pitch was changed. But what he struggled to recall was whether he had to increase or decrease the pitch. How would that famous football manager describe it? Ahhh that's it. "Squeaky bum time." Yes, it was definitely squeaky bum time. Closing his eyes, he envisaged Fu-ts'ang's flight through the air. Nearly out of time, with the weapon not far from level with Casey and the prone Richie, it was... NOW or NEVER!

Drawing back his arm, he marvelled at just how delicious the handle of the whip felt in his hand. Ohhh, how he was enjoying this. Memories of the cocky dragon standing between him and that fool Bentwhistle during their time at the nursery ring bubbled to the surface of his consciousness. A quiet peace flooded through him, as he pushed the memories aside. One word sprang to the forefront of his mind as he brought his arm forward. "PAYBACK!"

In the biggest gamble of his, and more importantly, Richie's life, Flash replicated the song, and increased the pitch as much as he could. The result was instantaneous. Having almost reached the point of no return in its path, where it would have been level with Casey and where any change in its direction would have been too late, Fu-ts'ang shivered slightly, before whipping around almost ninety degrees to its right, burying itself deep within Casey's left ribcage. As the chill from Fu-ts'ang passed instantly from muscle to muscle within him, the surprise on the dragon's face was palpable. As the blood around the wound congealed and then froze, the deadly whip clattered to the stony ground. He tried to move, tried to fight. But it was no good. Fu-ts'ang had him in his grip. Nothing could save him now.

Flash opened his eyes to see the hilt of his... his what? Friend? That sounded stupid, even to him, but that's how the bond between them felt. Imagine him... friends with a weapon. Strangely, when he said it like that, it seemed like a perfect match. With the hilt of his friend poking out of Casey's ribcage at an odd angle, the dragon torturer was entirely frozen, by the look of things. Wasting no time, Flash sprinted off, keen to be reunited with both of his friends, one lying on the ground, the other embedded in a dragon.

Wiping away two steady streams of tears, Janice could barely believe what she'd just seen. Sure that her weapon was going to miss, she was gobsmacked when, at the very last moment, it almost turned a corner to find its mark in the evil dragon. Heart pounding, she took off after Flash, eager to make sure Richie was okay.

Hook punched the air with his fist.

"Yes!" he screamed to no one in particular. Flash's throw was the single most amazing thing he'd ever seen, and that included all the events of the last few hours. He just had to know how it was done. He also had to know how Richie was, and so with that, he trotted off after Flash and Janice, the heavy water pack bumping his back ever so slightly as he moved.

Emma, Taibul, Angela and Sam stood, mouths hanging open, in the shadowed entrance to the alleyway which they'd been taking cover in. They could all barely believe what had happened. It had looked like Richie was a goner. Flash's throw had seemed impossible. All breaking into smiles simultaneously, they rushed to join the others, keen to know the extent of the lacrosse player's injuries.

All around the bazaar, the battle was coming to an end. Prisoners who'd been freed, residents of the underground ancient city, were putting an end to the remaining guards who'd turned their world so unexpectedly upside down. No mercy was shown, with the residents doubling, sometimes even trebling up on the, by now, terrified guards. Some begged for mercy, some put up a fight. Either way, it made no difference. They all died, some quicker than others, but all in the most brutal fashion.

47 OH, FOR SOME RUBBER GLOVES

Groggy but not too badly harmed, Richie pushed herself up on to her feet. Wobbling a little unsteadily as she did so, she tried to grasp exactly what had happened. Flash was the first to skid to a halt in front of her, a look of concern etched across his face.

"You okay?" he asked.

"Uhhh... yeah, I, uhhh, think so," she replied.

"That was about as close as it ever gets. Don't do that to me again... EVER!" Flash declared.

Throwing him her best grin, the one reserved for winning people over and giving her an edge, Richie stated,

"Can't promise that I'm afraid. How about promising not to make a habit of it?"

"Deal," he replied, leaning forward and embracing the lacrosse captain softly.

Janice arrived next, having stopped to pick up the laminium dagger that Richie had dropped as she'd fallen. Approaching Richie, Flash and the unmoving dragon, the young blonde rolled the dagger over in her hands. It certainly looked pretty, all the jewels shining brightly in the light, and it felt... solid, well made. But she figured there was more to it than that, and was sure that Richie should have it back at the earliest opportunity. Offering it out in front of her, to her bedraggled 'friend', she didn't know what kind of response to expect, but was almost knocked out when the young lacrosse player leaned in, kissed her on both cheeks and thanked her profusely. The biggest grin in the entire dragon domain spread rapidly across her beautiful face.

And with that, the others arrived: Hook, followed by Taibul, Emma, Angela and Sam, as well as some of the other dragons who'd been freed by Janice's heroics. Hook gave Richie a congratulatory pat on the back, which caused her to turn and give him the 'look'. Laughing, he told her that he'd seen her in a worse state on a lacrosse pitch. Smiling, she agreed. And then abruptly the tone turned more serious. One of the freed dragons plodded forward. The others stepped out of the way to let him through.

"Are you the one responsible for all this?" he boomed in a very deep voice.

"Well..." started Richie. It was only then that she remembered the old shopkeeper. Turning in the direction of where she'd last seen him, there amongst the wreckage of the market, his body was just visible on the ground. Others around her followed her gaze, most of them letting out little gasps. About to take off in that direction, Flash put his hand out in front of her.

"I'll go," he announced, and taking Janice and the others with him, sprinted off in the direction of the master mantra maker.

Turning around to face the dragon that had spoken to her, she pushed all thoughts of the mighty Gee Tee out of her mind.

"So, are you the one?" enquired the dragon once again.

Other freed dragons had congregated around them both, all wanting an answer to the question. Feeling as though she were under a giant microscope, that's how much scrutiny she was under, in true Richie style, she puffed out her chest and very brashly stated,

"I am."

Along with all the others, the big dragon in front of her gave her answer careful consideration as the moments ticked by.

As Flash knelt down by the old dragon's head, the skin on his own back, or distinct lack of it to be precise, sent waves of agony rippling throughout his beaten body. Gently, and with more than a little trepidation, he opened first the master mantra maker's left eye, and then his right.

'They look fine,' he thought on examination. But Gee

Tee continued to remain unconscious. Throughout, the human friends circled the huge dragon form, eager to help in any way they could. By no means a novice in this area, Flash's Crimson Guard training had included developing a full medical skill set, both for humans and dragons alike. But try as he might, he just couldn't find anything wrong. The old dragon was breathing, he could hear it, and the natural dragon smell of methane on his breath was almost overpowering, and that was to a dragon, albeit one stuck in human guise. His heart was beating, his circulation was fine and nothing was obstructing or blocking his airways. All things being equal, he should be standing up in front of them. Flash didn't know what to do. And then it hit him, much later than it really should have. TANK!

'Oh God,' he thought, turning around to see his friend still hanging up, over two hundred yards away. 'Why on earth haven't I got him down already?' Ordering the others to stay with Gee Tee, Flash, assisted by dragon power, sprinted off in Tank's direction.

Sweat dribbled down her back as she stared intently at the big dragon in front of her, mind filled with questions. What if they didn't know who she was? What if they were more concerned with how many dragon laws she'd broken, than with the fact that she'd rescued them? What if their battle rage still clouded their minds? Could she talk her way out of this? So many questions, and nothing in the way of an answer forthcoming from the dragons around her.

Reaching the metal monstrosity, Flash bounded straight up the side of it in two mantra enhanced leaps. Once at the top, he realised he should have brought Richie's dagger with him to cut the rope from which Tank swung. Silently, he cursed to himself... 'schoolboy error'. With no other option, he did something that he'd only ever done a handful of times in this particular form. Searching deep down in the core of his body, he found the tiny little spark that he was looking for. Just for a moment, he'd been afraid that he wouldn't find it, that it didn't exist, that it was somehow missing from this shell that he found himself inhabiting. But he recognised it and on doing so, pulled it upwards through his stomach and up into his throat. Feeling the familiar acidic tang precede what he needed, he leaned forward so that his head was almost touching the rope that held the binders to the structure, and then opened his mouth as wide as it would go. A small flame, blue and orange in colour, burst forth from between his lips, pretty much like you'd get from a Bunsen burner. Immediately, Tank started to fall. Flash leapt, somersaulting backwards, tucking his legs into his body, all the time ignoring the devastating pain that assaulted him. Before he hit the floor, he dived forward, catching in his outstretched arms the bulk of Tank's broken frame. Surprised at how much the strapping rugby player weighed, he supposed he shouldn't have been. Having caught him, he gently laid him on the cobbles, and started running through all the checks he'd done only a short time before with Gee Tee. After a while, it became clear things weren't looking good.

The rather fierce expression on the dragon that had asked Richie the question suddenly melted away as he offered out his hand to the talented lacrosse star.

"We all owe you our thanks, little one. And yes, we know exactly who you are. Thank you."

Richie let out her breath, not really aware that she'd been holding it in. It felt as though a great weight had been lifted off her shoulders, despite her battered and bruised body.

"You're all very welcome," she mumbled, not really

knowing what to say.

"Just one thing though," whispered the dragon. "Are you out of your tiny little mind? Bringing humans here?" Shaking his giant skull, the huge dragon roared with laughter. "Inspired, truly inspired."

Joining the dragon laughing, it was only then she wondered what she must have been thinking? Humans... saving dragons. Mad, absolutely mad. Quickly, the moment passed and, for her, it was back to the business at hand.

"What now?" she enquired, eyeing the motionless Casey suspiciously. She hadn't forgotten he was there, quite the opposite in fact. She was looking forward to someone extracting some information from him.

Kneeling down beside Tank, Flash looked over his shoulder to see if he could summon a little help. Richie, he could see, was deep in discussion with the group of local dragons, while the humans (he smirked at that, still not able to believe that they were here and more importantly, had saved everybody) remained gathered around the old shopkeeper, doing their best to rouse him. Help looked as though it wouldn't be forthcoming anytime soon. Deciding to fall back on his training, he'd already tried everything obvious, perhaps it was time for the unconventional.

Something that had always stuck with him was an afternoon spent alone with one of his dragon trainers, many decades ago. The trainer in question was thought to have been a little... long in the tooth both in age, and quite literally. His name was Smoking Bandit, and derived from his time raiding human settlements across Nepal, throughout the early seventeen hundreds. Once caught by the council, who at the time had no idea what to do with him, the death penalty had been one distinct possibility, but on closer cross examination they discovered that Smoking Bandit had an almost unrivalled knowledge of human weaponry and guerrilla fighting tactics. Arguing for many days, the council's vote eventually led to them giving him a training position, after using a mantra to bind him to the dragon domain, thus preventing him from ever seeing the surface of the planet again. And so it was that Flash found himself under the tutelage of the elderly dragon, who, on getting to know him just a little, was much more than he appeared. As well as being a human weaponry and battle tactics expert, Smoking Bandit had on occasion, mixed with the other dragon colonies on the surface. At that time, there weren't many, well, not in their natural form anyway. But tucked away, particularly in the more remote parts of Nepal, small enclaves of their race thrived in secretive communities. One of those communities had welcomed Smoking with open wings, letting him stay for a while, trying to encourage him to join on a more permanent basis. It wasn't really his thing though, but he had for a while enjoyed the company of members of his own race. And in doing so, he'd gained much in the way of knowledge, in particular, obscure mantras, a wealth of medicinal knowledge, and some rather bizarre and unlikely seeming cures for all sorts of dragon ailments. That afternoon, Smoking Bandit decided that Flash was worthy, well, those were his words, of being the custodian of all the information that he'd been entrusted with. Amongst everything that he'd gleaned that day, there was one mantra in particular called 'fanning the flames', that he always thought about. It was always kicking around inside his head at the end of every battle, especially if there were casualties of any sort. He'd never had to use it before, but since nothing else had seemed to work, he figured he had nothing to lose.

In front of them, the old dragon with the glasses who'd given them the weapons lay still on the cobbles. Flash had already determined that his breathing was okay, but every few minutes, one of the humans leaned in just to check this was still the case. They were taking it in turns, and it had come to be Janice's. Kneeling down next to his giant head, she rested one hand on the scales that ran down from his cheek, and moved her head slowly forward, turning it to one side as she did so. She could hear the air escaping his jaws, and there was no mistaking the fetid odour of methane. Rising back to her feet, she nodded to the others.

"He's still breathing," she uttered. They all nodded back, still not knowing what to do, desperate to help the old dragon; after all, without him, none of this would have been possible. Staring solemnly in silence, apart from Janice, who was keeping a close eye on Flash and Tank on the far side of the huge square, she wondered what was going on. Judging from the look of concern carved into Flash's bruised and beaten mug, he faced a dilemma of his own. In her head, she whispered a silent prayer for both Tank and the dragon sprawled out in front of her.

In response to the lacrosse playing dragon's question, the freed dragons, all local residents, had gathered into a huddle. Richie stood, looking on, wondering exactly what they were discussing. One of them she knew had to take charge... and soon! The situation called for it. They needed to collate everything they knew from everyone still alive, try to work out exactly what was going on, and formulate a plan. They needed a leader, someone to follow, someone to inspire... someone who could help them... WIN! Knowing they had little time to waste, she hoped their discussion would end soon. As always, she found waiting the hardest thing to bear. More importantly though, she was fully aware of everything around her. Although she hadn't looked in either direction, she knew that Gee Tee was lying prone off to her right, just as Flash was tending to Tank further off to her left. Desperate to see how her friends were doing, her instinct screamed inside her to wait here for the dragons' decision. Closing her eyes, taking a deep breath, she softly wished to be granted more patience, as every second that passed while she just stood there, seemed to ring out in her head.

'Come on, come on, how hard can it be?' she thought. 'It can't possibly take this long. You're all dragons, after all.'

Knowing what he had to do, oddly, the injuries inflicted by the sadistic Casey with his crackling energy whip made things easier. Tank lay on his back, his chest exposed for all to see, huge amounts of skin missing due to the welts of the whip. Just looking at the state of his friend made him want to throw up, although he himself had pretty much the same injuries, just not quite as deep, because Casey had taken more pleasure and put more energy into every stroke of the whip when he'd hit Tank. In some ways Flash thought himself lucky. But now he needed to ignore his own pain and concentrate on his friend. Bringing his left arm over and above Tank's damaged chest, Flash found a part that was bleeding profusely and pressed it firmly to a bloody section of his friend's torso. At precisely the moment of contact, Flash's head swam with more pain than he could cope with. It took him several seconds to regroup and push the pain to one side. He felt for Tank, fearing for him at the same time. The extent of the agony was truly staggering, very much off the scale. He'd been trained to deal with it, and almost couldn't cope, but his friend... Over the course of his colourful life, he'd heard of beings driven mad in such situations, and could now understand why. Aware of just how strong his friend was, he knew this would be the test of his life. Flash hoped with all his heart that Tank passed with flying colours.

The dragons' impromptu discussion broke up, all of them striding purposefully back in Richie's direction.

'About time,' was all she could think, desperate to offer Flash all the help she could, and see how Gee Tee was doing. Walking right up to her, the dragon who'd asked the question would be intimidating for most, not even close for Richie. As they gathered round, Richie's impatience got the better of her.

"Well?" she declared.

"We need someone to take charge, galvanise us, bring us together. Someone we can all get behind."

"And?"

With a totally passive face that Richie just couldn't read, the huge dragon studied her closely. Normally she'd have staked her life on her ability to tell what another dragon or human was thinking. But for once, she was well and truly stumped. And that was only the first shock.

"Looks like the job's yours."

"WHAT?" remarked Richie, sure she'd misheard.

"YOU! You're our leader."

There it was again. It occurred to her then that perhaps she was dreaming. There really weren't many other explanations left. And of course it would explain everything else away. That's it, she was dreaming.

"You don't seem to believe me little one, but I assure you... that's the decision we've made. We were all agreed... you're the best dragon for the job."

Running both hands through her brown, curly hair, she thought about the implications of what the dragon had just said. Moments later, she reluctantly came to the same conclusion. Perhaps, after all, she was the best choice. But to make the best choices from here on in, she needed information. And she needed it now.

Flash   traversed   the   rivers   of   blood,   swimming submerged well beneath the surface, on the lookout for something specific, but so far he'd seen no sign of it. With as much speed as he could muster, he pushed on.

'It must be here somewhere,' he thought, turning a sharp bend and then plunging headfirst into a steep downward slope. Thick, gooey red liquid closed in all around him.

It seemed she had little or no choice. Standing here arguing with a group of dragons could easily waste hours, if not days. So, although reluctant, she made the decision to accept what had been thrust upon her. With the decision made in her mind, she turned to address the group of dragons, and began doing what needed to be done.

"I need to know how all this started," she asked first of all. "But before one of you fills me in, are there any healers amongst you?"

Three dragons towards the back of the group raised their wings high above their heads.

"Can the three of you help with the healing please? The two over there that were being tortured look in desperate need of your help. Please, they're my friends, help them if you can. If two of you could do that, then perhaps the other could take a look at the old dragon over there, the one surrounded by the group of humans. And just so you know, that dragon is Gee Tee, the master mantra maker, and he's the one responsible for this rather unconventional rescue."

All three nodded, and after a brief discussion, two headed at top speed towards Flash and Tank, while the other shot off towards the old shopkeeper.

Taking a deep breath to calm herself down, Richie's heart was still beating furiously, so much so that she could almost feel the adrenaline pumping away inside her.

"So," she said, addressing the remaining group, "who

can tell me how this all started?"

Just as he was starting to question whether or not he should give up, Flash caught a fleeting glimpse of what he was looking for. Up ahead, just for a second, he'd seen the tiniest blue spark, dancing around erratically, exactly what he'd been taught to find. Although only his mind wove throughout Tank's battered and bruised body, it felt as though the rest of him was there as well. And as such, he had to throw all his body weight to his right to continue following the tiny blue glimmer. Thick red blood sloshed all around him as he sought another glimpse of the spark.

'There,' he thought, aware of everything around him. Again he used his weight to change direction, this time to the left, and instantly found himself falling. Strangely, the sensation reminded him of flying. Sadness enveloped him, at the thought of something he loved so much that he almost certainly would never experience again. Distracted, he almost lost focus. Almost, but not quite. Hanging on for all he was worth, he was determined to redouble his efforts and save his friend. But he was tired, and getting more so with every passing second. Moments later he realised he had nowhere near the reserve of strength it was going to take to catch the spark, the spark that held Tank's consciousness, the spark of life that made him who he was. Darkness started to shroud his vision.

"I'm so sorry," echoed out from the chapped lips of his tortured body, as tears ran across the deep cuts on his face.

Quietly and calmly, against the backdrop of the frozen Casey, dragons recalled the events leading up to the battle in the bazaar. They told how it had started with deception, one at a time. For two of them, dragons they didn't recognise had knocked at the door, claiming to be disorientated and confused. Of course they'd let the dragons in, why wouldn't you? But by then it was too late. Overpowered and overwhelmed, they found themselves bound and restrained. That's how it had started. After that, the dragons had moved on to the next house, and then the next. After the dragons had left, human shapes had come to march them to the bazaar. They looked human, but felt so utterly alien, dark, cold hearted and almost like they were trying to slither into your head. Amazingly, nearly all the dragons Richie quizzed used the word "slither". It seemed to her to be more than just a coincidence. As they continued, Richie began to get an idea of the much bigger picture of what had happened. They were all rounded up and taken to the square. Some were beaten ruthlessly, others killed without thought. Retaliation was not an option. As that was going on, some of the human shaped beings built the construction that Tank and Flash had been suspended from, with the occasional aid from a dragon guard or two to weld the metal together with the charged heat from their fiery breath. What astonished Richie the most as she listened, was the sheer scale of what had happened. Enemy dragon guards alone must have measured in their hundreds, with the human shaped enemies numbering even more. It was a bold move, and really quite staggering. It was also... unthinkable!

Continuing to methodically describe what happened next, the dragons mentioned a sort of human, not like any of the others, marching into the square, surrounded by a ring of guards and other unusual beings. The human shaped being, for they couldn't get a sense of what he really was, limped badly and was aided by a rather stunning looking walking stick. Immediately, she knew who it was, but waited for the dragons' descriptions to have her worst fears confirmed: stocky, receding brown hair, with soul destroying eyes.

'MANSON!' was the only thought that buzzed through her head. It wasn't just tears she fought back as the story continued, but the fear that threatened to inundate her very being. It was hard to believe he was even still alive, but of course it would explain so much. And with his previous form, the threat was ever more real. She knew just what he was capable of, with destruction, murder, and even mass murder a very real possibility. On top of all this, each one described a dragon, albeit in human form, being carried in a sedan chair by two other humans, who looked old, tired and barely awake for most of the time. But from the way he was looked after and addressed occasionally, they had to assume he was important. Things had just gone to a new level, and it wasn't only their lives on the line.

About to pull his bleeding hand away from Tank's battered body and sever the connection to his friend once and for all, suddenly he was engulfed in... energy. From being slow, sluggish, weary and on his last legs, he went to being renewed, invigorated... as full of power as it was possible to be, instantaneously. Thanking everything he knew that he hadn't cut the connection, with his new found energy and resolve he was confident he could achieve what he'd set out to do. At the back of his mind, swimming just beneath the well of energy he was drawing on, he could feel two dragons sharing their power with him, offering him hope and help, encouraging him with everything they had. It was a selfless gesture, with Flash realising it must have been two from the group of local residents that had surrounded Richie. Briefly, he sent them a message of thanks, on top of which he told them what he was going to do. They didn't fully understand, but waves of support emanated off both of them. Without further ado, he closed his mind to everything else and once again found the little blue spark that was his friend.

The group of friends made way for the hulking great

dragon that not a moment before had been amongst those surrounding Richie. Skidding to a halt, he then plodded forward, his giant feet making a slapping sound against the dark cobbles of the bazaar.

"So, little ones," he remarked, in a much softer voice than anyone would have thought possible. "What do we have here?"

Janice stepped forward to speak.

"Uhhh... his name is... Mr Gee Tee."

Throwing back his head, the dragon healer chortled uncontrollably. Moments later, he calmed down and looked at the startled, but beautiful blonde human.

"I don't think his name is Mr anything," he said, deeply amused. "But I know who he is, unlike all of you. Perhaps you could tell me what you've been doing for him?"

Hook stepped out.

"We've just been making sure he's been breathing really. That's all."

"Well, if that's all you've done... you've done a terrific job," answered the dragon.

A visible sense of relief rolled off the group. Just for a moment they thought they might be in trouble.

"Truth be told," declared the healer, "there isn't much else you could do. But what you've done is more than enough. I just hope that we're able to revive him. I hear he was responsible for this most dramatic of rescues."

Simultaneously, the friends all nodded.

"Because I think it's only fitting that he should witness the results of his outstanding and rather unconventional plan. Don't you?"

As the tiny, blue spark flittered about in the upper part of Tank's lungs, Flash's consciousness had it cornered.

'And now,' thought Flash, 'it's time.' Feinting one way, he knew full well the spark would leap the other. Sure enough, it did, but Flash was ready and dived headlong straight into the middle of it. A resounding ringing tone thumped Flash's ears, as more darkness encroached. It was also noticeably cold on the inside. Pushing all that to one side, having carried out his mission and reached his destination, it was now time to act. With all the willpower he possessed, and drawing on the well of energy provided by the healers, he opened the floodgates and started pouring it all into the spark, all the while sending hot, fiery thoughts through his subconscious. Fireballs, meteors, bubbling lava, a candle's flame, a roaring fire, a barbecue, a dragon's breath and finally a jumbo sized bonfire, were just some of the images he managed to bombard the spark with. It was working, he could feel it, feel it getting bigger, brighter, stronger... warmer.

She'd thought the recounting of what had happened at first was bad enough, but what she was hearing now made her feel physically sick. One by one, the group took it in turns to describe how, as the captured dragons watched, surrounded by guards, four dragons were frogmarched into the bazaar, all beaten sickeningly, all wearing restraints. The first two described were obviously Tank and Flash and she heard how they were immediately hung from the now completed structure. The currently immobile Casey was described as begging the leader, who she was pretty sure was Manson, to let him use his whip on the two prisoners. After some deliberation, the leader with the walking stick gave in and agreed. Depicted in some detail was the look of pure pleasure on Casey's face when this had happened. Richie could feel her blood start to freeze. A calculated evil nibbled away at her. She had the power; it had been granted to her. And he was only a few yards away. She could make him pay, make him beg for death, make him... suffer. No one here would object, that's for sure. In fact, most would fully understand. All she had to do was say the word. It was all she could think about, that is until the dragons started to explain what the other two prisoners looked like. Heart racing, her throat ran dry and a dreadful feeling took hold in the pit of her stomach. From the descriptions the dragons gave, she knew that the prisoners could have been none other than Peter and Tim, and there was no doubting the malice and intent with which they'd both been greeted by Manson. Her mind pondered this. She could understand Manson's interest in Peter given their history, but what did he want with Tim? In theory, he shouldn't even know who Tim was. It was after all, a closely guarded secret. But what if Manson knew? What if he knew that Tim was the dragon from the prophecy? What if he knew that the fate of the entire dragon domain was inexplicably linked to him? That feeling in the pit of her gut suddenly trebled in intensity.

'Things,' she thought, 'are looking worse than ever.'

And it might be that she was in charge of the only force capable of mounting a defence anywhere on the entire planet.

A tingling in his fingers signalled to Flash that he'd returned from his corporeal visit and was back firmly in his rightful place. Instinctively he pulled his hand away from his friend's devastated body. At least it should have been devastated and bloody, but it wasn't. Tank's body was covered in scars, bruises and bumps from the beating he'd taken at the claws of the brutal Casey, but the blood, the open wounds and the oozing welts had all disappeared. Flash was more than a little perturbed, as the little he'd been told about the task he'd just carried out seemed for all intents and purposes to save only the dragon's spirit, its soul, in a time of desperate need. He'd heard nothing to indicate that the dragon in question would be healed or even brought back to full health. Was it something he'd done? Perhaps a side effect produced by the other dragons sending him their power? Whatever it was, it was a welcome sight. As he knelt on the smooth dark cobbles, he just wished his friend would open his eyes.

Waiting patiently, the group of dragons expected some sort of response. Her mind hurriedly tried to process everything she'd been told. It appeared from what the captives had overheard, that Peter and Tim had been taken along with Manson. While they couldn't be entirely sure, a couple of the dragons had thought they'd heard the word 'London' mentioned. Ever more concerned, she tried to put the pieces together.

'What fate awaits Peter and Tim, goodness only knows,' she thought. 'But if Manson and his... army (yes, there are definitely enough of them to be classed as an army, and those are just the ones we know about) are on their way to London, it can only mean one thing: they plan to take over the entire dragon world, capture the council and the king, plunging the whole planet into chaos, and... BOOM! The earth's as good as theirs.' For the first time in her entire life... she felt genuinely scared. And not just a little. With fear pushing her on, her mind ran through every different scenario, every different plan, all the resources available to her.

'If it's a battle Manson wants,' she thought, 'a battle he will have.'

A racking cough spluttered from Tank's bruised mouth. Spittle shot up like a little fountain, before his eyes opened wide. The first thing he did was try to sit up. Before Flash could get there, a scale covered arm shot out, gently stopping Tank from sitting completely upright.

"Easy my friend," said a soft comforting voice. "Try and get your bearings first. Know that you are in safe hands, and there's no immediate threat." Carefully, Flash grabbed his friend's hand and pumped it gently. Tank looked over at Flash and nodded gratefully, seemingly aware of what had gone on. Flash smiled in return, glad his friend had survived. In all his life, he couldn't remember a time when he'd been more relieved. Releasing Tank's hand, he made to stand up.

"Not so fast, master of some very unusual knowledge," uttered one of the two healers.

Flash turned to face him, a puzzled look strung out across his bruised features.

"You're in no condition to go anywhere," announced the other dragon.

Opening his mouth, about to protest, the other healer shushed him before he had a chance.

"Just give us a couple of minutes, and then you can go. There's nothing you're needed for that can't wait that long."

Recognising a losing battle when he saw one, Flash nodded his agreement. Before his head had even finished moving, he felt a rush of warm energy wash across him. It was the best feeling he'd felt in days, no weeks, perhaps even longer. Sitting down, he watched his arms, legs and chest as the bright red blood retreated back inside his falsehood of a body, the gaping holes and rips slowly knitting themselves back together. Marvelling at just how good the healers were, he knew that even in the Crimson Guards they'd never had healers this accomplished. The speed with which they were repairing his and Tank's body beggared belief, even for him. So remaining sitting next to Tank, his mind wondered what was going on elsewhere, not only here, but across the entire domain. Thoughts turned to the king and the debt he felt he owed his monarch, hoping with all his heart he'd get the chance to repay it.

As they sat, Flash explained everything he knew about what had happened, well from his point of view anyway. At the first mention of Gee Tee, Tank was eager to get up and go over to the old shopkeeper. But the two healers waved him to sit back down, saying all would be done in just a few moments more. Reluctantly he complied. Gazing off into the distance, he could just make out Richie surrounded by some of the local dragons who he vaguely recognised. Not able to guess what was going on, it did however feel good to have his friend back where she belonged, even if her DNA suggested she shouldn't be here. A short smile drew across his face at the thought of that. At least Richie was a dragon, unlike their other visitors. The king and the council would have a fit when they found out. He'd only ever heard of the odd human ever stumbling across the domain, by complete and utter accident. When it did happen, as expected, there was uproar. It was all over the papers, a hot topic for the dragon councillors, and there were always calls for tighter safety regulations. Inevitably things always died down after a few days, until it happened again. But he'd never heard anything about a group of humans making their way in. And despite the fact that they'd initiated a rescue that had ultimately succeeded, and had saved a considerable number of dragon lives, he had no doubt at all that somewhere along the line, there would be hell to pay.

Both healers slumped to the ground, exhausted, their work done. Flash and Tank both rose to their feet, thanking the spent dragons profusely, before heading off in the direction of Richie and the group of local dragons. Nodding to each other, the two healers recognised the quality of the work they'd done. It had been decades since either had practised any healing at all, and both were slightly taken aback at producing what was probably their best ever work.

Richie was just about to tell the group of dragons what she'd decided, when over strode Tank and Flash, looking remarkably well considering what they'd both been through. Even though she couldn't help think inappropriate, she rushed over to greet them, practically throwing herself into Tank's huge arms. Immediately he returned the embrace. Flash found himself grinning from ear to ear. Up until his... 'accident', from which he still hadn't recovered and didn't know if he ever would, he'd been a loner. It had for all intents and purposes been all that he'd ever known. Having friends, dragons, people he could rely on, trust and share things with, was still relatively new to him. But as he watched Richie and Tank hold each other close, he felt sure that he couldn't be in better company than the small tightly knit group that he'd inexplicably found himself part of. Tank pulled away from his friend.

"Thanks for the save," he whispered. "It's good to have you back."

Richie held up her hand and showed him the ring.

"All thanks to Peter. Did you know?"

Tank shook his head.

"I didn't, no. But if I'm not mistaken, that ring used to belong to Gee Tee. It looks like the two of them have been conspiring again."

Richie smiled.

"Well all I can say is thank goodness they did."

"Anyhow," announced Tank, "I'd better go and revive the old dragon. If it's what I think it is, it shouldn't be too difficult."

Leaning forward, Richie kissed her friend on the cheek.

"I'll see you in a minute then."

Tank nodded and sped off towards the master mantra maker. Flash, meanwhile, thought it best to stay where he was, intrigued to see what was going on and if he could pick up any details about exactly how they'd been rescued.

The small group surrounding Gee Tee all took a step back as Tank arrived, well, all except Janice who much to his surprise, threw her arms around the strapping rugby player and gave him the same sort of hug Richie had only moments earlier. Smiling warmly at her, he noted the fear and panic etched across her face, the same look the other humans all had in varying degrees. As Janice released him, the others stepped forward to shake his hand. He recognised all of them, including Taibul, who he'd only ever spoken to in his restaurant role. Hook in particular was delighted to see his teammate, and gave him a big slap on the shoulder that, to Tank's surprise, resounded throughout the rest of his body. Pleased to see them all, he wanted to catch up with each and every one of them, but there was something important he had to do first. Turning to the dragon healer, he held out his hand in greeting. Grasping it firmly, the dragon healer declared,

"Well done, young one. To survive all that you have, you must have the strength of ten dragons."

"Thank you," replied Tank politely, "but I think it was more about luck, and the extraordinary efforts from my friend and the other healers."

"If you say so... young one."

"Can you tell me what's wrong with him?" asked Tank, motioning towards his aged boss.

"As far as I can determine... NOTHING! Everything appears fine, apart from the fact that we can't wake him. His breathing is regular, albeit a little shallow. I've tried to contact him telepathically, but there seems to be nothing there for me to contact. It's most odd."

Tank smiled to himself, having seen this on more than one occasion. In fact, both of them had put very specific protocols in place for exactly this. Kneeling down, Tank put the old shopkeeper's hand in his, closed his eyes and imagined a very specific image in his head. Holding that image for a count of ten, all the time projecting it in the direction of his employer, the time came for him to speak the name of the image. Using as much telepathic power as he dared, he yelled,

"JAM INFUSED MARSHMALLOWS!"

Instantly the old dragon shot bolt upright. Once there, his eyes opened wide behind his somewhat skewed glasses.

"I had the most horrendous dream," were the first words to leave his lips. Tank waited for what he knew would come next. Painstakingly slowly, Gee Tee gathered his wits about him and took in everything around him, including the group of stunned looking humans. Looking at his former apprentice, he just about managed to stammer,

"It wasn't a dream was it?"

Tank shook his head and laughed.

"Apparently not," he replied. "How are you feeling?"

"Like I could sleep for a hundred years. Oh and by the way, where are my jam infused marshmallows?"

Both the dragon healer and the stunned humans all had the same thought at exactly the same time:

'Why on earth does he want jam infused marshmallows?'

Tank continued to grin.

"I thought it was my best bet to bring you around. Looks like I was right. I think you might have to wait a while for them though."

"Well," said the old shopkeeper, almost back to his normal self, "I will expect some when we get back to the shop."

"And I'll make sure you get them."

Wrapping one of his giant wings around Tank as they both chuckled, the moment was over before it started, with the master mantra maker turning a touch more serious.

"Did we win?"

Tank nodded.

"Thanks to you, by all accounts."

"Flattery will get you nowhere, as you should be well aware. And I'm not going to forget about the marshmallows."

Any worries Tank had about Gee Tee's recovery had completely disappeared. From the look of things, the old shopkeeper was well and truly back to his antagonistic and stubborn self.

In about thirty seconds flat, Richie had bought Flash up to speed on events, despite the fact that the group of local dragons were getting impatient. She thought it important to include the ex-Crimson Guard, because of his experience in unusual matters. He was one of her main assets and she'd already decided in what role he'd be deployed. She only hoped he'd agree when the time came.

Much to the delight of the humans, the old shopkeeper had, one by one, embraced them all, praising their courage, telling them all that he'd been honoured to fight alongside them, even though he'd spent most of the time lying face down. The nervousness on their faces evaporated and they, Tank and the healer joined him as he walked back towards Richie, the group of local dragons and the ever present statue-like Casey.

Stepping forward, Richie enveloped the master mantra maker. In turn, he wrapped his wings around the talented lacrosse star, all the time giving her his best smile.

"I hear we did alright?"

"Slightly better than alright I think."

"Thanks to you," chipped in the old shopkeeper.

"Thanks to us all," ventured Richie.

Gee Tee nodded his agreement.

"So what happens now, little one?"

Swallowing involuntarily, Richie wondered how Tank and the old shopkeeper would react when they found out that she'd been put in charge.

'Still... no time to lose,' she thought, and added out loud,

"Those here have chosen me to lead them, for the time

being at least."

Tank was staggered. All he could think was that she wasn't qualified and wasn't really even a dragon at the moment. How on earth had they come to that conclusion? Gee Tee on the other hand, poked his glasses as far up his nose as they would go and pondered what he'd been told. Dragons and humans alike waited for his response. A ringing endorsement arrived.

"Do you think it was just chance that we bumped into each other, little one? I assure you it wasn't. I spent a long time searching for the right dragon, when all the time you were right under my nose, well... above my head. And once it dawned on me, there was never any doubt. I'd gladly put my life in your hands, time and time again. But more importantly, I trusted you with the life of my most valued FRIEND," at which point he motioned towards Tank with his wings. "I think that says it all. You have everything a great leader needs. Just look at what you've achieved here today already. A group of humans, here in the dragon domain... UNHEARD OF! Not only that, but a group of humans coming into the dragon domain to rescue DRAGONS! I truly believe you're the only individual on the planet who could, and would, have orchestrated that. So believe, little one. Use that much maligned confidence that you possess and follow your instincts. If you do both of these things, I truly believe we have a chance to overturn whatever evil is being perpetrated throughout our kingdom right at this very moment."

A few seconds of silence followed the old dragon's pronouncement. In that short time, everything hung in the balance. That is until the master mantra maker did something extraordinary and completely unheard of, something laced with more cunning and guile than one of Baldrick's plans. Very slowly he dropped down to one knee, not something easily achieved by a dragon of his age, but there he stayed, head bowed.

Tank was convinced he was dreaming. There wasn't a

reality in existence in which Gee Tee bowed to anyone, even the dragon king, let alone someone stuck in human form.

Flash was slightly more pragmatic and could see things for what they really were, and had nothing but admiration.

'You crafty old bugger,' he thought, watching a master at work. And not just a master mantra maker. 'By doing that, you give everyone here little choice but to follow. And with that, you give her little choice but to accept the task permanently, and to believe.' As he too dropped to one knee, he couldn't help thinking what a true stroke of genius he'd just witnessed.

As one, the group of local dragons followed suit. They'd been pretty sure she was the right choice before, and Gee Tee's words had only confirmed it.

Janice's head spun from the events of the last few hours. Here she was surrounded by 'real' dragons. Not only that, but she'd fought against 'real' dragons and emerged on the winning side. And now this. She couldn't imagine a day could get any crazier than this. But it had been her choice to follow Richie, who she now knew to be a dragon. In the end, the decision was straight forward. Janice still considered Richie her friend, and realised that she'd follow her again in an instant.

'At least I'm not going to be bored anytime soon,' she thought, dropping down to one knee.

Immediately the other humans followed suit, all in awe of the lacrosse playing dragon in front of them. Hook smiled as he hit the floor, wondering how on earth he was going to stand back up again with the incredibly heavy backpack still strapped firmly to his rear.

Aside from Casey and of course Richie, the only one left standing was Tank. Over a sea of dragon and human heads, the two friends gazed across at each other.

'How did it come to this?' he thought. 'She's my friend and has already been through so much, stripped of her necessary dragon DNA and then hung out to dry by the dragon council in the way that she was, just when she needed them the most. And now she's being asked to lead some sort of force to... to what? To fight? To die? To retake the dragon domain? She's too young. She should be getting on with her life, doing what she does best... playing lacrosse. Not carrying the burden of the entire planet on her shoulders.'

All this flashed through his mind as he locked eyes with his friend. But here, at this very moment... there was something else. Her delicate pale features were the same, stunning and yet innocent at the same time. All except her eyes. Her eyes were... cold, dark, chilling, dangerous. They had the look of... someone who'd do anything to get the job done. It was then that it hit him.

'They're right. She is the perfect one to lead us.' Dropping reluctantly to one knee, all he could think of was the toll this might take on his friend.

So here it was, confirmed by everyone, even Tank. Looking at them all, dragons and humans alike, heads all bowed, was a turning point for her. She hadn't asked for this. It had been unfairly thrust upon her. Maybe this was how it was meant to be. She had doubts of course, but not as many as most would have had. It occurred to her that this must be how the king felt, day in, day out. If it was, she decided there and then that she felt really sorry for him. But now was not the time to feel sorry. Now was the time to take decisive action. And the plan in her was a good one. At least, that's what she thought given all that she knew. That, however, was the problem. All that she knew. She needed every last scrap of information that she could get. And turning her head to look at the monument-like, frozen Casey, an idea formed as to exactly how she could get it.

"All of you stand," she commanded. They did as they were directed. "What we do next probably dictates the course of what we can achieve. It's important to get it right. However, as it stands, we don't know enough about exactly what's going on. I propose to change that," she said ominously, looking at the frozen bully off to her side. "This... thing, has information that we desperately need. He'll never give it up voluntarily, so we need to take it from him."

A ripple of unrest surged throughout the dragons, while the humans struggled to comprehend what was going on.

"And yes I know how extreme what I propose is, before you start. But it could ultimately save lives, and not just a few."

Flash stood and contemplated what Richie was planning to do. He couldn't disagree with it, and was surprised she had the 'scales' to do it. But it was a dreadful deed, something he'd never contemplated even on the gravest of missions as a Crimson Guard. Of course, he knew how, it had after all been part of his training, many decades ago. But it was a game changer in every sense of the word and not just for the victim, but also for the poor soul who had the job to go in and prise the information out.

'Good luck with that,' he thought, as Richie continued ever onwards.

Outlining exactly what she wanted to do, for Richie, it went something like this. Dragon telepathic abilities had been refined over millennia, with the skills they had now having been finely honed. It hadn't always been that way. A very long time ago, in much darker and more savage days, their telepathy had a more sinister purpose. We're talking about a time before man roamed the earth. Well, before intelligent man walked the earth. Humans were about, but not in the kind of numbers they are now, and not possessed of any kind of intellect. They were, then, just another item on the menu. To the dragons of that time though, they were barely just a side dish, with the main course tending to be... other dragons! It's hard to believe now, given how civilised they'd become, how in fact they ruled the planet from their hidden enclaves below the ground, but for a brutal period of their history, little talked about, largely forgotten, they had fought, killed and eaten one another. It was known as the 'age of barbarism', an unseemly and terrifying time to live in for any dragon. There was no cohesion, no cooperation, no teamwork. Individual dragons roamed the planet, fighting each other. Some worked in gangs with mercenary leaders who used their power and supremacy to control others. In the main, it was the physical threat that kept them in charge... but not always. Sometimes it was achieved by telepathy, for then that ability was just another weapon in a dragon's arsenal. And it was by no means pleasant, quite the opposite in fact. Many a dragon had been driven insane by other dragons invading their mind, mentally raping them if you like. Some dragons did this to learn their enemies' secrets. Others did it just because they could. Another long forgotten aspect of this was the belief at the time that by consuming another dragon, you gained their mental strength, adding it to your own. This has never been conclusively proven and is something that few dragons even know. But if you look deep enough into the past, the information is all there in the libraries, little clues dotted about in past issues of the telepathic papers. The whole idea of one dragon invading another dragon's mind is repulsive, repugnant and just downright evil. It is one of the most serious crimes and is punishable in the harshest way. No record exists of any dragon in recent history trying to do it, although the knowledge of how it is achieved remains out there to a certain few. Groups such as Flash's Crimson Guards have a working understanding of how best to carry out such a vile act, along with, no doubt, some other more powerful individuals. It was this knowledge that Richie was now looking for. She pleaded for anyone with the slightest inkling of what to do, to step forward. To say Flash was uncomfortable was something of an understatement.

Tank couldn't believe what he was hearing. Most of all, he couldn't believe anyone would have that kind of knowledge. It was barbaric and totally insane.

'And even if someone did have that kind of knowledge,' he thought, 'what kind of fool would step forward and admit it?'

Gee Tee felt sorry for her, he really did, and knew that it was partly his fault. After all, he'd roped her in, got her to lead the humans after giving them hope and weapons. And although he didn't like what he was hearing, he was proud of her for making what must have been a difficult decision in having to ask. So to his, and everybody else's surprise, particularly that of his former apprentice who was standing right beside him, he stepped forward.

Tank stood aghast, his eyes wide open.

'On reflection,' he thought, 'I should have known.' It felt as though the whole world was turning on its head.

'Humans saving dragons, torture, death, and now this. Where will it all end? With the deaths of us all, probably,' he thought, turning away, too disgusted to stay and watch.

'That's a shock,' she thought, as Gee Tee stepped forward. She'd assumed that Flash or maybe even one of the locals might have had the knowledge she was looking for, but the old shopkeeper? At this point it didn't matter who she obtained it from, only that she had it, and of course was able to use it on Casey.

"Before you get excited youngster," exclaimed the master mantra maker, "I have the knowledge that you're seeking, but as it stands at this very moment, I'm in no condition to help you. And even if I could, there's the question of whether I should."

Anger flared up inside Richie.

"Why bother to even tell me this? It's no help whatsoever. We need to know what he knows, and FAST! The slightest delay could cost us all dear."

The old shopkeeper's head lolled over to one side, his glasses nearly slipping from his nose, as he carefully worded his reply.

"To some degree you're right of course. But about using THAT mantra... you know nothing. Mantras aren't just tools to get the job done. Oh, sometimes that can be the case, but most of the time there are consequences to our actions. Every time a mantra is used, some of the energy is left over. Have you ever wondered what happens to that energy?"

Hardly able to believe what she was hearing, Richie wasn't alone. What the master mantra maker had just said was news to every dragon there, except Flash. While he hadn't known for certain, he'd heard rumours over the years and had also formed his own conclusion as a result of some of the missions he'd been sent on. Wondering if the old shopkeeper would go any further, deep down, he hoped he would.

"What difference does it make?" demanded Richie, barely keeping her temper under wraps.

"It makes all the difference in the world. Not just to you, but everyone here and across the entire planet. Some of that energy just bleeds off, but some of it is absorbed... by the caster."

"Surely that can only be a good thing," snapped Richie.

Gee Tee shook his head ever so slightly.

"I can understand why you would think so, but believe me, it's not nearly that simple. How and why you use the mantra in question play an important part, as does the mantra itself. Some make little or no difference to the user. But others containing more potent, ancient magic can... change an individual beyond recognition. The mantra you need for your plan is the worst of the worst. It would corrupt you, change you... destroy you. You were chosen by all of us for the qualities you possess. If you were to use this mantra, if any of us were... they'd be of no use as a leader. This isn't the way to go, my young friend. It's not worth it. You must find another way!"

She wanted to scream at him, tell him he was wrong,

wanting not to believe what he'd said. But the way he'd said it, the passion behind the words, meant she knew it was all true. Feeling alone, scared and as if she had nobody to turn to, she'd noticed Tank's disgust at what she'd suggested. Didn't they all realise she was trying to do her best, not just for them, but for everyone above and below ground? Standing entirely alone, she just stared back at all those looking to her for answers.

The old shopkeeper had shot up in Flash's estimation. He'd assumed that Gee Tee would have offered up the information on the mantra as soon as he'd stepped forward. But he hadn't. The old dragon had done what he should have, having warned her against using that particular mantra. And now they were back to square one. In fact, from the look of Richie, it might all fall apart at any second. He had to help, and thought he knew how.

Strolling past the old shopkeeper, he approached the young lacrosse captain.

"I can make him talk, at least I think I can."

"How?" demanded Richie.

"I was trained in the art of interrogation. I never needed to use that particular skill. But in theory I know what to do."

With dragons and humans looking on, she uttered two words.

"DO IT!"

Flash turned and called Janice over, remembering her affiliation with the very special weapon embedded in Casey.

"When I say, you're going to pull it out. Okay?"

"It has a name," Janice suggested.

Flash thought this over.

"Ahhh... that's right. Fu-ts'ang. Right, so when I say, you're going to pull Fu-ts'ang out of the wound, and just keep it close by. The first sign of trouble, you hit him again with it. Doesn't matter where, the slightest touch should be enough to incapacitate him again. Got it?"

Janice nodded, confident that she could do as Flash asked.

Strolling right up to Casey's contorted face, Flash told him what was about to happen.

"I'm going to take the weapon out now. Any funny stuff and I'll stick it somewhere where it hurts even more. Understand?"

Casey's left eye lid moved ever so slightly in response, despite the thin film of ice that had manifested itself across it.

Turning, he nodded to Janice. Gripping Fu-ts'ang with both hands, she slid the weapon out, in an almost cake cutting kind of way. Cold, misty breath filled the air as Tank and Flash's torturer exhaled. To rid his eyes of the ominous looking coatings, he blinked a few times. Up until then, he'd looked like a snake about to shed its skin. Quite an apt analogy really.

Poised to one side, Janice hovered Fu-ts'ang inches above Casey's damaged scales, sure she could make contact with the deadly blade before the evil dragon could even think about hurting her. Most importantly, she trusted Richie, Flash, Tank and... what was the old dragon's name? That's right... and Gee Tee, to keep her safe.

Flash looked up into Casey's prehistoric face as he addressed him.

"I think you'd better tell us everything you know," he suggested menacingly.

Casey wiggled his jaws. Janice stood by. Richie drew the laminium dagger from her belt, ready to intercede. A rumbling gurgle, followed by the swilling of liquid led to a splatter of frozen blood being spat in Flash's direction. Lightning reflexes kicking in, he ducked to one side before returning to his upright position.

"I won't be telling you ANYTHING!" boomed Casey. "You may think you've achieved something spectacular here today, but all you've managed to do is delay the inevitable." So great was the venom and aggression in his voice, that those surrounding him immediately took a step back, including Richie. But not Flash. He knew who it was that should be afraid, and it most certainly wasn't him. Taking two steps forward, he placed his human face right up against Casey's scaly jaw.

"Ohhhh... you're gonna tell us what we want to know, tough guy. Because if you don't, I'll make what you did to me look like a treasured memory. Now, where've they all gone?"

For a split second, Casey had been unsure, having seen a little fragment of something in Flash's eyes, and then it had gone. Either that, or he'd been mistaken. But he was certain this dragon, human hybrid, or whatever it was, offered little in the way of a genuine threat. And he was quite sure that the combined might of all present couldn't possibly match the damage that he'd already inflicted with his whip. So he spat out another huge gob full of green blood, and as it hit Flash full on in the face... smiled!

There were a couple of reasons his nickname was Flash, but the main one of course was because of his speed. Ever since he could remember, when he set his mind fully on something... he was quick. Not just a little quick either. Lightning quick. It was so fast, the humans all missed it, even Janice who was right there. Even to the dragons present, it was just a blur, and that was practically unheard of. In considerably less than a hundredth of a second, Flash had moved from right in front of Casey, to behind him on his right side by the exact point where his weak spot was situated. Normally so sure, it was at this point Flash started to question whether or not what he had planned would work. Having heard about Peter's battle with the twisted Manson on the Astroturf during the bonfire celebrations, when that story had been recounted to him by both the king and Peter himself, he'd found the most troubling part to be about Manson's weak spot. Peter had thought he'd killed him with the icicle, having slid it through his defences and scored a direct hit. But to no effect. Before supposedly dispatching Peter from the realm of the living, Manson had boasted how he and his cohorts could disguise their weak spots, thus making them nearly invulnerable. Just then Flash wondered why it was that nearly all baddies, evil geniuses, villains, call them what you will, felt the need to brag about how great they were and share the details of their so called plans. Constantly amazed at the number of Crimson Guard missions that had turned from failure to success at the last instant, purely because of his enemy's ego, he fervently hoped that would continue for a long time to come. Clearly it had saved Peter's life that day, and had saved Flash himself on many occasions. But what if it was a magically learnt ability, and Casey had been taught it? He found it hard to believe. Nevertheless, it was still a possibility.

'Oh well,' he thought as he thrust his hand up into Casey's weak spot. 'Here goes nothing!'

Casey couldn't comprehend what was happening. One moment the hybrid was standing right in front of him, the next, he'd disappeared totally. Just as he came to the end of this thought, the worst pain he'd ever felt in his entire life exploded into being from somewhere behind him and to his right. Frozen globules of blood showered the dark cobbles directly in front of him as his terrified scream carried across the square.

Flash was quite literally up to his elbow in dragon. If he had one wish at the moment, it was for a pair of really thick rubber gloves. Things had, however, gone as planned. Moving swiftly, he'd punched his way through Casey's weak spot, reached inside and found the small rounded protrusion beneath a layer of scales, about five inches up on the main body side of the cavity. In less time than it takes to blink, he'd run his hand upwards and found the fine ridge he was looking for. Parting the ridge with his fingers, he then thrust his hand inside what felt like a heavily laden pocket, but was in fact a layer of skin beneath Casey's protective scales. From there it was easy. A quick rummage with his hand led him to grabbing the biggest thing within, which was exactly what he was looking for... Casey's kidney! All he had to do then was... SQUEEZE! And he did.

As soon as it started, Tank wanted it to stop. He'd grown to think of Flash as one of his best friends, but he was repulsed by what he saw and heard, despite the fact that only a short while earlier Casey had nearly killed them both.

'Wow, this boy's got talent,' thought Gee Tee. 'I haven't heard a scream like that since the incident with the mantra, that amorous bear, that rather pompous upper class twit of a dragon and the huge pot of honey. Ahhh... happy days!'

With the exception of Janice, the humans all had their hands covering their ears, terrified, and rightly so. The sound wasn't so much inhuman as indragon, and would live with all of them for the rest of their lives, however long that might be.

Releasing his grip on Casey's kidney, the screaming stopped as the evil dragon's body visibly relaxed, only to be replaced by thick, heavy sobbing. Knowing time was of the essence, Flash soldiered on.

"Tell us everything you know... NOW!"

High pitched whimpers punctuated the sobbing, with the odd snuffle thrown in for good measure. But still Casey resisted.

"Go to hell!" he barely managed to snort.

'No more mister nice guy,' Flash thought, as he once again wrapped his fingers around Casey's kidney, squeezing for all he was worth.

Instantly the evil tormentor collapsed roughly to his knees. Janice only just managed to avoid being crushed, as she continued to hold Fu-ts'ang close to the dragon's scales, ready to pounce at a moment's notice.

For the life of her, Richie couldn't see how on earth this was a better way than reaching into Casey's mind and plucking the information from it. Of course there might have been risks, but surely that was better than pure and simple torture. But despite the screams, her mind had raced to what lay further ahead. She didn't consider herself squeamish, but the thought of what was to come truly turned her stomach. However, it was her responsibility. After all, they'd chosen her, and now wasn't the time to burden someone else with a deed like that. Not that she necessarily could, even if she'd wanted to.

The scream, or probably screams, it was so hard to tell now as they all seemed to blend into one, had increased considerably in pitch, so much so that even the surrounding local dragons had taken to covering their ears. Flash, meanwhile, had to shout at the top of his voice to make himself heard.

"I'm starting to lose my patience. Tell us what you know!"

Relaxing his grip just a little this time, Flash expected the foul dragon to finally concede defeat. Through the loud sobbing and the intermittent racking coughs, Casey mouthed two words. Flash couldn't quite make out the first, but the second one was most definitely, "OFF!"

With no thought about being watched, the former Crimson Guard reached down deep inside and found the agent persona of the dragon he used to be. Cool, calm and calculating jumped to the fore. It was time to show this scum sucking dragon who was in charge. Who was to be feared. It was time to unleash... the big guns!

Richie watched Casey mouth two words.

'Flash isn't going to like that very much,' she thought, surprised that her ex-classmate was still putting up a fight. Thinking about the outcome between the two dragons, as most of us do about decisions that affect us on a daily basis, it didn't take her long to make up her mind. There and then, she'd bet the house on Flash, and she'd have been right to do so.

With his hand still wrapped around Casey's twitching kidney, albeit not very tightly, Flash had already made his decision. As in a human body, a dragon's kidney is one of the most sensitive organs. Flash not only knew this, but he'd been counting on it as well. Now it was time to see just how sensitive it was. He didn't squeeze this time. Oh no. Instead, he pulled his fingers back ever so slightly, and then with all his might... dug in with his nails!

Dragons and humans alike threw themselves to the ground, all apart from Richie and the old shopkeeper, so abrupt and brutal was the sound coming from between Casey's jaws. Richie hadn't thought the pain could be ratcheted up any further, but quite clearly it had been.

'Flash hasn't been kidding about any of his exploits then,' she thought, looking on.

'Of all the assets I have, he could be the one to turn this in our favour. Even stuck in his human form,' she concluded.

Having dug his nails in for as long as he could, Flash pulled them out, tiny bits of kidney nestling underneath them. The noise subsided. Tears, saliva, blood and urine formed a moat around the spent looking dragon as he coughed, gurgled and cried. Once again, Flash spoke. Not so much a question, as an order.

"Tell us all you know!"

This time he did. Every last thing.

He told them how the enslaved nagas had little choice but to help with the plan, due to the internment of their king. He told them how some of the dragons were nagas in disguise. He told them how the monorail and all the telepathic newspaper nodes had been taken down across the entire planet. He told them about the prison in Antarctica, the one Flash had fleetingly visited. He told them how it would start with London, with the council and the king. He told them they knew about Tim's destiny and Peter's relationship with the king. That's why they'd been taken. He told them about the army of both dark dragons and nagas, here underground and on the surface. Ready to strike. Ready to die. He told them how the planet would be reshaped into something they would barely recognise. He told them it was unstoppable. He told them they had no chance. He told them every last detail.

It was done. She'd got what she wanted. Quite a big part of her wished she hadn't. If any of the others felt remotely like she did, then they'd be stunned, frightened... terrified for their very existence. But she couldn't afford to be any of those things now. Not here. Now she had to be strong. Be a leader. Show... no fear! Grim and determined, she stalked forwards towards Casey, who was by now curled up into a foetal position on the ground. Motioning to both Janice and Flash to move away, they did so.

"Get up!" she commanded, her voice full of steel and passion.

Casey just continued to shudder and whimper in his ball on the floor. Walking round to where his thick, scaly tail had curled up into the shape of a long deceased ammonite, she grabbed a section about a foot from the end firmly, and in a move so swift it would have rivalled anything Flash could have done, she drew the laminium dagger from her belt at the small of her back, whipped it around and sliced right through that part of Casey's tail. The howl that emanated from the broken dragon almost matched those from Flash's torture, for that's what it had been. As the foot long section of tail crumpled to the floor, Richie unrepentantly kicked it away.

"GET UP!" she screamed.

All the time howling, coughing and crying, he did.

As Richie stood and faced her former classmate, she held but one image in her head from when she'd first arrived on the scene. That of Tank and Flash swaying in the air, dangling from the metal monstrosity, their flesh shredded. It was meant to help her. It was meant to make things easier. It didn't.

She thought about words. Words to explain, to justify, to condemn. But there was simply no point. Words weren't the answer. The only answer was action. And so she took it. It was that simple. Almost without a thought, she brought the laminium dagger up and around from her side, all the time keeping that image in her head and channelling her intentions into the blade. It was easy. All too easy as a matter of fact. Having already chosen the point of impact, she hit it spot on. The laminium dagger cut through the scales, the arteries and the bone, much as a knife would cut through butter. There was little, if any, resistance. Time stood still, as the recognition of what had happened lingered on Casey's face for but a moment. Richie watched, totally disconnected, as his oversized severed head toppled off his thick, muscular neck, dropping end over end onto the dark cobbles, landing with a spectacular THUD. His body fell beside it.

Emma, watching from a distance with Angela, instantly threw up. Janice let out a surprisingly loud gasp, as the local dragons all bowed their heads, some whispering words that couldn't be made out. Tank stood agog, not knowing what to make of it. A tiny part of him had wanted Casey to pay for the horrific events of earlier, but not like this. Never like this.

'He could have been locked up somewhere, until the council were able to deal with him,' he thought. 'Things seem to be spiralling out of control.'

Flash had been surprised, and he didn't consider himself to be a dragon that was surprised easily. When Richie had told him that all the dragons had chosen her to lead them, he'd thought it a mistake. There was of course no doubting her confidence. But being a leader was more than just that, and goodness knows he'd been around a few. But this, this was something else. Despite her outward façade, he could tell that she wasn't happy about what she'd just done. Not that she looked happy in herself, she just looked kind of blasé about the whole thing. Most of the others would think just that, but he recognised the turmoil she was in.

'This,' he thought, 'bodes well. If she's willing to

recognise what needs to be done, and has the courage to take the responsibility herself in doing it, despite the fact that it goes against her very nature, she could well be the only being to lead us to any sort of victory.' Things were looking up.

Almost exactly the same thoughts were running through Gee Tee's mind. He knew, of course, that there was little choice but to kill the dragon Casey. For a start he was far too dangerous to keep alive, but also there was nowhere to hold him, and he'd seen far too much of what was going on here to be regarded as anything less than a massive risk. A tinge of guilt and sadness ran through him at all this. Guilt because he was primarily responsible for getting her into it... well, the leader part anyway. And sadness for the gruesome act which she had clearly not wanted to commit, but had done so anyway. He didn't doubt that she would be a fine leader, but worried that she herself would pay a high price much further down the line.

Looking down at the blade of the laminium dagger in her hands, she watched as tiny streams of green blood dribbled down it towards the tip. She'd never killed before. Never even thought about it before today. When Peter had described his battle with the evil dragon Manson on the Astroturf, she'd wondered what she would have done had she been in his position, considered the moment when he'd thrust the deadly looking icicle into what was supposedly Manson's weak spot. It hadn't turned out to be, but Peter hadn't known that. When he'd spoken about it all, she'd just assumed she would have done the same thing, with hardly a thought. But it had all played on her mind for days afterwards. Normally so sure of herself, she worried that she wouldn't have been able to do it, that she would have frozen at the last minute. Well, now she knew for sure. There was no turning back. She could kill if she had to. It felt horrible but... she could do it. Wiping the thick green blood off the shiny blade with the bottom of her T-shirt, she tucked the dagger back in place, and turned to face everyone.

Taibul, Sam, Emma and Angela were all comforting each other as best they could and had moved away from the rest of the group. The dragons stood straight and tall. Everyone looked as Richie turned around.

"Whether you agree with me or not... it had to be done. All we can do now is move on. We need to act on everything he told us if we're to stand any sort of chance. You've elected me as your leader, and as such I've come up with what I feel is the best way to deal with the situation. We will take two forces up to London. When we get there, I will lead one with the aim of saving the king and the council, seeing what help we can pick up on the way. YOU, master mantra maker," she stated, pointing at Gee Tee, "will lead the other. Your task will be to get the telepathic crystal nodes working so that we can spread the word across the planet and coordinate our efforts."

Both Gee Tee and Flash were surprised in equal measures. Gee Tee, because the last thing he felt qualified to do was lead anybody, especially given that he wasn't a people or dragon person and always much preferred his own company. Half thinking that this was Richie's revenge for him putting her in that position, he dismissed that almost immediately, knowing that she was only doing what she thought best. Flash's surprise was because he hadn't been chosen to lead the other group. Of everyone here, he was easily the most qualified, knew London like the back of his hand and had already proved his worth many times over today. I mean... he'd saved her life when Casey was about to finish her off, hadn't he? So why on earth hadn't she chosen him?

Looking across at Flash, as she knew he would, the ex-Crimson Guard was having trouble processing the fact that he hadn't been asked to lead. It was time to, quite literally, ask the world of him.

"Flash! Step forward," she commanded. He did so straight away, not knowing what was going to happen next. Keeping her voice strong, resolute, calm, but with just a hint of emotion, she spoke loudly enough for all to hear. "Your skills and experience have gone far in helping us achieve this small victory today. You saved my life, and countless others too. My respect, admiration and love for you is beyond measure."

Flash could hardly believe what he was hearing.

'Where on earth,' he thought, 'is this going?'

"And so it pains me," Richie continued, "to make this request of you. And yes, it is a request. You should feel free to turn it down, and know that it's not something I ask lightly. I believe you are the only one qualified and able to see it through, and ultimately think that its success is the key to returning the planet to some sort of normality."

Listening intently, Flash chided himself for believing briefly that Richie hadn't trusted him. From her words, it looked as though she trusted him only too well.

"Our deceased friend here described the army of nagas at Manson's disposal as titanic. I find it difficult to comprehend. But if it is as big as he described, then a dragon force a thousand times bigger than ours would have trouble defeating it. There seems to me to be only one way to counter this: to take away the threat hanging over their heads, and in doing so, stop them from working for Manson."

Now he understood. She was going to send him back to Antarctica. A cold shiver of fear ran up his back and arms at the very thought of returning. He'd had nightmares about his time there since returning. Not every night, but a few times a week. He'd wake up screaming, covered in sweat, his back burning with pain. And while the pain had subsided a little, the images that swam in and around his subconscious were as clear and frightening as ever. If there was one place on the whole of the planet that he never wanted to see again... IT WAS THERE!

"So you see, while you may have thought that I didn't trust you enough to lead the other London group, I actually need you to do something far more important... far more dangerous! And it's something I know you don't want to do because of your previous experience there. But it is precisely that experience that makes you the perfect dragon for the job. No one else knows what you do. No one else can make the rescue of the naga king work. So my mission for you, should you choose to accept it, is to make your way to Antarctica with all haste, via the latest monorail test borehole in Northern France, gathering help along the way if at all possible, and free the naga king from his icy hellhole. Hopefully, once this is achieved, the naga king will have some way to warn his race and can nullify that part of Manson's plan."

Richie made no mention of Peter's grandfather Fredric, but didn't doubt for one second that if Flash made it as far as the bleak, icy prison, he would go to great lengths to try and free him as well.

"So... what do you say?"

She made a compelling case, Flash thought, and knew that what they were trying to achieve would be almost impossible without somehow removing the naga threat. Unfortunately for him, he couldn't think of another way of doing that. And having been there already, he most certainly was the best dragon for the job. He just wished he wasn't. Reluctantly he nodded.

"I'm in," he declared.

"Thank you," replied Richie. "What do you need?"

Looking around at the meagre force gathered before them, ideally he needed an army about fifty times bigger than what there was here. Knowing that the more dragons he took from here, the less chance the groups in London would have, he felt unsure of what to do. But he knew he couldn't go alone.

'Hmmm,' he thought. 'Those healing dragons were fantastic, with their work of the highest standard. Yes, one of them would do fine.' And with that, he proceeded to tell Richie what he needed.

And so it was decided. There really wasn't much else to do. A phone call later (the signal boosted by some of Tank's mantra magic) and Yoyo was in, promising to be ready for Flash's arrival in Australia. He also alluded to something special that would help them in their quest to free the naga king. For Flash, it was just the boost he needed to know that Yoyo and whoever he could round up would be accompanying them. As well as that, one of the healers who'd assisted Flash in saving Tank agreed immediately to go to Antarctica, almost certainly not realising the full implications of the mission. With time of the essence, that's all there really was to it. Just as he was about to turn around and leave, Janice came running up to him. From her side, she pulled out Fu-ts'ang and offered it to him.

"You should take him," she whispered. "It sounds dangerous where you're going."

Flash smiled at the kind offer, both considering it and dismissing it in an instant.

"It will be downright dangerous where I'm going, but I think you should stick with it. I get the sense that it rather likes you. And besides, its most potent ability is the cold that its imbued with. There's too much cold where I'm going, so its effect may be nullified. Keep it, use it, let it protect you. I mean what I said about it liking you."

"I know," answered Janice. "Good luck," she whispered, not knowing what else to say.

"You too," added Flash, before turning and climbing up onto the healer dragon's back. But as he did so, something rather important occurred to him. Climbing back down, he strolled purposefully over to Richie. Leaning down slightly, he whispered delicately in her ear. For a moment, a rueful look crossed her freckled face. Flash pulled back. Richie stood on tiptoes, and kissed him gently on the cheek. Smiling, he turned and started to walk back towards the local healer that was his lift, not before a lumbering giant in the shape of Tank appeared right in front of him.

"I'm sorry you have to go back."

Flash nodded.

"It has to be me... for obvious reasons."

"I know," replied Tank, sadly, knowing full well just how much Flash hated and feared that place.

Reaching out, Flash clasped Tank's shoulder in a sign of friendship. Tank returned the gesture. Both stood silent, aware that they might never see the other again.

"Before you go, there's something you need to know," ventured Tank.

"I know my friend. I feel the same way too."

"Good," said Tank smiling. "Because it's not that. Well... it is, but there's something else. Something relevant to the mission."

"Go on," added Flash.

"The chains that hold the prisoners... Fredric and the naga king. They're unbreakable!"

Flash's face turned to stone.

"But all is not lost. Gee Tee and I have known for some time, and we've developed a mantra that will turn the chains into their most prominent base element... LAMINIUM!"

On hearing this, Flash's eyes took on the form of dinner plates, they were so wide. Leaning in close to his friend, Tank whispered the mantra to him. Flash's eidetic memory stored it safely away, knowing just how important it might be.

Again they stood in silence, until Flash whispered a heartfelt,

"Thank you, and good luck."

Tank nodded a silent reply, wishing his friend all the luck in the world, because he'd probably need it where he was going.

It was just at this point that Gee Tee noticed a thick bulge in the bottom of his Traveller's Bag of Capacity. Curious, he opened up the top and stuck in his giant, prehistoric head.

'Oh my!' he thought. Whipping his head out, with the speed of a hissing viper, the old dragon shouted across the market place,

"FLASH... HOLD ON A SECOND!"

About to hop onto his healer friend again, to start their epic journey to Australia, Flash obligingly turned and headed back towards the master mantra maker. Meanwhile Richie looked on, a little cross at yet another interruption, knowing that time was everything and even the odd second or two might make a difference in what they were trying to achieve. Striding over to the point where Flash and Gee Tee met, she was joined by Tank and Janice.

"I think we need to get a move on," she barked, at no one in particular.

Gee Tee's large, scaly head turned to one side, swivelling to look at her.

"Patience, little one," he whispered, more than a little patronisingly.

She was just about to snap and bark something very rude back at him, when out of the magical, seemingly bottomless bag he'd been carting around with him, he pulled a very old and scruffy looking pair of boots, dangling them right in front of everyone's faces.

Looking over at Tank, Richie turned one of her fingers around and around by her ear, trying to indicate that the old shopkeeper had finally, once and for all, lost the plot. In return, Tank held up his palm to stop her. Gee Tee had effectively saved them all today, and although Richie had officially been put in charge, it seemed at least prudent to hear the master mantra maker out. It was Janice that piped up first.

"Surely he's better off with the trainers he's wearing?"

"I couldn't agree more," chipped in Richie, so that only she and Tank could hear, well... supposedly. Gee Tee gave her a look.

"You've got to be kidding me!" exclaimed Flash in

excitement. "Are those really what I think they are?"

With the others looking on, more than a little puzzled, the old shopkeeper nodded in response to Flash's question.

"Amazing!" declared Flash. "I've only ever heard about them. Never seen a pair. Always wanted to though."

Richie shook her head.

"As your leader," she demanded, "can somebody please tell me what on earth is going on?"

"Boots of Fleeting... child!" announced Gee Tee, thrusting the worn and ropey boots in her face.

Flash laughed.

"Never heard of them."

"It's said that you could cover leagues in a simple step," announced Tank.

Flash and Gee Tee nodded in agreement.

"So what is it you're trying to tell me?"

"With those," said Flash, referring to the boots, "I'll be in Australia in no time at all."

"Really?" questioned Richie sceptically.

"Yep," replied Flash. "If I get the healer to get me above ground, I can put these on and it won't be long at all."

"Okay... if you say so."

Gee Tee handed over the boots, looking ever so pleased with himself. Flash tied the laces together and then hung them around his neck as he headed back towards the healer. After a quick discussion to tell him the change in plan, once again the former Crimson Guard leapt onto the back of the dragon. With a brief nod and a wave, the two dragons, one in human form hitching a ride and the other with a magnificent yellow and blue crisscrossing the scales of his entire body, took to the air. Circling once, they headed south across the city, flying dangerously low above the rooftops.

More than one of the group on the ground wondered if they'd ever see Flash again.

48 IF THE SHOE (OR BOOT) FITS...

'If anything, they look a little on the small side,' thought Flash, placing the boots on the ground after waving goodbye to Stinging Threat, the healer dragon who'd given him a lift to the edge of a desolate field on the outskirts of Salisbridge. Nagging doubts poked at his mind. If the boots were too small, how would he get them on? And if he couldn't get them on, how would he get to Australia? Automatically his training pushed the very real concerns to one side, those and his thoughts for the dragons... no, beings (as the humans were his friends as well, particularly given how well they'd just fought against overwhelming odds) that he'd just left behind underground, as he slipped off the borrowed trainers he'd been wearing.

Pulling back the tongue and making sure the laces were as loose as possible, carefully he edged his giant, sockless foot into the right boot while both his vision, and more importantly his brain, told him that it couldn't possibly fit into such a small space. As his toes disappeared from sight he felt a prickly, tingling sensation, right at the very tips of them. More than a little perturbed, he continued pushing his foot, which to his pleasant surprise was becoming more and more enveloped in the raggedy old boot. A moment later his heel slipped down the back of the shiny worn leather, producing a tiny little mushroom cloud of dust when it thudded down on the insole. Surprised at quite how comfortable his foot felt, tentatively he tugged on the laces, pulling them as tight as he dared, the fear of snapping them right at the front of his mind. With a double bow tied tight, he followed exactly the same process with the left boot. Standing up after he'd put them both on felt like walking on air.

Leaving the discarded trainers in a heap, he turned and faced the direction he needed to travel in. Just by looking into the distance, he could feel the power of the boots welling up, threatening to spill out, ready to be unleashed at his command. With his destination firmly set in his thoughts... he took a very small step. Instantly he was inundated with blurred lines of colour, that even his finely tuned and highly evolved dragons senses couldn't keep up with. What felt like a tornado whipped at his clothes, causing them all to flap like the wings of a demented seagull. A cold chill washed over him, gone as quickly as it had arrived, replaced instead by sheer exhilaration. Effectively, the world around him stopped. Momentarily he wobbled, thinking it was a side effect of travelling with the boots. It wasn't. He was perched precariously on top of some huge rocks, calm waves brushing gently at their base. In one small step, he'd reached the Dorset coastline. There, right in front of him, was the English Channel. Knowing exactly where he was, if he'd attempted that journey in a car it would have taken well over an hour to get there.

'These boots are amazing!' he thought, as he lifted up his left foot and took the biggest stride he could. Again the sights and sounds all washed over him, as in an instant the English Channel was but a memory, with the French countryside closing in all around him on all sides. Australia was getting closer and closer by the second.

49 ARE WE THERE YET?

With Flash disappearing off into the distance on the back of the magnificent healer dragon, Richie knew it was time for a decision. She also knew that it was her everyone was looking to, to make it.

'Oh to go back a few hours and be just a blissfully unaware human,' she thought, trying hard to compose herself. 'Two objectives, two forces, both going to the same city.' It made sense to stick together, at least until they reached the outskirts of London. Then they could split up, with a view to achieving their separate goals... re-establishing communications for the dragon world via the telepathic node system, and attempting to either rescue, reinforce or defend the king, depending on the situation. Unfortunately, with power to the monorail cut off, she was at a loss as to just how to get to London, short of heading back above ground which might prove a bit tricky with a small force of dragons in tow, especially given that, no doubt, their enemies would be watching and waiting there too.

Gathering everyone in, and her thoughts at the same time, she decided to put all her fears to one side about looking weak in front of them, and asked the question.

"As a force, we need to get to London. I suggest we go as one unit until we reach the very outskirts. Then we can split up and concentrate on our own objectives. Has anyone got any ideas about the best way to get there?"

"Can we not jury rig one of the monorail carriages with an independent power supply and go that way?" asked a younger dragon towards the back of the small gathering.

She'd already thought of that, but if she had, then so had they. As well, there was simply no telling how many stranded carriages would be on the line between here and the capital, and no way to know about them until a collision had already happened. Before she could speak, the master mantra maker spoke up.

"Impractical," he bellowed. "Our enemy will already have taken that into consideration."

"I take it above ground would be out of the question?" asked one of the remaining healers.

"I think the same thing applies," answered Richie, "as well as the problem of... THIS!" she stated, pointing at the shopkeeper with both hands.

Quiet acknowledgement rippled through the group, as an elderly female dragon stepped forward into the space at the front. Simply striking, with patches of intense purple fading to deep blue, her stomach edged with a scarlet stripe, she had every dragon's attention.

"We could use the flying tunnels of old," she announced confidently.

For Gee Tee, it was like a light bulb going off in his head, and he nodded his agreement enthusiastically.

'The flying tunnels... of course,' he thought. 'Before that blessed monorail, all we ever did to get around was use the now abandoned network of tunnels that were at that time the only way, other than on the surface, to travel between places. Most were three or four times the width of the biggest dragon's wingspan and served each and every major city, as well as many places in between. Once the monorail had announced its presence, there seemed little or no need for them anymore, so they were just discarded, like so many of us old things,' he thought.

"Weren't they destroyed?" responded Richie.

Before the master mantra maker could reply, the splendid dragon in front of them whose idea it had been answered.

"Not destroyed, their entrances were just blocked up. That shouldn't be too hard to sort out, and it should allow us to fly up to London totally unnoticed."

Richie liked the sound of that!

"Do you know where the entrance to the Salisbridge tunnel is?"

"I do," replied the elderly dragon female. "And it would be my pleasure to show you, and assist in unblocking it."

Richie nodded.

"Well... what are we waiting for?" Eager to get on with things, she let the elderly dragon lead the way.

Twenty five minutes later... they were in! A thick layer of rock which perfectly matched its surroundings, had been laid to waste, revealing a very wide, dark and cloying tunnel. The draught of warm air that had been released when they'd finally broken through had been an invigorating deep lava spa for most of the dragons there. Even Gee Tee seemed to take pleasure from it, puffing his chest out and pulling in great big lungfuls of air. It almost looked as if he were preening and showing off a little. That certainly couldn't be true... could it? And surely it would have nothing to do with the stunning female dragon whose brilliant idea it had been to use the tunnels... would it?

With the small, desperate force ready to go, it was only really a matter of working out who the humans and Richie would travel with. (A polite way of saying... ride upon.)Much to the amazement of all the humans there, Tank had transformed back into his natural dragon form. Sure it would terrify them, to his astonishment, they all came straight up to him to tell him how cool and wonderful he looked. It was indeed a strange old world they lived in. These last few hours had seemingly changed it forever. All they needed to do now was SAVE IT!

Richie bounded up across Tank's left wing, taking up a sitting position astride him, just behind his rippling, scaly neck. Not knowing what lay in store for them in the tunnels, it had been decided that he would fly at the front of the pack, with some of the more physically imposing dragons. Gee Tee and the humans hitching a lift with some of the other dragons, all of whom felt honour bound to take them given their heroics in rescuing them, all travelled in the centre of the small convoy, with the rest bringing up the rear, leaving a solitary few in Salisbridge to search the city for survivors and keep an eye out for any other threats.

Gripping the scales of her friend's neck tightly, Richie glanced over her shoulder at the most unusual group of beings to take up arms together since time had begun. As Tank flapped his powerful wings and leapt into the darkness, followed closely by the rest of the force, she wondered just what awaited them at the other end.

Her serious demeanour cracked just slightly as the darkness closed in around them. Just like the other humans, she couldn't see, couldn't access the so called dragon vision that assisted all the prehistoric shapes gliding all around her. But what had forced the tiniest smile across her face, in the midst of this most horrific crisis, was hearing Hook's hushed words, echoing in and around the tunnel they were all now trapped in.

"Are we there yet?"

50 GET READY!

Threatening to wake up the city of discarded computer towers at the front of the shop, the loud trilling of the phone echoed all around. Tina, for that was her human name, darted in and around the metal giants, her delicate feet just managing to find little islands of wooden floor as she ran. Eventually reaching the tiny front desk, she hurdled a pile of boxes and reached for the phone. Not out of breath in the slightest, despite her exertions, very politely she announced,

"DJ Hillier computer repairs... how may I help you?"

A voice she recognised followed the briefest of pauses.

"It's nice to know you're still awake... Tina."

'It's Yoyo!' she thought, tidying away some spare computer parts behind the desk, stacking them into their appropriate cubby holes. 'He never uses the phone. How odd.'

"Nice to hear from you, boss. What can we do for you?"

"That SPECIAL order, the one I came to see you about... is it ready?"

Tina thought...

'SPECIAL ORDER! Of course... the suits and the mantra.'

"I believe it's just being finished off as we speak," she replied.

"I'm about an hour out. I need it all ready for when I get there," exclaimed Yoyo urgently. "Also, I might need some of the staff to accompany me on a little... OUTING!"

"Understood," uttered Tina, intrigued about the 'outing' part. We'll see you when you get here."

"See you soon," answered Yoyo, and then he was gone.

Placing the phone back in its holder, Tina raced back the way she'd come, this time leaping computer towers three at a time, sprinting for the secret entrance that led her back to her friends, who were right at this very moment below her, putting the finishing touches to the dragon suits that their mentor had requested. They'd be both nervous and excited when she told them about the phone call, she knew, just as she was. Instead of using the hidden set of stairs, she palmed open the secret locker that was tucked behind an old upright vacuum cleaner, and after pulling open the dented metal door, leapt into the darkness, grabbing a very shiny metal pole and sliding down two storeys in no time at all.

Landing with a thump in full view of everyone else, she stood up and brushed herself down, before explaining what had just happened. Nervous excitement rippled around the room for a few seconds at least. But it didn't last, with the group quickly getting back to work, their minds fully focused on completing their assigned tasks. What would happen next was any dragon's guess, and not worth worrying over without knowing what it was. It would, no doubt, be revealed very shortly indeed.

51 REACHING THE END OF THE ROAD

All she could hear was the swishing of wings as the thick, dusty air washed over her. The darkness was all consuming. Even looking down to where she knew her hands were gripping the scales around Tank's neck, she couldn't actually see them, despite knowing they were most certainly there. Having lost all track of time in the tunnel, she had no idea how far they'd travelled given that she also had no idea of their speed. But she was hoping they were nearly there, if for no other reason than to stop for a drink.

'This heat is soul destroying,' she thought, as sweat poured off every part of her lithe body. 'Still, at least they all seem to be enjoying it.' All around her the flying dragons occasionally roared in approval at how hot it was in the confined space of the tunnel, with some murmuring that they couldn't remember it being like this when the tunnels were actually in use, before the monorail came along. Most seemed to think it was because all the entrances to the tunnels had long since been sealed up, preventing the air from circulating properly.

Gradually, she could feel Tank and the other dragons start to slow. Leaning forward as far as she dared, she spoke in her friend's ear. It was the first time she'd felt able to do so, as for the most part she'd been concentrating on clinging on and after that, the swooshing of wings and the rushing of passing air had made it all but impossible.

"What's going on?" she shouted. It came across to Tank as more of a whisper.

"It would appear that we can go no further. The tunnel is well and truly blocked."

"Have we reached London do you think?" she called, just as Tank landed on the uneven ground.

"I would hazard a guess that we're pretty close to the

outskirts," her friend replied, as others around her growled their agreement of his assessment.

By now, the entire group had landed all around them, the humans choosing to dismount their fabulous rides, all thanking the hulking prehistoric creatures who'd been honoured to carry them. With the pleasantries over, it was time for some light in the pitch black, provided of course by the master mantra maker. A mystical fountain of light welled up from the old dragon's hands, while all around him muted admiration from both humans and dragons alike shone out.

"I haven't seen him show off like this in years," whispered Tank in Richie's ear. "I think he might be smitten with the very graceful dragon who suggested the idea of using the tunnels."

Both looked on as the graceful dragon slipped around beside the master mantra maker, eager to learn about the mantra that had formed the exquisite well of light. In the meantime, the dragons who'd been at the front of the pack were examining the rock barricade that stretched across the tunnel before them, preventing the whole group from going any further.

Content to wait for their opinion, Richie stood next to Tank. All the humans came over to join them, breaking out some drinks which someone had thought ahead to pack. Richie was handed a small bottle of water by the diminutive Janice, which she downed in one go.

"That was a blast!" exclaimed Hook, having taken a long slurp of water, slapping Tank high on the thigh. Tank's huge scaly head twisted around, putting itself right in the rugby player's face. For a split second Hook looked mightily unsure of himself, that is until Tank broke out the biggest dragon smile in the world.

"No funfair ride in the world can beat riding on a dragon's back," he opined. All the humans nodded their agreement. Richie stood waiting, for once ignoring the good humoured banter. The dragons turned and came back, disappointment etched across their faces.

"No way we're getting through that anytime soon. Not without letting the whole of the capital know where we are."

As Richie racked her brain about what to do, Tank piped up.

"There was something, a kind of service tunnel or the like, about half a mile back, I'm sure."

One of the others agreed they'd seen something.

"Why don't we take a look?" suggested Tank.

"I'll go," said Richie.

Tank was just about to object, but Richie stopped him by holding up just one finger.

"Let me finish," she pleaded. "I'll go with the heavy squad here," she said, motioning to the dragons who'd been travelling at the front with them. "You stay and look after the others. We'll do a quick reconnoitre and hopefully be back in no time at all. So get comfortable, try and rest, and don't make too much noise. Post a couple of guards as well," she ordered.

Tank nodded, albeit reluctantly. Logically, he knew it all made sense, but that didn't stop him from wanting to go with her. Quickly, she shared the plan with the others and then set off into the darkness.

Tank tasked a couple of the dragons to take a watch in either direction, while they set up a makeshift camp. As well as the fountain of light, Gee Tee managed to produce a raging fire in the middle of their newly formed base, seemingly out of nowhere, procuring its energy from absolutely nothing. Already uncomfortable with the heat, the humans moved way back, while the dragons eagerly consumed the warmth and radiance the flames offered. Tank ordered them all to rest as much as they could, stating that undoubtedly they would need all the energy they could get later on.

All snuggled together, for the first time the humans had a chance to marvel at the situation they found themselves in, whispering in wonder to each other about it, much to the amusement of the dragons around them. After all, they were able to hear every last word with their superb enhanced hearing. This lasted more than half an hour, after which things became much quieter, with all the beings making up this bizarre group choosing to keep their counsel and rest.

Nearly two hours later, the guard nearest the entrance down which Richie had disappeared, alerted Tank's group that they had company. Rising to their feet, all the dragons adopted a fighting stance, with the humans and the master mantra maker protected behind them. They needn't have worried, as it turned out to be Richie's group returning. Tank was more than a little relieved to see her safe and sound, and of course the rest of the group.

Gathered around the fire, much to Richie's discomfort, they explained what they'd found. It turned out they'd reached the outskirts of London, as Tank had pretty much deduced, and had arrived in the urban dragon area of Molesey, close to Hampton Court and some way south west of their objective. In scouting the area, the group had been surprised to find so much devastation around them. Buildings had been looted, ransacked and set ablaze. Clearly, running battles had taken place between two forces, both of which were nowhere to be seen. They had, however, managed to find a source of relative safety... the Hampton Court nursery ring was still intact and untouched by whatever violence was ravaging the dragon domain. The *tors* on guard there had, on hearing about Richie and her group, offered them the chance to rest and replenish their supplies, which Richie had eagerly taken them up on, hoping that a few more dragons might decide to join her once they knew a little more about what was going on.

And so it was that the small, interesting band of fighters stalked through dusty, uneven streets, moving stealthily from shadow to shadow, always on the lookout for trouble, eventually reaching the temporary respite offered by the nursery ring.

Entering the small but beautifully formed and as yet untouched sanctuary, the young dragons, learning their way in life, were stunned to see actual humans, armed and below ground, bolstering the depleted fighting force. And they weren't the only ones. Whispered gripes passed from *tor* to *tor*, most only comfortable about expressing their displeasure to one another, despite most of those around them being able to hear what was going on. For the time being, Richie chose to ignore it, knowing that at the moment she needed all the allies she could get, to stand any chance of successfully carrying out what they were about to do. She hoped that once everyone heard the story of what had happened and how the humans had saved the day, with Gee Tee's help of course, it would bring them around to her side.

So as the small force sat down with all the dragons from the nursery ring and shared their food and water, in her head Richie practised the speech she would eventually have to give.

All around Flash, brilliant coloured lines rapidly slowed, as once more the world swam into view. Wavering a little, he fought off the urge to be sick as he looked around the dark, deserted concrete runway for any sign that he was in the right place. Exhausted, he decided even if he wasn't where he expected to be, he just had to sit down, for a few moments anyway. So he did, with the cool breeze doing little to stop the sweat pouring off him. He'd had no idea the boots would take such a toll, well, not physically anyway. Draining his reserves of mana, that was to be expected, but he hurt just about everywhere and felt more tired than he could ever remember being.

Abruptly, the faintest of noises rustled out of the darkness from behind him. Instantly he sprang to his feet, forcing the tiredness from his body, willing it to work.

Momentarily he thought about taking another step with the boots; it would at least get him clear of trouble, but as far as he knew, this was his supposed destination, and he had no idea where else to go.

Without warning, they appeared from out of the darkness, off to one side of the runway. First one, then two, followed by a whole group of them. In a couple of seconds he was surrounded by over fifteen of them. And by them, he meant... dragons! All in their natural form. Readying himself, his body tensed... just in case.

"You're actually thinking about it... aren't you?" came a familiar voice from off to one side.

A beaming smile broke out on Flash's face as several of the dragons parted to let his friend through.

"Well... you know. Old habits and all."

Yoyo burst into a trot and encompassed the ex-Crimson Guard, wrapping his giant wings all the way around him.

"It's so good to see you again," said the healer enthusiastically.

"I only wish it were under better circumstances," replied Flash, wary of the strangers. Yoyo stepped back.

"It's okay," he said. "They're with me. And I trust each and every one of them with my life, just as I do you."

Turning a full three hundred and sixty degrees, taking in each of the dragons before him, he had but one thought. 'Ragtag bunch of scallywags,' would barely do them justice. Some looked incredibly young... too young in fact. Most should still have been secreted in the nursery ring.

"I know what you're thinking," whispered Yoyo softly, "but often things are more complicated than we like to think, in actual everyday life."

"So they've never attended a nursery ring?" enquired Flash.

"For most... no!"

Flash's shoulders slumped as he shook his head in

resignation.

One of the dragons stepped forward, a look of righteous indignation scrawled across his face.

"Who the hell are you to judge us... human?!" he growled fiercely, full on into Flash's face.

'Clearly,' thought Flash, as he swept into action, 'Yoyo hasn't explained to them who I am.'

It happened so quickly, not a single one of them saw it, that's how fast he was. Having kicked one of the young dragon's legs away, Flash twisted his left wing behind his back and had produced a tiny little blade which was now hovering mere inches above the dragon's weak spot. Struggling for all he was worth, the youngster attempted to shake Flash off, but try as he might, he couldn't budge the ex-Crimson Guard. As one, the others exhaled at the sight of their friend in trouble.

Before things could get any further out of hand, Yoyo stepped in.

"Enough!" he ordered.

Looking up, Flash knew he'd made his point, and so slipped the concealed blade back where it had come from.

Two other dragons pulled the dazed youngster to his feet.

"Hillier! Apologise. Now!" Yoyo commanded.

A look of scorn on his face, the embarrassed dragon managed to mumble a barely coherent, "Sorry."

Looking on, Flash was pleased that his rightful place in the scheme of things had been returned.

"And you... dumbass!" exclaimed Yoyo, punching Flash fully in the arm, much to the former Crimson Guard's surprise. "I thought you of all beings would know that experience, courage, bravery and more importantly... help, comes in all shapes and sizes, and that you should never judge a book, or more crucially, a dragon, by its cover."

A wave of exhaustion washed over Flash, and suddenly he looked suitably chastised.

"They may not have had the education that you or I

have had, one that should be a given right for all dragons, but they're smart, courageous, loyal, brave and undeniably devious. All traits that I think could be put to good use at the moment. Plus, they've spent the last few months working on two things for just this very moment, should it ever come to pass. So for now... take my word that they're worthy allies."

Flash nodded.

"My apologies... to you all. I've had a long, exhausting journey, which of course is no excuse for my behaviour. I... I mean we... need all the help we can get. A bold play for the planet has been set in motion, and if we can't achieve what I came here for, then the dragon world, along with the human one above it, will cease to exist in any recognisable form."

Each and every dragon there looked on, shocked and stunned.

"And as for all of you," cried Yoyo, turning around in a giant circle behind Flash, his wings outstretched, "be sure you know exactly who you're dealing with here. This dragon is the bravest and mightiest warrior I've ever met. And yes... DRAGON! He eats death for breakfast, gorges on him for lunch, before taking him out for evening cocktails and kicking his ass! You saw, or not as the case may be, what he did to young Hillier here. No ordinary dragon is capable of that. So show him your respect, offer him your loyalty, pledge your allegiance to his cause. Because now is the time. Time to make a difference. I know none of you are stupid, and I know you've all been wondering what on earth has been going on over the last few months, about what I've had you doing in particular. Well... now you know. We need to go to the coldest and harshest place on the planet... Antarctica. To what end...? A rescue. Would that be right?" he asked, turning to Flash.

Flash nodded in response.

"Along with several other dragons, the king of the naga race is being imprisoned, and we need to free them all. I won't lie to you, it's not going to be pleasant. It might not even be possible. We might all die in the process. But if we don't at least attempt it, then everything's lost. The entire planet. What you witnessed on the news, the bombings, the devastation, the loss of life, is just the tip of the iceberg and will look like a picnic in the park compared with what's to come. I won't hold it against you if you don't wish to come. A more dangerous mission I can't possibly imagine." (Well, he could... just one! The one his friends on the other side of the planet were attempting, right at this very moment.) "But if Yoyo vouches for you, then you're fine by me. It's time to decide!"

A huddle of dragons on a cold, deserted, dark runway in the middle of nowhere never looked so strange. After fifteen seconds or so, it was decided.

"We're all in!" announced a young female dragon full of confidence.

Yoyo smiled and nodded at Flash.

"Then you'd better show him exactly what we have."

From out of the darkness appeared a huge canvas bag that took two dragons on each side to drag over to the runway. Everyone gathered round as the epic looking zip keeping it held together was run the length of the bag, almost longer than most school sports day races. Spilling open, the bag revealed layer after layer of shimmering material. Huge muscular dragon arms dipped in and pulled out one of the layers of fabric, holding it up to what little moonlight there was. Before Flash's very eyes, the material almost seemed to disappear.

'No... not disappear,' he thought, 'blend in. It blends in seamlessly to whatever the background is. For decades the Crimson Guards had dragons working on something like this, without much luck it had to be said. These youngsters can't possibly have come up with just that, in only a matter of months, can they?'

"I thought it would be much harder to shock you."

"That's quite some feat."

"I knew you'd know what it was. But that's only part of its secret."

That got Flash's attention.

'I wonder what else it does?' he thought, gaining more respect for the youngsters with every second that passed.

"The suit, as that's effectively what it is," announced Yoyo, holding up one of the pieces of material, "is a dynamic insulator, affording whoever wears it the ability to ward off the cold, as well as acting as a regulator for that being's thermal profile. In essence, it should provide suitable protection against even the harshest of environments, as well as providing camouflage so good that it should render its wearer practically invisible to all but the most adapted of species."

As everything Yoyo said sank in, Flash turned just in time to see one of the group of young dragons finish slipping her suit on. As soon as it embraced every living part of her... BAM! She simply disappeared, right in front of him. It was awe inspiring!

And then the thought hit him. All the suits were dragon sized. What was he going to do?

"I don't suppose one size fits all?" he piped up, hopefully.

"I'm afraid not," whispered the young female, who'd only just disappeared, from right behind him. Desperately, he tried to pretend she hadn't startled him as a glum look of disappointment formed on his face.

"But I'm assuming the human shaped one that Yoyo had us make is for you," she exclaimed, her head now the only part visible after having pulled down the hood. Flash turned to stare at his friend, who just smiled back and nodded.

It didn't take long for all the warm stealth suits to be handed out. In fact, it took longer to put them on for the dragons, than it did to pass them round. Some of the youngsters had real issues getting into them, needing assistance, much to the amusement of some of the others.

Yoyo also mentioned the heat specific search mantra that the team of brilliant individuals had come up with.

'For the first time in a while,' Flash thought, 'things are starting to look up.'

With them all suited up, Flash hitched a ride on the young female dragon, who was the only one to offer, seemingly amused to let another dragon ride her. Yoyo tucked Flash's boots in a specially designed pocket on his suit, so that they would be tucked away safely, and hidden from view. So in the darkness of the deserted airfield, the small, invisible dragon force took off, heading as fast as they could towards the icy plains of Antarctica, and the frozen hellhole that haunted Flash's nightmares.

The ever dwindling dragon force left alive in the deadly council building had been ordered to fall right back to the entrance of the king's private residence. Small cells of nagas had managed to infiltrate the council building, and that combined with whatever was causing the constantly opening, closing and locking of key doors in all areas of the building had proved costly to the remaining force left to protect the dragon monarch. A small contingent lay in wait just on the private residence side of the steep sided walkway, hugging the shadows of the rock face, barely noticeable at all. Most of the rest were beyond the entrance, a command post having been set up around the plinth, right in the centre circle of the ground floor of the magnificent building. For the most part, the king had been consulted on everything that was being done. Falling back hadn't been ideal, but under the circumstances, they'd had little choice. Taking on the small forces of nagas would have effectively been child's play, but for whatever was opening and shutting those doors at random, which changed the layout of the building almost every second, removing any advantage the dragons had. Whoever had devised that plan had certainly known what they were doing, and indeed it had cost them dearly, both in terms of lives lost and ground given away. Should he ever find out who was behind this, the king had a very specific idea of what he would do to the individuals, or individual, responsible.

A delicate (if that's what it could be described as, given the dragon producing it was renowned for being a formidable warrior) cough forced the king away from his thoughts of dark vengeance.

"Captain," said the king.

"Your Majesty," she replied, bowing a little.

"Enough with the formalities, Captain. We have more than enough to think about, without all that nonsense. What's on your mind?"

Amelia Battlehard smiled, well... a little at least. She'd had little contact with the monarch himself, and had only recently been posted here from the consulate in Paris. But often she'd heard other guard members comment on what a no nonsense dragon he was, and how he had an uncanny knack for cutting through all the crap, so to speak. To see it firsthand, despite the desperate situation they found themselves in, was refreshing. She supposed it helped that he used to be a knight and so must have had a good grasp of battleground tactics and close quarters fighting, something which it looked more and more like it might come down to. Taking him at his word, she decided to speak her mind.

"I'm a little concerned about the... eh... the basement of the council building, Sire."

"You mean the mythical beast capture and detain level, Captain?"

"Yes. It had been at the back of my mind all the time we were defending the building... what if the containment shut down, allowing everything down there out? I was glad it didn't, but couldn't understand why not; after all, the strange goings on affected everything else apart from that.

Having already taken a real shine to the young captain,

the king knew her to be a quick study, have an even quicker mind, and not be afraid to muck in with her troops, as well as being a gifted communicator. And although he was sure he could trust her (well he was, even at this very moment... with his life,) he wasn't sure he wanted to tell her why the mythical beasts were still contained. No good could come from her knowing that the release to the entire level wasn't controlled by any one dragon, or the computer, or some kind of electrical power supply, but by the magical ring throbbing away on his finger right at this very moment, the one with which they planned to power the shield which right now they were trying to set up at the entrance to this very building. Briefly, he wondered whether in actual fact he should set the mythical creatures free, to be recaptured at a later time. Before, it hadn't really been an issue, not when his force had been inside the council building, but now that they'd retreated back here, he could in fact let the creatures loose, in the hope that if nothing else they would damage the invading force that was heading their way, as well as not allowing said force to get their hands on some of those particularly dangerous creatures. It wasn't a decision he was willing to make at the moment.

"It's okay, Captain. I know why the basement remains locked down. And it's better that you don't know any more... for now at least. If things get desperate... well, more desperate," he smiled, "then I'll consider releasing the creatures. But it should only be as a last resort."

"I understand... Your..."

The king held up his hand and cut her off.

"Enough with all this nonsense. No more Your Majesty or Sire. Not until we've gained our, and everybody else's, freedom. Understood?"

"Understood," she answered reluctantly.

Just then one of the guards at the makeshift command post shouted over.

"Ummm... Captain, Your Majesty... you might want to

come and take a look at this."

Amelia Battlehard rolled her eyes at the king, something that greatly amused him, as they both strode purposefully over.

"Report!" ordered Captain Battlehard.

Swivelling around a high tech laptop sitting delicately atop the raised plinth, the guard had frozen its crystal clear screen on a piece of rather poor quality video footage.

"It suddenly occurred to us that some of the buildings in and around the Buckingham area are equipped with video surveillance."

Both the king and the captain alike raised their eyebrows.

"It's a hangover from a period before the council building was erected. Certain streets had a reputation for being a little... uncivilised," continued the guard. "Anyhow, we managed to hack into a couple of the cameras, the only ones that still seem to be online. You'd better take a look."

Hitting the resume button, the grainy footage on the screen started to play. The king vaguely recognised the end of the shadowy alley the camera was located on. But that wasn't what caught his attention. Looking out over the square, adjacent to the one in front of the council building, currently it contained a huge number of nagas, in their human forms by the look of things, and a complement of odd looking dragons, all marching together. They had to be outnumbered two or three hundred to one, just from what they could see, and that might just be the tip of the iceberg. Just when he'd thought it couldn't get any worse, his blood ran cold at the sight of something smack bang in the middle of said force. His face was a picture of hatred and anger, as both the captain and guard stepped back at once.

"What is it?" asked Amelia Battlehard.

Hitting pause on the touch screen, the king answered.

"There!" he said, pointing right into the middle of the throng of bodies.

Both dragons looked hard at the group surrounded by the guards, but it was difficult to make out, particularly with human, dragon and naga shapes all on view.

"That's who's responsible for all of this. That's who we'll be fighting."

"Do you mean the old man?" exclaimed the captain, taking a closer look at the screen.

"He might look like a harmless old man, Captain," replied the king, "but I'd recognise that being anywhere. And so should you, especially if you know your history. He's most definitely a dragon you won't forget in a hurry. I know I haven't. His name is... TROYDENN!"

Both the captain and the guard pulled abruptly back from the screen.

"Are you sure Sire?"

"Oh yes," answered the king. "Very, very, very sure."

"What could he possibly want, to go to all this trouble?"

"My head on a platter," replied the king softly, focusing in on the group in the picture once again. "Oh my God!" he exclaimed, recognising three of the other beings there.

"Sire?" enquired the guard.

Slumping down in the only vacant chair, dragons all around stopped what they were doing to watch.

"What is it Majesty?" asked Captain Battlehard. "We need to know."

Holding his head in his hands, too angry and frightened to look at the screen any more, he answered the dedicated soldier.

"Both human shaped captives are known to me. One is my best friend's grandson. The other is the 'white dragon' from the famed prophecy, newly arrived in our realm. Having both of these dragons prisoners does not bode well. But at least we now know who was responsible for the lovely goings on in the council building."

Both dragons once again looked closer at the screen. It was the getting-older-by-the-second captain who spoke first, or rather hissed,

"ROSEBLOOM!"

"So it would seem, so it would seem," muttered the monarch.

Amelia Battlehard stood up stock straight, surprising the guard beside her. Saluting, she announced,

"We won't let you down Sire. Not a chance. I'll die before I let those scum sucking traitorous leeches get hold of you."

"We all will!" growled the guard next to her.

"WE ALL WILL!" echoed from every guard, in every corner of the building.

Touched, almost to tears, the king knew they needed to see him strong, they needed him to give them strength. Standing, he turned slowly in a full circle.

"Know this! This is where we draw the line! This is where we make our stand! And notice I say WE! You and I... side by side. If this pervading threat wants to come into our home, our kingdom, our domain, then it does so at its own peril. I will not kowtow to evil, here or anywhere else. I promise to fight with you and for you. I will stand by your side. I will defend and protect you with my dying breath. I HAVE YOUR BACK! NOW AND ALWAYS!"

A rapturous cheer echoed around the room, the mood transforming instantly from one of distant hope, to a feeling that anything was possible. That... had been the king's intention. As destiny marched closer and closer, he just hoped that what they had would be enough to stave it off.

Through the tiniest slit in his bruised, battered and bloodshot eyes, Peter could just about make out where they were. If he was correct, then an epic showdown was all but impossible to stop. Abruptly he coughed, something inside him working its way up his throat. Despite the fact that he found it disgusting, he could do little else but to spit it out. Looking down at the uneven cobbles, he focused on what had just vacated his body. A huge glob of mucus wrapped in blood lay dribbling away just in front of him.

'Coughing up blood... that can't be good,' he thought, before the next regular shove in the back from the guard behind him forced his unwilling body ever forward. With his head bowed down, he took a tentative step, his knees nearly buckling from the pain. As it washed over him, he tried to put it away, compartmentalise it, as Flash had once described it to him. Plodding forward, aware of Tim struggling beside him more than he himself was, it would seem, his thoughts turned to his friends. Where was Flash and was he safe? He was supposed to have gone to the charity sports day... the one to raise funds for the rebuilding of the clubhouse, with Tank. He hoped they were both safe, but at the same time couldn't help wishing that the former Crimson Guard would suddenly make an appearance from out of the shadows, off to one side of the square they were in, with a view to putting a stop to all this... MADNESS! Right here, right now, he felt almost envious of Richie, not knowing about all this, not being involved. And although the consequences of what happened here would almost certainly reverberate around the world above at some point, just as they already had with the laminium bombs from that shocking attack, he hoped that currently she was enjoying being human and making the most of what little time the world as they knew it, had left.

Another sharp jolt in the back sent a spasm of pain straight up his back and into his neck. Fighting off the overwhelming urge to turn around and throw himself at the guard, he knew that if he reacted, he would only get hurt more, something the guard no doubt was trying to encourage, so he plodded on, biding his time, hoping against hope that either one of his friends or the king would be able to get himself and Tim out of this dire and seemingly deadly situation.

Nearly five hours had passed since they as a force had leapt into the air on the outskirts of Perth. For the most part it had all been freezing cold ocean beneath them, with rolling waves the size of houses crashing and bumping, the occasional piece of flotsam or jetsam breaking up the monotonous surroundings. The survival suits they'd been kitted up in had surprised Flash no end. Promises about just how good they were back on the deserted, dark runway had all seemed too good to be true... but they weren't. Knowing the temperature here would instantly incapacitate any dragon in their natural form, forcing them to spiral to a very unpleasant death in seas so cold that little smatterings of ice had recently started to break up the dark and foreboding waters, he appreciated even more the breakthrough work the eclectic group of young dragons had undertaken. To some degree it felt good to be back in the air, but of course it wasn't quite the same, catching a ride on the back of another dragon, when in fact he should have been flying himself. Memories of high speed chases on top secret missions in some of the remotest parts of the world dominated his thoughts, especially the ones in sunny climes, when pretty much as any other dragon would have done, he'd sailed high into the sky, allowing glorious rays of sunshine to wash over him. That all seemed light years away from where he was now. Although he had access to the vast majority of his magic, he missed the flying... as any dragon naturally would. A sudden change of direction by his ride exerted a considerable G force on his comparatively tiny, human shaped form. A stomach full of excitement threatened to spill over, as a tight turn combined with a speedy drop had his hair whipping out from underneath his suit, ever so slightly. Too afraid to use one of his hands to tuck the tiny strands back in place for fear of falling, he cast an experienced look into the distance and was rewarded with a view both breathtaking and frightening in equal measure. Far in the distance, his enhanced vision could just make out the contrasting bright colours of Casey Station, his former billet, albeit rather briefly. Smack bang in front of them, the rising peak of Law Dome jutted up out of the ice and snow, so high that it almost touched the very clouds themselves.

Due to the outstanding properties of the camouflage mantra entwined within the very fabric of the suits, Flash could only just make out the other members of the group. Approaching the mountain of ice, they all closed in on each other. Flash quelled the apprehension deep inside him that threatened to take him over. He didn't want to go back to that place... EVER! But he was here now and the fate of others, not just of this fighting force, but of all his friends on the opposite side of the world, his monarch, the naga king and Fredric Bluewillow, founder of the Crimson Guards and Peter's grandfather, all depended on his actions. Now it was time for everything he'd learned, everything he'd trained for, to come to the fore. Single-mindedness about his mission overtook him. Doubts turned to confidence in one swift stroke. The survival suits would give them an advantage, one that he planned to use to devastating effect. He would rescue the prisoners and change the whole complexion of the current situation in London and around the world.

From out of nowhere, Yoyo sidled up to the young dragon Flash was straddled across. Despite having grouped together and having slowed down, the wind howled like a banshee mistaking muscle rub for its pile cream.

"How do you want to do this?" the healer shouted.

Flash had given this particular question much thought on their journey here. His considered opinion was that if the prisoners were still in the same place, then provision for anyone coming in from the stream would no doubt have been changed after his escape. He was sure that wasn't a viable option. Also, the survival suits protected them from the cold and even, as far as he was aware, the icy chill of the water, but there was no provision for an air supply, and unlike the nagas' magical option for this, nobody here had a mantra that would replicate it or find a way around. So, like most problems in his life, he'd decided to deal with this one... head on! Slowly and loudly, he explained his plan to Yoyo, who for the most part nodded in agreement. They would fly to the summit and once there would use the heat seeking mantra to try and ascertain the whereabouts of the two captured dragons and the naga king. Once located, they would try and drill down into the rock and snow, creating a passage that should in theory allow the force to pass through, one at a time. Several one off mantras had already been procured, as well as some specific to laminium extraction and others required for the drilling stage of the plan. There were dozens of things that could go wrong, not least the fact that all the captives could already be dead, have been moved, or there could be a force of a thousand waiting there. It was impossible to know one hundred percent. So, for the most part, they'd be winging it... something Flash was born to do, in more ways than one.

A textbook landing brought about the end to their near three thousand mile journey. The entire group settled atop a snow covered ridge enclosed on two sides, offering a degree of protection, very close to the summit. Without fuss, the youngsters prepared to unleash the heat detecting mantra they'd spent so long working on. It was strange just to see the odd sliver of movement, Flash thought, his mind not being able to conceive how on earth the suits they all wore functioned. If he hadn't been looking for it, almost certainly it would have been impossible to detect. For sure, not a human being alive would have been capable of seeing through the almost faultless suits. But he knew the enemies they now faced would prove more inventive and more powerful than any his race had faced in centuries, if not ever. Determined not to be lax, complacent or let his guard down in any way, shape or form, he knew in that lay defeat, something he was too acutely aware of thanks to his rather unsuccessful last visit to this freezing hell. So, for now, he was content to stand and watch, coiled, full of energy and focus, ready to spring into action when the need arose, constantly aware of the seconds ticking away.

52 HAUNTED

Cold gnawed at the very heart of him. The decades he, Fredric Bluewillow, had been confined here were starting to take their toll. Brief moments of sleep against the freezing, icy walls of the cavern had deserted him recently, replaced by waking dreams... hallucinations if you like. Memories from his past barged in on his conscious mind, assaulting him, forcing him to live those moments over and over again. Of course, only the painful memories returned and there were plenty of those, particularly given the things he'd done. Back then it had all seemed so clear cut, so refined. But as it all came flooding back with crystal clarity, thanks to his eidetic dragon memory, his views became conflicted, his mind lost in turmoil.

'Oh no,' he managed to think in a daze. 'Not anything to do with World War 2 please, and especially not this one... anything but this one!'

He'd had his suspicions for some time now. All the late nights... early mornings even. But it was more to do with her change of character. And that had changed dramatically. Once kind, loving, full of empathy, just about the perfect... he'd almost said 'human being', but of course he meant dragon... she'd won awards for her caring and considerate nature during her time in the nursery ring. Out of everything, those had made him the most proud, the proudest father on the planet. But that all seemed like a long time ago. Longing for that time to return, the professional in him combined with his life experience told him it was gone forever. He hoped not, hoping against the odds that he could get it back. Tonight would be the first step to doing just that.

His spy craft was awesome, as you'd expect from the king's right hand man (or dragon, so to speak) and the founder of the Crimson Guards. So far he'd followed her across to Spain on the monorail, and was currently climbing up a rather well hidden ladder that led into the sewer system beneath Barcelona. Ahead of him by only a few minutes, it didn't matter because he'd used a mantra that was his stock in trade. Once cast, the mantra created a fine layer of magical dust, invisible to all but the caster, and once in contact with another being it formed a shimmering trail for the caster to follow, while remaining invisible to everyone else. Just as she'd been going out of the door, he'd made a point of standing in her way. Although she appeared sulky, defiant and determined, he hadn't made a big thing about it, quite the opposite in fact, but just as she'd stormed past him, he'd ruffled her hair, something he'd done all the time when she was younger, something she hated now, and she'd told him so in no uncertain terms. But with the magical dust, it had done the trick and enabled him to follow her at a distance, with a view to finding out exactly what was going on.

A tiny shaft of natural light filtered down through the rusty looking manhole above him. Searching far and wide with his dragon abilities, it soon became apparent that no one was about. Hastily he pushed open the cover, crawled out and was up on his feet instantly, all without a sound. Sticking to the shadows, he followed the glistening trail of dust from his daughter's hair, illuminating the way just for him, like Christmas lights on a housing estate. Following the trail, he avoided contact when he could, but the further he went, the more people appeared around him. When the shadows were of no use, he pretended to be drunk, weaving and staggering just enough for most to want to leave him alone. Still he carried on, that is until he turned a corner and stood across from a small piazza, around which a number of restaurants, bars and bistros were dotted. From the look of things, the enigmatic trail led into the most crowded bar on the other side of the street.

'This,' he thought, 'is where things might just get a little interesting.' Closing his eyes, he reached deep within his human guise, tucking all his dragon-ness into a small black box, sealed it up and slid it into the equivalent of a cupboard under the stairs within his mind. Appearing fully human and much, much older than he'd normally look, thanks to another stock in trade mantra, he strolled confidently across the piazza and walked straight into the crowded bar. Immediately he became alert (more so than he was already, and that was saying something) because through the haze of the smoke, the smell of sweaty humans and spilt alcohol, and above the noise of

*the very out of tune singer, nearly all the voices were speaking in...
German! This he hadn't expected. For all intents and purposes, this
was a very Spanish area, populated entirely by locals. The
Germans/Nazis, call them what you will, shouldn't have been
anywhere near here. But it looked as though they were, and rather too
many of them for his liking. Squeezing sideways past the suited and
booted clientele, most of the men wearing ties, nearly all having their
hair slicked back with grease, he reached the sticky wooden surface of
the bar and tried hard not to touch it. Offering him an enticing smile,
the busty brunette behind the bar headed his way. Returning the
gesture, he was just about to open his mouth and order a drink in
German, when a slender but powerful arm appeared almost out of
nowhere, its fist connecting fully with his jaw. Stumbling back, he
was surprised at how such a thing could happen and catch him off
guard. Abruptly, the singer stopped. The music too, with the patrons
having turned totally silent. Forming a circle around him, the group
closest had all taken three steps back. Shaking off the stinging pain
in his face, he spread his feet, bent his knees into the perfect fighting
stance, ready to defend himself against whatever attack might come.
He considered himself ready for anything, to take on the whole bar if
need be. But he wasn't ready for... THIS! As the German customers
slinked back, all the while smiling and nodding their approval as if
knowing what was to come, a petite figure, dressed in her usual brown
outfit, revealed itself, a savage, wolf-like grin burrowed into her face.*

*'Oh no. What have I done?!' he thought, desperately reassessing
the situation. But it was too late for that.*

*Stepping forward, much to the delight of the crowd, she hit him
once again, hard across the face.*

"YOU BASTARD!" she screamed.

"I... I... I... I..." he managed to stutter.

*"You spied on me, followed me here. Well... THAT'S IT! No
more. We're done!" she spat.*

*"B... B... But y... your mother. W... w... what about your
mother?"*

*"Leave her out of this, you stupid old man. We're done... for
good. Now... get the hell out of here!" she ordered, before the throng of
patrons folded in all around her, and then him.*

Righteous fury ignited inside him. She was his flesh and blood... his daughter! He wasn't about to leave her here... with these despicable beings.

'This is it!' he thought. 'No more.' Reaching into that mental cupboard under the stairs in his mind, he opened the box. His power exploded out of it deep inside him. It was then that he took in his surroundings. Guns were out... everywhere! Lugers, machine guns... the lot!

Swallowing nervously, something of a new experience for him, as he could count on the fingers of one hand the number of times in his long life that he'd been outgunned... on one finger actually, he ran through all the possible outcomes.

Weighing up the options, he'd already decided he could take them... well, maybe. Figuring it would be a close run thing, to him... it didn't matter. He wanted to do it so badly, just wanted her back in his arms more than anything else in the world right now. However, he knew how to control his emotions, knew that at times you needed to walk away, live to fight another day, when the odds were that much better. So his heart told him to fight for her, but his head told him to retreat. It was a draw, at least up until now. But somewhere in the multitude of beings that surrounded him, he felt a presence, something unusual, something odd, something dangerous... something definitely not human. Suddenly it wasn't just one. There was another, and another, and another. Things had just gone from bad to worse. He didn't know what it meant, his daughter being tied up with all this, all he knew was that he had to get out of there... now! Channelling all his dragon power, he spun as fast as he could, lashing out at those nearest. Immediately, they flew back into the crowd causing a domino effect, the first four or so rows all falling to the floor. Guns started firing in his direction. However, he was already on the move. Each arm whirled with uppercuts, smashing his way towards the front of the bar, the satisfying crunch of broken jaws music to his ears. Determined to stop him from leaving, the crowd flocked to the narrow entrance. But that was never his destination. Leaping up onto a three legged, circular, wooden table, he lashed out with his foot, catching one of them full in the face with his boot, blood splattering the nearest half a dozen or so patrons. And then he launched himself. It wasn't pretty *or graceful, but it was effective. Tucking into as much of a ball as he could, he hit the massive plate glass window shoulder first, the impact rippling through his body. But he didn't have time to worry about that, not with the tiny pin pricks from the flying shards of glass stabbing him all over. And then he hit the cobbles outside... HARD, taking the full force of the blow on his lower back. Sure he would pass out, the pain was out of this world. But he didn't, and knew that he had to act now. In a few seconds it would be too late, he'd be dead and his daughter lost forever. This thought alone spurred him on as he staggered to his feet, taking one last look over his shoulder at the baying crowd in the bar, frantically trying to get through the narrow entrance to give chase. But by then, he was on his way and assisted by more than a dab of dragon power. He sought refuge once again in the shadows, using a very different way to get back to the dragon domain, all the time hoping that she'd return to him. She never did! He never saw her again. Not an hour went by that he didn't ask himself where she was, what she was doing, and who she was with. His Crimson Guard had orders to look out for her and to report to him at the very first sign, but to no avail. It broke his heart.*

Tears raced from his eyes as despair, sorrow and the familiar underlying feeling of failure ripped through him. Freezing before they'd got halfway down his cheek, building steadily into some kind of stalactite formation, stubbornly he refused to wipe or chip them away. The pain from that particular memory hurt him the most. Through glazed eyes he looked across at the naga king, envious of him curled there, emotionless and stoic. Briefly he wondered if he too suffered from thoughts of all the things he'd done. But that was soon forgotten as the next memories faded in and out, tearing into parts of Fredric the cold just couldn't touch.

53 DRAGON'S HIDE

If in fact there had ever been one, the plan was to stay in the nursery ring for a few more hours, get some rest, try and recruit a few more dragons and then move on, splitting into two groups to carry out the separate missions agreed upon. The *tors* had other ideas though. They'd provided food and in the valued safety of the nursery ring, a climate for much needed rest. Gee Tee was utterly exhausted from the day's events and he wasn't the only one. Having fought valiantly, the humans, to one degree or another, were still intoxicated from the alcohol consumed on their night out. It was no state to go charging blindly into an all out battle for the planet's survival and so, reluctantly, Richie had agreed when the *tors* had insisted they stay, eat, drink and recover as best they could, at least until morning. That was some time ago now, with the food having been mostly packed away, a few remaining scraps scavenged for the trip ahead stowed here and there by dragons and humans alike. Young dragons, the *tors'* charges, roamed around the nursery ring, hardly daring to believe that real humans sat and slept amongst them. Too excited to sleep, they were starting to become a real distraction, and Richie wasn't the only one to think so.

Snoring away soundly in the far corner of the courtyard they all found themselves in, the master mantra maker grunted and wheezed occasionally, reminding everybody of his presence. The humans, well most of them anyway, had curled up against the back wall, asleep for the most part, Hook supporting two of the girls' heads on his hulking great thighs, saving them from bedding down on the uncomfortable flagstones. Hook himself sat upright against the wall, eyes shut, not entirely asleep. Taibul leant next to Sam, eyes closed, breathing shallowly. Midway between the sleeping old shopkeeper and the sportsmen and women from the surface, sat Janice, cross legged, awake and entirely lost in thought, all the time twisting and turning the legendary sword Fu-ts'ang in her lap, its frosty glow giving the skin tone of her face an odd, blue radiance.

Looking over, Richie knew full well what was on the young human girl's mind: Peter! It had to be. Nothing else could explain that faraway look. Well, perhaps the discovery of dragons, and the battle to end all battles, but she knew that look too well. It was one she herself was trying desperately to mask. Her worry for Tim would have to wait. She had given herself over to more important matters.

'Still,' she thought, 'I wonder where he is and what's happening?'

A large, powerful hand brushed her shoulder gently, startling her from all thoughts of her former, illicit boyfriend. Turning, she looked up into the friendly face of Tank.

"And how are you doing?" he whispered, plonking himself down on the floor beside her. On arriving at the nursery ring he'd transformed back into his human guise, much to some of the other dragons' surprise. Feeling that it was the right thing to do, for many reasons. Normally, he spent almost all his time in that form and having his human friends here, he hoped that by appearing as such, it might just put them a little more at ease, if that were at all possible. Given what they'd been through already today, they'd done remarkably well. And then there was Richie. Part of it was for her. She'd been amazing, despite having learned the truth about her past through some illegal and immoral action on Peter's behalf, with no doubt the sleeping shopkeeper having something to do with it... oh yes, he knew. Well, he didn't, but you didn't just stumble across a magical ring that could absorb and safely store a dragon's consciousness, not unless you were nearly five hundred years old and owned your own Mantra Emporium. They'd be having THAT conversation at some point, but only after they'd saved the world again, if indeed they could.

"Okay, I suppose," she replied softly.

"Really?" enquired Tank sceptically. "Not worried at all?"

"What you fail to understand, is that as leader of everything... I can delegate anything I like. Currently I have others worrying for me. You see... leadership... it's a piece of cake."

Tank chuckled quietly, so as not to disturb anyone.

"But really," he said more seriously, "are you okay? Is there anything I can do?"

Richie took stock of her thoughts. She hadn't quite made up her mind... well, not yet. But there was going to be something he'd have to do. And he really wouldn't like it. But that was for another time. Not here, not now.

"I don't think there's anything you can do at the moment," she replied thoughtfully. "We all just need to rest as much as we can... like the great dragon himself," she said, nodding in the direction of Gee Tee, who'd she'd just noticed was using his magical rucksack as some kind of pillow.

"Not only are his mantras legendary, but so is his snoring," added Tank, trying to lighten the mood. No easy task, given their current predicament.

Nodding in the direction of Janice, Richie said,

"Do you think she'll be alright?"

"She's worried about Peter... like the rest of us," replied Tank, looking deep into Richie's eyes, seeing there the fear he himself felt for his friend's safety. "But given her actions back at the square, I'd say she's every inch as tough as any dragon I've ever met. To think that I didn't approve of their relationship seems utterly ludicrous now."

"And not just theirs I might add."

"I know... and I'm truly sorry."

"It's alright... I understand. But one way or the other, the world as we knew it has already been turned totally on its head."

Tank muttered his agreement, as both friends snuggled up to each other, keen to gain as much rest as was possible in the dim light crackling forth from the fire in the centre of the courtyard.

Just then, two of the *tors* shepherded a group of youngsters into the area directly around the fire, the younglings keen to feel the warmth of its embrace.

"I think a little story might take the edge off everyone's nerves," announced the head *tor* to Richie as he strutted past. She nodded her agreement, hoping that he'd be as quiet as he could, allowing the others to sleep for as long as possible.

Almost as if reading her thoughts, and with the young dragons closed in all around him, his soft voice could just be heard over the crackle and hiss of the dying embers of the fire.

54 A PRIZE FIT FOR A...

Walking from the sink over to the wall with the lava running down it, holding her damp hands mere inches above the slow moving, molten rock, soaking up the heat, she decided that everybody in the world should dry their hands this way. Moving across to the bed, she lounged back, tired from lack of sleep. In a way, she didn't mind the waiting, but the worrying and not knowing how things were proceeding, now that was a different thing altogether. Slowly closing her eyes, her thoughts drifted off for the last time, back into the past.

'It was so easy,' thought Earth as she slipped unnoticed off the monorail, heading towards the secluded entrance to the human world above. Gnarled Wolf, her father's mission planner, had always had a soft spot for her. All it had taken was a flirty smile, the promise of a drink sometime and a tall tale about a family tragedy, to get him to reveal the details of her father Fredric's current operational deployment and exactly where they were in Germany. So easy. Smiling a sick, twisted kind of smile, pleased that she'd guessed right, she continued on her way. Of course Fredric hadn't told any of the other dragons about what had gone on between them, or most importantly about the events in Barcelona. Probably too ashamed, he was no doubt already planning her rescue from the clutches of the evil Nazis. If only he knew.

Slipping stealthily out into the moonlit forest, she followed the muddy tracks that she knew would lead her to the farmhouse headquarters. Once there, she would unveil her plan to capture the dragon agents without revealing the details about her father's identity and involvement. That she would save for later... personally presenting the dragon king's special envoy and head of the Crimson Guards, knowing this was her 'ticket' up the ladder. For some time now she'd been trying to get noticed by the hierarchy. This would be like a massive flare sailing up into the night sky, shattering the peace and quiet, lighting her up like a film star. They couldn't possibly fail to notice her after this. And best of all... she'd be rid of her interfering and do-gooding father, FOREVER!

Assigned half a dozen nagas to assist her, as well as having been warned in no uncertain terms that THIS was her last chance, and although not unexpected, the nagas had been a welcome addition. As for the warning... it had just made her laugh.

The group of three dragons led by her father stood no chance against her force, especially as they had no idea they'd been betrayed and that their little operation had been compromised.

Splitting the nagas up into three groups of two, each pair responsible for taking down one of the dragons, she was keen to assist with her father. Of course she could take him down alone; using her relationship with him could in itself be a very potent weapon, but she'd learned over the years not to underestimate him and for the sake of earning her freedom once and for all, she wasn't prepared to take any chances.

The teams had been on site for a week now, one posing as the manager of the hotel they were staying in, the rest disguised as either staff or guests. Being masters of concealment, the nagas had found it easy to blend in, especially given all the years of experience they'd had in the service of their new masters.

As the teams reported in, she marvelled at how professional, focused and ruthless they were. Nothing stood in their way, nothing was left to chance. She admired that a lot. Their mission so far had been a success. Two of the dragon agents had been assassinated, killed in cold blood, gunned down in a hail of machine gun fire, stuck fast in their human disguises, which was no way for a dragon to die. She knew they found it abhorrent, and knowing that they were missing out on a proper dragon burial was the icing on the cake for her and, in her opinion, nothing more than they deserved. Of course they could have been captured alive, but she'd ordered them to be killed, knowing that it would make the prize of her father all the more valuable.

Carefully she sneaked down the hotel stairs, always mindful, on the lookout for any traps. It appeared he was being careless, but she knew him better than that. Being on the run and having seen his comrades gunned down would be enough to make him dangerously angry and unpredictable, and he had an uncanny ability to spot anything out of the ordinary. Knowing all this didn't bother her at all, because the naga spell casters had smothered her with spell after spell, negating the signs of her presence and abilities. If spotted, she would appear totally human and of little threat to anyone. Tiptoeing down the last step, she edged cautiously along the wall towards the fire escape that led to the alley behind the hotel. The door was still ajar. Sneaking a peek through the thinly veiled gap, half fearing some kind of ruse, she glimpsed her father kneeling behind a perfectly polished black car, facing away from her, his back fully exposed as two naga assailants headed in his direction down the alley. Savouring the moment, just as you would with a fine wine or the first bite of a perfectly cooked meal, the thought of what she was about to do sent her enhanced senses into overdrive. With her moment of glory almost upon her, she knew exactly what to do and nothing now could or would stop her. Silently she slipped through the gap in the door, creeping ever closer to her father Fredric, his attention fully focused on the human shaped nagas marching in his direction from the other side of the alley, sweeping their automatic weapons from side to side as they did so. Three paces away. That's how far she was from him. A feeling of euphoria washed over her, despite not yet having completed her task, which would have been stomach churning to most. With her heart pumping furiously, she took one more step forward, the mantra already set to be unloosed by her bony, white fingers.

Preparing to unleash hell on those damn Nazis heading his way, the tiniest splash in the world reverberated out from behind him. Before it happened, he already knew it was too late. He didn't even have time to turn around. But that didn't matter. Instantly he let rip the hell he'd been preparing for those scum sucking soldiers who only minutes before had cut down his dragon comrades. As a surge of pain ripped through the back of his neck, instantly knocking him out, he released the power he'd been holding on to. Magic crackled furiously out from the entire length of his body, purple, blue, orange, red, yellow and green waves of unadulterated, unstoppable energy filled the alley.

The car saved the Nazi soldiers, or nagas as they were in their true form. Earth, well she wasn't nearly so lucky. Having flung nearly all her magic into her father's exposed back, she was caught off guard by the power that exploded out of him. Being so close, she caught the full force of it and more, with some being reflected back towards her from the shiny automobile Fredric was crouching behind. The magic behind the mantra Fredric had cast was not unlike the magic that his daughter had hit him with. Both father and daughter lay unconscious, side by side in the puddle littered alley, as the rain drizzled about them, before both being dragged off by the squad of nagas.

Fredric was condemned to his icy prison, never to return. Earth got what she wanted, well in a way. Upon waking, she had no recollection of her past at all. Nothing from before she was hit with her father's magic, and so was unable to reveal the importance of her prisoner, his identity, or anything else that she knew and had been saving up. But it didn't matter. From that day on, she became a high flyer, if such a thing were possible for a dragon that shunned its natural form. Nazi officers, as well as fiendish imposters, welcomed her with open arms, quite literally most of the time. Not once did she ever wonder about her father, indeed, how could she when she had no memory of him? Even if she had retained it, it's doubtful whether things would have been any different. That rainy night turned out to be of huge historical significance, something from which the world was still suffering.

55 QUEEN OF HEARTS, NECKS AND THROATS

It all happened so quickly. One minute she was curled up in a ball on the rickety old bed, in the cellar deep within the dragon domain, guarded by a squad of nagas. The next, she was being whisked through the shadows by her contingent of naga bodyguards, off to meet fate, and of course her love, thoughts of revenge on the dragons she hated so much, clouding her mind.

Tucked out of sight, hidden behind a stunning marble pillar situated at the top of the steps off to one side of the entrance to the council building, waiting to be introduced, she marvelled at the assembled army as it filed into the square in front of her.

Having bided her time for so long, a great sense of satisfaction breezed across her at having got this far, knowing it was very nearly PAYBACK TIME!

Trudging into the square past more pyres of dead dragons, the scale of what was happening finally hit Peter. Up until now, he'd thought it was just a renegade group and that they would be put down without mercy by the dragon authorities. But looking around at the burning towers of dead dragon guards, and the thousand upon thousand nagas in both human and their natural forms, as well as turncoat dragons, the reality of what was going on finally hit home.

'We're doomed,' he thought, still trying hard to keep in step with his marching captors and the equally shocked Tim.

The rebel army, as that's what they were, faced the steps leading up to the council building, the one that Peter had visited, the one that sat in front of the king's private residence. On either side of the steps, directly beside the swirling pools of mesmerising lava, poles with the heads of dragon guards lay on display for all to see. It was a terrifying sight, in so many different ways.

SMACK! Peter got a clout around the face for daring to look up at the council building off to his left.

"Keep your eyes forward," spat the nearest guard.

With his ears now ringing, his blood soaked face hurt even more than it had previously, something he wouldn't have thought possible. Desperately wanting to share a look with Tim, he was too afraid of being hit again to even try.

Turning slightly, the column of enemies made their way through a natural gap in the lines towards the very front of the building at the bottom of the steps, passing the fiercest and most frightening beings Peter had ever seen, giving him even more incentive to keep his gaze straight ahead, mostly looking at his feet. Abruptly, the guard in front of him stopped. Peter was too slow to react, and walked straight into the back of him. WHACK! The guard hit Peter with a powerful uppercut to the jaw, sending him flying up in the air, before spiralling down into a bedraggled heap, five yards away, blood flowing freely from his mouth, teeth littering the floor, much to the amusement of all the other guards around him. One of them grabbed his chains and forced him to his feet. When he got there, he swayed unsteadily.

"NO MORE!" issued the guard who'd picked him up, to the one who'd punched him. "The boss wants him in one piece, that's all I know." They shared a look, and then a nod.

Through the haze surrounding his mind, despite the pain and blood pouring from his face, his thoughts turned to the king, wondering where he was and if they had him. He hoped not. He hoped, even now, that he had a plan and that soon the evil out here would be wiped from their entire, miserable existence. As that thought circulated in his head, there was a commotion off to one side. Dragons and nagas alike were moving, no... kneeling in unison. Before he could see what was happening, powerful hands dug into his shoulders, forcing him to his knees. Trying to look up, a hand gripped his head, compelling him to look at the floor. Peeping out of the corner of his eye, he tried to see what was happening to Tim, but all he could see was the new dragon's knees, pressed to the cold floor just like his. Off to his right, people, no... beings, a group of them, sauntered past, making their way onto the steps.

A rush of air around the back of his neck told him the guards behind had dropped to their knees. Thoughts of escape bubbled up... ridiculous really, given the number of troops gathered in the square, all on bended knee before the council building. Silence, punctured by just the bubbles from the pools of lava in front of them, enveloped everything, the air sick with the smell of death... dragon death!

"Arise, my army!" bellowed a sickeningly familiar voice.

Immediately Peter's legs went weak, his stomach twisted as if a knife had been thrust into it, as the sound of thousands of beings all rising to their feet assaulted his ears. The guard behind him pulled him up by his hair, and he received a slap for daring to make a noise. The exact same thing happened to Tim next to him.

"My loyal subjects," Manson began from the top of the steps, looking down on all and sundry, "the time is nearly at hand, the new vision of OUR planet, within the grasp of a new dawn. The only thing that stands between that vision becoming reality, lies behind that door," he said, pointing to the top of the steps. "The so-called king and a few deluded dragons barricaded, trapped, delaying the inevitable by only a few hours. Pitiful really!"

Raising his hands in the air, each and every being in the square cheered loudly, with the exception of Peter and Tim.

"So, we're going to go in there and get them out... one piece at a time if need be." Another cheer rose up. "Except for the king. We're going to take him alive and make him suffer for what will seem like an eternity." Shouting and baying for blood, the crowd went wild. "But before we do that, I'd like to introduce you to someone that will have a major part to play in the way we shape the new world to come." Slowly, Manson stretched out his right arm towards a secluded area, off to one side of the building, somewhere the King's Guards had used to keep a sneaky eye on things. Not anymore. From out of nowhere, a stunning human woman, dressed from head to toe in to-die-for brown silk, strutted out onto the steps, head held high, shoulders back, looking immaculate and as if she owned the place. Diamonds in her ears and around her neck sparkled brightly. Her hair was HUGE, almost as if it had a mind of its own. It did, however, look magnificent. Peter and Tim both gawped, mouths hanging open. In all their lives, they'd never seen anyone so stunning. The rest of the crowd did likewise. So far, they'd only seen her profile, as she'd walked across the steps sideways on to the crowd.

"My... Queen!" declared Manson, getting down on one knee and holding out his hand, which she graciously accepted. Both nodded to each other before he rose to his feet. As she turned to gaze out at the crowd, there was much cheering, but what was obvious to Peter, was the undercurrent of shock and awe, something he was feeling in abundance. Because it was only as she'd turned to face the crowd directly, that they all caught a glimpse of her face: a visage littered with deep purple lines, a face stricken by madness, a face well known to the dragon community in the past for the atrocities that it had committed. Gazing upon that face, in an instant Peter knew that things had just plummeted downhill faster than an Olympic bobsleigh. He didn't know why, he just knew. Manson alone was one thing, dangerous, murderous, scheming and devious. But from the look of her, madness reigned supreme. Throwing in a big dab of insanity could do

494

nothing for the position of the king, the planet, and all the beings on it. Hopelessness and dread consumed the young hockey player; all his fears and more had been realised in only a few moments. If only he knew the truth!

"But before we march forward and claim what is rightfully ours, I have a gift for my beautiful Queen," shouted Manson, spreading his arms wide.

The queen looked quizzically at Manson, as he signalled with his hands for the guards to bring Peter and Tim to him. Bracing himself, Peter knew what was coming next, and he wasn't wrong. Both he and Tim stumbled, despite being ready for the huge shove from behind. As the two human figures were brought forth, the queen's eyebrows rose up in wonder. Twirling his walking stick in one hand as he moved, Manson trotted down to the bottom of the steps.

"This, my Queen," he announced, grabbing Tim by his hair, "is the so-called 'white dragon' from the famed prophecy that every dragon has been waiting for forever to be fulfilled. He's the whole reason dragons have protected and nurtured those pitiful humans for all this time. Pathetic!" he spat, slamming Tim's head down.

"And the other?" asked the queen, licking her shiny purple lips in anticipation.

Strolling across to Peter, Manson grabbed him by the hair, exposing his throat, as he pulled his head viciously back as far as it would go.

"This one is the luckiest dragon alive."

Strangely, Peter didn't feel like agreeing with him.

"A constant thorn in my side up until now, and someone the king has shown a real fondness for. But for you, my Queen, a sacrifice and someone to hone your dark arts on."

As she wandered down the steps to join her lover, the queen wondered why the king had any interest in the puny young dragon before her, and knew that he might yet have a part to play, as some kind of bargaining chip much later on in the siege. Approaching Peter, she brought her long nailed hands up to his exposed throat. Slowly, she ran the long, sharp nail on her index finger down the side of his neck, enabling blood to flow freely.

"Delightful," she whispered seductively.

At this point, it was all Peter could do to keep control of his bladder. Desperately, he tried to think of something else... Richie, Tank, Flash, Gee Tee, the king... anything. But nothing could take him away from the sheer terror of the moment. Oddly though, and he couldn't explain why, he felt an ill-fated sense of familiarity. His body though, was too busy shaking and worrying to even try and figure out the reason.

Letting go of Peter, the queen glided across to Tim, but not before licking Peter's blood off her fingernails. Peter nearly vomited.

"So... the White Dragon eh?" she observed, leaning right into Tim's face. "I look forward to killing you very slowly, taking away every dragon's last hope. Eventually, I'll gut you while you're still alive, so that you can watch your own beating heart after it's ripped from your chest."

Tim, wholly pale by now, relinquished all control of his bladder, urinating there and then, the watching crowd all guffawing at once. The queen slapped him hard across the face, a prelude of things to come. Manson moved forward, wrapping his arm around his love's shoulders.

"So now, my eager troops, it's time to let the chaos begin and bring the dragon king's reign to an end. This day will reward us all with a new dawn. Let us go forth and finish what we've started."

And so with Tim standing in a puddle of his own pee, and warm, fresh blood trickling down Peter's neck, the two of them were swept along into the council building on a wave of anger and retribution, Manson and his queen leading the way.

All the while billions of innocent beings on the surface were blissfully unaware of the imminent change in ownership of their entire planet.

The adventure continues in book 4, Earth's Custodians. Good vs evil has never looked so prehistoric. Read on for an extract...

Irritated, that's how the leader of the small group of nagas felt. Whatever was so important, why not just say it in person, he thought. Telepathic contact was so draining and unnecessary. No doubt he'd made some terrific discovery about one of the species down here. BOO HOO! There were hundreds of different varieties held captive here, and he was going to catalogue at least a dozen before it was time to go back and report to their so called leader. He knew if he didn't, things would go very badly. Although he'd not been told to do so, his imagination played out some brutal scenes, with Manson asking him time and time again as to why he hadn't used his initiative and made a note of some of the different types. So he was damn sure that's what he was going to do, and as far as he was concerned, the more the merrier.

Back towards the entrance to the underground enclosure, the relative silence was pierced by the ripping and twisting of metal, a small hole at first, made much larger in only a short space of time. Without warning a massive claw began to peel back the alloy of what only a few moments ago was the wall of one of the cells, and then another, and then another, until the gap was large enough for one of the creatures to clamber through. Which it did. A scorpion's body, nearly the size of a car, its venomous tail darting this way and that, clearly looking for a suitable target. Although unusual in itself, that wasn't the weirdest thing. Exactly where the head should have been, mid-way between two thick, meaty claws was instead the torso, head and arms of a human. Long, mangy, matted dark hair ran halfway down the back of the first male to make it out, anxious to see the outside of the prison he'd only just discovered had held him and his friends. It wasn't long before there were scorpion men as far as the eye could see, well if you had night vision, which indeed they all did. Their clacking pincers added to the ever building noise.

Elsewhere in the basement, creatures from only the darkest of nightmares roamed. Eagles with two heads soared above the cells, occasionally dive bombing other species. Pixiu... winged lions darted through the air, from one walkway to another. Asena... blue maned wolves, skulked in packs throughout the darkness, on the hunt, but on the hunt for what? Conaima... giant were-jaguars padded softly this way and that, most on the lookout for their next meal, the rest guarding their newly born young. The evil trumpeting and stamping of a giant elephant beast off in one corner caught the attention of more than one group of animals. All had the same reaction. Whatever that was, it was to be avoided at all costs. All of that combined with the shape-shifting venomous snakes, myrmecoleon, a sort of ant/lion hybrid, hundreds of fire breathing gnats, a group of scaled apes, all having four arms, a pack of vampiric lizards that were spitting lightning, and something called an asag, if the name on the cell was anything to go by, a giant hideous rock demon. More and more species were coming to the fore. How long would it be before they escaped the basement good and proper?

It started out of nowhere. Using one of their ancient hunting techniques, one single nifoloa had used its razor sharp tooth to secret itself beneath one of the alleyways, the rest of the swarm sitting on a wall just around the corner.

All aware that something was wrong, but not knowing exactly what, the group of nagas were more hesitant now. They slithered to a halt at a four way intersection, each facing in a different direction, all looking out for trouble.

Tapping into all his magic, he'd tried to contact his missing comrade telepathically, ironic given that he'd rejected his last communication. But there was nothing.

No contact... just a fuzzy kind of background static. He ordered the others to try, but they had no luck either. Something was wrong, and despite not having had any communication with the different species that were contained here, only moments before he'd come to the conclusion it was time to get out, even if it meant facing the wraith of Manson. His thick, forked, snake-like tongue hissed from his mouth as he opened it to tell the others of his decision. Excruciating pain blazed into existence deep within his tail, forcing him to temporarily lose his balance.

"Whoa... are you okay?" asked one of the others.

"I... I... I..." was all that the leader could get out.

Surrounding their stricken colleague, the others hoped to gain some insight into what had happened. But before they could, a fierce buzzing came out of nowhere, igniting their threat sense and alerting them to a much more imminent danger.

As one, the nagas slithered in closer to their wounded leader, instantly erecting magical barriers in front of themselves. Using their heightened magical senses, they focused in on the eerie buzzing heading their way. Similar in form to wasps, but with one long pointed tooth, seeming almost way too big for their bodies, especially in flight, the swarm circled around the trapped nagas, one of their number occasionally attacking the shield, a sharp electrical discharge and singed wings the cost of doing so.

Much closer to the entrance, the one which the group of nagas had spent many hours trying to open, the separated naga slithered silently through the darkness, encouraged at the thought of being so close to getting out, determined to barricade the door from the other side once he'd done so. Poking his head around a corner, he was rewarded with the outline of the outer door to the basement in the distance, backlit from the light outside. Making a madcap dash for it, he abruptly drew up as a darkened, four legged shadow stepped into his path. About four feet tall, and looking more than a little sorry for itself, the rays of light from beyond the door did just enough to illuminate the creature in all its splendour. Wary at first, that is until it became apparent to the naga exactly what creature, still shrouded by shadows, he was dealing with.

'A unicorn,' he thought to himself.

"Hello little fella," he whispered through the darkness, all the time snaking slowly towards its shady profile.

Stamping its feet gruffly, the foal let loose a little grunt, causing the naga to smile at the thought of having some good news for the maniac Manson. Unicorns were rare, rarer than rare. The fact that the dragons had some incarcerated down here boded well. Their magical powers were legendary, with numerous potions and possibilities available from their extracts. Sliding to a halt, the naga reached out with one hand to stroke the unicorn's mane. Nervously the unicorn shied away, understandably really, turning around a little to face the very pleased with himself naga. It was then that the pale beams of light, seeping through the door out of the basement revealed the real silhouette of the beast. Not one horn on top of its head, but two, something that changed the very nature of the being a hundredfold. Immediately, the naga slinked backwards, desperate to get away, but the ra-hoon, as that's what it was, was having none of it. Incisors bared, it stalked after the naga, the terrifying tapping of its hooves on the cold metal floor signalling impending doom. Petrified and desperate, the naga shimmied one way and then darted the other, hoping against hope that the beast was dumb enough to fall for a very over the top dummy, and that he could get out and close the door behind him. Not a hope. The ra-hoon whirled with the grace and speed of a stallion, clamping its fierce teeth around the naga's scaly tail, about two metres from the end.

"Aaaarrrrgggghhhhh!" screamed the naga in agony, trying to wriggle free.

With a snarl and a cunning look that gave away not

only its intelligence, but something of its devilish nature, the ra-hoon crunched down, severing the naga's tail from its squirming body. Shaking the tail free, tossing it ten metres in the air as it did so, the unicorn lookalike bore down on its prey. With no way to balance now, the naga toppled over, trying to access all its magic for what little it would be worth.

'Everyone knows that ra-hoon are immune to any kind of magic, don't they? What the hell are they doing here, in the council building?' were the last thoughts the naga ever had, before a group of much smaller ra-hoon trotted out of the shadows and began feasting for all they were worth.

Their leader strewn on the floor in the middle of them, the party of nagas were holding their own against the deadly nifoloa. The individual that had attacked their leader had been suitably blasted into smithereens by a crackling bolt of green lightning, preventing any more damage being taken from inside the magical shield that they all now shared. Currently the conscious nagas were having a telepathic discussion about just how they were going to get their leader back to the entrance. They'd pretty much just decided that they'd need to take out all the attacking nifoloa, something they thought was pretty much doable, when trouble started appearing on all sides.

The junction, or more like crossroads, that they were situated in the middle of, had just become a magnet for half a dozen species, hungry, desperate, down on their luck, and angry about having had the world they knew and loved torn away from them. Stumbling upon two enemies (the nagas looking like a prolific source of food) brawling pushed all the right buttons on their internal fight or flight decision making process. Flight was never really an option.

Half a dozen snarling wolves bounded towards the struggle, their fluffy blue manes ruffling as they took one last flying leap, the sound of their jaws snapping at the nifoloa echoing off into the darkness. Looking out from behind their magical shields, the nagas were unable to believe what they were seeing.

One of the wolves that had hung back was just about to join the rest of its pack, when four thick, meaty, brown scaled hands whipped it up off the ground, causing it to howl like a banshee briefly, before trying to strike out at its attacker with its claws and needle sharp teeth, to little or no effect. The grinning, prehistoric looking primate rolled its eyes, before snarling right into the face of the helpless beast. Its massive scaled muscles rippled as it tore each of the wolf's legs off, one by one, only to discard them and move in closer to where the real action was.

The sound from the fight was off the scale now. Buzzing, howling, snapping, clacking, the sound of breaking bones and agonising screams were like a beacon in the dark. The creatures contained here weren't timid and shy, but the worst of the worst the mythical world had to offer. That's why they were there. Most of them liked nothing more than a good fight and had no concept of losing. To them, this was why they lived. For the nagas at the centre of it all, things were just going from bad to worse, despite the fact that they were safely holed up behind their magical barriers.

As one of the wolves swallowed a nifoloa whole, and was about to look for the next one, a giant pincer ripped a swathe of its stomach open to reveal blood and internal organs. It slumped to the floor, barely able to pant, let alone call for help, as the scorpion men moved forward together, their pincers weaving in front of them, all the time nipping at the buzzing enemies in the air surrounding them.

In the recesses of one of the paths, just back from the main event, the scaled apes had been set upon by the frighteningly vicious winged lions known as the pixiu. At first the apes had thought nothing of the flying monstrosities, that is until in one fell swoop, one of the beasts had torn off half an arm at the elbow, biting clean through the primate's protective scales. This had sent the group into a wild frenzy, causing them to exact revenge. One of the pixiu had been downed by two apes working together, one throwing the other high up into the air when one of the creatures had dared to try and attack again. The sheer weight of the ape had brought the creature down and, while not defenceless on the ground, far from it, there were now three apes, rolling around beating the living daylights out of it.

Amidst the chaos of battle proper, two-headed eagles joined in the fun, constantly bombing the nagas' shield as they tried to pick off a nifoloa or two. One or two had been successful, while most had just been harmlessly turned away by the magic.

Inside the shield, things had just gotten worse, if that were possible.

"He's stopped breathing," said one, from down by the leader's side.

"I don't care about him," shouted one of the others. "You need to get back up here and help us reinforce these shields."

"Alright," he replied, giving his former leader one last look, before joining the remainder of the nagas.

"What if we gradually moved off in the direction of the exit, while still maintaining the shields? The beasts seem to be content fighting each other. Plus they might consider our former comrade's body as food, creating a distraction, and buying us some valuable time to form an orderly retreat."

As a group they considered this, despite all thinking it was deeply disrespectful to the naga that had led them for a few weeks now. But nobody could come up with anything better, so they decided to go with that. A few inches at a time the group, with their shields still up, steadily retreated back in the direction from which they'd arrived.

A scaled ape ran at full pelt towards his friend, well, brother actually, who held his hands out low in front of him, ready to use every ounce of strength he had to toss his sibling high in the air, ready to bring down another pixiu. So far the apes had managed to topple three of the nightmarish beasts, but at some cost. All but these two were missing arms, with one lying prone on the ground from a nasty head wound. The fast moving ape, getting his timing just right as one of the flying lions circled above, came sprinting up to his sibling, lifting his right leg up, straight into his brother's hands. With all the might he had, his brother lobbed him high up over his head, speeding towards his target.

BOOOOMMMMM!!!

A rocky fist the size of small car swung out of nowhere, punching the ape even further up into the air, accompanied by the sound of bones shattering. The ape died on impact. Its brothers and the flying pixiu scattered for all they were worth as the fist's body appeared from out of the darkness, revealing a giant, hideous rock demon. Walking like a constipated robot, each tiny step shook the walls and the floor of the basement, creatures of every kind scattering before it. Moss and lichen draped from its armpits and the top of its legs made it look like a swimmer having just exited an ocean full of seaweed. Mostly different shades of grey, occasional worn away rock revealed a subtle white undertone. Beneath its eye sockets, malevolent purple light shone out. From somewhere deep within, it roared.

Intrigued as to why the creatures were all scattering in different directions, the nagas watched in horror as the rock demon stomped ferociously out of the black, heading towards them. Panic and a sense of self preservation took over. Each naga made the same decision at almost the exact same instant. That decision went something like this: "Sod this! I'm off!" Each retracted their shields around just themselves and slithered off on any course other than the one from which the rock demon was coming, completely ignoring however many other enemies were in their way.

Amongst those still remaining where the nagas had made their stand, a strange sense of unity had arisen. Waves of creatures banded together and were hurling themselves at the rock demon, who in turn tried desperately to either stamp on them, or crush them with his mighty fists. For the most part he was too slow, but one or two of the wolves had caught glancing blows, sending them skittering back into the dark. The nifoloa had fared better, but hadn't so much as dented his thick, rock skin with their deadly teeth.

Of the nagas who had fled, only one was managing to stay ahead of the game. Two had been taken down by the group of four armed scaled apes, although not many of their complement still had the correct number of limbs. Using all of their magic and knowhow, the nagas gave everything in the struggle against the apes. The turning point in the whole encounter was the fact that the apes' scales, much to the nagas' surprise, offered an amazing amount of resistance to their magic. Brilliant green lightning bolts fizzled and sizzled, scorched, singed and burnt, but did little other than that. With little in the way of offence, the only real option for the two was to turn tail and flee, which they did, only to be tripped up in the darkness by the remainder of the apes' party. After that, it was all over, as the frenzied creatures pummelled and mashed their bodies into a disgusting slush, from which they could be seen slurping many hours later.

Another had slithered for all he was worth, but had become momentarily confused on leaving the running battle with the rock demon, and instead of heading towards the exit, had in fact travelled deeper into the basement. By the time he realised his mistake, for him, unfortunately, it was way too late. Being constantly harangued by two pairs of double headed eagles, his concentration was elsewhere when it should have been on his immediate environment. He never saw the punch that pierced his protective shield, catching him side on in the middle of his head, forcing him to roll off into the shadows and come up fighting. Conjuring up a raging ball of fire that illuminated his ambusher, a battered and bruised scorpion man, missing one of his pincers, he tossed the deadly magic towards its target, trying hard to ignore the ringing in his ears. Within feet of the scorpion man, the fireball exploded, causing him to rear up in surprise, all the time crying out in agony. With his target damaged and on fire, the naga assumed he'd done enough to earn a brief respite. Not so. Flames pouring from every part of him, the scorpion man gave one defiant charge just as one of the two headed eagles swooped out of the shadows and took an almighty chunk out the naga's tail. It was the tiniest of distractions, but it was enough. In what turned out to be the throes of death, the scorpion man, with one last Herculean effort, sidled around and brought down the huge stinger on the end of his tail, burying it straight into the bemused naga's chest. Both creatures collapsed where they were, both roaring with pain, both unable to move, the poison working in mere moments on the naga, while the scorpion man took much longer to die, in more pain than any being had a right to suffer.

That just left one. And he was snaking towards the exit at quite a rate, determined to raise the alarm. That is until a gentle hissing up ahead caught his attention. Wary beyond belief, he put as much of his magic into the shield around him as he could, and slowed to a halt. Peeking out from behind one of the gloomy corners, he could just make out a tangle of snakes slithering around in the middle of the path to the exit. Panting rapidly from having pushed himself so hard, for fear of death, from behind him the sound of many creatures racing to keep up sent a wave of fear rushing through him, as he considered all the options available. He had to get past, he just had to. But what to do? A flying leap was all that came to mind. It wasn't impossible, but it would need to be in excess of four metres from the look of things. That was pushing it he knew, however, he was out of options. So without any fuss or last thoughts, he shot off round the corner, knowing that speed was the key. Slithering from side to side on the cold stone floor, the reassuring heat he could feel from the friction gave him hope. He approached as close as he dared, the snakes seemingly oblivious to his presence, and then using the muscles in his tail, he kicked off, judging it to perfection, but for one thing. These weren't just any snakes. These were shape shifting snakes, and the moment he left the ground, two of their number dissolved completely, appearing a fraction of a second later as two hulking great snow beasts, eight feet tall, covered in thick, white matted fur all over and a set of teeth that would have put a great white shark to shame. Abruptly, the naga slammed into the first one's chest, bouncing off and landing smack bang in the middle of the band of snakes. Immediately he was peppered with bites, the serpents slithering over him, fighting for position. The poison here wasn't as quick to take his life, it just paralysed him. So there he lay for over an hour as not only the snakes tore tiny fragments off him, but the other creatures he'd been battling against earlier joined the feast, while at the same time fighting off the snakes. Through a gap in the wriggling and sliding serpents that covered his head, he could just make out the exit, the one they'd spent so much time trying to break into. If only he could go back, go back and change things. As his life force ebbed away, he watched all the different creatures, tentatively at first, make their way through the door and out into the council building proper. By the time he died, it was a positive free for all stampede of exotic and magical creatures.

ABOUT THE AUTHOR

Paul Cude is a husband, father, field hockey player and aspiring photographer. Lost without his hockey stick, he can often be found in between writing and chauffeuring children, reading anything from comics to sci-fi, fantasy to thrillers. Too often found chained to his computer, it would be little surprise to find him, in his free time, somewhere on the Dorset coastline, chasing over rocks and sand in an effort to capture his wonderful wife and lovely kids with his camera. Paul Cude is also the author of the Bentwhistle the Dragon series of books.

Thank you for reading...

If you could take a couple of moments to write a review, it would be much appreciated.

CONNECT WITH PAUL ONLINE
www.paulcude.com
Twitter: @paul_cude
Facebook: Paul Cude
Instagram: paulcude

OTHER BOOKS IN THE SERIES:
A Threat from the Past
A Chilling Revelation
A Twisted Prophecy
Earth's Custodians
A Right Royal Rumpus

Made in the USA
Columbia, SC
09 September 2019